THE DIVISION OF COMPETENCES BETWEEN THE EU AND THE MEMBER STATES

The issue of competence division is of fundamental importance as it reflects the 'power bargain' struck between the Member States and their Union, determining the limits of the authority of the EU as well as the limits of the authority of the Member States. It defines the nature of the EU as a polity, as well as the identity of the Member States. After over six years since the entry into force of the Lisbon Treaty, it is high time to take stock of whether the reforms that were adopted to make the Union's system of division of competences between the EU Member States clearer, more coherent, and better at containing European integration, have been successful. This book asks whether 'the competence problem' has finally been solved.

Given the fundamental importance of this question, this publication will be of interest to a wide audience, from constitutional and substantive EU law scholars to practitioners in the EU institutions and EU legal practice more generally.

Volume 79 in the Series Modern Studies in European Law

Modern Studies in European Law

Recent titles in this series:

Strengthening the Rule of Law in Europe:
From a Common Concept to Mechanisms of Implementation
Edited by Werner Schroeder

The Pluralist Character of the European Economic Constitution
Clemens Kaupa

Exceptions from EU Free Movement Law
Edited by Panos Koutrakos, Niamh Nic Shuibhne and Phil Syrpis

Reconceptualising European Equality Law: A Comparative Institutional Analysis
Johanna Croon-Gestefeld

Marketing and Advertising Law in a Process of Harmonization
Edited by Ulf Bernitz and Caroline Heide-Jörgensen

The Fundamental Right to Data Protection:
Normative Value in the Context of Counter-Terrorism Surveillance
Maria Tzanou

Republican Europe
Anna Kocharov

Family Reunification in the EU
Chiara Berneri

EU Liability and International Economic Law
Armin Steinbach

The EU and Nanotechnologies: A Critical Analysis
Tanja Ehnert

Human Rights Between Law and Politics:
The Margin of Appreciation in Post-National Contexts
Edited by Petr Agha

The European Union and Social Security Law
Jaan Paju

The Rule of Law in the European Union: The Internal Dimension
Theodore Konstadinides

For the complete list of titles in this series, see
'Modern Studies in European Law' link at
www.bloomsburyprofessional.com/uk/series/modern-studies-in-european-law

The Division of Competences between the EU and the Member States

Reflections on the Past, the Present and the Future

Edited by
Sacha Garben and Inge Govaere

·HART·
PUBLISHING
OXFORD AND PORTLAND, OREGON
2017

Hart Publishing
An imprint of Bloomsbury Publishing Plc

Hart Publishing Ltd
Kemp House
Chawley Park
Cumnor Hill
Oxford OX2 9PH
UK

Bloomsbury Publishing Plc
50 Bedford Square
London
WC1B 3DP
UK

www.hartpub.co.uk
www.bloomsbury.com

Published in North America (US and Canada) by
Hart Publishing
c/o International Specialized Book Services
920 NE 58th Avenue, Suite 300
Portland, OR 97213-3786
USA

www.isbs.com

HART PUBLISHING, the Hart/Stag logo, BLOOMSBURY and the Diana logo are trademarks of Bloomsbury Publishing Plc

First published 2017

British Library Cataloguing-in-Publication Data
A catalogue record for this book is available from the British Library.

ISBN: HB: 978-1-50991-348-0
ePDF: 978-1-50991-347-3
ePub: 978-1-50991-349-7

Library of Congress Cataloging-in-Publication Data

Names: Garben, Sacha, 1982-, editor. | Govaere, Inge, editor.

Title: The division of competences between the EU and the member states : reflections on the past, the present and the future / Edited by Sacha Garben and Inge Govaere.

Description: Portland, Oregon : Hart Publishing, 2017. | Series: Modern studies in european law ; volume 79 | Includes bibliographical references and index.

Identifiers: LCCN 2017022890 (print) | LCCN 2017023222 (ebook) | ISBN 9781509913497 (Epub) | ISBN 9781509913480 (hardback : alk. paper)

Subjects: LCSH: Competent authority—European Union countries. | Separation of powers—European Union countries. | Federal government—European Union countries. | European Union.

Classification: LCC KJE5086 (ebook) | LCC KJE5086 .D58 2017 (print) | DDC 341.242/2—dc23

LC record available at https://lccn.loc.gov/2017022890

Typeset by Compuscript Ltd, Shannon
Printed and bound in Great Britain by TJ International Ltd, Padstow, Cornwall

Foreword

The subject of this book—following an excellent seminar at the College of Europe, Bruges—proves to be a brilliant choice: all the more brilliant because it may have seemed, in some respects, a surprising one. After all, was not the division of competences between the Union and the Member States the object of a recent, and perhaps definitive, settlement in the Lisbon Treaty—the first occasion on which the Union's competences had been spelt out in Treaty form, and in a fashion which seemed satisfactory overall and largely in conformity with the case law of the Court of Justice? And did not the existing allocation of competences meet general approval? Including the apparent approval of the United Kingdom, which had very recently conducted its own thorough and official enquiry into the 'balance of competences'—an enquiry which now ranks as perhaps only a footnote in the history of the European Union?[1]

Moreover, the current allocation of competences has seemed, overall, to work reasonably well.

Yet, as the book superbly demonstrates, there are serious, indeed vital, issues that arise—some of the more important issues emerging just as the papers in

[1] The Review of the Balance of Competences between the UK and the EU was announced by the then Foreign Secretary, William Hague, in the House of Commons on 12 July 2012: 'The review will be an audit of what the EU does and how it affects us in the United Kingdom. It will look at where competence lies, how the EU's competences, whether exclusive, shared or supporting, are used and what that means for our national interest. These are issues that affect all EU member states and could have a bearing on the future shape of the EU as a whole.'

The Foreign and Commonwealth Office indicated that the Review would be an analytical and evidence-gathering exercise, which would not draw conclusions or make recommendations regarding the UK's future relationship with the EU, but would instead seek to inform public debate. The Review concluded in December 2014.

For the purposes of the Review, the Government adopted 'a broader definition of competence' than that used in the Lisbon Treaty. The Review would encompass 'all the areas where the Treaties give the EU competence to act, including the provisions in the Treaties giving the EU institutions the power to legislate, to adopt non-legislative acts, or to take any other sort of action.'

The Review was conducted over four 'semesters', with each semester resulting in 6–10 reports on individual competences. Before each set of reports was published, and in order to inform their content, the government departments responsible took evidence, by issuing Calls for Evidence to relevant stakeholders and parliamentary committees. Each report addressed an aspect of the competences listed under Title I of the Treaty on the Functioning of the European Union. EU law scholars were invited to take part and were questioned in meetings with officials. (I took part in one of these.) By the time the Review was completed in December 2014, 32 reports had been published.

The outcome was surprising and perhaps found disappointing by some who had promoted it. It appeared that the balance of competences was 'about right'. No proposals emerged from the Government for re-drawing the boundaries of EU competence. A party was even held by the FCO to mark the completion of the Review, admittedly in a room of imperial splendour under the watchful eyes of Lord Palmerston.

this book were being written. And the authors have come up with extraordinarily interesting ideas and suggestions for the future of the subject.

It is possible in this foreword only to highlight a few of the issues that emerge.

First, there are areas where the EU's competence seems seriously constrained. The most important example is indubitably the management of the euro. Because of the limited competences under the Treaties, it has been considered necessary to adopt emergency measures by way of international agreement, outside the Treaty framework, thus avoiding the constitutional limits imposed by the Treaties. That has been done even though it is widely recognised that at least some such measures could and should have been adopted under the Treaties. Would it not be preferable to act *within* the Treaties and to accept the need for emergency derogation from the normal constraints where that need was proved? Unforeseen emergencies do not prevail over the need to preserve the very existence of the Union currency. The law should not act on the basis *fiat Justitia ruat euro.*

Second, and conversely, there are serious issues which arise where EU law has extended beyond the field of the competences conferred by the Treaties. An example is the case law of the Court of Justice to the effect that, even where a Member State acts in a field outside the EU's competence, it remains subject to general principles of EU law. While that case law can be seen as having some justification in particular contexts, it may if taken too far have the effect of limiting Member States' competence in areas where they could expect to be free from the constraints of EU law.

Third, there are areas where unnecessary complications arise in the exercise of the EU's legislative competences. Where the legislation includes ancillary measures in different sectors, should not such measures more readily be adopted under a single competence? But there is a far bolder and far more interesting suggestion in this book: that the EU should have an entirely *general* legislative competence—exercisable of course subject to appropriate safeguards. That idea should certainly be considered in any future reorganisation of the EU.

A similar issue may arise in the EU's external competence—notably in its treaty-making power. It is not suggested that the EU should have a general treaty-making power, but there are problems with the scope of the existing competence. The EU's exclusive treaty-making power in the field of commercial policy may be seriously hampered by the need for mixed agreements, requiring ratification by all Member States, where the agreement includes ancillary measures in fields remaining within Member State competence. Where such measures can be regarded as ancillary, should they not be included within the EU's treaty-making competence, given the existing constitutional safeguards?

The practical difficulties which are now inherent in signature and ratification of mixed agreements by all Member States have been dramatically illustrated while the papers in this book were being written, notably in the near-debacle over the approval of the EU's treaty with Canada—with the possibility of further difficulties if a referendum is required by popular pressure in one or more Member States before ratification can be achieved. Indeed populist protest may reach the stage where mixed trade agreements can no longer pass at all. This might well seem an unsatisfactory triumph of populism over representative democracy, especially unsatisfactory given that the benefits of such trade agreements might well help those who protest against them.

These points are simply examples of the kinds of issue which now arise from examination of the competences of the European Union. Many more are considered in the excellent introductory chapter which follows, and still more are treated in the chapters of this outstanding book.

The book raises issues of great legal, constitutional and political importance. It should be read, and mulled over, by all who are interested in the future government of Europe.

Francis G Jacobs
December 2016

Contents

Notes on Contributors

Karen BANKS is Deputy Director-General in the Legal Service of the European Commission, in charge of "Quality of Legislation, Infringements and Information".

Kieran BRADLEY is special advisor to the Court of Justice of the European Union on the implications of Brexit for the institution and on certain staff matters.

Ton VAN DEN BRINK is associate professor of European Law at the Europa Institute of Utrecht University and is member of the management team of the Utrecht Centre for Regulation and Enforcement in Europe (RENFORCE).

Marise CREMONA is Professor of European Law and Co-Director of the Academy of European Law at the European University Institute.

Gareth DAVIES is Professor of European Law at the VU University Amsterdam and Visiting Professor at the College of Europe.

Mark DAWSON is Professor of European law and governance at the Hertie School of Governance.

Sacha GARBEN is Permanent Professor of EU law at the European Legal Studies Department of the College of Europe.

Gregorio GARZON CLARIANA is Professor of Law at Universitat autonoma de Barcelona.

Inge GOVAERE is Professor of European Law at Ghent University and Director of the Ghent European Law Institute (G.E.L.I.) as well as Director of the European Legal Studies Department at the College of Europe.

Pablo IBANEZ COLOMO is Associate Professor of Law at the London School of Economics and Political Science and Visiting Professor at the College of Europe.

Sir Francis JACOBS is Professor of Law and Jean Monnet Professor at King's College London and Visiting Professor at the College of Europe.

Päivi LEINO is Adjunct Professor of EU Law, University of Helsinki, and works as a Counsellor of Legislation, EU Law, at the Finnish Ministry of Justice.

María José MARTINEZ IGLESIAS is Director in the Legal Service of the European Parliament in charge of Legislative Affairs and Visiting Professor at the College of Europe.

Fritz SCHARPF is Professor and Emeritus Director of the Max Planck Institute for the Study of Societies in Cologne.

Robert SCHÜTZE is Professor of European Law and Comparative Constitutional Law at Durham Law School and Visiting Professor at the College of Europe.

Christiaan TIMMERMANS is former judge of the EU Court of Justice.

Takis TRIDIMAS is Professor of European Law at the Dickson Poon School of Law of King's College, London and Visiting Professor at the College of Europe.

Michael WAIBEL is a University Senior Lecturer in Law and a Fellow of the Lauterpacht Centre for International Law at the University of Cambridge.

Bruno DE WITTE is professor of European Union law at Maastricht University, and part-time professor at the European University Institute in Florence.

Part I

General Reflections

1

The Division of Competences between the EU and the Member States: Reflections on the Past, the Present and the Future

SACHA GARBEN AND INGE GOVAERE*

THE EVER-INCREASING IMPORTANCE OF THE COMPETENCE QUESTION

AS THE EUROPEAN Union presently moves from crisis to crisis, one may wonder whether it is the right time to revisit the discussion on EU competences. The European integration process is facing a host of pressing issues, among which a great influx of refugees, the aftermath of the euro- and economic/financial crisis and its social consequences, a range of terrorist attacks with cross-border implications, the prospect of UK secession—and more generally a faltering confidence in the European project among citizens and a rise of Eurosceptic parties across the EU. Perhaps all available intellectual resources should for now be directed at finding a solution to those problems, before EU scholars and practitioners can once again afford to turn their attention to constitutional niceties such as competences? And, furthermore, didn't the Lisbon Treaty finally resolve 'the competence problem'[1] that was one of the core issues in the decade-long 'Debate on the Future of Europe'?[2]

While the Lisbon Treaty certainly introduced a number of changes to the Treaties' competence arrangement aiming to make the division of competences between the EU and its Member States clearer and more effective at containing European integration, the various contributions to this book will show that not all the competence questions have been conclusively resolved—quite the contrary.

* Sacha Garben is Professor of EU law at the College of Europe, Bruges. Inge Govaere is Professor of European Law at Ghent University and Director of the Ghent European Law Institute (GELI) as well as Director of the European Legal Studies Department at the College of Europe. A very warm thanks to Valérie Hauspie for her invaluable assistance in the organisation of the conference on which this book is based, as well as her excellent editorial assistance.

[1] Term borrowed from P Craig, 'Competence: Clarity, Conferral, Containment and Consideration' (2004) 29 *European Law Review* 323.

[2] The Intergovernmental Conference held in Nice in December 2000 launched the 'Debate on the future of the European Union', aimed at answering the question 'how to establish and monitor a more precise delimitation of powers between the European Union and the Member States, reflecting the

It could furthermore be argued that underlying these various crises confronting the Union at present is in fact a problem very much intertwined with the matter of competences, namely that of finding the right balance between the containment and the empowerment of the EU. While agreement may lack on whether these crises stem from either too much European integration, or instead from insufficient empowerment of the EU institutions (or perhaps both), many would agree that the mechanisms for deciding what and how much the EU can do are crucial for effective government in Europe and that these crises are symptoms showing that these mechanisms still do not function properly.

In theoretical terms, this goes to the federal question of how to organise a system of multi-level governance in such a way as to reap the benefits of both central and local rule; how to ensure that the right levels of government are always implicated in the right situations.[3] In political terms, it raises the sovereignty issue. Nation states are concerned with preserving regulatory autonomy where possible but also heed the need to pool authority in certain situations, perhaps in reaction to the de facto limitation of their individual sovereignty due to pressures of globalisation and the externalities of policy making by other 'sovereign' jurisdictions. The competence question is the legal manifestation of this *problématique*, of how to organise the tasks, powers and modalities thereof among the various levels or sites of authority on a given territory. It goes to the core of a polity's constitutional settlement—in many ways, it is the concrete expression of that settlement.

The competence question is therefore of perennial, fundamental, and perhaps ever-increasing importance for any polity, let alone the European Union. The EU is a particularly dynamic system of multi-level government, in which nation states have voluntarily engaged in a unique and unprecedented sovereignty-sharing exercise, the limits of which have not been, and most likely cannot be, clearly defined and are continuously contested. As such, its constitutional arrangement is constantly evolving, and so is the competence question. Debates on the limits of Community powers are as old as the Treaties themselves, but they continue with growing intensity in the current, volatile, post-Brexit-referendum EU legal and political order. It is thus exactly the right time to revisit the competence discussion, looking at the way the concerns of the past have shaped the system of the present, and to reflect whether this is the appropriate arrangement to carry the European Union into the future.

THE LEGAL PRINCIPLES LIMITING EU COMPETENCE

The current Treaties feature a double-pronged approach of limiting both the *existence* and the *exercise* of EU competence. The exercise of competences is

principle of subsidiarity'. One year later, the Laeken Declaration of 13 December 2001 redrafted and concretised these issues. See Laeken Declaration on the Future of the European Union, Annex I to the Conclusions of the Laeken European Council, 14–15 December 2001, SN 300/1/01 REV 1.

[3] See D Halberstam, 'Federalism: A Critical Guide' (2011) *University of Michigan Public Law Working Paper* No 251.

limited mainly through three principles. The first and foremost is the principle of subsidiarity, which demands that all EU-level action be necessary in the sense that the policy goals in question cannot be achieved as effectively and efficiently on the national level.[4] The second is the proportionality principle, which requires EU action to be rational, in that it should be appropriate and necessary to achieve its aims, and that it should not limit individual (or Member State) autonomy too gravely (proportionality *stricto sensu*).[5] The third limitation is found in Article 4(2) TEU. Although the precise legal value of this provision has yet to be determined, the idea is that EU action should respect national diversity and 'core areas of constitutional identity'.[6] All three principles can form the basis of judicial review of EU legislation by the Court of Justice of the EU (CJEU). Furthermore, the principle of subsidiarity is policed by national parliaments through the so-called Early Warning System introduced by the Lisbon Treaty, described in further detail by María José Martínez Iglesias in Chapter 12.[7]

The limit on the *existence* of EU competences follows quite logically from the conferral principle, entailing that as any other international organisation, as distinguished from states, the EU only possesses those powers attributed to it. The importance of this principle to determine the structure, functioning and exercise of EU law can hardly be overestimated.[8] From a sequential perspective it is necessarily the very first of all the structural principles to be applied. It may be difficult if not impossible to establish a full sequential order of the various structural principles underlying EU law, but all the other EU law principles are triggered only once this initial hurdle has successfully been taken by the EU.[9] While the EEC Treaty referred to the principle of conferred powers only implicitly in Article 7(1) EEC,[10] over time, the Member States have felt the need to make the principle more explicit.[11] The Lisbon Treaty has both reinforced the wording and inserted multiple references to the principle of conferral.[12] Article 5(2) TEU now provides:

> Under the principle of conferral, the Union shall act only within the limits of the competences conferred upon it by the Member States in the Treaties to attain the objectives set out therein. Competences not conferred upon the Union in the Treaties remain with the Member States.

[4] See, for a discussion and overview of the wealth of academic literature on the subsidiarity principle, A Estella, *The EU Principle of Subsidiarity and its Critique* (Oxford, Oxford University Press, 2002).

[5] See T Harbo, 'The Function of the Proportionality Principle in EU Law' (2010) 16 *European Law Journal* 158.

[6] For an interesting recent account: F Millet, 'Respect for National Constitutional Identity' in L Azoulai, *The Question of Competence in the European Union* (Oxford, Oxford University Press, 2014).

[7] Art 69 TFEU, Protocol on the application of the principles of subsidiarity and proportionality.

[8] I Govaere, 'To Give or to Grab: The Principle of Full, Crippled and Split Conferral of Powers Post-Lisbon' (2016) 4 *College of Europe Research Paper in Law* 2.

[9] ibid.

[10] 'Each Institution shall act within the limits of the powers conferred upon it by this Treaty'.

[11] Article 3b EC (Article 5 EC) provided: 'The Community shall act within the limits of the powers conferred on it by the Treaty and of the objectives assigned to it therein'.

[12] I Govaere, 'Multi-faceted Single Legal Personality and a Hidden Horizontal Pillar: EU External Relations Post-Lisbon' (2011) 13 *Cambridge Yearbook of European Legal Studies* 87–111.

This central principle has been translated more concretely in a drafting technique that entails the specific and detailed attribution of competences in separate provisions scattered throughout the Treaty.[13] These legal bases, which generally refer to either a specific policy area or to a policy objective to be achieved, are defined with a precision that outmatches the precision of the constitutions of most federal states.[14] This reflects the contentious nature of the issue of competence demarcation, the most explosive of federal battlegrounds.[15] The idea is that each policy area has negotiated its own specific scope of competence and appropriate procedures, allowing for better Member State control—or at least the illusion of it.[16]

Since the Maastricht Treaty, some of these legal bases explicitly and specifically exclude the harmonisation of Member States' laws and regulations. The Lisbon Treaty reaffirmed and extended this technique of limiting legislative competence by applying it to the newly labelled category of 'supporting, coordinating or supplementary competences' in Article 2(5) TFEU.[17] It also amended the flexibility clause of Article 352 TFEU to prevent its use to adopt harmonising measures in those areas. Lisbon introduced two additional categories. The competences exclusive to the EU, such as the customs union and monetary policy for the euro countries, are set out in Article 2(1) and 3 TFEU. Competences shared between the Member States and the EU, such as in the internal market and agriculture, are governed by Articles 2(2) and 4 TFEU. The EU's coordinating powers in the area of economic, social and employment policy are mentioned separately in Article 5 TFEU, but are to be considered part of shared competences.[18] Finally, the Treaties feature an implicit category of exclusive Member State competences, namely those powers that are not conferred to the Union and hence fully remain with the Member States (Article 4(1) TEU). This category would seem to comprise national security, which Article 4(2) TEU identifies as 'the sole responsibility of each Member State'.

THE PROBLEM OF COMPETENCE CREEP

The categorisation of competences, the various reiterations of the principle of conferral,[19] the Early Warning System as well as a number of other changes, such as a reference to reducing competence in Article 48(2) TFEU, were introduced

[13] A Dashwood, 'The Relationship Between the Member States and the European Union/European Community' (2004) 41 *Common Market Law Review* 357.

[14] G de Búrca and B De Witte, 'The Delimitation of Powers between the EU and its Member States' in A Arnull and D Wincott (eds), *Accountability and Legitimacy in the European Union* (Oxford, Oxford University Press, 2002) 202.

[15] J Weiler, 'The Transformation of Europe' (1991) 100 *Yale Law Journal* 2403.

[16] S Garben, 'Confronting the Competence Conundrum: Democratising the European Union through an Expansion of its Legislative Powers' (2014) *Oxford Journal of Legal Studies* 5.

[17] See R Schütze, 'Co-operative Federalism Constitutionalized: The Emergence of Complementary Competences in the EC Legal Order' (2006) 31 *European Law Review* 167.

[18] Art 4 TFEU states that 'the Union shall share competence with the Member States where the Treaties confer on it a competence which does not relate to the areas referred to in Articles 3 and 6'.

[19] Art 7 TFEU, Arts 4, 5, 13(2) TEU, Declaration 18.

out of a concern for clarity and containment.[20] Indeed, one of the main purposes of the Constitutional Treaty, later modified into the Lisbon Treaty, was to make the competence arrangement more transparent, more coherent, and more effective at containing EU integration particularly in certain sensitive policy areas.[21] In essence, this was to heed the often-heard concerns about 'competence creep',[22] referring to a process whereby the powers of the EU were perceived as expanding in covert or somehow unclear ways, including into areas where Member States were supposed to remain fully in charge.

The main cause of competence creep is often considered to lie with the existence, and/or wrongful use and interpretation of, the functional powers of Articles 114 and 352 TFEU.[23] Of Article 114 TFEU it is argued that its harmonisation powers are being put to use for purposes only remotely connected with the functioning of the internal market.[24] While the Court of Justice has drawn some outer limits to the use of this provision in *Tobacco Advertisement*,[25] subsequent case law has taken something of the force out of these limits.[26] Gareth Davies argues in Chapter 5: 'it allows in principle for the removal of almost all legislative differences between Member States'. As for the flexibility clause of Article 352 TFEU, which was amended by the Lisbon Treaty partially to reduce its scope,[27] the persistent problems with containment were set out by the German Constitutional Court:

> [Article 352 TFEU] meets with constitutional objections with regard to the ban on transferring blanket empowerments or on transferring Kompetenz-Kompetenz, because the newly worded provision makes it possible substantially to amend treaty foundations of the European Union without the constitutive participation of legislative bodies in addition to the Member States' executive powers.[28]

But it is not because of the continuing existence of Articles 114 and 352 TFEU that the Lisbon Treaty has not been able to resolve the problem of competence creep.

[20] P Craig, 'Competence: Clarity, Conferral, Containment and Consideration' (2004) 29 *European Law Review* 323.

[21] S Garben, 'Confronting the Competence Conundrum: Democratising the European Union through an Expansion of its Legislative Powers', *Oxford Journal of Legal Studies* (2014) 2.

[22] S Weatherill, 'Competence Creep and Competence Control' (2004) 23 *Yearbook of European Law* 1.

[23] De Búrca and De Witte, above n 14, 204.

[24] M Dougan, 'Legal Developments' (2010) 48 *Journal of Common Market Studies* 172.

[25] Case C-376/98, *Germany v European Parliament and Council* [2000] 8419.

[26] Case C-380/03, *Germany v European Parliament and Council of the European Union*, C-491/01, *The Queen v Secretary of State for Health, ex parte British American Tobacco (Investments) Ltd and Imperial Tobacco Ltd*, C-210/03, *The Queen, on the application of Swedish Match AB and Swedish Match UK Ltd v Secretary of State for Health*, C-434/02, *Arnold André GmbH & Co KG v Landrat des Kreises Herford*.

[27] The unanimity requirement has always provided an important brake on this potential integration accelerator, and it is now made explicit that it cannot be used to harmonise areas where the direct legal basis for that area has excluded such harmonisation. Still, Art 352 TFEU remains a powerful provision, especially since it is no longer confined to the attainment of objectives in the context of the common market.

[28] *BVerfG*, 2 BvE 2/08 vom 30.6.2009, Absatz-Nr (1–421) para 328, available in English at: www.bverfg.de/entscheidungen/es20090630_2bve000208en.html, accessed 29 August 2014.

The legitimate criticism of overuse of these two provisions notwithstanding, it does not tell the full story about how exactly it happens that in spite of either a complete absence or a clear limit of EU competence in a certain policy area, that very area can nevertheless be subject to a significant degree of European integration. For a meaningful answer to that question, it would seem that the scope of the discussion on competences would have to be extended beyond its traditional confines. First, we should not only examine the principles limiting the EU, but also, and particularly, those limiting the competences of the Member States. Second, in considering the problems of competence containment, we should not only focus on EU legislation, but also take into account European integration from other sources.

THE LEGAL PRINCIPLES LIMITING MEMBER STATE COMPETENCE

EU law limits the competences of the Member States in several ways. The first and arguably only limit on the *existence* of Member State competence is by virtue of an exclusive EU competence. Before the Lisbon Treaty, the exclusive nature of an EU competence was identified by the CJEU in its case law. The Lisbon Treaty now declares such exclusivity in Article 3 TFEU, in the area of the customs union, the establishing of the competition rules necessary for the functioning of the internal market, monetary policy for the Member States whose currency is the euro, the conservation of marine biological resources under the common fisheries policy and common commercial policy.

The consequence of this constitutional exclusivity is, according to Article 2(1) TFEU, that in these areas only the Union may legislate and adopt legally binding acts, the Member States being able to do so themselves only if so empowered by the Union or for the implementation of Union acts. So, while there may be continuing Member State action in these areas, this is by way of delegation and not by virtue of a remaining Member State competence. As specified in Article 5(3) TEU, the subsidiarity principle does not apply to these areas. Furthermore, as Marise Cremona explains in Chapter 8, the Lisbon Treaty also codified existing case law on exclusive external competences. As a result, we have a group of policies which are explicitly exclusive, listed in Article 3(1) TFEU, such as the common commercial policy. In addition, the Treaties now provide that exclusive competence to conclude international agreements, under Article 3(2) TFEU,

> when its conclusion is provided for in a legislative act of the Union or is necessary to enable the Union to exercise its internal competence, or in so far as its conclusion may affect common rules or alter their scope.

The CJEU has firmly rejected an interpretation of the latter which would 'pick and choose' what prior case law would, or would not, survive the Lisbon Treaty reforms.[29]

[29] I Govaere, '"Setting the international scene": EU external competence and procedures post-Lisbon revisited in the light of ECJ Opinion 1/13' (2015) 52(5) *Common Market Law Review* 1277–1307.

As regards shared competence, Article 2(2) TFEU provides that both the Union and the Member States may legislate and adopt legally binding acts in that area. It specifies that the Member States shall exercise their competence to the extent that the Union has not exercised its competence, and that they shall again exercise their competence to the extent that the Union has decided to cease exercising its competence. This is an expression of the principle of pre-emption, which limits the *exercise* of Member State competences.[30] According to the Treaty, such pre-emption does not fully apply to all areas of shared competence; however, since in the areas of research, technological development and space, and development co-operation and humanitarian aid, Article 4(3) and (4) TFEU provide that the exercise of Union competence 'shall not result in Member States being prevented from exercising theirs'. Similarly, in areas where only minimum harmonisation is allowed, such as social policy, the pre-emption principle is mitigated.

The self-standing value of the principle of pre-emption and the exclusivity of EU competences is contestable. Arguably, they are both mere consequences of the fundamental principles of primacy, sincere co-operation and the effectiveness of EU law (*effet utile*). In fact, these principles better explain the actual functioning of the competence constellation in terms of the scope of Union versus Member State action, than the categorisation of competences as set out since Lisbon.

The most powerful illustration thereof is the limitation of Member States' exercise of their retained powers, namely those where the EU has no or only complementary competence.[31] As Christiaan Timmermans notes in Chapter 2 and Bruno De Witte sets out in further detail in Chapter 4, while the Treaties provide that such areas either 'remain with the Member States' or, respectively, that the exercise of EU competence shall not 'supersede' the competence of the Member States, the Court has often repeated, in slight variations of wording, that 'powers retained by the Member States must be exercised consistently with EU law'. This means that provisions of EU law in other policy areas may constrain (pre-empt?) the action of Member States in areas of retained powers. This logic is derived from the fundamental principles of primacy and *effet utile* of EU law, which do not allow policy areas to be carved out of the scope of application of the Treaty altogether. Particularly the internal market provisions powerfully cut through areas where the EU possesses no, or only limited, legislative powers, such as health, wages, education, culture and sport.[32] But this is just one of many examples. Pablo Ibáñez Colomo demonstrates in Chapter 7 that the state aid provisions can also have such pervasive effects. The same mechanism has furthermore led the Court to recognise a power for the EU legislator to specify that EU obligations in a legislative measure for environmental protection had to be implemented through criminal law, even if the EU did not at the time possess any specific competence

[30] R Schütze, 'Supremacy without pre-emption? The very slowly emergent doctrine of Community pre-emption' (2006) *Common Market Law Review* 1023–48.

[31] S Garben, 'Supporting Policies' in F Amtenbrink et al, The Handbook of European Union Law (Alphen aan den Rijn, Kluwer, 2017), forthcoming.

[32] ibid.

to do so.[33] Furthermore, the Union may very well restrict Member States' competences in these areas through the adoption of Union legislation on the basis of other Treaty provisions.[34]

The principles of primacy, effectiveness and sincere co-operation do not only limit the exercise of Member State competence in areas which primarily fall within their responsibility. As said, arguably these principles also explain the specific dynamics of 'pre-emption' in relation to shared competences and even constitute the very reason for the exclusive nature of certain areas of EU competence. The underlying logic of the exclusion of incompatible national law and policy based on the primacy and effectiveness of EU law is the same.

This explains why in certain areas of shared competence, the law-making powers of the Member States can be fully abrogated through progressive EU legislative action, while in other areas of shared competence, such as social policy, development co-operation and humanitarian aid such full pre-emption is not a priori possible: in pursuing those latter goals it is unlikely that continuing parallel action by the Member States will obstruct the EU in the achievement of its tasks or result in outright incompatibilities. However, in the hypothetical case that a Member State would unilaterally and knowingly act in clear conflict with EU action in such a field, there seems no reason why such action would not be precluded under the principles of primacy, loyalty and *effet utile*. It would furthermore seem that the very same mechanism lies behind the fact that Member States cannot act independently in areas of exclusive EU competence: the very nature of these policies demands that any unilateral national action would not be compatible with the supreme EU policy in place. Arguably, it is not because these fields are exclusive that Member States cannot act but because Member States can no longer act without contravening the established EU policy (or the very fact that it is supposed to be a common policy) that these competences are, or have become, exclusive. As Marise Cremona discusses in Chapter 8, the main rationales for exclusivity in external relations remain, also after Lisbon, the principles of *effet utile* and of sincere co-operation.

From this perspective, the categorisation of competences introduced by the Lisbon Treaty is problematic. It comes across, at best, as a theoretical exercise attempting to systematise the status quo at a certain point in time. It thereby fails to capture the inherently dynamic nature of the competence arrangement, which is shaped as the *acquis* progresses, with the principles of effectiveness, primacy and loyalty as driving forces. In light of changing political, legal and societal realities, some areas may see such an increase in European integration that they move from complementary to shared, or from shared to exclusive. For similar reasons, common policies can be decentralised and devolved. It remains to be seen to what

[33] Case C-176/03, *Commission of the European Communities v Council of the European Union*, EU:C:2005:542.

[34] S Garben, 'Confronting the Competence Conundrum: Democratising the European Union through an Expansion of its Legislative Powers' (2014) *Oxford Journal of Legal Studies* 8.

extent the rigid constitutional categorisation of the Lisbon Treaty will disrupt this fluid development of the competence arrangement. Probably the CJEU will simply continue its pragmatic, flexible and case-by-case approach to competence division, as Christiaan Timmermans and Marise Cremona suggest in Chapters 2 and 8 referring to the post-Lisbon case law. That would render the Lisbon categorisation progressively outdated and invalid.

As regards the retained powers of the Member States, the Lisbon categorisation is moreover highly misleading.[35] It pretends that certain policy areas are free from integration, or will only be subject to very limited EU action, while this is only true for the EU's direct legislative competences in those areas. More generally, this is because the competence categorisation fails to take account not only of the dynamic evolution of policy areas as mentioned above, but also their dynamic interaction. Contrary to the implicit assumption underlying the categorisation, no single policy area stands alone—all are to a certain extent inter-linked. For instance, as Michael Waibel explores in Chapter 6, while monetary and economic policy fall into different competence categories, they are highly interconnected especially in the context of the EMU. As Robert Schütze has noted in his work on EU federalism, the legislative reality within Europe 'is increasingly characterized by mutual interpenetration and interlocking laws', which is a natural consequence to the fact that 'an ever more interconnected social reality' cannot be divided into 'neat competence categories that mutually exclude each other'.[36] The Lisbon competence categorisation is an expression of dual federalism, while the EU legal order is characterised by co-operative federalism instead. Robert Schütze further explores these themes in a comparative setting in Chapter 3.

BEYOND LEGISLATIVE COMPETENCE: THE REAL SOURCES OF 'CREEP'

Apart from the above finding that the Lisbon competence categorisation fails to take the dynamic evolution and interaction of policy areas into account, it furthermore ignores another important piece of the puzzle: European integration from other sources than EU legislation. Such non-legislative integration is just as important for the underlying *problématique* of competence creep, as it too can significantly limit national autonomy and displace decision making to the European level. The most important of these non-legislative sources of European integration are: (i) CJEU case law, particularly concerning the EU's 'negative competences' as Gareth Davies calls them in the context of the internal market in Chapter 5; (ii) soft law, such as in the context of EU economic governance, as explained by Mark Dawson in Chapter 14; and (iii) parallel integration on the margins of the EU institutional framework, as discussed by Christiaan Timmermans in Chapter 2 and Sacha Garben in Chapter 18.

[35] ibid.

[36] R Schütze, *From Dual to Cooperative Federalism—The Changing Structure of European Law* (Oxford, Oxford University Press, 2009) 346.

As Gareth Davies points out in Chapter 5,

> when courts apply the Treaty prohibitions to national measures they restrain national policies, and so limit the remaining competences of the Member States. The competence division between the EU and its Member States, the subject of this book, is not just determined by which directives and regulations the EU can adopt, but also by the extent to which its primary texts constrain national freedom of action. Both what EU law allows itself, and what it prevents in Member States, are part of the division of powers.

Neither the discussions on competence containment, nor the various Treaty amendments aimed at improving that containment, have taken this form of negative integration sufficiently into account. While many scholars agree that the Court has taken a very wide approach to the free movement provisions, these considerations are not often enough integrated into the competence discussion.

This is misguided not only because it misses an important part of the picture, but also because when only (the existence and exercise of) positive, legislative EU competences are limited while 'negative competence creep' through the CJEU's case law is left entirely unaddressed, the result may be a regulatory gap, where neither the national nor the European legislator is able to protect the public interest. This would aggravate the asymmetry in European integration that Fritz Scharpf has identified,[37] the implications of which he explains in detail in Chapter 17. This risk of inadvertent deregulatory consequences due to an over-emphasis on EU legislation in the competence debate while ignoring the effects of negative integration is further heightened because the discourse on the need for 'Better Regulation' increasingly tends to feed into the competence debate. As the same concerns for national autonomy, subsidiarity and proportionality that inform the competence debate are deployed in the narrative of the Better Regulation Agenda, the latter may appear to be a natural ally in the search for competence containment. However, a very different agenda ultimately informs Better Regulation policy: one that is concerned with cutting 'red tape' and reducing 'regulatory burdens' as perceived obstacles to the competitiveness of businesses.

Mark Dawson points out in Chapter 14 that in fact, the Better Regulation Agenda itself seems to largely escape competence control because of its soft law character. Nevertheless, he points out, its potential effects, while non-juridical, are very real and its impact has been felt 'well beyond the political institutions'. Testimony is the creation of a 'Better Regulation watchdog' consisting of over 50 civil society groups joined to form of to oversee the impact of REFIT on citizen, worker and consumer rights out of concern for its possible deregulatory consequences. More generally, Mark Dawson warns us about turning a blind eye to the expansion of European integration through soft law:

> [A]ttempting to control EU power via judicial and political oversight of competence allocation may be important but it does not get to the heart of how power is exercised via soft law. Competence control is aimed at hard, juridical power: EU action under soft

[37] F Scharpf, 'The Asymmetry of European Integration, or Why the EU Cannot be a "Social Market Economy"' (2010) 8 *Socio-Economic Review* 211.

> law is simply not of this nature. This does not, however, obviate the normative need for control. The type of power and coercion being exercised via soft law may be just as real; it simply doesn't carry hard law's traditional repressive form.

From this perspective, it is curious that in the context of Impact Assessment of new legislation, the subsidiarity principle is operationalised through a default preference for soft law options. While often perceived as less intrusive than hard law, such soft norms can equally challenge the division of competences in the EU and the objectives of national regulatory autonomy and democratic legitimacy that ultimately underlie it.

For a powerful example, one only needs to consider the Country Specific Recommendations (CSRs) issued in the context of the European Semester—the EU's yearly cycle of economic policy coordination. The CSRs deal with a range of issues that lie outside the EU's direct competences, such as minimum wages and redistributive policies on health care, social protection and education.[38] While strictly speaking the recommendations are non-binding, they are issued in a highly structured and coercive framework with the possibility of financial sanctions for non-compliance in some cases, making them a particularly hard form of soft law. Similarly, the Memorandums of Understanding signed with countries receiving financial assistance in the context of the euro crisis undermine the division of national and European competences.[39] The exact legal status of these Memoranda is unclear,[40] which is troublesome in light of their scope and breadth,

> including very detailed instructions regarding the state budgets both on the revenue and on the spending side … affect[ing] policy choices in areas which are not within the EU legislative competence.[41]

The old concerns about competence creep, subsidiarity and the protection of national regulatory autonomy in the context of 'over-expansive and intrusive' EU legislation that gave rise to the constitutional reforms over the course of various subsequent Treaty revisions seem positively trivial when compared to the competence coup taking place through European economic governance.[42] This is further facilitated by the fact that part of this economic governance takes place outside the EU's legal and institutional framework, in an intergovernmental arena ostensibly governed by international law. As Christiaan Timmermans notes in Chapter 2,

> important pieces of the legislation adopted in the aftermath of the euro crisis have been enacted by intergovernmental agreements between Member States: the Treaty establishing the European Stability Mechanism, the Treaty on Stability, Coordination and

[38] S Garben, 'The constitutional (im)balance between "the market" and "the social" in the European Union (2017) 13 *European Constitutional Law Review*, 23.

[39] M Dawson and F De Witte, 'Constitutional Balance in the EU after the Euro-Crisis' (2013) 76 *Modern Law Review* 817–44.

[40] C Kilpatrick, 'Are the Bailouts Immune to EU Social Challenge Because They Are Not EU Law?' (2014) 10 *European Constitutional Law Review* 393, M Schwarz, 'A Memorandum of Misunderstanding' (2014) 51 *Common Market Law Review* 398–99.

[41] B De Witte, 'Euro Crisis Responses and the EU Legal Order: Increased Institutional Variation or Constitutional Mutation?' (2015) 11 *European Constitutional Law Review* 452.

[42] Garben, above n 38.

> Governance in the Economic and Monetary Union (the Fiscal Compact) and the Agreement on the Single Resolution Fund for banks. There is little doubt that the latter two texts could also have been decided as Union instruments. The Two Pack has already incorporated part of the Fiscal Compact into Union legislation. Moreover, both texts provide for their incorporation into Union law.

Another important instance of such parallel integration straddling the borders of the EU institutional framework is the Bologna Process, which has harmonised higher education systems through the introduction of a common Bachelor-Master-Doctorate system across Europe, as discussed by Sacha Garben in Chapter 18.

While the legality of such parallel integration is not contested, at least under the current interpretation of EU law in *Bangladesh* and *Pringle*,[43] its legitimacy is another question altogether. Avoiding the in-built checks and balances and democratic safeguards of the EU legislative process, with the involvement of the European Parliament as a co-legislator and national parliaments through the Early-Warning System, the judicial review of the Court of Justice to guarantee the rule of law and respect for fundamental human rights, and the weighted and balanced voting rules in the Council which help to mitigate traditional power politics, such intergovernmental integration suffers from various fundamental defects from the viewpoint of constitutional democracy. In stark contrast to the efforts to make the EU a democratic, balanced, fair and transparent platform for transnational governance, it brings us back to all the flawed characteristics of traditional international co-operation: 'redistribut[ing] domestic power in favour of national executives by permitting them to loosen domestic constraints imposed by legislatures, interest groups, and other societal actors'[44] and suffering from grave 'executive dominance and … parliamentary exclusion'.[45] Similar legitimacy concerns could be levelled against soft law,[46] and against negative integration by the CJEU where highly political decisions are displaced from the legislator (at national and European level) to the judiciary, as Fritz Scharpf explains in Chapter 17.

IMPLICATIONS FOR LEGAL PRACTICE

The competence picture that emerges is rich and complex. While there has always been agreement that there should be some limits to what the EU can do,[47]

[43] Case C-181/91, *Parliament v Council and Commission* and Case C-370/12, *Thomas Pringle v Government of Ireland, Ireland and The Attorney General.*

[44] A Moravcsik, 'Why the European Union Strengthens the State: Domestic Politics and International Cooperation' (1994) 52 *Harvard University Centre for European Studies* WPS 1.

[45] D Chalmers, G Davies, and G Monti, *European Union Law* (Cambridge, Cambridge University Press, 2010) 132.

[46] For instance, on the OMC, see M Dawson, *New Governance and the Transformation of European Law: Coordinating EU Social Law and Policy* (Cambridge, Cambridge University Press, 2011), in particular 203, 207 and 280 on the role of national parliaments.

[47] Even the Court of Justice in its most revolutionary and federalist judgment to date recognised that Member States have limited their sovereign powers only in 'limited fields': Case 26/62, *NV Algemene Transport en Expeditie Onderneming van Gend & Loos v Netherlands Inland Revenue Administration* [1962] 1 para 3. In 1991 the CJEU, however, spoke of 'ever wider fields': Opinion 1/91 on the draft EEA Agreement [1991] 6084.

there remains much confusion and disagreement about where those limits actually lie, where they should lie, and what form they should take. As Christiaan Timmermans notes:

> it may pose a challenge to law professors but create confusion for legal practice. Indeed, in individual cases it might not be so easy to establish the precise impact of Union law, where it starts, where it stops and what the exact margin is for Member States to apply their own rules.

This statement appears to be well-founded, as Päivi Leino reports in Chapter 13:

> when working as a legal advisor for a Member State government and solving competence problems before national parliamentary committees, I was often faced with the difficulty of giving a clear-cut answer to a legal basis question. Outcomes of EU discussions on the choice of legal basis were hard to anticipate, no matter how objective they were claimed to be. Equally difficult was it to identify absolute national competence reserves.

One thing is clear: the Lisbon Treaty's competence categorisation fails to grasp the complexity of the competence constellation.

For practitioners, the competence question usually translates more concretely in that of the choice of legal basis, and this fact remains unchanged after the Lisbon reforms. To know exactly the scope of EU powers and the various conditions and modalities of its exercise in relation to a specific action, issue or area, it will still be necessary to refer to the applicable specific legal basis or legal bases as scattered throughout the Treaties. But as Karen Banks describes in Chapter 11, the Lisbon categorisation is also used:

> Issues of exclusive or shared competence, and indeed the question whether the EU has any competence at all over a given matter, figure largely in the daily work of the Commission. From fisheries to public health matters, from disputes with Member States over whether a proposed international agreement is covered by the exclusive EU competence for trade matters to the question whether and how the EU can step back from full harmonization of a sector in order to restore a competence to the Member States, questions touching on competence arise constantly, and are the subject matter of vigorous debates both internally and with the other Institutions.

In a way, competence categories are just another instrument in the toolbox of legal argumentation that can be used in competence disputes. As Päivi Leino describes, legal concepts such as competences essentially serve as the 'rules of the game', framing political choices and power politics, rather than providing clear and conclusive answers in themselves.

This practical context clearly brings to the fore the importance of the horizontal, that is inter-institutional, dimension of competence division. In competence litigation, each institution or actor will inevitably seek to enhance its own powers and position, to 'defend its prerogatives', as also María José Martínez Iglesias invokes with respect to the European Parliament in Chapter 12. Still, there tends to be an indirect federal dimension also to such horizontal inter-institutional wrangling, as some institutions naturally tend to represent the national level's interest (the Council, the national parliaments) and others naturally side with the interest of the EU level (the Commission, the Parliament). This can be seen clearly from Karen Banks' discussion of the areas of trade and the conservation of marine biological resources where the Commission closely guards the EU's exclusive competence against the Council and the Member States. That discussion also shows that while exclusivity of EU competence could be argued, as explained above, to be a simple expression of the principles of primacy, loyalty and effectiveness, in practice it matters a great deal whether an issue falls into that category or not.

Indeed, it is arguably in this practical context that competences are, ultimately, most relevant. For upon reading the preceding sections, one could be forgiven for thinking that competence division is redundant, as the EU's scope for action is virtually unlimited, especially if one takes into account non-legislative forms of European integration. However, the CJEU has established that the doctrine of the choice of legal basis has 'constitutional significance'.[48] Hence, for legal practice, especially that in the European institutions, competences, particularly in their concrete expression of legal bases, are of crucial significance, as also a large and dense body of case law testifies. Alan Dashwood wrote in a seminal article on competences two decades ago: 'much of my time at the Council was spent in worrying whether this or that proposal by the Commission was based on the correct Treaty provision or whether it was not, perhaps, entirely beyond Community powers'.[49] It transpires from the contributions by our practitioners in Part III of the book that for them this is still the case.

THE WAY FORWARD

Nevertheless, the fact that competences have real and important consequences does not necessarily mean that they, in the larger scheme of things, are useful. If they are eventually found to do little to contain European integration, because their delimitation can be so easily undermined by resorting to soft law, intergovernmental co-operation and negative integration, then they do not seem to serve their ultimate purpose: namely to protect the rule of law and democratic decision making.[50] Of course, the choice of legal basis can have an impact on the democratic and constitutional legitimacy of EU action: the more direct the competence, and the more democratic the procedure (that is, co-decision in the ordinary legislative procedure), the more legitimate the action. But then, would European integration overall not be much more legitimate if all of it took place on the basis of legislation adopted through the Community Method? Is perhaps the (de)limitation of EU competences in itself an important part of the competence

[48] CJEU, Opinion 2/00, Cartagena Protocol [2001] 664 para 5.

[49] A Dashwood, 'The limits of European Community powers' (1996) *European Law Review* 21(2) 113.

[50] S Garben, 'Confronting the Competence Conundrum: Democratising the European Union through an Expansion of its Legislative Powers' (2014) *Oxford Journal of Legal Studies*.

problem, at least as long as it can be undermined by less legitimate, covert forms of integration?

That train of thought has led Sacha Garben to propose the introduction of a general legislative competence for the EU, coupled with limits on integration 'by stealth' through soft law, parallel integration and CJEU case law, as further explained in Chapter 18. This is a far-reaching and provocative proposal, meant as much to highlight the shortcomings of the current system as to stimulate debate. What is perhaps most important to take away from it, is the call for the reinstatement of the Community Method and for EU legislation as the main mode of governance of European integration. Instead of caving in to the self-flagellating narrative of EU 'over-regulation'[51] and thus implicitly giving credence to the destructive discourse of a power-hungry EU that spreads itself too thinly and too widely by intruding in a range of issues that is none of its business, the merits and benefits of the European legislative process should be trumpeted and taken pride in. In theoretical terms, it remains the most stunning accomplishment of transnational democratic government and constitutionalism. In political terms, it is a well-balanced and carefully weighted procedure that provides both for federalist safeguards and majoritarian-ism. In practical terms it delivers, more often than not, high standards of protection of the public interest to the benefit of Europe's citizens.[52]

This is not to say that there is no scope for improvement of the European legislative process. Päivi Leino mentions the important practice of trilogues: informal negotiations that 'are increasingly taking over as the main legislative deal-making forum between the three institutions'. While arguably increasing the effectiveness of EU governance, they are ill at ease with a transparent democratic process. In Chapter 16, Gregorio Garzón Clariana describes the expanded powers of the EU's most democratic institution, but also identifies remaining problems, such as the special legislative procedures where the Council appears as sole legislator and 'the continuing effect of acts adopted in the past in accordance with obsolete procedures that are no longer applicable to their subject matter, or even that no longer exist in the law of the European Union' which 'perpetuates inappropriate limitations to parliamentary scrutiny'. In Chapter 15, Ton van den Brink puts forward the argument that national discretion should be addressed in a more systematic and careful fashion in EU legislative processes. In Chapter 17, Fritz Scharpf criticises the multiple-veto character of the ordinary legislative procedure constraining the capacity for effective political action.

What finally emerges in the normative, theoretical discussion on the issues that underlie the competence conundrum, is a fallacious opposition of the effectiveness of governing in Europe on the one hand, and its democratic and constitutional legitimacy on the other. Some argue that the EU should be seen as, first and

[51] D Kelemen, paper presented at the workshop '*The EU Better Regulation Agenda: Critical Reflections*' organised at the College of Europe on 10 October 2016.

[52] ibid.

foremost, a problem-solving platform for national leaders, and that its legitimacy would ultimately be dependent on the results it delivers. As the ends would justify the means, democratic and constitutional legitimacy would be of secondary importance; a 'nice-to-have' rather than a 'have-to-have'. However, as Fritz Scharpf points out in Chapter 17:

> democratic legitimacy presupposes effective governing and problem-solving capacity. Hence the failure of output legitimacy may undermine or even destroy the possibility of input legitimacy—a risk for which the fate of the Weimar Republic remains a most disturbing memento (Brecht 1955). At the same time, however, the lack of input legitimacy in the present European context will constrain and may ultimately destroy the effectiveness of measures based on non-accountable supranational authority.

In his chapter, Fritz Scharpf postulates the root causes of the 'self-inflicted crises' and proposes to redress the various ways in which the legislator (at national and European level) is displaced in crucial areas of European integration, by loosening the institutional constraints on democratic political action on both levels.[53] As regards re-empowering the national legislator, Scharpf points at the need to limit the CJEU's negative integration in the internal market. As regards the re-empowerment of the European legislator, 'the theory of deliberative democracy offers a legitimation of majority rule that is generated by the process of political communication and policy-oriented deliberation itself'. Together, these proposals constitute an ambitious democratic vision for Europe.

FINAL THOUGHTS

This introductory chapter has attempted to provide the overall narrative of this edited volume. While convinced that the various contributions can indeed be joined into a coherent overall account of the competence conundrum as seen from the past, the present and the future, we have not meant to gloss over the differences in approach of our collected authors. There are as many interpretations of the issues connected to competences in the EU legal and political order, as there are minds to reflect upon them. The richness of the topic of our inquiry merits such diversity, thus the editors have welcomed it and hope the readers will too. Ultimately though, what binds all chapters together, no matter how critical their account of the current status quo or different their approaches to the topic, is a genuine concern for the welfare of the European project and thus a firm commitment to it.

[53] For this argument concerning the social dimension of European integration, see Garben, above n 38.

2

The Competence Divide of the Lisbon Treaty Six Years After

CHRISTIAAN TIMMERMANS*

GENERAL OBSERVATIONS

THE NEW REGIME on competences established by the Lisbon Treaty (Articles 2–6 TFEU),[1] as it has been applicable since the entering into force of that Treaty, is it a failure, a success, something in between or simply irrelevant?

As far as the Court of Justice is concerned, there is not much case law specifically regarding the competence divide according to the Lisbon Treaty. What case law there is mostly concerns the external relations field.[2] In that regard one may provisionally conclude that the Court maintains and continues its pre-Lisbon case law. The Lisbon regime until now has not meant a new start or a rupture with the past, neither for the internal nor for the external competence divide. In a way this confirms the analysis often made in literature according to which the Lisbon regime constitutes a codification of existing case law. The Court has still not referred to the pre-emption rule of Article 2(2) TFEU where it could have.[3] It has seen no reason because of the wording of Article 3(2) TFEU to change its *AETR* case law as further developed pre-Lisbon.[4] There are no really new developments to be found

* Former Judge, EU Court of Justice.

[1] See L Azoulai (ed), *The Question of Competence in the European Union* (Oxford, Oxford University Press, 2014).

[2] See M Cremona, 'EU External Relations: Unity and Conferral of Powers' in Azoulai, above n 1 at 65; I Govaere, 'Setting the international scene: EU external competence and procedures post-Lisbon revisited in the light of ECJ Opinion 1/13' (2015) *Common Market Law Review* 1277; PJ Kuijper, 'Litigation on External Relations Powers after Lisbon: The Member States Reject their own Treaty' (2016) *Legal Issues of Economic Integration* 1. See also A Rosas, 'EU External Relations: Exclusive Competence revisited' (2015) *Fordham International Law Journal* 1073.

[3] Case C-47/09 *European Commission v Italian Republic (Pure Chocolat)* EU:C:2010:714.

[4] See Case C-114/12 *Commission v Council* (Neighbouring Rights of Broadcasting Organisations) EU:C:2014:215; Opinion 1/13, Convention on the civil aspects of international child abduction EU:C:2014:2303.

in the post *Vodafone* case law[5] with regard to control of the subsidiarity principle.[6] Most importantly, the case law with regard to the inroads by EU law into the fields of competences retained by Member States has been fully maintained and further developed.

Indeed, the Treaties have not provided a catalogue of subjects for which Member States remain exclusively competent. Even if the Lisbon Treaty has increased the number of policy fields for which Union regulatory competence is limited excluding for instance any harmonisation of national laws (see Articles 2 para 5, 4, para 3 and 4, 6 TFEU), no policy fields have been declared immune from any interference by EU law. The national identity clause of Article 4 para 2 TEU might be the exception. I shall come back to that. However, before and after Lisbon, Member States are bound to exercise their competences in conformity with EU law whether or not there exist EU regulatory competences or specific EU rules for the subject concerned. The origins of these inroads are well known but their relevance in an individual case sometimes comes as a surprise. To mention the most relevant ones:

— In exercising retained national competence, Member States must respect the fundamental Treaty freedoms, including the free movement rights of Union citizens. The consequences of this obligation might affect national policies for which the Union itself could not claim regulatory competence. The case law concerning nationality laws gives a good example.[7]
— Even in areas where Member States have retained full competence, situations might arise which fall within the scope of Union law. If so, Member States have to respect general principles of EU law[8] and fundamental rights as now codified by the EU Charter. Since its entering into force the Charter has started to play an ever-increasing role in the case law. The Charter is of course in the first place addressed to the Union itself, its institutions, bodies and agencies. Member States, however, also have to respect the Charter but only when they are implementing Union law (Article 51(1) EU Charter). This notion of 'implementing' has been given a wide interpretation by the Court. It covers not only cases in which Member States transpose Union law (for instance directives) into national law or apply it, but also situations

[5] Case C-58/08 *The Queen, on the application of Vodafone Ltd and Others v Secretary of State for Business, Enterprise and Regulatory Reform* EU:C:2010:321.

[6] See more particularly Cases C-547/14 *Philip Morris Brands SARL and Others v Secretary of State for Health* EU:C:2016:325, C-477/14 *Pillbox 38* EU:C:2016:324, C-358/14 *Poland v Parliament and Council* EU:C:2016:323, C-508/13 *Estonia v Parliament and Council* EU:C:2015:403. See also X Groussot and S Bogojevic, 'Subsidiarity as a Procedural Safeguard of Federalism' in Azoulai, above n 1 at 234.

[7] See Cases C-369/90 *Mario Vicente Micheletti and others v Delegación del Gobierno en Cantabria* EU:C:1992:295, C-135/08 *Janko Rottman v Freistaat Bayern* EU:C:2010:104. See also L Boucon, 'EU Law and Retained Powers of Member States' in Azoulai, above n 1 at 168.

[8] See eg the application of the proportionality principle in *Rottmann*, above n 7. See also Joined Cases C-201/10 and C-202/10 *Ze Fu Fleischhandel GmbH and Vion Trading GmbH v Hauptzollamt Hamburg-Jonas* EU:C:2011:282.

where Member States act within the scope of Union law. The latter formulation is certainly more vague and difficult to define in the abstract.[9] One might say that it concerns situations in which a Member State's action shows sufficient links with Union law to require that it respects the fundamental values of the Union legal system. This is the underlying rationale of the judgment in *Akerberg Fransson*.[10] In fact, the Court follows and maintains in this judgment the approach it earlier developed to define the situations in which Member States have to respect the general principles of Union law. That case law also applied to fundamental rights before the entering into force of the Charter, those rights being qualified as pertaining to the general principles. In my view it can only be welcomed that the Court in *Akerberg Fransson* has maintained the parallelism in the scope of application for the Member States of both the general principles and the fundamental rights. Indeed, treating both differently in that regard would have been difficult to justify. This judgment has met with criticism. When reading only Article 51 of the Charter, the criticism is understandable. However, the Charter, as also the EU Treaty itself (Article 6(3)), tells the Union and the national courts to interpret the Charter giving due regard to the explanations accompanying the Charter. These explanations refer explicitly to earlier case law in which the Court applies the criterion of the scope of Union law to determine the situations in which Member States are bound to respect general principles, including fundamental rights.[11] One may infer that it has not been the intention of the authors of the Charter to overrule this case law.

— As a third inroad reference should be made to the principle of national procedural autonomy allowing Member States in the absence of EU rules to apply national procedural rules for protecting Union rights provided the principles of equivalence and effectiveness are respected. This is long-established case law and needs no further comment.[12] However, this principle is sometimes also applied to substantive rules.[13] This means that on a subject for which Member States remain competent because there exists no substantive EU regulation, nevertheless national rules are made subject to the tests of equivalence and effectiveness. On a dogmatic level this is far from

[9] See M Dougan, 'Judicial Review of Member State action under the general principles and the Charter: Defining the "scope of Union law"' (2015) *Common Market Law Review* 1201.

[10] Case C-617/10 *Åklagaren v Hans Åkerberg Fransson* EU:C:2013:105.

[11] Cases C-260/89 *Elliniki Radiophonia Tiléorassi AE and Panellinia Omospondia Syllogon Prossopikou v Dimotiki Etairia Pliroforissis and Sotirios Kouvelas and Nicolaos Avdellas ao* EU:C:1991:254 and C-309/96 *Daniele Annibaldi v Sindaco del Comune di Guidonia and Presidente Regione Lazio* EU:C:1997:631.

[12] Case 33/76 *Rewe-Zentralfinanz eG and Rewe-Zentral AG v Landwirtschaftskammer für das Saarland* EU:C:1976:188.

[13] See eg Joined Cases 6/90 and C-9/90 *Andrea Francovich and Danila Bonifaci and others v Italian Republic* EU:C:1991:428 para 43; Joined Cases C-46/93 and C-48/93 *Brasserie du Pêcheur SA v Bundesrepublik Deutschland and The Queen v Secretary of State for Transport, ex parte Factortame Ltd and others* EU:C:1996:79 paras 67–74, 83–90; Case C-591/10 *Littlewoods Retail Ltd and Others v Her Majesty's Commissioners of Revenue and Customs* EU:C:2012:478 paras 27–34.

obvious. How to apply the test of effectiveness if there exist no substantive EU rules? But, if such rules exist, the normal compatibility test should be applied. Merely controlling whether the application of the EU rules is made impossible or excessively difficult, would be too lenient a test.[14]

— Finally, the strict standards sometimes imposed by the Court in reviewing respect of secondary EU rules by Member States should also be mentioned. National competence should not be so exercised as to jeopardise the aims or functioning of a secondary law regime and thus deprive it of its effectiveness (*effet utile*). This is a rule of conflict with a very wide scope indeed. This case law was particularly developed in the field of agricultural market organisations[15] but also applied elsewhere.[16]

When reading the definitions of the various categories of competences in Article 2 TFEU one should be aware of these inroads by EU law. This holds particularly true for the definition of shared competence ('The Member States shall exercise their competence to the extent that the Union has not exercised its competence.') Indeed, the various inroads of Union law may considerably qualify this freedom of Member States to exercise their competence. That this case law has been maintained does not surprise. The Lisbon regime has not explicitly dealt with it.

The picture of the competence divide resulting from all this is rich but fairly complex. It may pose a challenge to law professors but create confusion for legal practice. Indeed, in individual cases it might not be so easy to establish the precise impact of Union law, where it starts, where it stops and what the exact margin is for Member States to apply their own rules, for instance procedural rules. A recent judgment gives a good example. The Supreme Administrative Court of Lithuania had questioned the Court of Justice about the division of the burden of proof and the assessment of evidence with regard to establishing an anticompetitive behaviour, in this case a concerted practice of companies. In its preliminary ruling the Court combines different elements, first derived from secondary law (Regulation No 1/2003 on competition rules), then the principle of procedural autonomy, more particularly, the principle of effectiveness and finally also the fundamental right of the presumption of innocence according to Article 48(1) of the Charter.[17]

While the preceding observations lay emphasis on the continuity of the case law after Lisbon with regard to the competence divide, there are also some interesting new developments to be mentioned.

[14] Further developed in my contribution 'Looking behind the scene of judicial cooperation in preliminary procedures' to the forthcoming publication F Cafaggi and S Law (eds), *Judicial Cooperation in European Private Law*.

[15] See for a recent example Case C-333/14 *Scotch Whisky Association and Others v The Lord Advocate and The Advocate General for Scotland* EU:C:2015:845.

[16] See eg Case C-290/14 *Criminal proceedings against Skerdjan Celaj* EU:C:2015:640. For a more detailed analysis concerning this rule of conflict see my contribution (ECJ Doctrines on Competences) in Azoulai, above n 1 at 155.

[17] Case C-74/14 *'Eturas' UAB and Others v Lietuvos Respublikos konkurencijos taryba* EU:C:2016:42.

NEW DEVELOPMENTS POST LISBON

Protection of National Identity

Potentially the most important innovation of the Lisbon Treaty for the competence divide is the obligation imposed on the Union to respect national identity (Article 4(2) TEU). This provision, by referring also to the fundamental political and constitutional structures, national security etc, is much more detailed than its predecessor in the Maastricht Treaty (Article F(1) TEU). It may be read as defining the hard core of national sovereignty, which must remain immune from Union intervention. Is it overcoming absolute primacy, as has been said?[18] The national identity clause imposes an obligation under Union law and as such should also benefit from the primacy principle. This becomes relevant when considering the question of judicial control.

Article 4(2) being of horizontal application it could in principle also be invoked to oppose the inroads by Union law into the domains for which Member States remain fully competent.

This makes the question of judicial control and the scope of that control the more important. Indeed, contrary to the situation under the Maastricht Treaty the Court now has jurisdiction over the identity clause. Obviously, it is not for the Court to determine what forms part or not of the fundamental constitutional structures of a Member State. What, however, the Court could and should control, is the pertinence or better the plausibility—its control will necessarily have to remain limited—of the reasons submitted by a Member State justifying the application of this clause. Merely invoking it cannot be sufficient.

There is also an obvious need for such control. Article 4(2) cannot legitimise protection of elements of a national constitutional identity, which could not be considered in conformity with the fundamental values of the Union itself (Article 2 TEU). One might think of certain constitutional developments in Hungary or Poland.

The case law the Court has now started to develop is cautious and tentative, understandably so with regard to a Treaty provision with such great potential impact on the competence divide. In any event, the Court has fully assumed

[18] A von Bogdandy and S Schill, 'Overcoming Absolute Primacy: Respect for National Identity under the Lisbon Treaty' (2011) *Common Market Law Review* 1417. See furthermore about the national identity clause L Besselink, 'Annotation of Case C-208/09 *Ilonka Sayn-Wittgenstein*' (2012) *Common Market Law Review* 671; M Safjan, 'Between *Mangold* and *Omega*: Fundamental Rights versus Constitutional Identity' (2012) *Il Diritto dell'Unione Europea* 452; G Di Federico, 'Identifying National Identities in the Case Law of the Court of Justice of the European Union' (2014) *Il Diritto dell'Unione Europea* 769; FX Millet, 'The Respect for National Constitutional Identity in the European Legal Space: An Approach to Federalism as Constitutionalism' in Azoulai, above n 1 at 253; E Levits, 'L'identité nationale des Etats Membres selon l'article 4, § 2, du T.U.E. en tant qu'élément de la structure constitutionnelle de l'Union Européenne' in *La Cour de Justice de l'Union européenne sous la Présidence de Vassilios Skouris (2003–2015) Liber Amicorum Vassilios Skouris* at 387.

responsibility for controlling the application of this provision, including the reasons invoked to that effect.[19] This case law demonstrates at the same time the need for this control. Indeed, in a number of cases the arguments put forward could be easily dismissed as irrelevant because they are based on an erroneous interpretation of Union law, have no bearing on that interpretation or are simply irrelevant to the case.[20]

As to the scope of the Court's control, there is not yet a clear line. Sometimes, the Court seems to interpret Article 4(2) not as a self-standing obligation but as a legitimate objective that could justify derogations from Union law, possibly also balancing respect of this objective with other interests protected by Union law.[21] The latter approach in my view does not do full justice to the unconditional nature of the obligation to respect national identity. This might also explain the implicit criticism (if at all intended) of the *Bundesverfassungsgericht* (*BVerfG*) in the *Gauweiler* case according to which Article 4(2) as interpreted by the Court of Justice could not be a sufficient basis to meet the constitutional objections raised by the German Constitutional Court against the OMT Decision of the European Central Bank.[22] In this respect the *Gauweiler* preliminary reference gives a signal to be taken seriously. Indeed, Article 4(2) also has an important role to play as a platform for the judicial dialogue between the national Supreme and Constitutional Courts and the Court of Justice to channel possible conflicts.

In my view, Article 4(2) should not be interpreted as implying a legitimate objective possibly to be balanced against other Union interests, such as upholding the fundamental freedoms. It should be applied as a hard and fast obligation. Judicial control should of course extend to probing the reasons submitted

[19] See, apart from the cases referred to in the following note, Cases C-208/09 *Ilonka Sayn-Wittgenstein v Landeshauptmann von Wien* EU:C:2010:806, C-391/09 *Malgožata Runevič-Vardyn and Łukasz Paweł Wardyn v Vilniaus miesto savivaldybės administracija ao* EU:C:2011:291, C-393/10 *Dermod Patrick O'Brien v Ministry of Justice, formerly Department for Constitutional Affairs* EU:C:2012:110 para 49, C-202/11 *Anton Las v PSA Antwerp NV* EU:C:2013:239. See also the Opinion of AG Mengozzi in Case C-115/14 *RegioPost GmbH & Co KG v Stadt Landau in der Pfalz* EU:C:2015:566 paras 82–84 and that of AG Poiares Maduro in Case C-213/07 *Michaniki AE v Ethniko Symvoulio Radiotileorasis and Ypourgos Epikrateias* EU:C:2008:544 paras 31–35.

[20] Case C-276/14 *Gmina Wrocław v Minister Finansów* EU:C:2015:635 para 40; Case C-127/12 *Commission v Spain* EU:C:2014:2130 paras 61–63; Joined Cases C-58/13 and C-59/13 *Angelo Alberto Torresi and Pierfrancesco Torresi v Consiglio dell'Ordine degli Avvocati di Macerata* EU:C:2014:2088 paras 53–59; Case C-151/12 *Commission v Spain* EU:C:2013:690 para 37; Case C-3/10 *Franco Affatato v Azienda Sanitaria Provinciale di Cosenza* EU:C:2010:574.

[21] See *Runevic-Vardyn*, above n 19 paras 87–91. *Sayn-Wittgenstein*, above n 19, may be considered a precursor of *Runevic-Vardyn* but the reference to Art 4(2) TEU reads more as an obiter, the justification being entirely based by the Court on grounds of public policy. The recent Case C-438/14 *Nabiel Peter Bogendorff von Wolffersdorff v Standesamt der Stadt Karlsruhe and Zentraler Juristischer Dienst der Stadt Karlsruhe* EU:C:2016:401 is in a way combining the approaches of *Sayn-Wittgenstein* and *Runevic-Vardyn* by first accepting that the German constitutional rule in question, as an element of the national identity referred to in Art 4(2) TEU, may be taken into account as an element of justification but subsequently link the justification to public policy. One notes that the AG in *Bogensdorff* does not refer at all to the national identity clause. See furthermore also Case C-51/08 *Commission v Luxembourg* EU:C:2011:336 para 124.

[22] *BVerfG*, 2 BvR 2728/13, § 29.

for applying the provision as the Court is actually doing. This control should also imply a proportionality control. But it should remain light-touch and not include the third stage of that control whereby the importance of the interest protected is balanced with the negative impact on the Union interest.[23] Indeed, that balancing has already been done by the authors of the Treaty in favour of the protection of national identity. The *Sayn-Wittgenstein* case gives an example of a sober proportionality test,[24] which moreover fully conforms to pre-Lisbon precedents like *Omega Spielhallen*.[25] Of course, if the Court in an individual case would uphold an argument based on Article 4(2) justifying a Union rule not to be applied, that would disrupt the uniform application of that rule between Member States. This seems to me a logical consequence of Article 4(2). It would by the way not represent a new development in the case law. The result of the approach followed by the Court in *Omega Spielhallen* and *Sayn-Wittgenstein* was exactly that.

The *Pringle* Case[26]

The judgment in this case brings some interesting new elements to the debate about the competence divide. I limit myself to three comments.

First, so the Court decides, the Treaty amendment adding a new third paragraph to Article 136 TFEU allowing the Member States of the euro zone to set up a stability mechanism does not encroach upon existing Union competences because the Treaties do not provide for a specific competence for the Union in that regard. Therefore, having regard to Articles 4(1) and 5(2) TEU, the relevant competence remains with the Member States.[27] The Court refers also to earlier case law confirming this conclusion.[28] According to that case law when a Union competence is not exclusive, Member States remain free to act, also collectively by concluding an agreement inter se.[29] However, the *Pringle* judgment seems to go beyond this principle. The Court did accept Member States' competence to set up the European Stability Mechanism, not because there existed a non-exclusive Union competence but because there was no specific Union competence. That seems to have to imply that should such a specific competence exist, Member States would be barred from

[23] On the desirable scope of the proportionality test in this context see also F De Witte, 'Sex, Drugs & EU Law: The Recognition of Moral and Ethical Diversity in EU Law' (2013) *Common Market Law Review* 1545.

[24] *Sayn-Wittgenstein*, above n 19.

[25] Case C-36/02 *Omega Spielhallen- und Automatenaufstellungs-GmbH v Oberbürgermeisterin der Bundesstadt Bonn* EU:C:2004:614.

[26] Case C-370/12 *Thomas Pringle v Government of Ireland, Ireland and The Attorney General* EU:C:2012:756.

[27] *Pringle*, above n 26 paras 64–68 and 105.

[28] *Pringle*, above n 26 para 68.

[29] Joined Cases C-181/91 and C-248/91 *Parliament v Council and Commission* EU:C:1993:271 para 16; Case C-316/91 *Parliament v Council* EU:C:1994:76 para 26 and Case C-91/05 *Commission v Council* EU:C:2008:288 para 61.

acting. Could one indeed read the judgment (*a contrario*) as implying that the mere existence of a specific Union competence would exclude an intergovernmental approach? If so, that would be quite innovating.

Second, the Court's conclusion that, in the absence of a specific Union competence to set up a stability mechanism, the competence to do so remains with the Member States having regard to Articles 4(1) and 5(2) TEU, is somewhat surprising. According to the latter provisions competences not conferred upon the Union remain with the Member States. However, the Court did not conclude in *Pringle* that the Union lacked the necessary competence, only that no specific competence was granted to the Union. Indeed, in discussing the possible use of the subsidiary competence under Article 352 TFEU the Court has not said that the article could not be used as a legal base. It only concluded that this article does not provide for a specific competence, furthermore that there is no obligation to use the subsidiary competence.[30]

Third, it is interesting to note that the Court accepted to discuss the argument according to which accepting Member States' competence to act collectively would be contrary to Article 3(2) TFEU, the derived exclusive external competence because of the *AETR* effect.[31] By dealing with this argument the Court seems to accept that the *AETR* effect could also be invoked with regard to agreements concluded between Member States without the participation of a third country. Such agreements must of course respect Union law. But that Member States could lose their competence to act collectively because of the *AETR* criteria being satisfied, would be a new development in the case law, I think. It has been said that the Court was mistaken to accept the applicability of Article 3(2) TFEU in this context.[32] If so, it would be a deliberate one, the Advocate General in *Pringle* having already dismissed the argument based on Article 3(2) TFEU as irrelevant. And, one might ask, is there not indeed at least some analogy in the sense that also by concluding an intergovernmental agreement Member States could affect common Union rules or alter their scope. On the other hand, the Court could also have refused to discuss the argument on the basis of Article 3(2) TFEU and dealt with it instead referring to the rule of pre-emption under Article 2(2) TFEU. The outcome would not have been different but prima facie the *AETR* test seems to be stricter than the pre-emption test.

WHAT ABOUT THE RECENT CRISES AND THE COMPETENCE DIVIDE?

Do the euro crisis, the migrants crisis or the Brexit crisis shed any new light on the competence divide? Do they reveal deficiencies in the Lisbon regime of competences or is the competence divide not at all the problem?

[30] *Pringle*, above n 26 para 67.

[31] *Pringle*, above n 26 paras 99–107.

[32] See B De Witte and T Beukers, 'Annotation Pringle' (2013) *Common Market Law Review* 805 at 834.

Euro Crisis

Questions of competence divide have certainly played an important role and continue to do so: where to draw the line between monetary policy and economic policy, the scope of competences of the European Central Bank, the relationship between Union competences and intergovernmental agreements, between the Union method and the intergovernmental method? The *Pringle* judgment gives the beginning of an answer.[33]

Important pieces of the legislation adopted in the aftermath of the euro crisis have been enacted by intergovernmental agreements between Member States: the Treaty establishing the European Stability Mechanism, the Treaty on Stability, Coordination and Governance in the Economic and Monetary Union (the Fiscal Compact) and the Agreement on the Single Resolution Fund for banks.[34] There is little doubt that the latter two texts could also have been decided as Union instruments. The Two Pack[35] has already incorporated part of the Fiscal Compact into Union legislation. Moreover both texts provide for their incorporation into Union law.[36]

The Agreement on the Single Resolution Fund, particularly, illustrates the tension between the Union and the intergovernmental method. The Fund forms part of the Single Resolution mechanism for banks adopted by Union legislation.[37] The Fund itself is set up by that legislation. However, it is the Agreement that regulates its financing and internal organisation. This leads to an intertwining of Union and intergovernmental instruments of such intensity that the relevant Union legislation cannot function without the Agreement and is in itself incomplete and deficient.

One could have doubts about the legality of such a construct. Adopting an EU regulation that leaves essential elements to be decided by Member States seems

[33] See also more elaborated on these issues my contribution 'Intégration Européenne, Démocratie et Rôle de la Cour de justice: Quelques Remarques eclectiques' in *Liber Amicorum Vassilios Skouris*, above n 18, 633 at 635–43.

[34] These texts are unfortunately not available at EUR-Lex but can be found on the website of the European Council (www.european-council.europa.eu/media).

[35] Regulation (EU) No 472/2013 of the European Parliament and of the Council of 21 May 2013 on the strengthening of economic and budgetary surveillance of Member States in the euro area experiencing or threatened with serious difficulties with respect to their financial stability; Regulation (EU) No 473/2013 of the European Parliament and of the Council of 21 May 2013 on common provisions for monitoring and assessing draft budgetary plans and ensuring the correction of excessive deficit of the Member States in the euro area. Both regulations have been published in OJ 2013 L 140.

[36] Art 16 of the Fiscal Compact and Art 16(2) of the Agreement on the Single Resolution Fund.

[37] Directive 2014/59/EU of the European Parliament and of the Council of 15 May 2014 establishing a framework for the recovery and resolution of credit institutions and investment firms and amending Council Directive 82/891/EEC, and Directives 2001/24/EC, 2002/47/EC, 2004/25/EC, 2005/56/EC, 2007/36/EC, 2011/35/EU, 2012/30/EU and 2013/36/EU, and Regulations (EU) No 1093/2010 and (EU) No 648/2012, of the European Parliament and of the Council, OJ 2014 L 173. See moreover Regulation (EU) No 806/2014 of the European Parliament and of the Council of 15 July 2014 establishing uniform rules and a uniform procedure for the resolution of credit institutions and certain investment firms in the framework of a Single Resolution Mechanism and a Single Resolution Fund and amending Regulation (EU) No 1093/2010, OJ 2014 L 225.

hardly compatible with the principle of legal security.[38] Could it not also be argued that if the EU legislator in a field of shared competence regulates a specific issue, he cannot stop halfway, change tack and leave it to the Member States to regulate essential elements by deciding collectively outside the Treaty framework? Should that not be considered contrary to the rule of pre-emption implied in Article 2(2) TFEU?

I do not think the judgment of 2 March 1994 concerning the European Development Fund could be invoked as a relevant precedent.[39] That case also involved a combination of an intergovernmental agreement and a Council instrument. Member States had concluded an Internal Agreement about the financing of development aid within the framework of the Lomé Convention fixing their respective contributions, further financial rules being decided by Council Regulation. The Court accepted that construct because in the field of development co-operation Member States could still exercise their competence, also jointly with the Community (now the Union, see also Article 4(4) TFEU). Moreover, the Council regulation in question was of a hybrid nature. It had been enacted outside the framework of the Treaty on a mandate given by the Member States, a possibility already accepted in principle by the Court in the *Bangladesh* case.[40] In that respect the case of the Resolution Fund is different because the resolution mechanism decided by the EU legislature is based on the Treaty and thus forms full part of Union law.

The possible problems arising from mixing Union legislation with intergovernmental agreements are not due to the Lisbon regime of competences. The problem is much more a political one: the reticence of Member States, at least some of them, to use existing Union competences because of fear of losing sovereignty, more particularly when important financial consequences could occur. The Lisbon codification of the competence divide has not drawn a clear line in cases of shared competence determining when Union law still allows the intergovernmental method to be used, particularly in combination with adopting Union instruments. However, this need not necessarily be a deficiency. Decision-making practice needs some flexibility in this regard, particularly to find a way out in case of a political deadlock. Herman van Rompuy once said, in commenting on the euro crisis legislation, that sometimes the choice was not between using the Union or the intergovernmental method but between an intergovernmental instrument and no solution at all.

Obviously, future steps to complete the Economic and Monetary Union will again give rise to important questions of competence divide.[41]

[38] cp also Case 23/75 *Rey Soda v Cassa Conguaglio Zucchero* EU:C:1975:142.

[39] Case C-316/91 *European Parliament v Council* EU:C:1994:76.

[40] Joined cases C-181/91 and C-248/91 *European Parliament v Council and Commission* EU:C:1993:271.

[41] See the so-called Five Presidents' Report of March 2015, Completing Europe's Economic and Monetary Union, Report by Jean-Claude Juncker in close co-operation with Donald Tusk, Jeroen Dijsselbloem, Mario Draghi and Martin Schulz. See also the Van Rompuy Report of 5 December 2012 'Towards a Genuine Economic and Monetary Union' and the Commission's 'Blueprint for a Deep and Genuine EMU' of 2012, COM(2012) 0777 final.

Migrants Crisis

The tortuous road the Union is following to reach agreement on solutions to manage the massive inflows of migrants is not so much a problem of competences. Title V of Part 3 TFEU on the Area of Freedom, Security and Justice provides for adequate legal basis to adopt the necessary legislation: to reinforce control at the external borders; to set up and adequately equip hotspots in Member States most confronted with massive inflows like Greece and Italy, hotspots allowing for registration and expedited procedures for granting international protection; to decide on relocation between Member States of migrants whose right to international protection has been recognised, and on resettlement of such migrants directly from third countries. All that to be decided in full respect of the principle of solidarity and fair sharing of responsibility, including its financial implications, between the Member States. I am just quoting Article 80 TFEU.

Thus, the problem is not so much one of competences but again one of political will to adopt the necessary legislation and, equally important, getting that legislation fully implemented by Member States.

That being said, also in the context of the migrants crisis, the tension between the Union and the intergovernmental method has become manifest. The relocation saga gives the most obvious example.[42] Member States are very reluctant or flatly unwilling to decide on relocation or resettlement of refugees by EU instrument. In May 2015 the Commission proposed a Council Decision for a scheme allowing 40,000 persons to be relocated from Greece and Italy, and divided between the other Member States.[43] Two months later Representatives of Governments of Member States adopted in an intergovernmental setting a Resolution on relocation of about 40,000 persons and distribution between them. Subsequently, the Council adopted a Decision on relocation referring to that resolution.[44] We see here another example of an intricate mix of intergovernmental and Union decision making. About a week later the Council adopted a second Decision on the relocation and division between Member States of an additional 120,000 persons, this time without an intergovernmental component.[45] The Decision was taken with qualified majority against the opposition of Hungary, the Czech Republic, Slovakia and Romania, Finland abstaining. However, according to the agreement between the EU and Turkey of 18 March 2016 about the migrants crisis, the resettlement of migrants from Turkey to the Union and the division between Member

[42] See with further references Editorial Comments, 'From eurocrisis to asylum and migration crisis: Some legal and institutional considerations about the EU's current struggles' (2015) *Common Market Law Review* 1437 at 1447–49.

[43] COM(2015) 286 final.

[44] Council Decision (EU) 2015/1523 establishing provisional measures in the area of international protection for the benefit of Italy and Greece, OJ 2015 L 239.

[45] Council Decision (EU) 2015/1601 establishing provisional measures in the area of international protection for the benefit of Italy and Greece, OJ 2015 L 248.

States of these migrants will be arranged by Member States on a voluntary basis, that is one presumes by intergovernmental agreement.[46]

Another dimension of Union decision making, which reinforces the intergovernmental element, is the overall dominance of the European Council. The just-mentioned agreement between the EU and Turkey about the migrants crisis gives a telling example. That agreement is clothed in the form of an EU-Turkey Statement. However, the Statement in spelling out partly fairly detailed commitments agreed between the parties, reads like an international agreement. Does this mean that the European Council may claim Treaty-making power? The answer to that question is not so difficult (Article 218 TFEU).

Brexit

As far as I know the United Kingdom has not fundamentally put into question the general Lisbon regime of competences. Nevertheless, the Decision of the Heads of State or Government, meeting within the European Council, of February 2016 concerning a new settlement for the United Kingdom within the European Union (hereafter the Brexit Decision or the Decision),[47] if entering into force, will have consequences for the exercise of existing Union competence and the competence divide. That the more so because most new elements, arrangements, mechanisms agreed by Member States or announced to be agreed, will be of general application and not be limited to the United Kingdom alone. In fact, the only measure expressly limited to the UK is the derogation from the reference to ever closer union.

The outcome of the Brexit referendum of 23 June 2016 has not made the Brexit Decision meaningless, at least not yet. As long as the exit procedure under Article 50 TEU has not been completed, the Brexit decision remains of more than just academic interest.

The arrangements with regard to ensuring better respect of the subsidiarity principle, the red card mechanism more particularly, will affect the exercise of existing Union competences, not so much the competence divide. That may be different for attempts to impose specific restrictions on the interpretation of Treaty texts. The most striking one concerns the references in the Union Treaties to the process of an ever closer union. The Decision stipulates that these references 'do not offer a legal basis for extending the scope of any provision of the Treaties or of secondary legislation. They should not be used either to support an extensive interpretation of the competences of the Union or of the powers of its institutions as set out in the Treaties. Similarly, the Decision insists that the national identity clause of Article 4(2) TEU 'confirms that national security remains the sole

[46] EU-Turkey statement, 18 March 2016, see www.consilium.europa.eu/en/press/press-releases/2016/03/18-eu-turkey-statement/.

[47] See Annex I Conclusions European Council, 18 and 19 February 2016, Doc no ST 1 2016 INIT.

responsibility of each Member State' and that this 'does not constitute a derogation from Union law and should therefore not be interpreted restrictively'.

These messages from the Heads of State or Government might be more particularly addressed to the Court of Justice. It is true that in the *Rottmann* case (C-135/08) the Court has accepted to take into consideration the Edinburgh Decision of Heads of State or Government as being an instrument for the interpretation of the EC Treaty.[48] However, the contents of that decision were much more innocent. In any event, the Treaties cannot be changed by intergovernmental decision. In my view these interpretations of the EU Treaties dictated by the Heads of State or Government cannot be considered to be binding for the Court of Justice.

On balance, the wording of both statements is such that their interpretative effect might remain limited. Of course the reference alone to an ever closer union cannot constitute a legal basis; and what constitutes an extensive interpretation leaves quite a margin for debate. Personally, I share the statement that the national identity clause is not a derogation and therefore should not be interpreted restrictively.

We see here the intergovernmental hand attempting to steer the institutional mechanisms of the EU. There are more quite interesting examples. The Decision contains instructions addressed to representatives of Member States for future decision making in the Council programming in advance their position (red card mechanism, protection of the opt-outs from the Area of Freedom, Security and Justice). The most far-reaching example might be the draft decision relating to the effective management of the banking union and of the consequences of further integration of the euro area (appeal mechanism to protect the Member States not participating in the euro).[49] The Council is instructed to adopt this Decision, fully drafted in advance by the Heads of State or Government, on the date of entering into force of the Brexit decision.

Finally, Section D of the Brexit Decision on Social Benefits and Free Movement by announcing future amendments of secondary legislation, which will introduce more flexibility for Member States, all Member States, will have some consequences for the competence divide.

However, all in all, the Brexit Decision leaves the competence regime of the Lisbon Treaty intact. As far as the competence divide is concerned, the most interesting are the intergovernmental elements just mentioned.

CONCLUSION

Overlooking the three crises and the issues they have raised with regard to matters of competence, two obvious conclusions may be drawn.

[48] Case C-135/08 *Janko Rottman v Freistaat Bayern* EU:C:2010:104 para 40.
[49] See Annex II of the Brexit Decision.

First, there is the all-embracing role played by the European Council and the Heads of State or Government in a more intergovernmental setting. The European Council is *the* crisis manager, it has become the ultimate governing body of the EU. In view of the magnitude of these crises and the challenges they have raised for the future of the Union it is only logical and to be welcomed that those responsible on the highest political level in the Member States have taken responsibility for dealing with and finding solutions for these issues. In fact, they had no choice. But there is also a negative side. The normal institutional mechanism of the Union with its own checks and balances allowing reconciling national and Union interests are largely neutralised. Thus, the legitimacy of the Union's decision making, which is already weak, might be further undermined. This risk is the more serious since the dominant role of the European Council goes hand in hand with a growing importance of intergovernmental elements in its decision making. That is my second obvious conclusion: to get the necessary solutions accepted—and that applies to all three crises—intergovernmental instruments have appeared to be indispensable.

Having said that, what does the balance sheet for six years' experience with the Lisbon regime of competences look like? Has the regime appeared to be successful, deficient or largely irrelevant?

In fact, time has been too short to allow clear answers, either to the negative or the positive. However, as far as the control of subsidiarity is concerned, the general feeling seems to be that there still is room for improvement both for the control ex ante and the control ex post. Additional safeguards to that effect have now been put into place.[50] But more generally, the regime must first be further tested before firm conclusions can be drawn.

In that respect the development of the case law with regard to the protection of national identity clause will be critical. One would hope that the potential of this clause as a safety valve in case of tensions in the dialogue between courts, but also more generally, will be fully explored.

Thus, my conclusion is not that the system has failed or appeared to be irrelevant. One might perhaps even say that the system has proven itself by leaving sufficient flexibility for having recourse in real crisis situations to intergovernmental solutions as an emergency exit however dubious these solutions might sometimes be from an institutional point of view. At the same time, the crises the EU has to confront, to some extent show the relativity of the issue of competences. The substantive issues these crises have raised and how to solve them are in the end more important than the issue of competences. Once a possible solution emerges, the necessary legal instrument will be found or created. In times of real crisis the law becomes malleable. Of course, this is a factual statement, not a normative one.

[50] See the Interinstitutional Agreement between the European Parliament, the Council of the European Union and the European Commission on Better Law-Making, OJ 2016 L 123.

3

Classifying EU Competences: German Constitutional Lessons?

ROBERT SCHÜTZE*

INTRODUCTION

ONE OF THE central tasks of every Union of States is the division of powers between the 'federal' and the state level. This division of powers is principally a division of legislative powers. The 1787 United States Constitution thus lists the Union's legislative competences in its Article I;[1] while, with regard to executive and judicial competences, the text had remained taciturn.[2] It therefore seemed that the division of legislative competences would equally inform the dividing line with respect to these two governmental functions.

What was the nature of the legislative powers conferred onto the federal Union? Unlike the 1777 Articles of Confederation,[3] the 1787 Constitution contained no verbal reference on the nature of the federation's powers. A first answer thus drew on the idea of 'dual sovereignty': 'The United States are sovereign as to all the powers of Government actually surrendered: Each State in the Union is sovereign as to all the powers reserved.'[4] The Union and the States were here seen as 'equal' and 'co-ordinate' within their respective spheres. This 'dual federal' solution stipulated a division of legislative powers that were mutually 'exclusive'. This first solution would, however, disappear in the course of the

* Professor of European Union Law and Co-Director, Global Policy Institute, Durham University. Visiting Professor, College of Europe (Bruges). Warm thanks go to the editors, as well as to the European Research Council (EU Framework Programme 2007-13: ERC Grant Agreement No 312304).

[1] Art I, Section 8 of the 1787 US Constitution.

[2] Art II of the US Constitution only stated that '[t]he executive power shall be vested in a President of the United States of America' (Section 1), while Art III vested the judicial power in 'one Supreme Court, and in such inferior courts as the Congress may from time to time ordain and establish' (Section 1) with the Union having jurisdiction, inter alia, in 'all cases, in law and equity, arising under this Constitution, the laws of the United States, and treaties made, or which shall be made, under their authority' (Section 2).

[3] The 1777 Articles of Confederation seemed to have answered this question in their text, whenever they gave 'the United States in Congress assembled' '*the sole and exclusive right and power*' to act (see only ibid Art IX).

[4] *Chisholm v State of Georgia*, 2 US 419 [1793] 435.

early twentieth century; and by 1950, dual federalism was pronounced dead.[5] For the United States had—with a famous exception—abandoned the idea of exclusive powers and embraced a 'sharing' of legislative competences under which the Union and its component States could both act. And within the (almost) undivided universe of 'shared' competences, the principle of legislative pre-emption would become the primary tool to demarcate the federal boundary between the Union and the States.[6]

By contrast, German federalism has retained its character as dual 'competence' federalism. The division of legislative competences between the Union and the States (*Länder*) here continues to be primarily seen through the prism of mutual exclusivity. The German constitutional order has nevertheless adopted a complex classification of legislative competences according to the degree of power conferred onto the Union. What are these competence categories; and how successful have they been in explaining the division of legislative powers? We shall discuss the German constitutional perspective below,[7] after which we examine the 'competence question' within the European Union. For the European Union has, with the Lisbon Treaty, expressly adopted a 'Germanic' competence classification that distinguishes between various types of competences. And while the (specific) theoretical and practical problems with these competence categories will be discussed in subsequent chapters, this chapter aims to offer a general overview of the constitutional ideas behind each category.[8] A Conclusion will try to distil some 'lessons', offered by German federalism, for the European Union.

GERMAN COMPETENCE FEDERALISM: DUAL FEDERALISM

The intellectual history of German federalism has been divided by two World Wars into three constitutional periods: the period of the German Reich, the Weimar Republic, and the Bonn-Berlin Republic.[9]

[5] ES Corwin, 'The Passing of Dual Federalism' (1950) 36 *Virginia Law Review* 1.

[6] For this point, see R Schütze, *From Dual to Cooperative Federalism: The Changing Structure of European Law* (Oxford University Press, 2009) 94 et seq.

[7] This part will draw heavily on an unpublished chapter of my original EUI doctoral thesis; see R Schütze, *From Dual to Cooperative Federalism: The Changing Structure of the Legislative Function in the European Union* (European University Institute, 2005), Chapter III. It will concentrate on 'legislative' competences and not explore the division of executive or judicial competences. Importantly, however, and unlike the US solution, the German constitutional order has not adopted a symmetric solution for its legislative, executive and judicial competences. Instead, the States are here generally competent and even obliged to execute and arbitrate federal law under an arrangement known as 'executive federalism' ('*Vollzugsföderalismus*'). A similar solution applies, mutatis mutandis, to the European Union; and on the constitutional *asymmetry* between legislative and executive powers here, see R Schütze, 'From Rome to Lisbon: 'Executive Federalism' in the (New) European Union' (2010) 47 *Common Market Law Review* 1385.

[8] This part will draw heavily on a number of published chapters and articles, and here in particular my *European Constitutional Law* (Cambridge University Press, 2015), especially Chapter 7.

[9] All quotations from the German *Grundgesetz* (GG) will use the official 2014 translation offered by the German Parliament, see www.btg-bestellservice.de/pdf/80201000.pdf, which—while far from perfect—offers a common linguistic version.

The vertical separation of legislative competences represents the very heart of German federalism.[10] The German *Grundgesetz* (GG) thereby follows three important principles. First, it positively enumerates the powers of the federation, leaving the residual powers to the Member States (*Länder*); and according to Article 30, this constitutional technique applies to all three branches of government.[11] Article 70 GG repeats the principle of enumerated powers specifically for the legislative function: 'The *Länder* shall have the right to legislate insofar as this [*Grundgesetz*] *does not confer legislative power on the Federation*.'[12] Second, the Constitution differentiates between different types of competences. Each competence category thereby shapes the degree of federal legislative power *vis-à-vis* the Member States. Each type represents a defined mode of federal regulatory power. Third, German constitutionalism recognises the 'statehood' of the Member States,[13] which, in turn, is taken to imply a minimum of legislative power reserved for them as the 'quintessence' of statehood.[14]

Dual Federalism and the 'Perfected' Competence Order

The theoretical foundation of modern German federalism is the indirect bequest of an influential 'Weimar scholar': Hans Kelsen. Kelsen considered the relationship between the Union and the States as one of coordination and equality; and he consequently defined their respective legislative spheres as coordinate and mutually exclusive.[15] What did this mean for the relationship between the competences of the Union and its States? While never officially embracing the theory of dual

[10] While the 1871 Imperial Constitution did not expressly distinguish between different kinds of competences, there were already references to the idea of exclusive competences (see only Art 52: 'Dem Reiche ausschließlich steht die Gesetzgebung über … zu.'). By contrast, the Weimar Constitution expressly contained a competence catalogue that listed exclusive competences (ibid Art 6) and non-exclusive competences (ibid Arts 7–9).

[11] Art 30 GG states: 'Except as otherwise provided or permitted by this Basic Law, the exercise of state powers and the discharge of state functions is a matter for the *Länder*.'

[12] Art 70(1) GG (emphasis added).

[13] While this was not undisputed in Imperial and Weimar constitutionalism, the *Bundesverfassungsgericht* spoke, early on, a 'Machtwort' (*BVerfGE* 1, 14—*Südweststaat* (1951), 34 (emphasis added)): 'Die Länder sind als Glieder des Bundes *Staaten* mit eigener—wenn auch gegenständlich beschränkter—nicht vom Bund abgeleiteter, sondern von ihm anerkannter staatlicher Hoheitsmacht.'

[14] For this imperative requirement, see P Laband's concept of 'legislative autonomy' as the hallmark of the member states of a federation. A federal organisation requires 'daß den Einzelstaaten ein Gebiet staatlicher Tätigkeit und Macht verblieben ist, auf welchem sie, und nicht das Reich, die Herren sind' (P Laband, *Das Staatsrecht des Deutschen Reiches*, Band I (Mohr, 1911) 106). In the present German Constitution, this springs from Art 79(3) GG—the so-called 'eternity clause'. See in particular: *BVerfGE* 34, 9—*Besoldungsvereinheitlichung* (1972).

[15] The Kelsen theory of the federal state famously postulated a third constitutional entity comprising both the federal state and its member states. This aggregate state or 'total state' (*Gesamtstaat*) would be hierarchically superimposed over the federal state and the member states: '[The Union] is part of the total federal state, just as the central legal order is part of the total legal order of the federal order of the federal state … The federal state, the total legal community, thus consists of the federation,

sovereignty,[16] German constitutionalism has traditionally adopted a dual federal philosophy in which the doctrine of federal supremacy is seen to violate the 'sovereign' equality between the federal and the state governments: 'The proposition: "Federal law breaks State Law" contradicts the federal principle because it transforms the equality between the Union and its Member States in a centralizing manner.'[17] This philosophy of dual federalism has traditionally also shaped the constitutional federalism of Austria,[18] as well as Switzerland.[19]

The intellectual cornerstone within this 'Germanic' competence federalism is the idea of a 'perfected' competence order, which is governed by the principle of mutual exclusivity.[20] The distribution of legislative competences is here seen as a strict vertical separation of powers in which no competence overlaps occur. Each competence can only belong to *either* the federal level *or* the state level:

> The federal dichotomy rests on a *separation* of competences between the Union and the States. According to the Constitution, competences are conferred to *either one or the other side (principle of alternativity)*. The same task and the same competence can therefore always only be exercised by one side at one time; and even if concurrent competences may move from one side to the other, at each point in time Article 72(1) GG determines who alone holds the competence … For competences are exclusive competences (principle of exclusivity) … This even holds true for framework competences, which exclusively

a central legal community, and the component States, several local legal communities. Traditional theory erroneously identifies the federation with the total federal state' (H Kelsen, *General Theory of Law and the State* (Russell & Russell, 1945) 317). And by assuming a third level above the union and the states, Kelsen could 'explain' the legislative equality between the union and its member states.

[16] But see A Bleckmann, *Staatsorganisationsrecht, Grundlagen, Staatszielbestimmungen und Staatsorganisationsrecht des Bundes* (Heymanns, 1993) 385 rn 874: 'Ich möchte deshalb der im 19. Jh. vertretenen Theorie der geteilten Souveränität den Vorzug geben, nach welcher sowohl der Bund als auch die Gliedstaaten souverän sind.'

[17] H Kelsen, 'Aussprache' (1929) 6 *Veröffentlichungen der Vereinigung deutscher Staatsrechtslehrer*, 57.

[18] For the Austrian federal order, see LK Adamovich and BC Funk, *Österreichisches Verfassungsrecht* (Springer 1985) 185–86: 'In engem Zusammenhang damit steht der Grundsatz der Kompetenztrennung (Exklusivität der Kompetenzbereiche von Bund und Ländern). Nach diesem Grundsatz kann ein und dieselbe Rechtsmaterie immer nur einem einzigen Kompetenztatbestand zugeordnet werden … Die Trennung der Kompetenzbereiche besteht nicht nur auf der Ebene der Gesetzgebung, sondern setzt sich auch im Bereiche der Vollziehung fort[.]'

[19] For the federal order of Switzerland, see M Usteri, *Theorie des Bundesstaates* (Polygraphischer Verlag AG Zürich, 1954) 275–76: 'Dem gegenüber möchten wir die These begründen, daß der Begriff der konkurrierenden Kompetenz im Bundesstaat überhaupt unmöglich ist … Im Bundesstaat sind eben die Kompetenzen geteilt, was das Gegenteil von konkurrierend ist … Und ganz allgemein erscheint der Begriff der konkurrierenden Kompetenz im Bundesstaat als ein Unding. Der Begriff der konkurrierenden Kompetenz ist wohl—wie der Satz "Bundesrecht bricht Gliedrecht" als Relikt aus dem ganz anders strukturierten alten deutschen Reich der Feudalzeit zu betrachten.'

[20] See only R Scholz, 'Ausschließliche und konkurrierende Gesetzgebungskompetenz von Bund und Ländern in der Rechtsprechung des Bundesverfassungsgerichts' in M Drath and C Starck (eds), *Bundesverfassungsgericht und Grundgesetz: Festgabe aus Anlaß des 25jährigen Bestehens des Bundesverfassungsgerichts* (Mohr, 1976) 252 at 256: 'Das Kompetenzsystem der Art 70 ff GG ist in sich geschlossen und "perfektioniert". Es verfügt eine prinzipiell lückenlose Abschichtung der Kompetenzen von Bund und Ländern, gibt einer Vorrangentscheidung im Sinne einer (generellen) Kompetenzvermutung also von vornherein keinen Raum.'

> belong to the Union, while it falls exclusively within the competence of the States to adopt complementary legislation.[21]

The principle of exclusivity constitutes 'the' intellectual essence of German competence federalism (even with regard to 'non-exclusive' competences). Its central task is the clear 'division of competence spheres'.[22] These competence spheres are meant to be mutually exclusive, and the German Constitutional Court has thus traditionally prohibited 'shared' or 'dual' competences ('*Verbot der Doppelzuständigkeiten*'): 'The idea of shared competences on the basis of which both the Union and the States may legislate on the same subject-matter differently is foreign to the German competence order, since it would violate the *separation principle established by Article 70(2) GG*.'[23] There can therefore always only be one 'competent' legislator for a given social issue.[24] *Legislative* conflicts consequently represent a constitutional anomaly. For in Kelsian terms, they signify that the 'total state' had not properly distributed legislative competences!

But did that mean that all federal competences were exclusive competences? The exclusive competences of the Union are defined in Article 71 of the German *Grundgesetz*: 'On matters within the exclusive legislative power of the Federation, the *Länder* shall have power to legislate only when and to the extent that they are expressly authorised to do so by a federal law'; and Article 73 GG positively enumerates the exclusive powers of the Federation.[25] Exclusive competences are here seen as double-sided entities: they are both shield and sword. On the one hand, they entitle the federal level to legislate, while they also contain a constitutional prohibition: State laws falling within the scope of an exclusive competence will be *unconstitutional* (unless expressly authorised). The meta-constitutional rationale behind exclusive powers is thereby the belief that certain matters belong *by their very nature* to the Federation.[26]

[21] J Isensee, 'Idee und Gestalt des Föderalismus im Grundgesetz' in J Isensee and P Kirchhof (eds), *Handbuch des Staatsrechts der Bundesrepublik Deutschland*, Band IV (CF Müller, 2003) 517 para 134 (my translation, emphasis added).

[22] ibid, para 179: 'Das Grundgesetz geht von der Trennung der Kompetenzräume von Bund und Ländern aus.'

[23] *BVerfGE* 36, 193—*Zeugnisverweigerungsrecht* (1973) 202 (my translation, emphasis added).

[24] HJ Vogel, 'Die bundesstaatliche Ordnung des Grundgesetzes' in E Benda, W Maihofer and HJ Vogel (eds), *Handbuch des Verfassungsrechts der Bundesrepublik Deutschland* (W de Gruyter, 1994) 1041 at 1073: '[N]ach dem Verteilungsprinzip des Grundgesetzes kann jeweils nun *ein* Gesetzgeber die Befugnis zur Reglung beziehungsweise zur Rahmen- oder Grundsatzregelung der jeweiligen Materie haben.'

[25] The Bonn Constitution lists, among others, external relations, self-defence, free movement and immigration as exclusive legislative competences of the federal level (Art 73(1) and (3) GG). This enumeration is not exhaustive. The existence of implied exclusive competences was recognised by German constitutional doctrine at an early stage. Implied exclusive competences can particularly arise through the constitutional acknowledgement of '*Kompetenzen kraft Natur der Sache*'.

[26] Exclusive competences arise naturally 'wo nach der Natur des zu regelnden Gegenstandes bei seiner rechtlichen Ordnung regionale Verschiedenheiten grundsätzlich nicht geduldet werden können oder gar nicht denkbar sind, dem Bund die ausschließlichen Kompetenz zusteht', *cf BVerfGE* 18, 407—*Verordnung als Landesrecht* (1965) 414.

'Concurrent' Competences as 'Subsequently Exclusive Competences'

In addition to exclusive competences, German constitutionalism also recognises concurrent competences;[27] but the constitutional dogma of dual federalism has also shaped this second type of legislative competence.

The nature of concurrent competences is captured by the positive definition found in Article 72 GG: 'On matters within the concurrent legislative power, the *Länder* shall have power to legislate *so long as and to the extent that the Federation has not exercised its legislative power* by enacting a law.'[28] This formulation is the fountain of the—dynamic—nature of German 'competence federalism'. The wording already indicates a clear departure from the US conception of shared competences. For under German constitutionalism, concurrent competences are *not* shared competences: the States will never exercise their competences alongside the Union. In line with the philosophy of dual federalism, at no point in time should two legislators act on the same issue. The term 'concurrent competence' is thus profoundly misleading for the two levels will never be actually concurring.[29]

The very essence of concurrent competences is that their *exercise* limits the very *existence* of state competences. For to the extent that the Union has legitimately exercised its concurrent competences, the Member States *lose* their legislative power. State laws falling in an area in which the Union legislator has made use of its concurrent competence will consequently be considered '*ultra vires*' for lack of legislative competence. To quote the German Constitutional Court:

> Article 72(1) GG forms part of the competences order. It changes the normal rule that, within the sphere of concurrent competences, it is first the States that will be competent; for from a particular point onwards—the moment when the Union exercises its concurrent competence—it will *only be the Union that is competent for the regulated area* … It therefore follows that it is *not a conflict between State legislation and the hierarchically higher Union legislation that causes the former's invalidity, but the State law's incompatibility with the German competence order* within which the State legislator lacked the very competence to adopt its law.[30]

The important point is thus this: the *exercise* of legislative competences changes the competence *order* within the federation. While the States had a competence in the past, the 'activation' of a concurrent competence by the Union 'negatives' the state competence. State laws that were previously adopted henceforth

[27] The majority of federal competences are concurrent competences. Thirty-plus competence titles are listed under Art 74 GG as matters pertaining to the concurrent competences of the federation. Among the most generous competence here are those for 'civil law', 'criminal law' and 'economic law'.

[28] Art 72(1) GG (emphasis added).

[29] *cf* J Ipsen, *Staatsorganisationsrecht* (Justische Lehrbücher, 1998) 100: 'Die "konkurrierende" Gesetzgebungszuständigkeit des Bundes bedeutet entgegen ihrer mißverständlichen Bezeichnung keineswegs, daß Bund und Länder nebeneinander zuständig sind … Die Zuständigkeiten bestehen vielmehr hintereinander, so daß man die konkurrierende Bundeszuständigkeit besser als subsidiäre Landeszuständigkeit bezeichnet.'

[30] *BVerfGE* 36, 342—*Niedersächsisches Landesbesoldungsgesetz* (1974) 342, 362–63 (my translation, emphasis added).

lose—like a rug pulled from under the state law's feet—their constitutional base. The German doctrine of 'pre-emption' is thus one of 'constitutional pre-emption'. The pre-emptive effect here derives directly from Article 72(1) GG and not from federal legislation. Exercised concurrent competences are thus seen as subsequently exclusive competences:

> The term 'concurrent' legislative powers is admittedly misleading when it creates the impression that we are dealing with parallel legislative competences under which there is a partially competitive relationship between federal and state *legislation*. That is not intended. In determining the relationship between the Union and the State legislator, *Article 72(1) has favoured an alternative-exclusive division over a cumulative-shared distribution of competences*; and the former mode simply does not allow for the continuous co-existence of two legislators—and with it the possibility of legislative conflicts ... In relation to a specific provision, there never exists a normative co-existence but only the temporal succession of two legislators.[31]

Viewed in this light, Article 72(1) GG triggers a 'transfer of legislative competences from the States to the Union'.[32] The dynamic nature of the German competence order here contrasts strikingly with the traditional US constitutional belief in a static competence order.

The Rise and Fall of 'Framework Competences'

In the past, a third type of competence belonging to the Union was defined as 'framework legislation'. According to Article 75 GG the Union was here confined to adopt a legislative 'framework'. Framework competences represented a constitutional minus: they simultaneously entitled and limited the Union to setting only a general 'frame' within which the States had to remain free to pursue their autonomous policies.

What were the contours of this legislative 'frame'? Past jurisprudence defined the concept as follows:

> Frame means that the Union law *cannot exist on its own* but that it was designed to be complemented by State legislation. Wherever the Union is given a framework competence, the States thus remain principally competent to legislate; yet in the interest of the common good these state competences are federally limited without however the Union ever being able to exhaustively legislate within the area. Whenever the Union legislator adopts framework laws it must therefore leave something to the States, *and that something must be of a substantial weight*. While State laws must fit into the federal frame, *the federal frame itself must consequently leave to the States the possibility of complementarily regulating the subject-matter according to the special circumstances in the State.*[33]

[31] W März, 'Artikel 31' in C Starck (ed), *Das Bonner Grundgesetz* (Franz Vahlen, 2000) rn54, 55 (my translation, emphasis added).

[32] G Leibholz and HJ Rinck, *Grundgesetz für die Bundesrepublik Deutschland* (Schmidt, Stand April 1992), Art 72, para 1.

[33] *BVerfGE* 4, 115—*Besoldungsgesetz von Nordrhein-Westfalen* (1954) 129–30 (my translation, emphasis added).

In this early pronouncement on the nature of framework competences, the German Constitutional Court indeed highlighted a number of characteristic features. *First*, the concept of 'frame' seemed to refer to a concrete piece of legislation and not to the abstract competence title in Article 75 GG. The federal legislator could thus never totally pre-empt state legislators.[34] *Second* and more precisely, States should theoretically remain co-legislators of 'substantial weight' within the regulated policy field. (Where exactly the federal legislator crossed the 'substantial weight' threshold was however an issue clouded by linguistic indeterminacy).[35] And *third*, while single sections of a federal statute could regulate a matter exhaustively,[36] the constitutionality of these exhaustive sections within the federal law was, dependent on a 'particularly strong and legitimate interest for uniform regulation of the matter'.[37]

Yet despite these strong principles, framework legislation became ever more detailed in constitutional practice, and the Länder's discontent finally translated into a constitutional amendment in 1994.[38] This Article 75 amendment was designed to sharpen the constitutional contours around framework laws so as to better safeguard the legislative competences of the States. The new Article 75(2) GG henceforth clarified that 'only in exceptional cases' could framework laws contain detailed or directly effective provisions;[39] and this constitutional mandate was subsequently interpreted in *Juniorprofessor*.[40] The Court here famously struck down a framework law on the ground that it had overstepped the constitutional limits imposed on 'framework' legislation:

> *Materially, the presence of an exceptional case must be determined on the basis of quantitative and qualitative criteria.* With regard to quantity, Article 75(2) GG decrees a

[34] *BVerfGE* 36, 193—*Zeugnisverweigerungsrecht* (1973) 202: 'Zwar kann eine Vollregelung für einzelne Teile einer Gesetzgebungsmaterie auch aufgrund der Kompetenz zur Rahmengesetzgebung getroffen werden; dann ist aber Voraussetzung, daß sie im Zusammenhang eines Gesetzeswerks steht, das—als Ganzes gesehen—dem Landesgesetzgeber noch Spielraum läßt und darauf angelegt ist, von ihm aufgrund eigener Entschließung ausgefüllt zu werden[.]'

[35] The German Constitutional Court here retreated to a casuistic judicial approach, claiming that the degree of sufficiency is contingent on the policy title under Art 75 of the Constitution.

[36] *BVerfGE* 66, 270—*Schleswig-Holsteinisches Hochschulgesetz* (1984) 285: 'Der Bundesgesetzgeber darf beim Erlass von Rahmenregelungen für einzelne Teile einer Gesetzgebungsmaterie auch eine Vollregelung treffen, namentlich dann, wenn an der einheitlichen Regelung dieser Frage ein besonders starkes und legitimes Interesse besteht und die Einzelregelung im Zusammenhang eines Gesetzeswerkes steht, das—als Ganzes gesehen—dem Landesgesetzgeber hinreichend Spielraum belässt und auf Ausfüllung angelegt ist.'

[37] *BVerfG* 43, 291—*Numerus Clausus* II (1977) 343: 'Bei Erlaß von Rahmenvorschriften darf der Bundesgesetzgeber für einzelne Teile einer Gesetzgebungsmaterie auch eine Vollregelung mit unmittelbarer Wirkung namentlich dann treffen, wenn an der einheitlichen Regelung dieser Frage ein besonders starkes und legitimes Interesse besteht, sofern die Einzelregelung im Zusammenhang eines Gesetzeswerkes steht, das—als Ganzes gesehen—dem Landesgesetzgeber noch Spielraum läßt und darauf angelegt ist, von ihm aufgrund eigener Entschließung ausgefüllt zu werden.'

[38] 42. Gesetz zur Änderung des Grundgesetzes vom 27.10.1994.

[39] The inserted Art 75(2) GG read: 'Rahmenvorschriften dürfen nur in Ausnahmefällen in Einzelheiten gehende oder unmittelbar geltende Regelungen enthalten.'

[40] *BVerfGE* 111, 226—*Juniorprofessor* (2004).

> norm-exception relationship that will already be violated when those provisions that exhaustively regulate a matter numerically dominate the federal law. But more importantly: qualitatively, these exhaustive federal norms must never break the framework character of the Union law ... These norms must therefore, when viewed against the background of the norm-exception relationship established by Article 75(2), be necessary in a qualified sense. *An exceptional case for detailed or directly effective federal rules thus only exists when framework legislation could not have been adopted without them, that is: where these exhaustive norms are virtually indispensable* ('schlechthin unerläßlich').[41]

Following this seminal judgment, framework legislation seemed to be subject to two strict conditions. Quantitatively, the number of exhaustive harmonising provisions within a federal law could never outnumber those provisions that allowed for supplementary state action. (The Court had designed this primitive quantitative criterion as a preliminary test.) The more refined qualitative dimension would—secondly—proceed to ask if those exceptionally exhaustive provisions were 'necessary'.[42] The necessity test, suggested by the Court, was thereby highly qualified: only where the detailed provisions were 'virtually indispensable' for the operation of the legislative scheme as a whole would the federal legislator be entitled to adopt the act.

Despite some spirited denial,[43] the constitutional philosophy behind framework competences was that of co-operative federalism.[44] They were therefore always a '*Fremdkörper*' within the competence order established by the German Constitution. And indeed: in line with dual federal ideas, the 2006 German Federalism Reform removed them altogether; yet simultaneously introduced a new type of legislative competence called 'derogation competence'.

Derogation Competences as True 'Concurrent Competences'?

Article 72 GG now distinguishes between three variants of 'concurrent competences': full concurrent competences,[45] concurrent competences whose exercise

[41] ibid para 94 (my translation, emphasis added).

[42] In an earlier part of the judgment, the Court also confirmed that framework laws 'müssen der ergänzenden Gesetzgebung der Länder substantielle Freiräume lassen, damit diese politisch selbstverantwortlich Recht setzen können' (ibid, para 83).

[43] I have explored this doctrinal point further in R Schütze, *From Dual to Cooperative Federalism*, above n 7, 65–66.

[44] *BVerfGE* 4, 115—*Besoldungsgesetz von Nordrhein-Westfalen* (1954) 129: 'Wenn der Bund von seiner Gesetzgebungskompetenz nach Art 74 GG Gebrauch macht, werden die Länder insoweit von ihrem Gesetzgebungsrecht ausgeschlossen. In den Sachbereichen, in denen der Bund gemäß Art 75 Rahmenvorschriften erläßt, bleibt die Gesetzgebungsbefugnis der Länder erhalten; Art 75 setzt sogar ein entsprechendes Tätigwerden des Landesgesetzgebers voraus.' This was confirmed in *BVerfGE* 111, 226—*Juniorprofessur* (2004), para 81: 'Art 75 GG ist auf kooperative Gesetzgebung von Bund und Ländern angelegt.'

[45] Art 72(1) GG.

is subject to a 'subsidiarity' test,[46] and—since 2006—there also exist concurrent competences whose exercise will not prevent the States from adopting derogating legislation. This third variant has come to be known as 'derogation competences'; and among the six areas listed, the most important competence here relates to the protection of the environment.[47]

What is the nature of this new competence type? Article 72(3) GG defines it by the fact that the States 'may enact laws at variance with' federal legislation and moreover states: '[a]s for the relationship between federal law and law of the *Länder*, the latest law enacted shall take precedence'.[48] This represents a revolutionary new idea: the introduction of a competence in which both the Union and the States can act and within which federal and state law enjoy hierarchical parity. Article 72(3) GG indeed qualifies, albeit within limited fields, the principle of (federal) precedence established in Article 31 GG.[49] For derogation competences are concurrent competences 'in a literal sense'.[50] The Union and the States truly 'compete' as the principle of supremacy is replaced by the principle of posterity: a later state law can overrule an earlier federal law (as much as a later federal law can overrule an earlier state law).[51] Importantly: the *lex posterior* only 'disapplies' earlier law with neither the federal nor the state law 'invalidating' the other. For that reason derogation competences have been said to constitute an 'atypical duplication of legislative competence' within German competence federalism.[52] Yet derogation competences still come closer to dual federalism than to co-operative federalism. For not only is the equality between the Union and its States—the central tenet behind dual federalism—here preserved; Union law and state law can never 'co-operate' *together*; since, on the contrary, the either-or

[46] Art 72(2) here states: 'The Federation shall have the right to legislate on matters falling within clauses 4, 7, 11, 13, 15, 19a, 20, 22, 25 and 26 of para (1) of Art 74, if and to the extent that the establishment of equivalent living conditions throughout the federal territory or the maintenance of legal or economic unity renders federal regulation necessary in the national interest.' This 'necessity' is akin to a 'subsidiarity' test because the 'necessity' of the federal legislation here relates to the necessity of a uniform—as opposed to diverse—legislation. Importantly, Art 72(4) GG adds that whenever the Union legislator finds that the 'necessity' has disappeared, it may decide to re-open the sphere for State law: 'A federal law may provide that federal legislation that is no longer necessary within the meaning of para (2) of this Article may be superseded by Land law.'

[47] Art 72(3) No 2 GG: 'protection of nature and landscape management (except for the general principles governing the protection of nature, the law on protection of plant and animal species or the law on protection of marine life)'. As the wording suggests, not all environmental legislation will fall within the 'derogation competence' but some 'derogation-resistant' core is expressly excluded.

[48] Art 72(3) GG.

[49] Art 31 GG: 'Federal law shall take precedence over Land law.'

[50] L Michael, 'Abweichungsgesetzgebung als experimentelles Element einer gemischten Bundesstaatslehre' (2011) 59 *JÖR* 321 at 325.

[51] M Kloepfer, 'Die Neue Abweichungsgesetzgebung der Länder und ihre Auswirkungen auf den Umweltbereicht' in R Pitschas and A Uhle (eds), *Wege gelebter Verfassung in Recht und Politik: Festschrift für Rupert Scholz zum 70. Geburtstag* (Duncker & Humblot, 2007) 651 at 659.

[52] C Seiler, 'Die Freigabe von Bundesrecht zur landesrechtlichen Gesetzgebung' in M Heintzen and A Uhle, *Neuere Entwicklungen im Kompetenzrecht: Zur Verteilung der Gesetzgebungszuständigkeiten zwischen Bund und Ländern nach der Föderalismusreform* (Duncker & Humblot, 2014) 239 at 241.

logic is resumed in such a way that either the Union or the States will 'govern' a particular field.[53]

The advantages of this new competence category have been said to be manifold. Not only would it offer more legislative freedom *to the States* by means of the hierarchical parity between federal and state law. The *Union*, too, would equally enjoy greater legislative freedom because it could henceforth adopt fully developed legislative solutions that need not reserve legislative space to the States.[54]

EUROPEAN FEDERALISM: CO-OPERATIVE FEDERALISM (WITH A DUALIST STREAK)

The European Union is a federal union,[55] which is based on the principle of conferred powers. The principle can be found in Article 5(2) TEU and states: 'Under the principle of conferral, the Union shall act only within the limits of the competences conferred upon it by the Member States in the Treaties to attain the objectives set out therein. Competences not conferred upon the Union in the Treaties remain with the Member States.' Unlike the German competence catalogues in Articles 73 and 74 GG, the EU Treaties generally grant legislative competences within each policy area.[56] Yet since the Lisbon Treaty, the European constitutional order also expressly acknowledges the idea of distinct competence categories.[57] Article 2 TFEU here reads as follows:

> 1. When the Treaties confer on the Union exclusive competence in a specific area, only the Union may legislate and adopt legally binding acts, the Member States being able to do so themselves only if so empowered by the Union or for the implementation of Union acts.
>
> 2. When the Treaties confer on the Union a competence shared with the Member States in a specific area, the Union and the Member States may legislate and adopt legally binding acts in that area. The Member States shall exercise their competence to the extent that the Union has not exercised its competence. The Member States shall again exercise their competence to the extent that the Union has decided to cease exercising its competence.

[53] For this point, albeit in the analogous context of Art 125a(2) GG, see: *BVerfGE* 111, 10—*Ladenschlussgesetz III* (2004) 29: 'Aus dieser Rechtslage folgt im Umkehrschluss, dass es den Ländern verwehrt ist, bei Fortbestand der bundesrechtlichen Regelung einzelne Vorschriften zu ändern. Die andernfalls entstehende Mischlage aus Bundes- und Landesrecht für ein und denselben Regelungsgegenstand im selben Anwendungsbereich wäre im bestehenden System der Gesetzgebung ein Fremdkörper.'

[54] M Kloepfer, above n 51, 654.

[55] R Schütze, 'On "Federal" Ground: The European Union as an (Inter)national Phenomenon' (2009) 46 *Common Market Law Review* 1069.

[56] We thus find the Union's competence on environmental protection (Art 192 TFEU) in the treaty title dedicated to the environment (Title XX of Part III of the TFEU).

[57] For the pre-Lisbon 'unwritten' competence categories established by constitutional practice, see R Schütze, 'The European Community's Federal Order of Competences: A Retrospective Analysis' in M Dougan and S Currie (eds), *50 Years of the European Treaties: Looking Back and Thinking Forward* (Hart Publishing, 2009) 63.

> 3. The Member States shall coordinate their economic and employment policies within arrangements as determined by this Treaty, which the Union shall have competence to provide.
>
> 4. The Union shall have competence, in accordance with the provisions of the Treaty on European Union, to define and implement a common foreign and security policy, including the progressive framing of a common defence policy.
>
> 5. In certain areas and under the conditions laid down in the Treaties, the Union shall have competence to carry out actions to support, coordinate or supplement the actions of the Member States, without thereby superseding their competence in these areas. Legally binding acts of the Union adopted on the basis of the provisions of the Treaties relating to these areas shall not entail harmonisation of Member States' laws or regulations.

The EU Treaties here recognise four general competence categories: exclusive competences, shared competences, coordinating competences and complementary competences; and Articles 3–6 TFEU correlate the various Union policies to a particular competence category. The existence of exclusive competences shows that the Union legal order does recognise elements of dual federalism;[58] yet the great majority of its competences are shared (or weaker) competences. Indeed, shared competences are the 'ordinary' competences of the European Union: unless the Treaties expressly provide otherwise, a Union competence will be shared.[59] This general principle is, however, severely qualified in the external relations sphere; and as Article 2(4) TFEU acknowledges, a very special competence category will here also apply to the Union's common foreign and security policy.

Let us explore some of these competence categories in more detail.

Shared Competences and Co-operative Federalism I

Within a shared competence, 'the Union *and* the Member States may legislate'.[60] And the Court has time and again held that whenever the Union has legislated within an area, the Member States will *not* lose their competence to legislate within the same area; on the contrary, the Court here explores whether there is a legislative conflict—whether jurisdictional or substantial—between Union *legislation* and state *legislation*.

Was Article 2(2) TFEU therefore inspired by the philosophy of co-operative federalism? If that is the case, then the definition of shared competences offered

[58] Art 3(1) TFEU here states: 'The Union shall have exclusive competence in the following areas: (a) customs union; (b) the establishing of the competition rules necessary for the functioning of the internal market; (c) monetary policy for the Member States whose currency is the euro; (d) the conservation of marine biological resources under the common fisheries policy; (e) common commercial policy.'

[59] Art 4 TFEU states that EU competences will be shared 'where the Treaties confer on it a competence which does not relate to the areas referred to in Art 3 and 6', that is: areas of exclusive or complementary EU competence.

[60] Art 2(2) TFEU (emphasis added).

is far from perfect. For the formulation '[t]he Member States shall exercise their competences to the extent that the Union has not exercised its competence' invokes the geometrical image of a divided field: the Member States may only legislate in that part which the European Union has not (yet) entered. Within one field, *either* the European Union *or* the Member States can exercise their shared competence.[61]

When viewed against the constitutional status quo ante, this is a fundamentally misleading definition of shared competences. For in the past 60 years, shared competences have generally allowed the Union and the Member States to act *in the same field at the same time*. The exception to that general rule concerns situations where the Union field-pre-empted the Member States.[62] The formulation in Article 2(2) TFEU seems to be based on that exception. It appears to demand 'automatic [field] pre-emption of Member State action where the Union has exercised its power'.[63] This must—in my view—have been a 'German' mistake: the drafters of the provision must have taken their cues—directly or indirectly, actually or potentially—from the German competence paradigm and its insistence that every exercise of a concurrent competence will lead to (constitutional) field pre-emption.

Will the technique of minimum harmonisation—allowing for higher national standards and so common within European law—thus be in danger? This seems doubtful, since the EU Treaties expressly identify minimum harmonisation competences as shared competences.[64] However, the bad formulation within Article 2(2) TFEU has dialectically forced the Treaty-drafters to clarify a 'special' type of shared competence in Articles 4(3) and (4) TFEU. Both paragraphs separate the policy areas of research, technological development and space, as well as development co-operation and humanitarian aid, from the ordinary shared competences. For according to paragraphs 3 and 4, the 'exercise of that competence shall not result in Member States being prevented from exercising theirs'.[65] This special type of shared competence has been described as parallel competence;[66]

[61] The Union may, however, decide to 'cease exercising its competence'. This reopening of legislative space arises 'when the relevant EU institutions decide to repeal a legislative act, in particular better to ensure constant respect for the principles of subsidiarity and proportionality'. See Declaration (No 18) 'In relation to the delimitation of competences'.

[62] On the various pre-emption types, see below.

[63] P Craig, 'Competence: Clarity, Conferral, Containment and Consideration' (2004) 29 *European Law Review* 323, 334. The Treaties, however, clarify that such field pre-emption would 'only' be in relation to the legislative act (see Protocol (No 25) 'on the Exercise of Shared Competence': 'With reference to Art 2 of the Treaty on the Functioning of the European Union on shared competence, when the Union has taken action in a certain area, the scope of this exercise of competence only covers those elements governed by the Union act in question and therefore does not cover the whole [competence] area.').

[64] See Art 4(2)(e) TFEU on the shared 'environment' competence.

[65] In the words of the Final Report of the Working Group V 'Complementary Competences' (CONV 375/1/02 Rev 1), within these areas Union activities 'would never preempt the competence of the Member States' (ibid 9).

[66] D Wyatt A Dashwood et al, *European Union Law* (Sweet & Maxwell, 2011) 104.

yet in actual fact it only describes the effect an ordinary shared competence should have under the philosophy of co-operative federalism.[67]

Shared Competences and Co-operative Federalism II

What are the legal consequences following the exercise of a shared Union competence? The two governing principles within European law here are the principles of (legislative) supremacy and pre-emption.[68]

With regard to the principle of supremacy, the Union legal order has thereby adopted an absolute perspective under which all Union legislation prevails over all forms of national law. Yet what are the legal consequences of supremacy? Must a national court 'hold such provisions inapplicable to the extent to which they are incompatible with [Union] law', or must it 'declare them void'?[69] The classic answer to this question was given in *Simmenthal II*,[70] where the Court found that the supremacy of European law would not render national law void but only 'inapplicable'. Not 'invalidation' but 'disapplication' was required under the supremacy principle.[71] The Union legal order, while integrated with the national legal orders, is thus not a 'unitary' legal order. European law leaves the 'validity' of national norms untouched; and it will never negate the underlying legislative competence of the Member States. (And while the national *legislator* will be required to amend or repeal national provisions that give rise to legal uncertainty,[72] this secondary obligation is not a direct result of the supremacy doctrine but derives from Article 4(3) TEU).[73]

What about the principle of pre-emption? The important question behind the doctrine of pre-emption is this: to what degree will Union law displace national

[67] Importantly: unlike the German idea of 'derogation competences' the principles of supremacy and pre-emption will however apply here. Whenever the Union adopts legislative norms under Arts 4(3) and (4) TFEU, Union law will thus prevail over prior and posterior national legislation!

[68] For an overview of the two principles, see R Schütze, *European Constitutional Law*, above n 8, Chapter 4.

[69] This very question was raised in Case 34/67 *Firma Gebrüder Luck v Hauptzollamt Köln-Rheinau* [1968] ECR 245.

[70] Case 106/77 *Amministrazione delle Finanze dello Stato v Simmenthal SpA* [1978] ECR 629. But see also Case 48/71 *Commission v Italy* [1978] ECR 629.

[71] This was subsequently confirmed in Joined Cases C-10-22/97 *Ministero delle Finanze v IN.CO. GE.'90 Srl and others* [1998] ECR I-6307.

[72] See Case C-185/96 *Commission v Hellenic Republic* [1998] ECR 6601, para 32: 'On that point, suffice it to recall that, according to established case-law, the maintenance of national legislation which is in itself incompatible with [European] law, even if the Member State concerned acts in accordance with [European] law, gives rise to an ambiguous state of affairs by maintaining, as regards those subject to the law who are concerned, a state of uncertainty as to the possibilities for them of relying on [European] law.' See also Case 367/98 *Commission v Portugal* [2002] ECR I-4731, esp para 41: 'The Court has consistently held that the incompatibility of provisions of national law with provisions of the Treaty, even those directly applicable, can be definitively eliminated only by means of binding domestic provisions having the same legal force as those which require to be amended.'

[73] See eg Case 74/86 *Commission v Germany* [1988] ECR 2139, para 12.

law on the same matter? Unlike German competence federalism, the European pre-emption doctrine is a 'relative' doctrine. Three pre-emption categories may here be distinguished: field pre-emption, obstacle pre-emption, and rule pre-emption.[74] Field pre-emption refers to those situations where the Court does not investigate any *material* normative conflict, but simply excludes the Member States on the ground that the Union has exhaustively legislated for the field. In contrast to field pre-emption, obstacle and rule pre-emption—our second and third pre-emption categories—require some *material* conflict between European and national law. The most concrete form of conflict will here occur where national legislation literally contradicts a *specific European rule.* Obstacle pre-emption is, however, wider than rule pre-emption. The Court will not go into the details of the legislative scheme, but will simply find that the national law somehow interferes with the proper functioning or the objectives of the Union legislation.

The European doctrine of pre-emption consequently acknowledges the possible co-existence of Union and national legislation and therefore represents the co-operative idea of shared—not concurrent—competences.

European Competences as 'Framework Competences'?

Having lost the battle on the *scope* of Union competences early on,[75] the Member States of the European Union soon adopted a different constitutional strategy by trying to 'contain' the *nature* of Union competences. The three 'containing' competence types that were introduced into the Union legal order since the Single European Act are here: 'minimum harmonisation' competences, coordinating competences and complementary competences. This subsection will particularly analyse the first and the third competence category in light of the German category of framework competence.[76]

Minimum Harmonisation Competences: Soft or Hard Constitutional Frame?

Starting with the Single European Act, a first attempt to contain Union competences was the introduction of 'minimum harmonisation' competences. The constitutional regime for environmental policy is paradigmatic for this type

[74] R Schütze, *European Constitutional Law*, above n 8, 134— which is based on my 'Supremacy without Pre-emption? The Very Slowly Emergent Doctrine of Community Pre-emption' (2006) 43 *Common Market Law Review* 1023.

[75] For an analysis of the expansion of Union competences in the past, see R Schütze, *From Dual to Cooperative Federalism*, above n 6, 132 et seq.

[76] Coordinating competences shall not be discussed here. The genesis of this type of competence appears to have been accidental (Presidium CONV 724/03 (Annex 2), p 68); and the addition of a new competence type was, arguably, unnecessary in light of Art 2(6) TFEU.

of (shared) competence. According to Article 193 TFEU, European laws 'shall not prevent any Member State from maintaining or introducing more stringent protective measures'. Union laws are consequently confined to laying down minimum standards that must permit national 'opt-ups'.[77] The central question, however, is this: must all EU environmental laws be minimum harmonisation measures, or does Article 193 TFEU only 'softly' require the Union legislator to leave some—abstractly defined—legislative space to the national legislators? Surprisingly, after almost three decades of constitutional practice, the issue has not been definitely resolved.

Two views are possible. According to a first view, Article 193 will not constitutionally prevent the Union legislator from adopting specific legislative acts that totally harmonise all matters within their scope.[78] This first view therefore only deposits a strong *presumption* against field pre-emption—codified in Article 193; while the Union legislator faces no absolute *constitutional limitation* to exhaustively harmonise a specific environmental issue. By contrast, a second view argues that Article 193 TFEU refers to every single piece of European legislation. Each Union act must thus leave a degree of autonomous space to the national legislators; and there are heavy legal arguments in favour of this *hard* constitutional solution. First, the very wording of Article 193 points in that direction. For the frame of reference for the higher national standard is not the Union environmental *policy*, but the specific Union *measure(s)*. Second, from a teleological perspective, the aim of achieving a high level of protection within the Union would always be better served by allowing Member States to go beyond the federal compromise represented in European legislation.[79] And third, requiring the Union legislator to leave regulatory space to the national legislators *within the scope of the Union act* would provide a more concrete 'jurisdictional' standard that would better safeguard the Member States' legislative autonomy.

What are the judicial guidelines from the European Court of Justice? The nature of European environmental legislation had—partly—been addressed in *Fornasar.*[80] The Court was here asked to interpret the exhaustiveness of the Union legislation on hazardous waste, in particular Directive 91/689. One part of the ruling thereby signalled the Court's support for the hard constitutional solution. '[European] rules do not seek to effect complete harmonisation in the area

[77] This is different from the 'opt-out' mechanism in Art 114(4)–(9) TFEU, which allows for a *derogation* from European legislation.

[78] JH Jans, *European Environmental Law* (Europa Law Publishing, 2000) 118.

[79] G Winter, 'Die Sperrwirkung von Gemeinschaftssekundärrecht für einzelstaatliche Regelungen des Binnenmarkts mit besonderer Berücksichtigung von Art 130 t EGV' (1998) 51 *Die öffentliche Verwaltung* 377 at 380.

[80] Case C-318/98 *Fornasar et al v Sante Chiarcosso* [2000] ECR I-4785.

of the environment'.[81] This absolute statement was however subsequently relativised in a second part of the ruling, where the Court specifically analysed the legislative regime established by the Directive; and since the latter expressly entitled Member States to supplement the Union law, it could be construed as a 'minimum harmonisation' measure.

This evasive ambivalence has been repeated in subsequent jurisprudence.[82] However, in *Azienda Agro-Zootecnica Franchini*,[83] the Court appears to have given a strong push in favour of the hard constitutional frame. The case concerned an Italian law under which it was forbidden to construct new wind turbines within a 500-metre buffer zone of a 'special protection area'—a prohibition that was claimed to violate a number of Union directives, and in particular the Birds and Habitats Directives. In its pre-emption analysis, the Court reasoned as follows:

> It should be noted in this regard that European Union rules do not seek to effect complete harmonisation in the area of the environment. Article 14 of the Birds Directive provides that Member States may introduce stricter protective measures than those provided for under that directive. *There is no provision in the Habitats Directive that is equivalent to Article 14 of the Birds Directive. Nevertheless, since that directive was adopted on the basis of Article 192 TFEU, it should be noted that Article 193 TFEU provides that Member States may adopt more stringent protective measures* ... It follows that legislation such as that at issue in the main proceedings which ... imposes an absolute prohibition on the construction of new wind turbines in those areas, pursues the same objectives as the Habitats Directive. To the extent that it provides for a stricter system of protection than that established by Article 6 of that Directive, it therefore constitutes a more stringent protective measure within the meaning of Article 193 TFEU.[84]

The Court here appears to suggest that even in the absence of a *legislative* clause expressly allowing for the adoption of stricter national standards within Union legislation, the Member States would always be allowed to go beyond the relevant Union standard because of the *constitutional* guarantee offered in Article 193 TFEU. If that constitutional frame argument was consistently accepted, minimum harmonisation competences would come close to (German) framework competences.

[81] ibid para 46.

[82] The Court did not resolve this ambivalence in Case C-6/03 *Deponiezweckverband Eiterköpfe v Land Rheinland-Pfalz* [2005] ECR I-2753. The Court, again, started out with a broad constitutional statement (ibid para 27): 'The first point to be noted is that the [European] rules do not seek to effect complete harmonisation in the area of the environment.' However, in a second step, the Court found—again—that the specific Directive only set minimum standards (ibid para 31): 'The wording and broad logic of those provisions make it clearly apparent that they set a minimum reduction to be achieved by the Member States and they do not preclude the adopting by the latter of more stringent measures.' And—again—it found that 'Art [193 TFEU] *and the Directive* allow the Member States to introduce more stringent protection measures that go beyond the minimum requirements fixed by the Directive' (ibid para 32 (emphasis added)).

[83] Case C-2/10 *Azienda Agro-Zootecnica Franchini sarl and Eolica di Altamura Srl v Regione Puglia* [2011] ECR I-6561.

[84] ibid, paras 48–52 (emphasis added).

Complementary Competences as Non-legislative Competences?

The term 'complementary competence' is not used in Article 2(5) TFEU. However, it appears to be the best way generically to refer to 'actions to support, coordinate or supplement the actions of the Member States'.[85] A good example here is the Union competence to protect human health, which is formulated as follows:

> Union action, which shall *complement* national policies, shall be directed towards improving public health, preventing physical and mental illness and diseases, and obviating sources of danger to physical and mental health … The Union shall encourage cooperation between the Member States in the areas referred to in this Article and, if necessary, lend support to their action. *It shall in particular encourage cooperation between the Member States to improve the complementarity of their health services in cross-border areas.*[86]

The contours of this competence type are largely unexplored by jurisprudence. However, after the Lisbon reform, it appears to be a defining characteristic of complementary competences that they do '*not entail harmonisation* of Member States' laws or regulations'.[87] The formulation suggests the Union's intent to guarantee legislative space to the Member States.

But what exactly is the prohibition of harmonisation supposed to mean? Two views can be put forward. According to the first, the exclusion of harmonisation means that Union legislation must not limit national legislative competences. However, considering the wide definition given to the concept of 'harmonisation' by the Court of Justice in *Spain v Council*, any legislative intervention on the part of the Union will unfold a *de facto* harmonising effect within the national legal orders.[88] From this strict reading, the exclusion of harmonisation would consequently deny all pre-emptive effect to European legislation.[89] A second, less restrictive view argues that the Union's legislative powers are only trimmed so as to prevent the de jure harmonisation of (existing) national legislation.[90] *Both*

[85] Art 2(5) TFEU. The Working Group V 'Complementary Competencies', above n 65, felt that '[t]he term *complementary competence* is inadequate' (ibid 1); yet its reasons are hard—if not impossible—to follow. For it is simply a mistake to argue that the term 'complementary competence' misleadingly suggested that the Union was competent 'in fields where Member States are fully competent' (ibid 1); or that it was misleading because 'Member States have not transferred their legislative competence to the Union' (ibid 3). Something our constitution makers could have—should have!—known is that in line with the principle of conferral, the Union can only act—even for legally binding 'supporting measures'—when it has a competence; and a quick look at some of the 'competences' that they identified as 'supporting measures' were actually 'legislative competences'.

[86] Art 168(1) and (2) TFEU (emphasis added).

[87] Art 2(5) TFEU—second indent (emphasis added).

[88] Case C-350/92 *Spain v Council* [1995] ECR I-1985. In that judgment, the Court found the adoption of a Regulation not beyond the scope of Art 114 TFEU because it aimed 'to prevent the heterogeneous development of national laws leading to further disparities' in the internal market (ibid para 35).

[89] *cf* A Bardenhewer-Rating and F Niggermeier, 'Artikel 152' para 20 in H von der Groeben and J Schwarze, *Kommentar zum Vertrag über die EU* (Nomos, 2003).

[90] For Lenaerts, 'incentive measures can be adopted in the form of Regulations, Directives, Decisions or atypical legal acts and are thus normal legislative acts of the [Union.]' '[T]he fact that a

views appear, however, problematic. National legislators are—still—quicker in passing legislation than the Union legislator. Will the Union therefore never be able to adopt a European standard? If so, it would be difficult to speak of a truly independent Union *policy* as the European legislator simply cannot make its own *policy* choices.[91] In light of these uncertainties, the definition of complementary competences in Article 2(5) TFEU represents a failure. For their 'classification' has hardly added any clarity to the constitutional status quo ante.

External Competences and the Logic of Dual Federalism

With regard to their nature, the Treaties do not—as a rule—distinguish between internal and external competences; and indeed, within the areas of Union competences listed in Articles 3–6 TFEU, we find a number of external competences.[92] There nevertheless exist two very important exceptions to this rule. Not only does Article 2(4) TFEU specifically isolate the Union's CFSP competence from the ordinary competence categories listed in Article 2 TFEU; Article 3(2) TFEU moreover provides an additional source of exclusivity for the conclusion of international agreements. Let us explore these two exceptions in this last subsection.

The Union's CFSP Competence: A Sui Generis Competence?

The nature of the Union's CFSP competence has been a legal problem ever since its inception. According to an early view, EU law adopted under a CFSP competence was 'classic' international law that contrasted with supranational European law adopted under the 'ordinary' of the Union.[93] A second view, by contrast, argued that the CFSP was part of one and the same European legal order.[94] The Lisbon Treaty has reinforced this second view. While recognising that the CFSP 'is subject

[European] incentive measure may have the indirect effect of harmonizing … does not necessarily mean that it conflicts with the prohibition on harmonization' (K Lenaerts, 'Subsidiarity and Community Competence in the Field of Education' (1994–95) 1 *Columbia Journal of European Law* 1 at 13 and 15).

[91] The national 'pre-emption' of Union action would only be lifted where the diverse national laws create genuine obstacles to intra-European trade and/or distortions of competition. The Union would then be entitled to have recourse to Art 114 TFEU.

[92] For example, the common commercial policy is listed under the Union's exclusive competences (see Art 3(1)(e) TFEU), environmental policy is listed as a shared competence (but see Art 191(4) TFEU: 'Within their respective spheres of competence, the Union and the Member States shall cooperate with third countries and with the competent international organisations. The arrangements for Union cooperation may be the subject of agreements between the Union and the third parties concerned'); and public health is listed as a complementary competence (see Art 6(a) TFEU and Art 168(3) TFEU: 'The Union and the Member States shall foster cooperation with third countries and the competent international organisations in the sphere of public health').

[93] M Pechstein and C Koenig, *Die Europäische Union* (Mohr Siebeck, 2000) 5 et seq.

[94] K Lenaerts and T Corthaut, 'Of Birds and Hedges: the Role of Primacy in invoking Norms of EU law' (2006) 31 *European Law Review* 287 at 288.

to specific rules and procedures',[95] the Treaty on European Union and the Treaty on the Functioning of the European Union confirm that the two treaties 'have the same legal value'.[96] This includes secondary CFSP law. For indeed, the CFSP competence will be exercised by the 'ordinary' legal instruments of the Union legal order,[97] yet unlike 'ordinary' Union law, the direct effect of CFSP law appears to be exceptional.

How shall we best characterise the CFSP competence? The Treaties treat the CFSP competence as distinct from the Union competences referred to in Articles 3–6 TFEU.[98] But what is its exact nature? We might find a first key to this question in Article 24 TEU dealing with the nature of the CFSP competence. The provision declares that '[t]he adoption of legislative acts shall be excluded' within the CFSP area. If the reference to 'legislative acts' were given a formal meaning, that is, referring to acts adopted under a legislative procedure, then Article 24 TEU would state the obvious. By contrast, if the formulation is given a material meaning, then Article 24 TEU signalled the exclusion of *generally* applicable CFSP norms. A second key might be found in Declaration 14 to the European Treaties, which underlines that the CFSP competence 'will not affect the existing legal basis, responsibilities, and powers of each Member State in relation to the formulation and conduct of its foreign policy, its national diplomatic service, relations with third countries and participation in international organisations'.[99] This formulation comes close to the idea of a parallel competence, but the better view insists that the CFSP competence is a 'special' or '*sui generis*' competence within the Union legal order.[100]

Article 3(2) TFEU: Subsequently Exclusive Treaty-making Competences

We find a second major exception to the 'ordinary' competence categories of the Union legal order in Article 3(2) TFEU. The provision offers a special rule for the Union's competence to conclude international agreements and states:

> The Union shall also have exclusive competence for the conclusion of an international agreement when its conclusion is provided for in a legislative act of the Union or is necessary to enable the Union to exercise its internal competence, or in so far as its conclusion may affect common rules or alter their scope.

[95] Art 24(1) TEU.

[96] Art 1 TEU and Art 1 TFEU.

[97] That is: decisions and international agreements. Prior to the Lisbon Treaty, the CFSP competence was to be exercised by a number of special legal instruments, such as 'joint actions' and 'common positions'.

[98] Art 40 TEU makes a clear distinction between the CFSP competence and 'the Union competences referred to in Arts 3–6 of the Treaty on the Functioning of the European Union'.

[99] Declaration (No 14) concerning the Common Foreign and Security Policy.

[100] M Cremona, 'The Draft Constitutional Treaty: External Relations and External Action' (2003) 40 *Common Market Law Review* 1347 at 1354.

In addition to the constitutionally fixed exclusive competences—mentioned in Article 3(1) TFEU—the Union legal order thus acknowledges the *dynamic* growth of exclusive external competences. The latter thereby grow if one of three situations is fulfilled.[101] According to the first situation, the Union *gains* an exclusive Treaty-making power when the conclusion of an international agreement 'is provided for in a legislative act'. This formulation corresponds to the 'WTO Doctrine' established in *Opinion 1/94* on the compatibility of the WTO Agreement with the Treaties.[102] The second situation mentioned in Article 3(2) TFEU grants the Union an exclusive Treaty power, where this 'is necessary to enable the Union to exercise its internal competence'. This formulation aims to codify the 'Opinion 1/76 Doctrine'.[103] Finally, the third situation in Article 3(2) appears to refer to the Court's '*ERTA* doctrine'. Under the *ERTA* doctrine,[104] the Member States are deprived of their Treaty-making power whenever the exercise of those powers affects internal European law; and the Union here acquires an exclusive competence.

What are we to make of the idea of subsequently exclusive external competences? The EU Treaties normally take great care to clarify that the question of competences is a 'constitutional' question; yet within the external sphere, this is not the case. The dynamic nature of external competences has indeed been expressly confirmed by the European Court of Justice:

> The exclusive or non-exclusive nature of the [Union]'s competence does not flow solely from the provisions of the Treaty but may also depend on the scope of the measures which have been adopted by the [Union] institutions for the application of those provisions and which are of such a kind as to deprive the Member States of an area of competence which they were able to exercise previously on a transitional basis.[105]

The European Court here espoused a theory that comes close to the German conception of (ordinary) 'concurrent' competences. For as soon as the Union exercises its (internal) competences, the Member States 'lose' their external competence to conclude international agreements. And while common under German constitutionalism, this 'competence federalism' may nevertheless be criticised. For from a theoretical perspective, the scope of the Union's exclusive competences should be a constitutional question and, as such, their scope should only be extended by means of constitutional amendment. It thus seems a feat of legal alchemy to permit the Union to modify its order of competences, especially because this would allow the European institutions to escape the reach of the subsidiarity principle.[106] The exclusive competence reading does also raise problems from a descriptive perspective. For in light of elements of 'co-operative' federalism within

[101] On the three judicial doctrines, see R Schütze, *Foreign Affairs and the EU Constitution* (Cambridge University Press, 2014) 256 et seq.

[102] Opinion 1/94 *(WTO Agreement)* [1994] ECR I-5267.

[103] Opinion 1/76 *(Laying-Up Fund)* [1977] ECR 741.

[104] Case 22/70 *Commission v Council* [1971] ECR 263.

[105] Opinion 2/91 *(ILO Convention 170)* [1993] ECR I-1061 para 9.

[106] C Callies, *Subsidiaritäts- und Solidaritätsprinzip in der Europäischen Union* (Nomos, 1999) 95.

the external sphere, one may wonder whether the mutually exclusive field logic of dual federalism truly offers the best analytical key to understand the jurisprudence of the Court.[107]

CONCLUSION(S)

Every federal order will be based on a division of (legislative) competences; yet only some of them will classify their competences into different types. Ever since the Laeken Declaration on the Future of the European Union, it has been a reform aim of the Union to achieve '[a] better division and definition of competences in the European Union';[108] and one central objective here was 'to clarify, simplify and adjust the division of competences between the Union and the Member States' in the form of 'clearer distinctions' between the various types of competence.[109] Has the Lisbon (Reform) Treaty fulfilled that mandate? Leaving the detailed answers to this question to later parts of this book, this chapter has tried to offer a general overview of the various classificatory choices.

We saw above that the Union legal order has—unlike the American legal order—adopted the 'Germanic' technique of competence categories. According to this technique, the Union's enumerated powers are divided into different types of competences—with each type supposedly representing a special balance in the power held, respectively, by the Union and the Member States. Article 2 TFEU thereby distinguishes four ordinary competence types (plus a special one for the CFSP). Like the German competence order, the European Union thereby recognises exclusive competences; and within the external relations sphere, it also acknowledges the existence of concurrent or subsequently exclusive competences. However, unlike the dual federalist philosophy underlying German federalism, the European Union legal order is based on a co-operative federalist philosophy. It has—like the US federal order—allowed for 'shared' competences that permit both the Union and its Member States to operate within the same sphere at the same time.

The constitutionalisation of this co-operative federalism is best illustrated by the rise of minimum-standard competences. These Union competences largely replicate the (by now repealed) German category of 'framework competences'; yet, the Lisbon Treaty makers—inexplicably—classified them as (ordinary) shared competences; and that despite the dual federalist definition of shared competence in Article 2(2)! This definitional mishap is not the only one if one considers the continuing uncertainty surrounding 'coordinating' and 'complementary' competences. Importantly: the latter can—formally—be

107 On this point, see R Schütze, *From Dual to Cooperative Federalism* above n 6, 329 et seq.
108 Laeken Declaration of 15 December 2001 on the Future of the European Union.
109 ibid.

legislative competences;[110] yet their material character may limit them to the adoption of non-regulatory acts. But even complementary competences can be the basis of—supreme—Union law and in that sense they differ from 'derogation competences'. This latter type of competence therefore remains a 'specialty' of German federalism; yet it is up to future constitution makers to reflect on whether or not they should also develop in the European Union legal order.

[110] The Treaty defines legislative competences formally as competences that envisage the application of the ordinary or a special legislative procedure; and in this sense, many complementary competences are legislative competences (*cf* Art 168(5) TFEU).

Part II

Areas of Complementary, Shared and Exclusive EU Competence

4

Exclusive Member State Competences—Is There Such a Thing?

BRUNO DE WITTE*

INTRODUCTION

AS THE COMPETENCES of the European Union expanded over time, leading it to deal with what were traditionally considered to be 'core state powers', such as monetary policy, immigration and defence,[1] some Member State governments became more keen to assert the existence of a range of exclusive competences, that is, policy domains in which they could freely decide and from which the EU institutions are excluded. This concern may seem odd at first sight since, legally speaking, the European Union remains an organisation with limited competences. The logical consequence of this, now explicitly drawn in Article 4(1) and Article 5(2) TEU, is that 'competences not conferred upon the Union in the Treaties remain with the Member States', and therefore there would seem to be no need to emphatically assert the existence of exclusive Member competences.

On further reflection, the simple notion of 'competences not conferred on the Union in the Treaties' can refer to two different things: to policy domains not mentioned in the Treaties as EU competences; and to specific actions which the Treaty text does not allow the Union to undertake in policy domains entrusted to it. An example of the former type of non-conferred competence is nationality law: nowhere in the Treaties is the EU given competence to regulate the conditions for the acquisition or loss of the nationality of the Member States, which might mean that this matter remains within the exclusive competence of the states. An example of the latter type can be found in Article 153(4) TFEU, which states that EU action in the social policy field, as defined in that article, 'shall not affect the right of Member States to define the fundamental principles of their social security systems and must not significantly affect the financial equilibrium thereof'.

* Bruno de Witte is Professor of European Union Law at Maastricht University and at the European University Institute in Florence.

[1] P Genschel and M Jachtenfuchs (eds), *Beyond the Regulatory Polity? The European Integration of Core State Powers* (Oxford, Oxford University Press, 2014).

The mirror image of these two kinds of limitation of EU actions is formed by two kinds of preserved Member State competences: they can either be implied (in the absence of competences given to the EU) or explicit (resulting from Treaty language prohibiting EU action). In this chapter, we will use the expression *retained competences* for the former category, and *reserved competences* for the latter. We will discuss both types of exclusive Member State competences separately, namely retained competences and reserved competences; in both cases, we will trace the evolution until the adoption of Lisbon Treaty, and the main emphasis will be on the interpretations given by the Court of Justice. We will deal with new developments in and after the Lisbon Treaty, in relation to both retained and reserved competences. The reason for this chronological distinction is that the Treaty reform process leading up to the Lisbon Treaty was openly concerned with the question of whether and how to preserve exclusive Member State competences, and the final result of that discussion, the Lisbon Treaty, includes some traces of that concern. The question underlying the analysis in this chapter, as posed in its title, is whether some or all of the retained and/or reserved competences can truly be considered as *exclusive* Member State competences. In a famous sentence written in 1990, the current president of the Court of Justice, Koen Lenaerts, put this in doubt when stating that 'there simply is no nucleus of sovereignty that the Member State can invoke, as such, against the Community'.[2]

RETAINED COMPETENCES

As regards retained competences, the central principle established by the Court of Justice is that the silence of the Treaties does not imply a green light for the Member States; the fact that the European Union is not entrusted with competences in a given policy domain does not imply that the Member States can freely act in that domain. This is rendered by the 'retained powers formula', a typical sentence adopted by the Court of Justice in a long series of cases since the mid-1990s.[3] The formula takes the form of a 'no, but' argument: *no*, the European Union has no competence to deal with subject X, *but* this does not mean that the Member States can do whatever they want on that subject; their competence is, rather, constrained by the need to respect certain legal obligations stemming from EU law.

The *Schwarz* judgment of 2007 provides a good illustration of the use and function of the formula. The case concerned a German tax scheme offering a reduction

[2] K Lenaerts, 'Constitutionalism and the Many Faces of Federalism' (1990) 38 *American Journal of Comparative Law* 205, 220.

[3] For a general analysis of the use of this formula by the Court, see L Azoulai, 'La formule des compétences retenues des Etats membres devant la Cour de Justice de l'Union européenne' in E Neframi (ed), *Objectifs et compétences dans l'Union européenne* (Bruxelles, Bruylant, 2013) 341, and L Boucon, 'EU Law and Retained Powers of Member States' in L Azoulai (ed), *The Question of Competence in the European Union* (Oxford, Oxford University Press, 2014) 168.

of income tax to compensate for the payment of school fees to private schools established in Germany. The Schwarz family was denied the tax reduction for school fees they were paying to a private school established in the UK. The Court of Justice used the retained competences formula in two consecutive paragraphs, in relation to direct taxation and education respectively:

> According to well-established case-law, although direct taxation falls within their competence, the Member States must none the less exercise that competence consistently with Community law' … Similarly, whilst Community law does not detract from the power of the Member States as regards, first, the content of education and the organization of education systems and their cultural and linguistic diversity … and, secondly, the content and organisation of vocational training …, the fact remains that, when exercising that power, Member States must comply with Community law, in particular the provisions on the freedom to provide services.[4]

Based on this reasoning, the Court came to the conclusion that Germany acted in breach of the freedom to provide services by restricting tax deduction for educational expenses to schools situated within Germany. Despite the fact that the German authorities are fully responsible for the organisation of their education system, and have retained the competence for direct taxation as well, EU law obligations forced them to adapt their taxation and education policies.

The same, or a very similar, formula is used in numerous judgments dealing with such diverse subjects as social security,[5] laws on nationality,[6] rules on name giving,[7] civil status of persons,[8] and the registration of ships.[9] As was noted by Azoulai,[10] those policy areas are not all similarly situated from the point of view of EU competences. Indeed, some of those domains, such as direct taxation and social security, belong to the shared competences of the EU; others, such as education and culture, belong to the supporting competences of the EU; and still others, such as nationality and name giving, are matters which can seem to be more truly 'retained', as no competence at all is given to the EU institutions. The Court of Justice does not distinguish between those three domains, but one might say that the retained powers formula does not apply equally well to all three of them. In particular, it does not seem quite right to state that direct taxation falls within the competence of the Member State, given the fact that EU legislative measures in this domain can be, and have been, adopted on the basis of Article 115 TFEU. Yet, although these policy domains fit in different categories from the point of view of EU competences, they can be said to share a common characteristic, namely

[4] Case C-76/05 *Schwarz* EU:C:2007:492, para 69 and 70.

[5] Case 238/82 *Duphar* EU:C:1984:45; Case C-157/99 *Geraerts-Smits and Peerbooms* EU:C:2001:404, paras 44–46; Case C-84/11 *Susisalo* EU:C:2012:374, paras 26–27.

[6] Case C-135/08 *Rottmann* EU:C:2010:104, paras 39 and 41.

[7] Case C-148/02 *Garcia Avello* EU:C:2003:539, para 25.

[8] Case C-267/12 *Frédéric Hay* EU:C:2013:823, para 26.

[9] Case C-221/89 *Factortame* EU:C:1991:320, para 17.

[10] L Azoulai, 'La formule', above n 3, 358.

that they are expressions either of core elements of national sovereignty (taxation, nationality) or of key components of national welfare states (education, social security).[11]

The retained powers formula does sound somewhat contradictory: how can the Court say that EU law does not 'detract' from Member State powers if the exercise of those powers is limited by EU law obligations? It seems, in fact, that the 'no detract' wording should not be taken literally: EU law does in fact detract from the Member States' competences since their policy choices (the 'exercise' of the competences) are limited by EU law norms. Those norms of EU law are, in most of the cases, the fundamental freedoms of the common market, which have an inherent tendency to apply to a wide range of domains of national laws; but the same effect has been ascribed to other norms of EU law, such as Union citizenship[12] and the principle of non-discrimination; thus, in a recent case relating to discrimination on grounds of sexual orientation, the Court stated: 'marital status and the benefits flowing therefrom are matters which fall within the competence of the Member States and … EU law does not detract from that competence. However, in the exercise of that competence the Member States must comply with EU law, in particular the provisions relating to the principle of non-discrimination.'[13]

Still, there is nothing shocking in the Court's doctrine. Does the same effect not occur when states conclude other international Treaties? The obligations contained in an international Treaty surely restrict the exercise of state competences, without those competences themselves being transferred to the international level. For example, a state's environmental policy may be restricted by the commitments it undertook under the international climate change regime, and its criminal procedure may be affected by its obligations under the ECHR. The CJEU's retained powers formula could be seen as expressing that same, hardly revolutionary, idea. Seen from this perspective, the fact that (for example) obligations accepted by EU Member States to allow for the free movement of persons and services may cause limitations to the exercise of their education policy is hardly shocking. What distinguishes EU law, though, is the broad sweep of the free movement obligations (affecting a vast range of domestic policies), the fact that the scope of the limitations thus imposed on the Member States is ultimately decided by an independent court (the CJEU), and finally the fact that these same free movement provisions do not just act as negative limits to Member States' retained powers, but also form the basis for positive measures of Union law that make inroads into these same retained domains.

[11] L Boucon, 'EU Law and Retained Powers', above n 3, 182.

[12] See eg Case C-438/14 *Nabiel Peter Bogendorff von Wolffersdorf* EU:C:2016:401, para 32 (in relation to the rules on name giving).

[13] Case C-443/15 *David Parris v Trinity College Dublin* EU:C:2016:897, para 58. Earlier cases in which EU norms on sex equality were found to limit the exercise of the states' retained powers in the organisation of their armed forces were Case C-273/97 *Sirdar* EU:C:1999:523, and Case C-285/98 *Kreil* EU:C:2000:2.

The latter phenomenon is well known, but deserves to be highlighted in this context because it has contributed in no small part to the uneasiness of some Member States about what they perceived as a competence drift in retained policy areas. The EU's internal market competence, as is often highlighted in the literature, is a functional or purposive competence.[14] Unlike other shared competences, it is not defined by a particular sector of activity (such as agriculture or transport), or by the existence of a policy field (such as environment or immigration), but by the underlying purpose of the EU's action to improve the smooth functioning of the internal market. Yet, that internal market purpose need not be, and cannot logically be, the only purpose of internal market legislation. Such legislation also invariably and legitimately pursues other public policy objectives. Internal market legislation is always also 'about something else', and that something else may in fact be the main reason why the internal market measure was adopted.[15] Even if a given non-market objective corresponds to a domain of retained Member State competence (as is the case for health, culture or education), the internal market competence can still be used. Thus, in its *Tobacco Advertising* judgment, the Court at no point sought to determine whether the health protection objective of the directive was dominant or ancillary to the internal market objective. In later tobacco-related cases, the Court accepted with so many words that health protection was the *decisive* factor in the adoption of the act.[16] In other words, the Member States' retained powers are not only *constrained* by the fact that they must respect EU law obligations when exercising those powers, they can also be *complemented* by harmonisation measures adopted by the European Union institutions.

RESERVED COMPETENCES

The text of the EEC Treaty was, right from the start, littered with derogation provisions, through which Community law norms were made subject to exceptions which Member States could invoke for listed reasons of public interest. The most well-known examples are the public policy exceptions to the free movement of goods, of services and of persons, which are still contained in the current text of the Treaties. For example, Article 36 TFEU states that the rules on free movement of goods contained in other articles of the same Treaty chapter 'shall not preclude' national restrictions that are justified on a wide list of grounds, which are both very general (public morality, public policy and public security) and quite specific (such as the protection of national treasures and of intellectual property).

[14] See G Davies, 'Democracy and Legitimacy in the Shadow of Purposive Competence' (2015) 21 *European Law Journal* 2.

[15] See B De Witte, 'A Competence to Protect—The Pursuit of Non-Market Aims through Internal Market Legislation' in P Syrpis (ed), *The Judiciary, the Legislature and the EU Internal Market* (Cambridge, Cambridge University Press, 2012) 25.

[16] Case C-210/03 *Swedish Match* EU:C:2004:802, para 31.

The intention of the Member States, when including these derogation clauses in the original text of the EEC Treaty, may well have been to create EC-free zones, in which the Member States would be permitted to do as they pleased as long as their actions could plausibly be linked to one of the grounds listed in the Treaty text. But, as we know, this is not the approach adopted by the Court of Justice. Very early on, it took an approach which it has stubbornly confirmed ever since and is now very much 'settled case law'. In the *Simmenthal* case, decided by the Court in 1976, the Italian government presented the argument that Article 36 EEC (the forerunner of current Article 36 TFEU) 'leaves the matters to which it refers to be dealt with by Member States under their sovereign powers', to which the Court replied that 'Article 36 *is not designed to reserve certain matters to the exclusive jurisdiction* of Member States but permits national laws to derogate from the principle of the free movement of goods to the extent to which such derogation is and continues to be justified for the attainment of the objectives referred to in that article.'[17]

In one of the more recent judgments in this long line of cases, the Court sums up its position as follows:

> While Member States essentially retain the freedom to determine the requirements of public policy and public security in accordance with their national needs, which can vary from one Member State to another and from one era to another, particularly as justification for a derogation from the fundamental principle of free movement of persons, those requirements must nevertheless be interpreted strictly, so that their scope cannot be determined unilaterally by each Member State without any control by the institutions of the European Union.[18]

Here, as with the retained powers formula discussed in the previous section of this chapter, the Court's formula is marked by a logical contradiction, as it affirms in the same breath that the states 'retain the freedom to determine the requirements' and 'that their scope cannot be determined unilaterally by each Member State'. Of those two statements, it is only the latter that counts; the states are *not free* to determine public policy requirements that restrict free movement; they take the initiative to formulate those requirements but the Court can judge whether they are acceptable or not. The public policy derogations, thus, do not create an EU-free zone.

More strongly formulated competence reservations were laid down (again, since the early days of the Treaty of Rome) in Articles 295 and 296 EC (now Articles 345 and 346 TFEU). Article 345 TFEU states: 'The Treaties shall in no way prejudice the rules in Member States governing the system of property ownership'; and

[17] Case 35/76 *Simmenthal v Italian Minister of Finance* EU:C:1976:180, at paras 13 and 14, respectively (emphasis added in the second quotation). The same, or very similar, sentences appear in numerous other judgments of the following years, see eg Case 153/78 *Commission v Germany* EU:C:1979:194, para 5; Case 72/83 *Campus Oil* EU:C:1984:256, para 32.

[18] Case C-348/09 *PI v Oberbürgermeisterin der Stadt Remscheid* EU:C:2012:300, para 23.

Article 346 contains a more detailed set of provisions, the core of which is that 'any Member State may take such measures as it considers necessary for the protection of the essential interests of its security which are connected with the production of or trade in arms, munitions and war material'. These reservations sound more robust than the ones previously discussed because they apply across the board (rather than in relation to one particular field of EU law), and also because of the use of words like 'in no way' and 'as it considers necessary'. These Treaty articles could therefore convincingly be read as giving *carte blanche* to the Member States when regulating their property laws or their military material.

Yet, the Court of Justice decided to transpose to these domains the approach it had adopted in relation to the derogations from fundamental freedoms, and it held that these more boldly worded derogations should also be interpreted strictly.[19] More specifically, it held that, despite the words 'as it considers necessary' used in Article 296 EC (as it then was), 'that Article cannot ... be read in such a way as to confer on Member States a power to depart from the provisions of the Treaty based on *no more than reliance on those interests*';[20] rather, the states have to *prove* that the derogation is really necessary to protect their essential security interests, and the Court scrutinises this closely, especially when the derogation affects the operation of the internal market. In relation to the safeguard clause on the system of property, the Court took a similarly reductionist approach. It has been convincingly argued that the reason for the inclusion of this clause in the original text of the EEC Treaty was to express the Treaty's neutrality as to the choice between public and private ownership of particular companies, and to preserve the Member States' discretion to nationalise companies or entire sectors.[21] Neither the Court nor the EU legislator ever interpreted it as a 'hands off' rule from property law in general. However, even in the specific matter of the regime of public vs private ownership, the Court adopted a restrictive view of the exception. This was illustrated most clearly in a series of disputes about 'golden shares', where the Court of Justice took the view that Article 295 EC 'does not have the effect of exempting the Member States' systems of property ownership from the fundamental rules of the Treaty and cannot, therefore, be relied on by way of justification for obstacles, resulting from privileges attached to the position of Member States as shareholders in privatised undertakings, to the exercise of the freedoms laid down in the Treaty'.[22]

[19] Case C-387/05 *Commission v Italy* EU:C:2009:781, para 46.

[20] ibid para 47 (emphasis added).

[21] See the discussion of the original meaning of this Treaty article by B Akkermans and E Ramaekers, 'Article 345 TFEU (ex Article 295 EC), its Meaning and Interpretations' (2010) 16 *European Law Journal* 292, 299–302.

[22] Case C-171/08 *Commission v Portugal* EU:C:2010:412, para 64. Quasi-identical wording had been used in a number of earlier cases dealing with public participation in private companies, eg in Case C-463/00 *Commission v Spain* EU:C:2003:272, para 67. And see also a much earlier case, dealing with compulsory acquisition by the state of private property, in which the Court adopted the same approach: Case 182/83 *Fearon* EU:C:1984:335, para 7.

A more ambiguous reservation is the one in the current Article 153(5) TFEU (originally inserted by the Treaty of Amsterdam) which excludes pay, the right of association and the right to strike from the scope of the social policy competences listed in the other paragraphs of that article. It is not entirely clear whether the drafters of that Treaty provision sought to exclude any EU measures affecting these subject matters (which was probably their intention), or whether EU measures can still exceptionally be adopted under other legal bases elsewhere in the Treaties. Whatever the scope of this reservation, the Court gave it the same treatment as to the other reservation clauses of the Treaty. In the *Viking Line* case, the Danish government argued that the reservation of the right of collective action and the right to strike implied that the exercise of those rights by trade unions could not be challenged for breach of the EU freedom of establishment of companies. The Court answered in the usual manner:

> even if, in the areas which fall outside the scope of the Community's competence, the Member States are still free, in principle, to lay down the conditions governing the existence and exercise of the rights in question, the fact remains that, when exercising that competence, the Member States must nevertheless comply with Community law.[23]

Interestingly, in support of this statement the Court referred to precedents in the field of social security and direct taxation, which were cases of *retained* rather than *reserved* powers. In other words: it does not really matter whether Member State competences are retained (that is, implicitly kept away from the EU) or reserved (that is, explicitly denied to the EU), as in both cases the exercise of those powers by the Member States can still be judged on its compatibility with obligations arising out of EU primary or secondary law.

A rather different kind of reservation was introduced in the Treaties at Maastricht. In fields such as education, culture and health, the Member States reluctantly accepted to grant limited competences to the European Union, but added no-harmonisation clauses to circumscribe those competences and also added provisions seeking to preserve policy control by the Member States. Thus, Article 165 TFEU (previously numbered as Article 149 EC) on education states that the Union should fully respect 'the responsibility of the Member States for the content of teaching and the organisation of education systems and their cultural and linguistic diversity', and Article 168 TFEU (previously Article 152 EC) states: 'Union action shall respect the responsibilities of the Member States for the definition of their health policy and for the organisation and delivery of health services and medical care.' These 'angst clauses'[24] are, unlike the previously discussed derogation clauses, not formulated as 'carve-outs' denying action by the Union, but rather as constraints on the content of EU policies in these domains of welfare or

[23] Case C-438/05 *International Transport Workers' Federation v Viking Line* EU:C:2007:772, para 40.

[24] An expression used by A von Bogdandy and J Bast, 'The Federal Order of Competences' in A von Bogdandy and J Bast (eds), *Principles of European Constitutional Law*, 2nd edn (Oxford, Hart Publishing, 2010) 276, 286.

social policy. They do not seem to have played a meaningful role in the case law of the Court of Justice. In the *Schwarz* case, mentioned above, the German government referred to the educational clause of Article 149 EC in order to oppose the view that it would be forced to give financial assistance to parents sending their children to private schools abroad; indeed, German private schools were part of the German educational system and subject to basic requirements in this respect, whereas the German government had no influence on the organisation of private schools abroad or on the content of their teaching.[25] The Court of Justice did not bother to respond to this objection and found the tax scheme to be an unjustified obstacle to the freedom to provide services and the exercise of the free movement of Union citizens.

THE LISBON TREATY REFORM: NEW GUARANTEES FOR EXCLUSIVE MEMBER STATE COMPETENCE?

By the time the Nice Treaty was negotiated, in 2000, the reform of the system of delimitation of competences had found its way to the top of the EU's political agenda, due, in large part, to the concerns in some countries that the Treaties did not seem to offer an effective limit to 'competence creep' by the EU institutions. The issue was kept away from the Nice reform process itself, but on the insistence of the German government (pressed by the *Länder*, who controlled the ratification of the Nice Treaty by means of the *Bundesrat*), competence became one of the four key questions to be addressed in the post-Nice process, according to the Declaration on the Future of the Union attached to the Treaty of Nice.[26] More precisely, the Declaration called for reflection on 'how to establish and monitor a more precise delimitation of powers between the European Union and the Member States, reflecting the principle of subsidiarity'. The competence theme was taken up again, and spelled out in greater detail, in the Laeken Declaration adopted one year later, in December 2001, which gave the go-ahead to the Convention on the Future of the Union; and that Convention engaged, from February 2002 until July 2003, in a project of wholesale reform of the EU's competence regime which was included in the text of the Constitutional Treaty and transposed in almost identical terms, some seven years later, into the Lisbon Treaty.

The Laeken Declaration devoted three important paragraphs to the competence question, which set the scene for subsequent events:

> Citizens often hold expectations of the European Union that are not always fulfilled. And vice versa—they sometimes have the impression that the Union takes on too much in

[25] Case C-76/05 *Schwarz* EU:C:2007:492, paras 50–52.

[26] See MW Bauer, 'The German Länder and the European Constitutional Treaty: Heading for a Differentiated Theory of Regional Elite Preferences for European Integration' (2006) 16 *Regional and Federal Studies* 21, 24. The 'Nice Declaration' was published as part of the Final Act of the Nice Treaty in OJ 2001, C 80/85.

areas where its involvement is not always essential. Thus the important thing is *to clarify, simplify and adjust the division of competence* between the Union and the Member States in the light of the new challenges facing the Union.

A first series of questions that need to be put concerns how the division of competence can be made more transparent. Can we thus make a clearer distinction between *three types of competence: the exclusive competence of the Union, the competence of the Member States and the shared competence* of the Union and the Member States?

Lastly, there is the question of how to ensure that a redefined division of competence does not lead to a creeping expansion of the competence of the Union or to encroachment upon the exclusive areas of competence of the Member States and, where there is provision for this, regions. How are we to ensure at the same time that the European dynamic does not come to a halt? In the future as well, the Union must continue to be able to react to fresh challenges and developments, and must be able to explore new policy areas. Should Articles 95 and 308 be reviewed for this purpose in the light of the 'acquis jurisprudentiel'?[27]

The second of those three paragraphs, in particular, could be read as an invitation to draft a comprehensive list of reserved Member State competences, and this option was discussed in the Convention on the Future of the Union, more precisely in its Working Group V on Complementary Competences. The Group quickly abandoned that idea in order to avoid the wrongful impression that the Member States derived their competences from the Union, or that Union action may never impact on these fields.[28] Instead, the Working Group proposed to clarify that the Union should respect certain 'core responsibilities' of the Member States. Two such areas of core national responsibilities were initially identified, namely on the one hand *the fundamental structures and essential functions of a Member State* (including matters such as regional and local self-government, national citizenship, territory, the legal status of churches and religious societies, national defence and the organisation of armed forces, and the official use of languages); and on the other hand *basic public policy choices and social values of a Member State* (including taxation, social welfare, education, public health and cultural heritage). Such a provision would, according to the Working Group, contribute to safeguarding the role and importance of the Member States in the Treaty, while at the same time allowing the necessary room for flexible institutional practice. In the final version of the Constitutional Treaty, the 'core responsibilities' clause was considerably shortened, and moved from the chapter on competences to a provision entitled 'Relations between the Union and the Member States'.[29] In the Lisbon Treaty, that shorter version was incorporated in Article 4 TEU, which we will discuss below.

[27] *Laeken Declaration on the Future of the European Union,* Annex I to the Conclusions of the Laeken European Council, 14–15 December 2001, SN 300/1/01 REV 1 (emphasis added).

[28] Final report of Working Group V, CONV 375/1/02 REV 1.

[29] On the origins of the provision, see B Guastaferro, 'Beyond the Exceptionalism of Constitutional Conflicts: The Ordinary Functions of the Identity Clause' (2012) 31 *Yearbook of European Law* 263.

While it proved impossible to draw up a list of exclusive Member State competences in the Convention, the traces of the concern about 'competence creep' are scattered all over the current text of the Treaties; there is now an 'overabundance of provisions limiting the Union's competences in the Treaties'.[30] One striking, though mainly symbolic, expression of that concern is the repetition in two consecutive articles (Articles 4 and 5 TEU) of the very same negative formula, namely that competences not conferred to the Union remain with the Member States. Another example of this competence concern can be found in Article 51(2) of the Charter of Fundamental Rights, stating that 'The Charter does not extend the field of application of Union law beyond the powers of the Union or establish any new power or task for the Union, or modify powers and tasks as defined in the Treaties', a statement which is, needlessly but significantly, repeated in the revised text of Article 6(2) TEU, as well as in Declaration No 1 concerning the Charter of Fundamental Rights of the European Union.

These generic statements are not, by themselves, effective guarantees of Member State competence. Instead, two other changes made by the Treaty of Lisbon can be seen as attempts to protect the exclusive competences of the Member States: the additional conditions for the use of the flexibility clause of Article 352 TFEU; the national identity clause and security exemption of Article 4(2) TEU. We will briefly consider these two changes, starting with the amendments made to ex-Article 308 EC in the new Article 352 TFEU.

(1) As we saw, the former Articles 95 and 308 EC had been singled out by the Laeken Declaration as suspect tools of competence creep. Those two provisions were eventually 'decoupled'[31] in the process of Treaty reform culminating in the Lisbon Treaty. Whereas the new Article 352 TFEU hedges the use of the residual competence with some additional safeguards for Member State autonomy, Article 114 TFEU corresponds exactly to the previous Article 95 EC, with no attempts being made to circumscribe its use more rigidly than before—despite the fact that, arguably at least, the internal market competence had been, and still is, the most powerful tool for the expansion of EU legislative activity. Article 352 TFEU, like its predecessor Article 308 EC, allows the European Union to adopt measures necessary for attaining the objectives of the Treaties, where no other, more specific powers can be used. It has thus served, for many years now, as a residual competence to fill gaps in the system of conferred competences. The German Constitutional Court, in its *Maastricht* judgment, called it a 'competence extension provision' (*Kompetenzerweiterungsvorschrift*). There was widespread concern in the 1990s that this article was used by the Council as a basis for the surreptitious erosion of national and regional competences. Various proposals for reform of Article 308 had been made in the context of the various Treaty revisions, and again

[30] L Azoulai, 'The 'Retained Powers' Formula in the Case Law of the European Court of Justice: EU Law as Total Law?' (2011) 4 *European Journal of Legal Studies* 192, 196.

[31] S Weatherill, 'The Limits of Legislative Harmonization Ten Years after Tobacco Advertising: How the Court's Case Law Has Become a Drafting Guide' (2011) 12 *German Law Journal* 827, 855–57.

during the debates of the Convention on the Future of the Union in 2002–03, but the idea of deleting it altogether never gathered much support. Whereas the Lisbon Treaty kept the residual competence in existence, it modified its formulation somewhat, and it added some State safeguards in additional paragraphs of the new Article 352 TFEU. More particularly, a 'non-circumvention' clause was added, according to which Article 352 cannot be used to adopt harmonisation measures in cases where other Treaty provisions exclude harmonisation.[32] This non-circumvention clause was referred to in 2012 by a number of national parliaments in the framework of the subsidiarity monitoring mechanism, as an argument to reject a draft regulation on the right of collective action. The Commission's proposal was based on Article 352 TFEU for lack of a more specific legal basis elsewhere, but several national parliaments pointed out, rather convincingly, that since Article 153(5) TFEU does not allow the EU to regulate the right to strike and to take collective action, such regulation could not be enacted 'by stealth' on the basis of Article 352.[33] As the Commission decided to withdraw its proposal, this particular controversy was quickly laid to rest. One should also keep in mind that the main avenue through which no-harmonisation clauses have been 'undermined' in the past was not Article 308 EC but rather Article 95 EC and other internal market competences which, as discussed above, are regularly used to harmonise national laws pertaining to no-harmonisation areas such as health, education and culture. All in all, the modifications made to Article 352 TFEU by the Lisbon Treaty have not resulted in an effective protection of reserved Member State competences.

(2) The enigmatic Article 4(2) TEU imposes the obligation on the EU to respect the 'national identities' and 'essential State functions' of the Member States, which includes 'ensuring the territorial integrity of the State, maintaining law and order and safeguarding national security. In particular, national security remains the sole responsibility of each Member State.' As was recalled above, this provision has its origin in the attempts made during the preparatory stages of the Constitutional Treaty to counteract the impact that the use of functional powers had had on certain policy fields that Member States consider particularly sensitive. Yet, with the exception of the last sentence, this provision is not clearly formulated as a competence reservation for the Member States. In particular, the need to respect the national identity of the Member States is formulated as a substantive obligation for the EU institutions when exercising their competences, rather than as a competence reservation for the states. As Advocate General Kokott stated in a pending case, '[t]he European Union's obligation under Article 4(2) TEU to respect the national identities of its Member States does not in itself support the

[32] 'Measures based on this Article shall not entail harmonisation of Member States' laws or regulations in cases where the Treaties exclude such harmonisation'.

[33] For discussion of this 'yellow card' drawn by national parliaments, and of the role of the competence issue therein, see F Fabbrini and K Granat, 'Yellow Card, but No Foul: The Role of the National Parliaments under the Subsidiarity Protocol and the Commission Proposal for an EU Regulation on the Right to Strike' (2013) 50 *Common Market Law Review* 115.

inference that certain subject areas or areas of activity are entirely removed from the scope of Directive 2000/78. It requires rather that the application of that directive must not adversely affect the national identities of its Member States.'[34] The same seems true for the 'essential State functions': Article 4(2) TEU recognises the primary responsibility of the states in this respect, and directs the EU institutions to respect that responsibility, but it does not define policy areas as being 'off-limits' for the EU. Only the final sentence whereby 'national security remains the sole responsibility of each Member State' strikes a different note, mainly due to the word 'sole', which could be interpreted as guaranteeing the exclusive competence of the Member States for national security. Yet, once again, this is not the way the Court of Justice seems inclined to read that sentence.

The existing, pre-Lisbon, text of the Treaties was already marked by a number of public security derogations, which had been treated by the Court in much the same way as all other derogations (see our comments on Article 346 TFEU above). In a case, *Commission v Italy*, decided on 15 December 2009, two weeks after the entry into force of the Lisbon Treaty, the Court attributed the label 'settled case-law' to the following formula: 'although it is for Member States to take the appropriate measures to ensure their internal and external security, it does not follow that such measures are entirely outside the scope of Community law'. It repeated that the EC Treaty only contained specific derogations and that '[i]t cannot be inferred that the Treaty contains an inherent general exception excluding all measures taken for reasons of public security from the scope of Community law'.[35]

One might have wondered whether this approach could be maintained after the entry into force of the Lisbon Treaty which *did* introduce a general security exemption within Article 4(2). In a post-Lisbon case concerning a decision of the UK authorities refusing a French national entry to the UK on grounds of public security, the Italian government argued that the preliminary reference should be declared inadmissible, because it fell outside EU competence: because of Article 4(2) TEU and Article 346(1)(a) TFEU, state security was the sole responsibility of the Member States and the question referred thus related to an area governed by national law. The Court rejected the plea: 'although it is for Member States to take the appropriate measures to ensure their internal and external security, the mere fact that a decision concerns State security cannot result in European Union law being inapplicable';[36] and the Court referred, in support of that view, to its pre-Lisbon judgment in case C-387/05 mentioned above. The Court then dealt with the substance of the dispute as a traditional case of the limits which states may impose on free movement of persons for reasons of public security. Apparently, the entry into force of the Lisbon Treaty, with its new provisions ring-fencing national security as a *sole* Member State competence, had not modified

[34] Case C-157/15 *Samira Achbita*, Opinion of AG Kokott EU:C:2016:382, para 32.

[35] Case C-387/05 *Commission v Italy* EU:C:2009:781, para 45.

[36] Case C-300/11 *ZZ v Secretary of State for the Home Department* EU:C:2013:363, para 38 (the argument of the Italian government is mentioned in para 35).

the pre-existing situation. It must be said, in support of the Court's position, that declaring national security to be a genuinely exclusive Member State competence would directly contradict the many provisions of the TFEU conferring either shared or supporting competences to the EU institutions in matters of security; indeed, constructing an area of freedom, *security* and justice is listed among the shared competences of the Union in Article 4 TFEU. Nor can one say that the EU plays only a minor role in questions of security. In 2015, the European Council endorsed the idea of an internal security strategy for the EU,[37] and in 2016 the Commission revamped its European agenda on security and proposed to work towards 'an effective and genuine Security Union'.[38] So, it would seem that the little phrase of Article 4(2) TEU, despite its sharp wording, is not a genuine competence reservation clause either.

CONCLUSION

At the end of this analysis, we can revert to the question posed in the title of this chapter: are there any exclusive Member State competences or was Lenaerts right when he wrote, back in 1990, that there is no nucleus of sovereignty that the Member State can invoke, as such, against the European Union? If one follows the line taken by the Court of Justice, then neither the retained competences, nor the many reserved competences scattered all over the text of the Treaties, effectively shield the Member States against the impact of EU law. With regard to the retained powers, we have argued that this position is logical and corresponds, in fact, to the widely accepted way in which international obligations can constrain the exercise of national competences even in areas for which no powers have been conferred to an international organisation. With regard to the reserved powers, the Court's position would seem more contestable, were it not for the fact that the manner in which these reservations are expressed by the Treaty text is either ambiguous (ie not clearly laying down a competence reservation; see the national identity clause of Article 4(2) TEU) or logically unsustainable (as with the 'sole responsibility for security' which contradicts other provisions in the Treaties that do vest competences for national security in the EU institutions).

This conclusion lends support to the views of those who are sceptical about the possibility for legal competence delimitation and argue that the protection of Member State interests should happen through the political process rather than through ineffectual competence limitation clauses.[39] However, the notion of

[37] European Council conclusions of 26 June 2015, EUCO 22/15, p 5.

[38] Commission Communication, *Delivering on the European agenda on security to fight against terrorism and pave the way towards an effective and genuine Security Union*, COM(2016) 230 of 20 April 2016.

[39] See in particular S Garben, 'Confronting the Competence Conundrum: Democratising the European Union through an Expansion of its Legislative Powers' (2014) 35 *Oxford Journal of Legal Studies* 55.

exclusive national competence retains a practical significance in today's European Union, for two complementary reasons. First, because the Member States have retained the exclusive competence, to be exercised collectively, to define, increase and reduce the Union's competences. This meta-competence is not only recognised by the Treaties (and emphasised in Article 1 TEU) but is also required by the constitutional text or jurisprudence of many Member States. Furthermore, the Member States have also retained the competence, to be exercised individually, to withdraw from the EU and thereby to reclaim potentially all the competences they had previously conferred on the EU. Second, even apart from the 'extreme' circumstances of Treaty revision or withdrawal from the EU, exclusive Member State competences are a legal concept embedded in the constitutional law of certain Member States, and developed by some national constitutional courts, most clearly but not exclusively by the German Constitutional Court in its *Lisbon* judgment. Even if the Court of Justice fails to recognise the existence of truly reserved competences of the states, national courts may take a different view on that matter. The ultra vires review that those constitutional courts are prepared to exercise may relate to the wrongful use of conferred powers by the EU institutions, but also to EU action that affects what are considered to be exclusive and inalienable areas of national policy.[40]

[40] On this question of competence reservation by national constitutions and national constitutional courts, see M Claes and JH Reestman, 'The Protection of National Constitutional Identity and the Limits of European Integration at the Occasion of the *Gauweiler* Case' (2015) 16 *German Law Journal* 917 (see in particular the comparative analysis at 940–67). See also several contributions in T Giegerich, OJ Gstrein and S Zeitzmann (eds), *The EU Between 'an Ever Closer Union' and Inalienable Policy Domains of Member States* (Baden-Baden, Nomos, 2014).

5

The Competence to Create an Internal Market: Conceptual Poverty and Unbalanced Interests

GARETH DAVIES*

INTRODUCTION

THE MEASURES TAKEN by the EU to create an internal market continue to be among the most impactful, politically inflammatory, and contentious of all its actions. The internal market is defined in Article 26 TFEU as an area of free movement for persons, capital, goods and services and all of these factors of production have revealed themselves to touch on matters of extreme national sensitivity: from early debates over the undermining of product standards and the consequences for national food cultures,[1] through fiercely fought battles over the impact of free movement of services on the welfare state,[2] to the Brexit phase, with a City of London desperately fighting to preserve its access to the capital and services market and where, most prominently, the free movement of workers has emerged as sufficiently contested to fragment and potentially explode the Union itself. Defining and using market competences in a way that attracts public and political support has become a matter of existential importance for the Union.

The role of the law in this is, at least, four-fold. First, it should be functional: it should have a clear and practical nature which allows it to be used for its

* Gareth Davies is Professor of European Law at the University of Amsterdam and Visiting Professor at the College of Europe.

[1] See H-C von Heydebrand und der Lasa, 'Free movement of foodstuffs, consumer protection and food standards in the European Community: has the Court got it wrong?' (1991) *European Law Review* 391.

[2] See eg G de Búrca (ed), *EU Law and the Welfare State* (Oxford, Oxford University Press, 2005); M Dougan and E Spaventa, *Social Welfare and EU Law* (Oxford, Hart Publishing, 2005); E Spaventa, 'Public Services and European Law: Looking for Boundaries' (2002) *Cambridge Yearbook of European Legal Studies* 271; G Davies, 'The Process and Side-effects of Harmonisation of European Welfare States' (2006) Jean Monnet Working Paper No 2/06; C Newdick, 'Citizenship, Free Movement and Healthcare: Cementing Individual Rights by Corroding Social Solidarity' (2006) 43 *Common Market Law Review* 1645; C Newdick, 'Disrupting the Community—Saving Public Health Ethics from the EU Internal Market' in J van de Gronden, E Szyszczak, U Neergaard and M Krajewski (eds), *Health Care and EU Law* (The Hague, Asser Press, 2011) 211.

purposes, and to achieve those purposes. Second, it should provide concepts and a framework which encourage substantively good results, by ensuring that relevant interests are adequately represented in the legal and legislative processes. Third, it should provide limits: the EU is a creature of conferred powers, and the legitimacy of those powers is partly dependent upon them being defined in a way that does not unduly undermine residual national competences and amount to an open-ended conferral. Fourth, the law should provide the basis for a legitimating discourse. It should contain principles and concepts which make evident that what is permitted or prohibited is so for good reasons. It should, in short, contain persuasive reasons for the scope of EU power.

These four functions are of course intertwined. They do not represent independent legal tasks for the Court or the legislator. Rather, they provide different perspectives from which to examine the law and consider whether it is doing its job well.

The suggestion in this chapter is that only the first task is done adequately. There is a generous mandate provided to the legislature to adopt rules, and relatively limited constraints on its functional freedom.[3] However, what the law does less well is provide balance, limits, or legitimating language. As the Court has interpreted them, internal market competences are overly focused on EU goals, and not enough on affected national interests;[4] they lack meaningful limits; and the law framing them displays a conceptual poverty which makes the internal market seem perhaps even more unbalanced than it is.

The chapter has three sections subsequent to this introduction. The next section considers what EU internal market competences are, and what matters are at stake in them. The following section considers how these have been interpreted, and the problems of this interpretation. The final section then concludes.

THE LEGAL BASIS OF INTERNAL MARKET COMPETENCES

Internal market competences have two aspects. On the one hand there are the legal bases allowing adoption of legislation, notably Article 114 TFEU, but also including several specific legal bases associated with particular aspects of freedom of movement, and allowing the adoption of harmonising or co-ordinating directives or regulations.[5] Many of these, and particularly Article 114, are relatively open and ambiguous in their wording: Article 114 allows legislation for measures whose object is the establishment and functioning of the internal market. That is a quite

[3] See S Weatherill, 'The Limits of Legislative Harmonisation Ten Years after Tobacco Advertising: How the Court's Case Law Has Become a Drafting Guide' (2011) 12 *German Law Journal* 828; A Dashwood, 'The Limits of European Community Powers' (1996) 21 *European Law Review* 113.

[4] G Davies, 'Democracy and legitimacy in the shadow of purposive competence' (2015) 21 *European Law Journal* 2.

[5] eg Arts 46, 48, 50, 52, 53, 59, 74, 75, 115 TFEU.

deliberate, and perhaps appropriate, deferral of difficult interpretative and applicatory decisions by the Member States in signing the Treaty. As often noted, they concluded an incomplete bargain, and left it to the EU institutions to complete it. The guarantee that the internal market would further develop in accordance with Member State wishes was not provided by substantive constraints on its scope, but instead by a legislative procedure and institutional structures which they clearly felt gave them, as states, sufficient continuing control.

What they may not have foreseen was that the Court of Justice would take such a central role.[6] Its interpretations of the legislative competences have become much more important than the Treaty text itself. In particular, it has determined that, broadly speaking, internal market legislative powers may only be used for measures which remove either obstacles to movement, or appreciable distortions of competition.[7]

This 'definition' of the internal market as an area without obstacles to inter-state movement or distortions of inter-state competition raises many issues, but what it also does is link the positive and negative competences of the EU.[8] For in order to understand what it means to remove an obstacle to movement we must have some definition of what such obstacles are, or perhaps of what it means to move freely. These definitions are found in the case law on free movement, those judgments in which the Treaty prohibitions on restrictions on movement of persons, services, capital or goods are given direct effect. This is a vast, and vastly discussed, body of law, which in defining free movement becomes part of the law on competence.[9]

It is also a body of law which in itself deserves to be seen as comprising an EU competence, the second aspect of the EU's internal market powers. For when courts apply the Treaty prohibitions to national measures they restrain national policies, and so limit the remaining competences of the Member States. The competence division between the EU and its Member States, the subject of this book, is not just determined by which directives and regulations the EU can adopt, but also by the extent to which its primary texts constrain national freedom of action. Both what EU law allows itself, and what it prevents in Member States, are part of the division of powers.

THE CONCEPTUAL BASIS OF THE INTERNAL MARKET

Both the legislative (positive) and negative competences of the EU rest on a small number of judicially developed concepts. Central is the idea of an obstacle to

[6] See G Davies, 'The European Union Legislature as an Agent of the European Court of Justice' (2016) 54 *Journal of Common Market Studies* 846.

[7] Case C-376/98 *Germany v Parliament and Council (Tobacco advertising)* EU:C:2000:544.

[8] G Davies, 'Can Selling Arrangements Be Harmonised?' (2005) 30 *European Law Review* 370.

[9] ibid. See for the law on free movement C Barnard, *Substantive Law of the EU*, 5th edn (Oxford, Oxford University Press, 2016); C Kaupa and F Weiss, *EU Internal Market Law* (Cambridge, Cambridge University Press, 2014).

movement, and a justified restriction on such movement. In addition, the Court uses the idea of undistorted competition. Finally it uses the ideas of subsidiarity and proportionality to provide limits to EU powers.

Alongside this are more procedural aspects of the law, such as the requirement for legislative impact assessment, the quality of evidence required both in such impact assessment and in assessing derogations,[10] the requirements of procedural correctness and the taking into account of the opinions of national parliaments.[11] These are all important legitimating factors which may well do much to save the internal market, but they are not considered in further depth in this chapter for the following reason: they are not to do with how the market itself is defined, but how choices about it are made. Assessing impact is important, but the prior question is which impacts matter. The question here is what kind of market the law imagines, rather than how the procedural aspects of creating it are supervised.

Nevertheless, the relationship between the procedural side of market-building and its substantive definition is more complex than the paragraph above suggests. For while one criticism made in this chapter is that certain interests are underplayed or ignored in market definition, these interests may well be represented in the political, and even in the administrative aspects of preparing legislation. The internal market may be a more rounded and justifiable creation than the law suggests. However, if that is the case, while it may offer encouraging avenues for justification, it does not defuse the critique that the law itself performs poorly, in that it does not in fact guarantee, nor explain, nor supervise, such a rounded representation of interests. It does not, in itself, tell a persuasive and justified story about the internal market.

THE MOST PERFECT MARKET: FULL HARMONISATION OR MANAGED DIVERSITY?

The legislative internal market competences may be used, the Court has found, for the removal of obstacles to movement or appreciable distortions of competition.[12] In pursuing these goals other interests should be taken into account, but those other interests do not provide independent justification for use of the legal base.[13] The case law since these ideas emerged has added many nuances and details to the law, concerning specific situations and problems, but the fundamental principles

[10] K Lenaerts, 'The European Court of Justice and Process-Oriented Review' (2012) 31 *Yearbook of European Law* 3; Case C-58/08 *Vodafone* [2010] ECR I-04999.

[11] M Zalewska and OJ Gstrein, 'National Parliaments and their Role in European Integration: The EU's Democratic Deficit in Times of Economic Hardship and Political Insecurity' (2013) Bruges Political Research Papers 28/2013; F Fabbrini and K Granat, '"Yellow Card, But No Foul": The Role of the National Parliaments under the Subsidiarity Protocol and the Commission Proposal for an EU Regulation on the Right to Strike' (2013) 50 *Common Market Law Review* 115.

[12] Case C-376/98, above n 7.

[13] ibid. See Davies, 'Democracy and legitimacy', above n 4.

remain. The primary purposes of any internal market legislation are one or both of the two above.

This interpretation of the Treaty is both too broad, and too narrow.

It is too broad because it allows in principle for the removal of almost all legislative differences between Member States.[14] Obstacles to movement have been persistently presented by the Court in primarily subjective terms: a measure is not analysed in the light of its global effects on economic activity or market structure but in terms of its consequences for the actors in the lawsuit in question.[15] As a result, almost all differences between legislation can, in some context, be regarded as creating obstacles to movement and be potentially harmonisable.[16] Similarly, the idea of a distortion of competition is understood to arise when regulatory burdens differ between states, but this is the default state of affairs where rules differ, rather than an exception.[17] Other than the essentially indeterminate limit of 'appreciability' the internal market is once again understood to entail the complete removal of regulatory difference.

The problem with this judicial understanding is that it suggests the internal market will be 'complete' when there are no differences in law left, since only in this situation would there be no obstacles or distortions in the sense that the law understands these ideas. Almost total homogeneity is implicitly, maybe even explicitly, the ideal to be pursued.

However, this is not an ideal: it is not a worthy goal for the European Union or its Member States and it does not correspond to a desire that is present to any significant extent among the public, or even among elites or politicians. A destination is sketched that almost no-one would in fact want to reach, for legal differences between Member States are widely regarded as desirable to at least a significant extent; they reflect the individual characters, preferences and circumstances of the state, as well as being expressions of autonomy per se. The capacity to make local choices is a democratic good in itself, quite independently of the additional good entailed in being able to match those choices to local needs and preferences. If a completed single market really entails legal homogeneity, then the EU should not strive for a completed single market, but rather for a more nuanced goal, for an optimal balance between market integration and other interests. The absoluteness of the Court's understanding is so at odds with good policy that it cannot reflect what was intended, and for that reason nor is it a plausible interpretation of the Treaty text.

[14] Weatherill, 'The Limits', above n 3; Dashwood, 'The Limits', above n 3. See also G Davies, 'Subsidiarity, the wrong idea, in the wrong place, at the wrong time' (2006) 43 *Common Market Law Review* 63.

[15] E Spaventa, 'From Gebhard to Carpenter: Towards a (non) economic European constitution' (2004) 41 *Common Market Law Review* 743; D Regan, 'An Outsider's View of "Dassonville" and "Cassis de Dijon": On Interpretation and Policy' in M Poiares Maduro and L Azoulai (eds), *The Past and Future of EU Law* (Oxford, Hart Publishing, 2010); *cf* G Davies, 'Understanding Market Access' (2010) 11 *German Law Journal* 671.

[16] Davies, 'Subsidiarity', above n 14.

[17] ibid.

Moreover, the idea that the most perfect or complete market is the most legally homogenous one is open to critique even on market or economic grounds. First, harmonising law does not create competitive equality if the background conditions are different. Where economic actors are subject to many rules and burdens, harmonising just a few of these does not necessarily make for a more level playing field. It may do, possibly, but the effects of measures and of harmonisation can only be assessed in their complete context. Given how widely the background conditions for business in European states vary—not just the laws, but the costs, the quality of infrastructure, the availability of personnel, business cultures, distance from relevant markets, tax levels, and so on—a piecemeal approach to harmonisation is hard to explain or justify. It looks far more like an authorisation to respond to ad hoc political lobbying than a pathway to a better market. Even if harmonisation were carried to the extreme of uniform European law, this would not create some ideal or perfect market. It would simply entrench advantages created by natural circumstances, social and behavioural differences, or other non-legal factors.

In practice, of course, total harmonisation is completely unrealisable anyway,[18] making the harmonisation programme even harder to explain, for selective harmonisation of law surely has little to do with creating competitive equality except in the most particular circumstances. What is required is a means of identifying those particular circumstances, the ones where harmonisation does level the playing field rather than just moving its bumps. The idea of a 'distortion' is intended to capture this, referring pejoratively as it does not just to differences, but to those whose elimination would enhance equality. However, nothing in the law provides the basis for an enforceable distinction between difference and distortion. There are of course economic theories on this, but they are both contested and narrow.[19] Economic models of undistorted competition use a more limited vision of what factors are relevant to making competition beneficial than this chapter argues should be the case. They may contribute to thinking about what should be harmonised, but they do not answer the question alone.

Second, diversity of law is one of the fuels of European economic activity. Local law, reflecting local circumstances, is more likely to be locally optimal, and also allows for experiment and change on a local level. Both the fact of local control over the shape of regulation, and the fact of being able to compare and contrast it with what the neighbours do, is likely to make a contribution to economic and social vibrancy.

When law is harmonised, the burden of adaptation to difference is transferred from individuals to jurisdictions. Instead of a business having to take account of

[18] S Weatherill, 'Harmonisation: how much, how little?' (2005) 16 *European Business Law Review* 533; G Teubner, 'Legal Irritants: Good Faith in British law or How Unifying Law ends up in New Divergences' (1998) 61 *Modern Law Review* 11.

[19] R Van Der Laan and A Nentjes, 'Competitive Distortions in EU Environmental Legislation: Inefficiency versus Inequity' (2001) 11 *European Journal of Law and Economics* 131.

different rules in another state, it is the state itself which must adapt to those differences, by bringing its own laws into line with an agreed common model. There is no particular reason to think that it is always more desirable or efficient to put the burden entirely on the state and never on the economic actors. Indeed, they are ultimately one and the same: almost all citizens are consumers, and all consumers are economic actors.[20] The real question is how we should adapt to the fact of difference with our neighbours: as individuals, or collectively. The presumption that collective adaptation is inherently better has no obvious basis. Either form of adaptation represents a cost that must be absorbed in the goal of cross-border business, but which form entails the best cost-benefit outcome is likely to be complex and case-specific.

More concretely, this means that harmonising as many laws as possible is unlikely to be a recipe for maximum economic activity or vibrancy. We might end up with a market which was more perfect in a certain legal formal sense, but was in fact less active, and in which even cross-border trade was reduced because of this. One may make a comparison with a team of workers: each may have their own style of work, and getting the best out of them will require giving them a certain freedom of action and choice. Yet getting the most out of the team as a whole requires facilitating their co-operation, which may require adopting certain common patterns and methods. Yet even getting such patterns and methods to be adopted may be difficult—it may happen more effectively if the level of compulsion is low, and individuals are induced to learn from and listen to each other, rather than if rules are simply laid down. Hence the optimal team is not one in which there is a maximum degree of commonality, nor a maximum degree of agreed rules, but rather one with an optimal balance between diversity, commonality, compulsion, and liberty. How that balance is arrived at is the art of management, but it will be at least to some extent context-specific: that means there will be no universal formula.

So in the internal market: a market which increases wealth, and in which trade and even cross-border trade is maximised and becomes easier and more usual, is not simply one in which there is the most intense framework of common regulation, but rather one in which the optimal culture- and context-specific balance of commonality, difference, compulsion and liberty is achieved. The ideal expressed in the law should not be that uniformity is good and necessary, but that the EU is committed to finding the best balance between uniformity and difference, not just in the name of diversity as such and non-economic interests, but even in the name of the market itself: the best, most complete, market is not the most legally homogenous, but the one in which social, cultural, economic and other conditions encourage economic actors to look easily and comfortably across borders. Just as self-confidence may facilitate relationships, autonomy at home may, by giving the self-confidence to face the world, facilitate trade.

[20] See G Davies, 'The consumer, the citizen and the human being' in D Leczykiewicz and S Weatherill (eds), *The Images of the Consumer in EU Law* (Oxford, Hart Publishing, 2016) 325.

What the law should seek to express is then the search for the right balance, not a unidirectional march towards ever more uniformity.[21] The best, and therefore the proper, understanding of the competence to create an internal market is that the EU is authorised to adopt rules which seek to enhance our economic openness to each other. This will entail taking account of the importance of local autonomy for creating economic success and actors with the capacity and desire to act internationally, as well as the importance of a legal framework which minimises the practical difficulties that they should have, and a search for the right balance between these when they conflict. The law should seek to voice and express the ways in which autonomy and difference can enhance the market and the capacities of its actors, as well as the ways in which uniformity can do so, so that the legislature can locate and debate their choices within a convincing legal framework.

WHAT PLACE FOR NATIONAL INTERESTS IN INTERNAL MARKET COMPETENCES?

Existing law does not go far along this path. It has little language to explain the distinction between desirable and undesirable differences. *Keck* was a hesitant step in that direction, with its half-presumption that rules concerning circumstances of sale, rather than product features, are likely to have a socio-economic importance that outweighs any impact on trade.[22] However, the Court has never really developed its first thoughts, and its use of the idea of selling arrangements has been intermittent and half-hearted, and in recent years it seems to want to marginalise their role in the law, without ever formally overruling *Keck*.[23] There was here the opening for serious thoughts about the kinds of rules that are presumptively desirable to remove in the name of trade, and about the kind of national interests that are at stake, but those thoughts never came. Hence there simply is no voice given in the law to the importance of national autonomy and diversity to social and economic success and to the success of a pan-European market.

A somewhat similar pattern is visible in the law concerning derogations from free movement. These are important to the division of competences in two ways.

[21] See M Dani, 'Rehabilitating Social Conflicts in European Public Law' (2012) 18(5) *European Law Journal* 621; F De Witte, 'Transnational Solidarity and the Mediation of Conflicts of Justice in Europe' (2012) 18(5) *European Law Journal* 694; M Everson and C Joerges, 'Reconfiguring the Politics-Law Relationship in the Integration Project through Conflicts-Law Constitutionalism' (2012) 18(5) *European Law Journal* 644; G Davies, 'Free movement, quality of life, and the myth that the Court balances interests' in P Koutrakos, N Nic Shuibhne and P Syrpis, *Exceptions from Free Movement Law* (Oxford, Hart Publishing, 2016) 214.

[22] Joined Cases C-267 and 268/91 *Keck and Mithouard* EU:C:1993:905.

[23] P Pecho, 'Good-Bye Keck?: A Comment on the Remarkable Judgment in Commission v Italy, C-110/05' (2009) 36 *Legal Issues of Economic Integration* 257; T Horsley, 'Annotation' (2009) 46 *Common Market Law Review* 2001–2019; E Spaventa, 'Leaving Keck behind? The free movement of goods after the rulings in Commission v Italy and Mickelsson and Roos' (2009) 24(6) *European Law Review* 914; P Wenneras, 'Selling arrangements, keeping Keck' (2010) 35(3) *European Law Review* 387.

For one, they demarcate the extent to which national policies can be defended against the Treaty prohibitions, showing the limits to national competence. However, they are also important to legislative powers, as the way that these derogations are described in the law is relevant to the role that they should be accorded in compiling legislation.[24] Are the interests at stake matters to be taken more or less seriously, to be harmonised as fully as possible, or to be left to national discretion?

The starting point for the Court when adjudicating on either 'mandatory requirements' or Treaty derogations is that they should be interpreted restrictively, because they represent limitations on the fundamental freedoms of Europeans.[25] A restriction on free movement involves a Member State pleading special interests in order to deprive a European of the freedoms that are part of their legal 'heritage' and so this must be strictly supervised and regarded as exceptional.[26]

This has a certain rhetorical grandeur, but is substantively nonsense. When national laws conflict with free movement there is substantive legitimacy on both sides. One can equally phrase the situation as free movement law restricting the choices made by democratic processes within the national constitutional order. Respect for national constitutional orders,[27] for substantive subsidiarity, and for democracy entails that free movement must in such a situation be interpreted restrictively.

Certainly, there seems little to be gained from a rhetorical battle to see whether it is national democratic choices or free movement which can be phrased in ways seeming to give them the most legitimacy. However, the Court's choice to put one side of the conflict on a high moral ground while the other is then treated as implicitly less important does not seem to rest on any objective view of what might give rules or policies legitimacy or moral weight. Rather than interpreting restrictions restrictively, they should simply be interpreted fairly: the interests represented should be respected, albeit not misused. A derogation is something that is regarded as more important than the policy derogated from, not less: that is what makes it a derogation.

In treating the derogations as matters to be reluctantly tolerated,[28] the Court assumes a particular role, as an agent of the EU, rather than an adjudicator for the body of Europe as a whole.[29] As in other federal systems, there are states' rights and states' interests, and there are federal competences and interests, and the logical function of the Court of Justice as an adjudicator between these, serving neither, and with no interest in one more than the other.[30] The Treaties have traditionally

[24] Davies, 'Can Selling Arrangements?', above n 8.

[25] Case 41/74 *Yvonne van Duyn v Home Office* EU:C:1974:133.

[26] Case 26/62 *NV Algemene Transport- en Expeditie Onderneming van Gend & Loos v Netherlands Inland Revenue Administration* EU:C:1963:1.

[27] Art 4 TEU.

[28] See Case 120/78 *Rewe-Zentral AG v Bundesmonopolverwaltung für Branntwein* ('Cassis de Dijon' case) EU:C:1979:42 para 8; national measures protecting certain interests 'must be accepted'.

[29] See Davies, 'Subsidiarity', above n 14.

[30] ibid.

regarded it differently, however: until Lisbon it was entrusted, with the other institutions of the EU, with the purposes of the EU, almost an invitation to treat EU law as a mission to be pursued and national laws and policies as matters to be pushed as far as possible to the side.[31] That particular entrustment clause has now been softened somewhat: the new Article 13 TEU provides that Union institutions should serve its interests but also those of the Member States. On the other hand, it still provides that the institutions, including the Court, should seek to advance the objectives of the Union, without any parallel provision for the Member States. Could one imagine the American Supreme Court being commanded to advance the objectives of the Federal government? In any case, it is hardly controversial to say that the Court's judgments display a commitment to EU policies and goals that is not matched by a similar commitment to protecting and assisting national policies and goals.

Partly this may be explained by jurisdictional matters; the Court has no competence to interpret national law, only European.[32] However, a system such as the EU requires a court whose adjudicatory starting point is that both EU and national law must be interpreted with due respect for each other, neither more restrictively than the other, and the legitimate policies and competences of each must be protected from encroachment and hindrance by the other.[33] Of course, no-one would really deny this statement if forced to take a stand on it, but it is not the rhetorical or even substantive perspective which the Court has chosen to adopt. The result is relative under-prioritising of legitimate national concerns.

Yet despite all these ways in which national competence is squeezed while EU competences are interpreted broadly, there is another way in which internal market legislative competences can be seen as too narrow: in the goals that may be pursued.[34]

ESTABLISHING A DISEMBEDDED MARKET

For what does it mean to establish a functioning internal market? What is required? One can argue that it requires trust between communities, effective communication, perhaps a certain shared understanding and expectations. Cultural and educational similarities can make trade easier, as can a shared language. One can also certainly argue, and indeed it is fiercely argued by many in these days of permanent economic crisis, that a market without redistribution cannot truly work—that it will lead to stresses and inequalities that will ultimately destroy it or the fabric of the societies in which it is embedded. It may be that an internal market requires a

[31] Former Art 7 TEC.

[32] Case 6/64 *Flaminio Costa v ENEL* EU:C:1964:66.

[33] See T Horsley, 'Reflections on the Role of the Court of Justice as the Motor of European Integration: Legal Limits to Judicial Lawmaking' (2013) 50(4) *Common Market Law Review* 931.

[34] Davies, 'Purposive Competence', above n 4.

high degree of political and economic integration. To 'establish', it may be noted, implies creating a thing in a way that is solid and rooted. An established market is not a disembodied one, but one that is solidly connected with and rooted in its society.

Who should take such decisions about what market establishment requires? It seems evident that it must be the legislature, or the Member States, but not the Court of Justice, for the matters at stake are as intensely contested and political as can be. Surely in choosing to make Article 114 so open the Member States were deferring the interpretation of 'establishment and functioning' to the legislature, with the function of the Court being to guard outer limits, rather than to impose a particular view.

Yet in limiting the possible uses of this Article to only two, the Court does seem to be imposing a substantive interpretation of what a market is and requires. Suppose the legislature does take one of the mainstream views that establishing a functioning market entails, for example, shared values or redistribution. It would seem that the Court will not allow them to pursue this path with law.

It could be said that this is merely a functional, practical understanding of Article 114, limiting it to actually facilitating trade, rather than making it available for all the other things that a trading society may need. Surely such other policies, however important, should have their own legal bases? The principle of conferral would seem to support this kind of limited, technocratic approach to the Treaty.[35]

This presentation seems to give the Court's limited approach a sensible, neutral colour, as if all the other values at stake in a market are not being denied, but merely pushed to their proper legal place. However, there is nothing neutral about the proposition that establishing a market requires merely movement and competition. This is a particular political standpoint, and a very contentious one. It is close to what is commonly referred to in critique as 'neo-liberalism' and however vague and misused that term may be, it is hard to fully rebut claims that the EU is a neo-liberal project as long as its core competence is not permitted to be used in any other than a neo-liberal way: as long as establishing a market and making it function cannot include ensuring that it is embedded in wider society.[36]

For a market is not separate from its context. It is not a place where abstract contracts exist without contracting parties, but rather a place where parties, often individuals, contract. A functioning market, one can certainly suggest, means that not just the contracts but the contracting parties are functional: then the human, social, context in which a market exists is inseparable from the functioning of that market. Hence, many might say that a market which undermines social institutions or the quality of life is dysfunctional.[37] EU law would seem to disagree,

[35] Arts 4 and 5 TEU.

[36] See and *cf* J Caporaso and S Tarrow, 'Polanyi in Brussels: Supranational Institutions and the Transnational Embedding of Markets' (2009) 63 *International Organization* 593.

[37] ibid. G Davies, 'Internal market adjudication and the quality of life in Europe' (2015) 21(2) *The Columbia Journal of European Law* 289.

in that measures whose primary aim is making people or institutions market-resilient would not appear to fall within Article 114.

It is, admittedly, possible that such measures could be adopted. The functional constraints imposed by the Court are fairly weak: many measures could be argued to promote movement or fair competition in some sense, and it is possible to slip quite a range of pork-barrel clauses into a fundamentally trade-orientated measure and call it preventing side effects. Health, harmony and the protection and promotion of good things can enter the law by being taken account of and respected within the trade-promoting project.

Yet there is an element of dishonesty to this approach. If the need is for redistribution or protection of weaker actors or greater trust and understanding, then it should be possible to overtly put these matters as the goal of legislative measures. Their contribution to the market may not be that they make movement easier or create more of it, but that they make it *better*: they make the market a less dysfunctional one. If such measures are adopted but under a false label, as if they are all about promoting trade, making more of it and removing obstacles in a concrete, narrow, sense, this distorts the politics and legitimacy of the EU legislative process. It is as if public health measures could only be adopted by a parliament if they could be shown to be cost-saving. Perhaps one can argue that the promotion of public health generally does save costs, if one looks at a big enough picture, but why should it be illegitimate to wish to protect public health even at the expense of some wealth? Requiring a certain frame and purpose sends a clear message about values and legitimacy, which can have a profound impact on society and on the legislating institution.[38] On the one hand it can corrupt society, by promoting a view in which certain values are treated as not worth pursuing on their own, as marginal to the economic.[39] On the other hand it can undermine the institution,[40] because so long as the public retains a robust sense of morality and decency they will slowly turn against a legislature which appears to be fixated on a political vision that they do not share. Both processes are arguably at work in the European Union. While the corruption of society may be more subtle and diffuse, the alienation of the EU from the public is evident, and if populist rhetoric does indeed reflect popular views then at least a part of this alienation comes from the promotion of the market as a body independent of its human and social consequences.

Thus while Article 114 is only weakly constrained functionally, the conceptual constraints are of great political importance. They may affect European consciousness and will certainly affect European views of the EU, and of its internal market. The Union should be able to do the things necessary to create a well-functioning

[38] CR Sunstein, 'On the Expressive Function of Law' (1995) 144 *University of Pennsylvania Law Review* 2021; W Van der Burg, 'The Expressive and Communicative Functions of Law, especially with Regard to Moral Issues' (2001) 20 *Law and Philosophy* 31.

[39] B Tamanaha, *Law as Means to an End; Threat to the Rule of Law* (Cambridge, Cambridge University Press, 2006).

[40] ibid.

market, which includes creating a market-ready society—fair, tolerant, lacking opportunities for exploitation, redistributive, mutually understanding, sceptical of economics, not too materialistic, protective of its weaker members and areas, and with a job-market which allows welfare-enhancing participation in that market for all: or at least this is one mainstream European political view—and it should be able to say openly that it is doing this, and not have to always pretend that it is merely seeking to facilitate and expand trade, for that is just one tiny part of what establishing a market may be thought to entail.

SUBSIDIARITY AND PROPORTIONALITY

As well as helping to shape the meaning of the internal market, one of the judicial functions is to police its principled limits.[41] The concepts of subsidiarity and proportionality are core here: they, in slightly different ways, indicate lines that the internal market competence should not be allowed to cross.[42]

Unfortunately, neither of them has the substance to do the work required. Proportionality is widely understood by the Court merely as a principle of effectiveness, requiring the Union (or Member State) to go no further than necessary.[43] This is, in itself, a banal proposition, difficult to object to, but not addressing the important and challenging situations where a measure which is necessary for one actor or level to achieve its preferences conflicts with a measure which is necessary for another actor or level to achieve theirs. That situation could be brought within proportionality, via the balancing process which is classically regarded as its third element,[44] but there is little evidence of a judicial taste for this in the law.[45] There are few cases where it occurs, and the general rule appears to be that the Court will not ask whether an EU measure is actually *worth it*; whether it is worth having given the disruptive consequences that it may have for national policy. Perhaps the Court regards this as too political, a decision best left to the legislature. Yet surely then it should be adopted explicitly into the procedural supervision of proportionality, so that the Court will regularly want to see, upon judicial review of EU measures, that such a cost-benefit analysis has been made. That is not the same as a mere impact assessment, which focuses on how a measure may promote trade and the trade and economic benefits which may arise from it, but the more difficult and less quantitative question of how much adjustment it may demand of states, how easy this will be, how negatively it will be experienced, and whether the expected benefits justify this. It may be that the

[41] Horsley, above n 33, 931–64.

[42] Art 5 TEU.

[43] W Sauter, 'Proportionality in EU law: A Balancing Act?' (2013) 15 *Cambridge Yearbook of European Legal Studies* 439; J Jans, 'Proportionality Revisited' (2000) 27 *Legal Issues of Economic Integration* 239.

[44] J Snell, 'True Proportionality' (2000) 11 *European Business Law Review* 50.

[45] Jans, 'Proportionality Revisited', above n 43; Sauter, 'Proportionality in EU law', above n 43.

enhanced role of national parliaments in the legislative process in recent years will help bring these questions to the political fore,[46] but there is still a role for the Court in ensuring that they have been adequately addressed.

Subsidiarity is of marginal importance because of its exclusive focus on EU needs.[47] It insists that the EU should not act where *its* goals—the EU goals—can be achieved by the Member States. This makes it a principle of delegation, rather than one of protecting national autonomy. It simply does not address the question of conflicts of interest or policy, nor of the value of local autonomy, diversity and decentralisation.

It should be noted that this is not the only imaginable form of subsidiarity. The version above follows from the way subsidiarity has been given textual shape in the Treaties and is the version which both Court and Commission use. However, subsidiarity is a principle with a life and history outside the EU, and there are those who argue that the traditional and best understanding of it is far more radical—that higher-level units of government should be truly subsidiary.[48] They should be residual, in the sense that they act only to complement or enhance lower-level action, never to undermine or contradict it.[49] It would be a challenge to give such a view of subsidiarity legal form in a way that did not entirely undermine the functioning of the EU and essentially make all compliance with its law discretionary.[50] However, the historical and philosophical roots of what may be called radical subsidiarity do display how the limited version placed in EU law is a particular and non-inevitable choice. The virtues of local decision-making are recognised, but in a way which keeps them quite clearly subordinate to the policy requirements of the higher level. This choice is understandable given that the EU is intended to have the capacity to restrain states, and that is widely understood as one of its strengths, but one should be aware of its political nature. The public discourse around subsidiarity in the EU tends to use it as a shorthand for the general safeguarding of decentral choices, when this is not in fact its function, thereby adding a further potentially disillusioning layer of deception to speech about the EU.

CONCLUSION

The Court has always taken a purposive view of the internal market, and required Member States to adapt to the requirements of inter-state trade. It concedes certain derogations and it concedes the protection of certain interests in this process,

[46] See K Auel and T Christiansen, 'After Lisbon: National Parliaments in the European Union' (2015) 38 *West European Politics* 261.

[47] Davies, 'Subsidiarity', above n 14.

[48] M Cahill, 'Theorizing Subsidiarity: Towards an Ontology-Sensitive Approach' (2017) 15 *International Journal of Constitutional Law.*

[49] ibid.

[50] G Davies, 'Theorizing Subsidiarity: Towards an Ontology-Sensitive Approach: a reply to Maria Cahill' (2017) 15 *International Journal of Constitutional Law.*

but they are minimised, or appended to the needs of trade. A certain vision of the market, as a trading framework unembedded in national institutions or policies, prevails.

This might have been challenged by the legislature, but they have shown little inclination, largely following the Court's cues and codifying them into law.[51] The combination of a broad functional competence mandate, combined with a narrow conceptual one, may have been attractive, allowing powerful and disruptive law to be adopted while only requiring a relatively limited range of political discussion or debate. Or it may simply be that the political sophistication and rootedness required to think and argue about what a market is does not yet exist on the European level, at least to a sufficient extent. It may well be that the enhanced role of national parliaments, with their more ideologically coherent and socially connected political parties, in EU legislation post-Lisbon will bring a change to this.

Such a change is needed to make the internal market legitimate and to ensure that it contributes as much as possible to the well-being of Europeans. However, that is not to say that the Court's role has always been opposed to such well-being. Rather, it has adopted an approach to the law which is easy to understand and sympathise with in the context of the early years of European integration, when building a robust EU could easily have been seen as both vital and challenging: as a project essential to a peaceful and contented Europe, and yet continually threatened by entrenched national structures, protectionism, nationalism, and backward-looking ideologies. Respect for national democratic processes may well have been seen as a less urgent priority than other more pan-European issues. The 'effectiveness' of EU law has traditionally indeed been one of the Court's most used and powerful ideological tools.[52]

Times change. The EU is in a different phase now, in which many states feel their competences threatened, and fear for their ability to shape the environment of their state in ways reflecting the values and preferences of their citizens.[53] Whether or not their fears are always correct, in the current phase of integration it would seem appropriate to take these fears very seriously, and to amend the law to reflect the fact that for most Europeans the direct facilitation of inter-state trade is not their most important political priority, whereas the possibility to shape their state via national political processes is deeply prized, or at least profoundly aspired to. Establishing an internal market, in the current phase of integration, may mean above all helping Member States become ready for that market, which

[51] G Davies, 'The EU Legislature', above n 6.

[52] See E Herlin-Karnell, *The Constitutional Dimension of European Criminal Law* (Oxford, Hart Publishing, 2012).

[53] See Treaty of Lisbon, 2 BvE 2/08 para 249, *Bundesverfassungsgericht* (*BVerfG*) [Federal Constitutional Court], 30 June 2009, available at www.bundesverfassungsgericht.de/SharedDocs/Entscheidungen/EN/2009/06/es20090630_2bve000208en.html. ('European unification on the basis of a treaty union of sovereign states may, however, not be achieved in such a way that not sufficient space is left to the Member States for the political formation of the economic, cultural and social living conditions'). See also paras 257–59.

may sometimes entail leaving them to work out their choices, and at other times assisting them with strengthening their institutions and social structures.

It is likely that the crude trade measures which have been the heart of internal market competences in the past should come to play a much smaller role. Let obstacles and distortions remain—they are often not so important. Traders can adapt to many burdens and circumstances, and that adaptability should be used and prized to relieve Member States and their populations of some of the economic pressures which they appear to find threatening to a considerable degree. For if states and their populations feel strong and self-confident, then a successful and active market will grow, and differences in law will be part of the texture and richness of that market, not something opposed to it at all.

6

Monetary Policy: An Exclusive Competence Only in Name?

MICHAEL WAIBEL*

INTRODUCTION

MONETARY POLICY FOR those Member States whose currency is the euro is one of the European Union's few formally exclusive competences. Yet despite formal allocation of monetary policy competence to the Union, this chapter argues that the practice of monetary policy decision making reflects the EU's nation-state structure. It tells us one side of the story about the balance of power for the conduct of monetary policy. If exclusive competence at bottom means that Member States have no say in devising policy, then monetary policy is not at present a genuinely exclusive competence. Instead, the chapter contends that monetary policy is an exclusive competence of the EU in name only. At the very least, the position is more nuanced than the label of exclusive competence suggests.

The first section compares competence for monetary policy with related areas, specifically economic policy, and closely connected thereto, education, health, labour and social policy. It also briefly discussed how the Eurozone crisis has affected the vertical balance of responsibilities between the EU and its Member States in these areas. The second section examines the asymmetric allocation of competence for economic and monetary policy, and the fuzzy boundary between the two, through the prism of the two key Eurozone crisis cases before the CJEU, *Pringle* and *Gauweiler*. The third section examines why, contrary to first appearances, the EU does not at present have a genuine exclusive competence for monetary policy.

* Michael Waibel is University Senior Lecturer in International Law at the University of Cambridge, Co-Deputy Director of the Lauterpacht Centre for International Law and a Fellow of Jesus College. Contact mww27@cam.ac.uk. Thanks to Hannah Dixie for her help in the preparation of this chapter.

COMPETENCE FOR EUROZONE MONETARY POLICY AND RELATED POLICY AREAS

Article 3 TFEU states unambiguously that '[t]he Union shall have exclusive competence [for] monetary policy for the Member States whose currency is the euro'. By contrast, Article 4 TFEU states that the Union only has a coordinating competence with respect to economic policy.[1] For social policy, the Union's competence is lesser still, providing only for Union 'initiatives to ensure coordination':

> the Member States shall co-ordinate their economic policies within the Union. To this end, the Council shall adopt measures, in particular broad guidelines for these policies. The Union shall take measures to ensure co-ordination of the employment policies of the Member States, in particular by defining guidelines for these policies. The Union may take initiatives to ensure co-ordination of Member States' social policy.

The competence literature typically focuses on legislative competence.[2] Indeed, most of the enumerated powers in the Treaties are legislative powers. By contrast, monetary policy is at its core an executive competence, though one delegated to an independent monetary policy authority.[3] This focus on executive action by an independent agency sets monetary policy apart from most other EU competences. As the third section explains, the Eurosystem[4] is an independent, executive policy-making body that is independent from the political branches at national and EU level.

In Garben's view, a tension 'between the need for containment and for conferral of the EU level' characterises EU economic policy.[5] Member States have been 'legitimately concerned about granting the EU a hard competence in this area',[6] fearing 'it may become a blank cheque for the EU to decide on highly sensitive decisions of re-distributive nature at the core of their sovereign powers'[7] which

[1] A Hinarejos, 'Economic and Monetary Union' in C Barnard and S Peers (eds), *European Union Law* (Oxford, Oxford University Press, 2013); F Fabbrini, *Economic governance in Europe: comparative paradoxes and constitutional challenges* (Oxford, Oxford University Press, 2016) 203.

[2] R Schütze, 'Organized change towards an "ever closer union": Article 308 EC and the limits to the Community's legislative competence' (2003) 22 *Yearbook of European Law* 79 and R Schütze, 'From Rome to Lisbon: "Executive federalism" in the (new) European Union' (2010) 47(5) *Common Market Law Review* 1385.

[3] To a lesser extent, the same observation applies to economic policy. Another example of a policy domain where the emphasis is also on executive functions is competition law. Legislative or harmonising measures play only a minor role; see Chapter 7 by Pablo Ibáñez Colomo in this volume.

[4] The Eurosystem is made up of the ECB and the national central banks of those EU members that have adopted the euro. *cf* Art 282 TEU, 2nd sentence: 'The European Central Bank, together with the national central banks of the Member States whose currency is the Union, which constitute the Eurosystem, shall conduct the monetary policy of the Union.'

[5] S Garben, 'The Constitutional (Im)balance between "the Market" and "the Social" in the European Union' (2017) *European Constitutional Law Review* at 21.

[6] ibid.

[7] ibid at 21–22.

are arguably 'beyond the EU's limited legitimacy'.[8] However, she concedes that 'the closely intertwined European economies and the common currency would seem to necessitate a strong European-level capacity to decide on the crucial elements of this economic and monetary union'.[9]

Given the limited co-ordinating competence, the EU Commission in 2010 devised the European Semester as a mechanism to enhance EU surveillance of Member States' economic policy and achieve better co-ordination of economic policy.[10] Under this framework, the Council ostensibly 'adopts country specific recommendations as part of the coordination of Member States' economic and employment policy'.[11] But it has attracted the criticism that it pursues 'a neo-liberal, deregulatory agenda'.[12] Grahl and Teague have been particularly critical, stating: 'With the "rescue-cum-retrenchment" regimes imposed on the states accepting bailout funds, virtually all social policy autonomy is lost.'[13] They note that even where the Commission does not demand specific social policy changes, 'the intensity of the pressure for rapid fiscal consolidation makes them inevitable'.[14] As for any suggestion of consolidating core social policies at the EU level, they refute this as 'completely unrealistic'[15] in the aftermath of the euro crisis: 'Since no resources were committed by the EU to achieve its social policy targets, since there are no effective levers to influence policy in the stronger states and since the weaker ones have to subordinate social objectives to deficit reduction, the targets are empty aspirations.'[16]

The euro crisis brought these tensions to the fore. Dahan empirically investigated the EU-IMF financial stabilisation programme for Latvia in 2011–2012. He concludes that:

> the IMF practice has shown that various social policies have entered the Fund's discourse. Social development and poverty reduction seem to have become priorities of IMF-supported programmes. Yet, the IMF lacks expertise in social policy and has a limited view of its mandate which prevents it fully engaging with such policies. Although a learning process has taken place in the IMF practice, this shift in policy thinking has not fully translated into practice. Social development may become a pillar of the IMF mandate, but it does not yet constitute a primary goal.[17]

[8] ibid at 22.

[9] ibid.

[10] A Steinbach, *Economic Policy Coordination in the Euro Area* (2014) 124; A Hinarejos, *The Euro Area Crisis in Constitutional Perspective* (Oxford, Oxford University Press, 2015) 30; Garben, above n 5 at 24; Fabbrini, above n 1 at 30.

[11] Garben, above n 5 at 24.

[12] C Barnard, 'EU Employment Law and the European Social Model: The Past, the Present and the Future' (2014) 67 *Current Legal Problems* 199, 204.

[13] J Grahl and P Teague, 'Reconstructing the Eurozone: the role of EU social policy' (2013) 37 *Cambridge Journal of Economics* 677, 685.

[14] ibid at 686.

[15] ibid.

[16] ibid.

[17] S Dahan, 'The EU/IMF Financial Stabilisation Process in Latvia and Its Implications for Labour Law and Social Policy' (2012) 41 *Industrial Law Journal* 305, 326; C de la Porte and E Heins, 'A new

Subsequent EU crisis resolution efforts, particularly in Greece, led to sharp criticism and concern about the social consequences resulting under stabilisation programmes that countries such as Greece and Portugal adopted.[18] Borrowing countries reduced spending on social welfare, education and health. Greece, for instance, cut hospital budgets by 40 per cent and experienced shortages of staff and medical supplies.[19] In addition to lack of adequate access to health care, unemployment, mental disorders[20] and suicide rate increased.[21] In 2015, the International Labour Organisation warned that 'serious health hazards are emerging because of the fiscal consolidation measures introduced since 2008'[22] and also attributed 'high unemployment, lower wages and social protection expenditure cuts'[23] to the economic adjustment programmes in crisis countries. For Barnard, this is unsurprising, given that 'social policy has always been seen as the poor relation to the EU's economic dimension'.[24] Some go so far as to argue that elements of the adjustment in the Greek programme have breached Greece's and the lender's human rights obligations.[25]

Social policy has traditionally been a matter for the Member States, an area deemed within 'the rightful purview of politics',[26] thereby demanding 'democratic legitimacy'.[27] One objective in establishing the monetary union was to insulate monetary policy from national politics. However, as Hinarejos has pointed out, this aim 'soon faltered, as it became apparent that it is not possible to separate the market from the political, as both spheres overlap or clash'.[28] She continued: 'This, together with the fact that EU law had been given direct effect and primacy over national law, meant that the economic and social policy choices made at the national level were bound to be overridden by EU rules created to protect and foster the single market and undistorted competition.'[29] As a result of the euro

era of European Integration? Governance of Labour market and social policy since the Sovereign debt crisis' (2015) 13(1) *Comparative European Politics*; Communication from the Commission to the European Parliament and the Council, 'Strengthening the Social Dimension of the Economic and Monetary Union' COM(2013) 690.

[18] eg M Karanikolos et al, 'Financial crisis, austerity, and health in Europe' (2013) 381 *The Lancet* 1323, 1324.

[19] ibid.

[20] ibid at 1327.

[21] ibid.

[22] International Labour Organisation, *World Social Protection Report*, 2015, available at www.ilo.org/wcmsp5/groups/public/---dgreports/---dcomm/documents/publication/wcms_245201.pdf, 135.

[23] ibid at 137.

[24] Barnard, above n 7; Dahan refers to the 'pre-eminence of fiscal over social policy': S Dahan, 'The EU/IMF Financial Stabilisation Process in Latvia and Its Implications for Labour Law and Social Policy' (2012) 41 *Industrial Law Journal* 305, 326; Hinarejos refers to the 'new social deficit', above n 10 at 81.

[25] O De Schutter and ME Salomon, 'Economic Policy Conditionality, Socio-Economic Rights and International Legal Responsibility: The Case of Greece 2010–2015' (Legal Brief Prepared for the Special Committee of the Hellenic Parliament on the Audit of the Greek Debt (Debt Truth Committee)).

[26] Hinarejos, above n 10 at 80.

[27] ibid.

[28] ibid.

[29] ibid.

crisis, social policy became de facto more centralised in programme countries.[30] Hinarejos has summed up the result:

> while in theory Member States' choice in social policy remains their own, in practice these choices are progressively curtailed by an ever higher degree of control and surveillance as regards economic and fiscal policy. This interference can happen in various ways: because the increased control in economic and fiscal policy requires a Member State to cut spending, thus indirectly impacting its social policy spending; because recommendations adopted within the European Semester seek to nudge Member States to adopt certain policy choices; or in the clearest cases, because of Memoranda of Understanding require certain policy choices of Member States in receipt of financial assistance.[31]

Similarly, Garben contends that EU economic policy is 'affecting a wide range of other—highly sensitive—policy areas in unprecedented ways'.[32] She refers to 'a competence *coup* taking place through European economic governance'[33] whereby Member States 'are given detailed instructions about the level of their wages and the procedures for setting them, about their pensions, their health care and education systems, and face political and financial sanctions or bankruptcy if they fail to obey'.[34] The implication of this development is that social policy, once 'the only remaining instrument governments could use to mitigate external economic pressures'[35] is now being removed from the competence of Member States. Social policy is thus a competence area where there is at least some disconnect between the formal position in the Treaties—a Member State competence with only a limited co-ordinating function for the EU—and the de facto position—an area of competence in which there are increasingly spillovers from decisions taken at the EU level pursuant to monetary policy competence. As the third section shows, a similar, but reverse disconnect exists for the formally exclusive EU competence of monetary policy.

THE FUZZY BOUNDARY BETWEEN EU COMPETENCE FOR 'ECONOMIC' AND 'MONETARY' POLICY

The Treaties sought to establish an '*Economic* and Monetary Union' for the European Union. Yet EU competence for 'monetary' and 'economic' policy is allocated asymmetrically. As the previous section discussed, monetary policy is deemed to be an 'exclusive' competence[36] whereas economic policy is only a

[30] ibid at 81.
[31] ibid.
[32] Garben, above n 5 at 28.
[33] ibid at 29.
[34] ibid.
[35] Grahl and Teague, above n 13 at 684.
[36] However, the next section contends that this formal characterisation does not stand up to closer scrutiny.

'co-ordinating competence'.[37] Authority for economic policy remains at the national level. Article 121 requires Member States to regard their economic policies as matters of common concern and to co-ordinate them within the Council. One policy instrument is the Broad Economic Policy Guidelines. These are non-binding and merely seek to co-ordinate national policies, without being backed up by an effective enforcement mechanism. The EU's current economic and monetary governance arrangements are the result of a lot of ad hoc *bricolage*.[38]

In *Pringle*, an Irish Member of Parliament contended that the European Stability Mechanism (ESM), an intergovernmental institution established by the Eurozone in 2011 to provide stability support to its Member States and protect the euro, should be classified for competence purposes as 'monetary policy' under the exclusive competence of the EU, as stipulated in Article 3(1)(c) TFEU.[39] Accordingly, and in line with Article 2(1) TFEU, the claimant argued that EU Member States lacked the competence to adopt any legally binding acts, such as the ESM, in this area. In contrast, the Member States submitted that the ESM was a measure of 'economic policy', falling outside the exclusive competences of the EU. The pivotal question for the CJEU to consider was therefore whether the creation of the ESM fell within the scope of monetary or economic policy.

In qualifying the establishment of the ESM as 'economic policy', the CJEU ultimately sided with the Member States. Acknowledging that the TFEU lacked any definition of 'monetary policy', the Court recognised that the ESM must be considered in light of both its objectives and its instruments so as to determine which competence head its establishment pertained to.[40] It held that the objective pursued by the ESM, namely 'to safeguard the stability of the euro area as a whole',[41] was 'clearly distinct from the objective of maintaining price stability, which is the primary objective of the Union's monetary policy'.[42] In drawing this distinction, the Court held that 'though the stability of the euro area may have repercussions on the stability of the currency used within that area, an economic policy measure cannot be treated as equivalent to a monetary policy measure for the sole reasons that it may have indirect effects on the stability of the euro'.[43] The Court emphasised that 'any effect of the activities of the ESM on price stability is not such as to call into question that finding. Even if the activities of the ESM might influence the rate of inflation, such an influence would constitute only the indirect

[37] R Schütze, 'Lisbon and the federal order of competences: a prospective analysis' (2008) 33 *European Law Review* 709; A Arnull and D Chalmers, *The Oxford Handbook of European Union Law*, 1st edn (Oxford, Oxford University Press, 2015) 87; Hinarejos, above n 10 at 68–69.

[38] Pisani-Ferry, as quoted in J-V Louis and R Lastra, 'European Economic and Monetary Union: History, Trends, Prospects' (2013) 32 *Yearbook of European Law* 196.

[39] Case C-370/12, *Thomas Pringle v Government of Ireland, Ireland and The Attorney General*, Judgment of the Court (Full Court) of 27 November 2012.

[40] Case C-370/12, *Pringle*, para 53.

[41] ibid at para 56.

[42] ibid.

[43] ibid.

consequence of the economic policy measure adopted'.[44] The Court thus concluded that the 'close link'[45] between the ESM and the TFEU provisions 'relating to economic policy and the regulatory framework for strengthened economic governance of the Union'[46] rendered the ESM an economic policy measure. Consequently, the Court found that Articles 3(1)(c) TFEU and 127 TFEU did not preclude the agreement, and subsequent ratification, of the ESM Treaty by Member States.[47]

The Court followed Advocate General Kokott's opinion on how to qualify the establishment of the ESM. Although the concept of monetary policy was not directly defined in the Treaty, she considered Chapter 2 of Title VII of the TFEU, which relates to monetary policy. First, the provision of credit facilities of the kind envisaged by the ESM was not a task which Article 127(2) TFEU ascribed to the European System of Central Banks (ESCB). Second, she submitted that 'Articles 123 and 124 TFEU, which directly concern the conditions governing the financing of Member States, are to be found in the chapter on economic policy and precisely not in the chapter on monetary policy'.[48] Third, the ESM does not constitute monetary policy simply because it may impact on money supply. She noted that neither is the ESM 'a commercial bank which by the extending of credit can create money',[49] nor does it indirectly affect the price stability in the euro area. The contrary conclusion would mean that 'the entire economic policy would be reserved to the ESCB and the rules of the Treaty on the coordination of economic policy within the Union would be devoid of meaning'.[50]

The judgment has attracted significant criticism in the academic literature. For example, Craig considered there to have been 'force in the contention that the ESM was in reality directed towards monetary policy',[51] highlighting 'the wording of Articles 2 and 12 ESM, which predicate assistance on the fact that it is indispensable to the financial stability of the euro area as a whole'.[52] He criticised the Court's reasoning on this point as 'strained'[53] and accused it of 'legal formalism'.[54]

In the second central crisis case, *Gauweiler*,[55] the claimants before the German *Bundesverfassungsgericht* (*BVerfG*) contended that the European Central Bank (ECB) had 'transgressed its competence' by implementing the Outright Monetary

[44] ibid at para 97.
[45] ibid at para 60.
[46] ibid.
[47] ibid at para 98.
[48] Opinion of AG Kokott, C-370/12, *Pringle*, para 82.
[49] ibid at para 84.
[50] ibid at para 85.
[51] PP Craig, 'Pringle: Legal Reasoning, Text, Purpose and Teleology' (2013) 20 *Maastricht Journal of European and Comparative Law* 1, 5.
[52] ibid.
[53] ibid.
[54] ibid.
[55] *Gauweiler*, *BVerfG*, Case No 2 BvR 2728/13 (14 January 2014).

Transactions (OMT) programme.[56] They alleged that the OMT programme amounted to 'economic policy' which fell beyond the ECB's monetary policy mandate. The Constitutional Court set out its preliminary view that the OMT programme was unlawful under EU law before making its first ever preliminary reference to the European Court of Justice.

The role of the ECB is to conduct monetary policy for the euro area within the narrow remit provided by the Treaties. The main opposition to the OMT programme was prompted by the ECB's purchasing of government bonds on the secondary market, conditioned upon the relevant Member State obtaining financial assistance from the ESM or the European Financial Stability Facility (EFSF). The pivotal issue was whether the OMT programme was a measure of monetary policy, and therefore within the competence of the ECB, or economic policy, and thus beyond its competence. Several features combined to lead the *BVerfG* to the conclusion that the OMT programme was economic in character. First, it assessed the programme's objectives. Second, it questioned its selectivity given the targeted nature of the purchases. Finally, it queried the links with the ESM assistance programme.

To determine the character of the OMT programme, the *BVerfG* referred to the CJEU's earlier judgment in *Pringle*[57] in considering the programme's 'immediate objective'[58] and 'the instruments envisaged to achieve the objective'.[59] This aspect of the Court's judgment has attracted academic criticism. Borger pointed out that 'the ECJ did not say in *Pringle* that regard should be had specifically to immediate objectives. It just stated that one should look at objectives, full stop.'[60] He argues that by so confining itself, the *BVerfG* ignored the ECB's longer-term indirect objective of 'safeguarding price transmission and singleness of its monetary policy, and its ultimate aim of safeguarding price stability'.[61] Indeed, the *BVerfG* viewed the ECB's proposed monetary policy transmission mechanism[62] with scepticism. According to Craig and Markakis, this scepticism 'resonated through [the *BVerfG*'s] judgment, with the emphasis on the economic rationality of interest rate spreads and the assumption that any attempt to address this under the Treaty necessarily constituted economic policy that was ultra vires the ECB'.[63] Rather, agreeing with the submissions of the Bundesbank, the German Constitutional Court determined that 'the primary objective (or at least the necessary

[56] PP Craig and M Markakis, 'Gauweiler and the legality of outright monetary transactions' (2016) 41(1) *European Law Review* 4, 6.

[57] Case C-370/12, *Thomas Pringle v Government of Ireland, Ireland and The Attorney General*, Judgment of the Court (Full Court) of 27 November 2012.

[58] *Gauweiler*, *BVerfG*, Case No 2 BvR 2728/13, para 63.

[59] ibid.

[60] V Borger, 'Outright Monetary Transactions and the stability mandate of the ECB: *Gauweiler*' (2016) 53 *Common Market Law Review* 139, 171.

[61] ibid.

[62] *Gauweiler*, *BVerfG*, Case No 2 BvR 2728/13, para 7.

[63] Craig and Markakis, above n 56 at 18–19.

intermediate objective) of the purchases is the reduction of the interest rates the Member States that benefit have to pay on the capital markets for new government bonds',[64] with the OMT programme intended to 'neutralise spreads on government bonds of selected Member States of the euro currency area'.[65] Consequently, the Court deemed such efforts to 'safeguard the current composition of the euro currency area'[66] to be 'obviously not a task of monetary policy but one of economic policy, which remains a responsibility of the Member States'.[67] Relying once again on *Pringle*, it reasoned that, just as 'an act could not be treated as equivalent to an act of monetary policy for the sole reason that it might have indirect effects on the stability of the euro',[68] equally 'purchases of government bonds may not qualify as acts of monetary policy for the sole reason that they also indirectly pursue monetary policy objectives'.[69]

On the matter of selectivity, the Court expressed concern over 'targeting the secondary bond markets of euro economies that were in serious difficulty',[70] which it found 'highly problematic, because it thereby undermined the sanctity of interest spreads',[71] thus falling outside the ECB's monetary policy remit. The *BVerfG* also criticised the conditionality of the OMT, asserting 'the fact that assistance via the OMT programme was conditional on economic policy reform showed that purchase of government bonds on the secondary markets was a measure of economic, not monetary policy.[72]

The *BVerfG* dismissed the argument that the OMT programme simply supported economic policy, which the ESCB is entitled to pursue under Articles 119(2) and 127(1) TFEU. It did so because the ESM might 'considerably broaden'[73] the scope of its assistance through the purchase of government bonds thereby potentially thwarting 'underlying political decisions'[74] above 'mere "support" of the economic policy in the Union'.[75]

In the view of the *BVerfG*, only 'a very limited version'[76] of the OMT is thus permitted under EU law and the German Constitution. However, as Hinarejos has recognised, the difficulty with this interpretation is that 'such a limited

[64] *Gauweiler*, *BVerfG*, Case No 2 BvR 2728/13, para 55.
[65] ibid at para 70.
[66] ibid at para 72.
[67] ibid.
[68] ibid at para 64.
[69] ibid.
[70] Craig and Markakis, above n 56 at 10.
[71] ibid.
[72] ibid.
[73] ibid.
[74] ibid at para 83.
[75] ibid.
[76] A Hinarejos, '*Gauweiler* and the Outright Monetary Transactions Programme: The Mandate of the European Central Bank and the Changing Nature of Economic and Monetary Union' (2015) 11 *European Constitutional Law Review* 563, 574.

reading of the Programme could arguably deprive the latter of its usefulness'.[77] Unsurprisingly, therefore, the CJEU chose to adopt a different approach.

The CJEU, as it had done in *Pringle*, underlined at the outset that the TFEU 'contains no precise definition of monetary policy but defines both the objectives of monetary policy and the instruments which are available to the ESCB for the purpose of implementing that policy'.[78] It continued to note that 'under Articles 127(1) TFEU and 282(2) TFEU, the primary objective of the Union's monetary policy is to maintain price stability'[79] and, further, that 'without prejudice to that objective, the ESCB is to support the general economic policies in the Union, with a view to contributing to the achievement of its objectives, as laid down in Article 3 TEU'.[80] The Court's first task was thus to determine whether the OMT programme fell within the scope of economic or monetary policy, as the *BVerfG* had endeavoured to do. It reached the opposite conclusion, namely that the monetary policy competence was an appropriate legal basis for the OMT programme.

Settling on the same approach, the CJEU heeded the *Pringle* judgment in recognising the need to uncover the underlying objectives of the OMT programme. However, unlike the *BVerfG*, it considered both direct and indirect objectives.[81] The ECB submitted that the aim was 'not to facilitate the financing conditions of certain Member States, or to determine their economic policies, but rather to "unblock" the ECB's monetary policy transmission channels'.[82] The CJEU considered this to contribute to the ultimate objective of monetary policy, namely maintaining price stability. Echoing its earlier judgment in *Pringle*, the Court held that 'a monetary policy measure cannot be treated as equivalent to an economic policy measure merely because it may have indirect effects on the stability of the euro area'.[83]

On the question of instruments, the Court turned to Article 18.1 of the Protocol on the ESCB and the ECB to demonstrate that the right of the ECB to 'operate in the financial markets by buying and selling outright marketable instruments in euro'[84] is made explicit, thereby underlining the monetary policy character of the OMT programme. Addressing the *BVerfG*'s concerns over the selective nature of these bond purchases, the Court held: 'the mere fact that the programme is specifically limited to those government bonds is thus not of a nature to imply, of itself, that the instruments used by the ESCB fall outside the realm of monetary policy.'[85] While the *BVerfG* was therefore right to suggest that 'the monetary policy

[77] ibid.
[78] Case C-62/14, *Peter Gauweiler and others v Deutscher Bundestag*, Judgment of 16 June 2015, para 42.
[79] ibid at para 54.
[80] ibid at para 43.
[81] Borger, above n 60 at 173.
[82] Opinion of AG Cruz Villalón, *Gauweiler* (C-62/14), para 104.
[83] Case C-62/14, *Gauweiler*, para 52.
[84] ibid at para 54.
[85] ibid at para 55.

framework of the European System of Central Banks does generally not have a targeted approach',[86] the CJEU contended that this selectivity by no means indicated the programme's economic nature, pointing out that 'no provisions of the FEU Treaty require the ESCB to operate in the financial markets by means of general measures that would necessarily be applicable to all the States of the euro area'.[87] Selectivity, in the Court's view, was simply 'the natural consequence of its initial focus on monetary policy transmission'.[88]

The CJEU went on to reject the notion that the OMT's attendant conditionality upon compliance with the ESM or EFSF financial adjustment programmes (which concern economic and fiscal policy) would impact on this conclusion. While conceding that 'a government bond-buying programme may, indirectly, increase the impetus to comply with those adjustment programmes and thus, to some extent, further the economic-policy objectives of those programmes',[89] the Court noted that 'such indirect effects do not mean that such a programme must be treated as equivalent to an economic policy measure, since it is apparent from Articles 119(2) TFEU, 127(1) TFEU and 282(2) TFEU that, without prejudice to the objective of price stability, the ESCB is to support the general economic policies in the Union'.[90] The CJEU thus openly accepted that the OMT programme 'had some impact on economic policy in the Member States undergoing severe financial difficulty',[91] which it deemed 'reflective of the interconnection between economic and monetary policy',[92] but refuted the deduction that 'economic policy was the principal rationale for the intervention'.[93]

Borger has given three reasons why conditionality upon ESM adjustment programmes does not alter the monetary character of the policy. First, because the TFEU 'specifically allows the ESCB to support the general economic policies in the Union'.[94] Second, because the link is a testament to Article 119(3) TFEU, which recognises 'sound public finances' as a guiding principle of economic and monetary policy, intended 'to make sure that States cannot free themselves from adjustment programmes because their financing constraints are eased due to OMT purchases'.[95] Third, because 'even though bond purchases tied to compliance with adjustment programmes constitute economic policy when carried out by the ESM [as in *Pringle*], the same cannot be said when they are conducted by the ESCB'.[96]

[86] *Gauweiler*, *BVerfG*, Case No 2 BvR 2728/13, para 73.
[87] Case C-62/14, *Gauweiler*, para 55.
[88] Craig and Markakis, above n 56 at 10.
[89] Case C-62/14, *Gauweiler*, para 58.
[90] ibid at para 59.
[91] Craig and Markakis, above n 56 at 19.
[92] ibid.
[93] ibid.
[94] Borger, above n 60 at 161.
[95] ibid at 161–62.
[96] ibid at 162.

While at first glance this seems inconsistent, the CJEU justified the difference on the basis of the different underlying objectives in each case.[97] As Borger explained:

> Whereas the emergency fund aims to protect the stability of the euro area, the ESCB focuses on safeguarding price stability through restoring the transmission of monetary policy. Activation of its OMT programme is therefore specifically tied to the condition that this transmission is disrupted.[98]

Pringle and *Gauweiler* illustrate that the boundary between 'economic policy' and 'monetary policy is fuzzy.[99] Whether the OMT programme is economic or monetary policy seemingly depends on the eye of the beholder. And this is not a sound basis for competence allocation in this crucial area. Craig and Markakis claim that 'the respective starting points of the Bundesverfassungsgericht and the CJEU shaped their conclusions as to whether the OMT fell within the ECB's powers'.[100] These different perspectives underlined their respective judgments; they note: 'the former's focus on interest spreads reflecting its view that the OMT schema was really about economic policy, while the latter's focus on monetary policy transmission reflected the alternative assumption that OMT could legitimately be regarded as falling within the sphere of monetary policy.'[101]

Not only is the allocation of competence to the EU for 'monetary' and 'economic' policy asymmetrical as mentioned earlier in this section, but these two categories have (1) no natural correspondence in economics; (2) a strict separation between them is impossible in practice, especially when it comes to unconventional central bank measures such as quantitative easing; and (3) the prevailing narrow conception of monetary policy risks hamstringing the Eurosystem in preserving financial stability.

First, to economists, monetary policy is a constituent part of economic policy. The term 'economic policy' in economics is a generic term that compromises both monetary and fiscal policy.[102] The crucial distinction is between fiscal policy—government spending and taxation, on the one hand, and monetary policy—money supply, exchange rates, interest rates, on the other hand. Yet the Treaties use 'economic policy' rather than 'fiscal policy'—the former, as the more generic term, is likely to be interpreted more broadly (as happened in *Pringle*).

[97] Hinarejos, above n 76 at 569.

[98] Borger, above n 60 at 162.

[99] See generally T Tridimas, 'Competence after Lisbon: The Elusive Search for Bright Lines' in Diamond Ashiagbor et al (eds), *The European Union after the Treaty of Lisbon* (Cambridge, Cambridge University Press, 2012) 47; A Mody, 'Did the German Court do Europe a favour?' (2015) 10 *Capital Markets Law Journal* 6.

[100] ibid at 8.

[101] ibid at 17.

[102] See eg the coverage of both monetary and fiscal policy by the influential journal Economic Policy; *cf* also F Snyder, 'EMU—Integration and Differentiation: Metaphor for European Union' in PP Craig and G de Búrca (eds), *The Evolution of EU law*, 2nd edn (Oxford, Oxford University Press, 2011) 694.

Second, the dividing lines between internal market competences, EU economic policy coordination, and monetary policy are difficult to draw. '[E]ach policy area should ideally correspond to one competence category', but it does not.[103] A good illustration is quantitative easing, which crosses the boundary between monetary and fiscal policy. Because central banks engage in large-scale purchases of sovereign or private sector debt on large scale and over time, these measures are quasi-fiscal in nature.[104]

Despite the fact that judges and academics highlighted the grey zone between monetary and economic policy, these competence 'crutches' remain influential. Beaumont and Walker presciently remarked in 1999:[105]

> The final instance which could give rise to legal action is in some ways the most interesting. It concerns the boundaries between monetary and economic policy. The Treaty Articles make it clear that while the ECB has considerable power and autonomy over the former, the Commission and the Council have the primary say over the latter. Economics as a discipline does not, however, respect formal Treaty boundaries. The line between monetary policy and economic policy may not always be pristinely clear, and in any event the two obviously interact, a point recognised forcefully in the Luxembourg European Council meeting in December 1997. There might well therefore be cases brought by the ECB which raise issues on the borderline between economic and monetary policy.

Judge Gerhardt, in his dissenting opinion in the *BVerfG* decision, similarly commented: 'Monetary and policies relate to each other and cannot be strictly separated.'[106] Advocate General Cruz Villalón expressed the same doubts over the purported dichotomy between economic and monetary union in his Opinion in *Gauweiler*, in which he stated:

> Although it may appear self-evident, it is important to make the point that monetary policy forms part of general economic policy. The division that EU law makes between those policies is a requirement imposed by the structure of the Treaties and by the horizontal and vertical distribution of powers within the Union, but in economic terms it may be stated that any monetary policy measure is ultimately encompassed by the broader category of general economic policy.[107]

Hinarejos has also criticised the efforts to draw a sharp divide between economic and monetary policy, recognising that:

> while the Court could be accused of drawing an arbitrary line between measures of monetary and economic policy, it seems impossible not to engage in arbitrary distinctions

[103] R Schütze, *European Constitutional Law* (Cambridge, Cambridge University Press, 2012) 163.

[104] A Haldane, 'How long can you go', Speech at the Portadown Chamber of Commerce, Northern Ireland, 18 September 2015, available at www.bankofengland.co.uk/publications/Documents/speeches/2015/speech840.pdf.

[105] PR Beaumont, R Paul and N Walker, *Legal framework of the single European currency* (Oxford, Hart Publishing, 1999) 115.

[106] Dissenting Opinion of Justice Gerhardt, *Gauweiler*, Case No 2 BvR 2728/13, para 17.

[107] Opinion of AG Cruz Villalón, *Gauweiler* (C-62/14) para 129.

> of some kind—an arbitrariness that seems imposed not by the Court itself, but by the problematic separation of competences at the heart Economic and Monetary Union.[108]

Meanwhile, for Craig and Markakis, the 'contestation as to the legal divide between economic and monetary policy under the Lisbon Treaty is reflective of the inherent factual linkage between the twin components of economic and monetary union'.[109] In their view, this 'inherent factual link'[110] between the two elements renders 'the search for a pristine legal dichotomy with an unequivocal boundary'[111] between the two 'doomed to failure'.[112] The authors recognised that this 'may be uncomfortable in legal terms, given that EU competence in the respective areas differs'[113] but simply stated:

> Legal categories of competence cannot, however, change the inherent factual connection between the constituent components of EMU, nor can they alter the fact that measures adopted to deal with macro-financial malaise will commonly have an impact on both limbs of EMU.[114]

Borger contends that there is little sense in defining monetary policy 'by juxtaposing it with economic policy, especially not by looking at a measure's objectives',[115] believing it to be not only difficult but often futile, as 'the two policy areas overlap and can at times be hard to distinguish in practice'.[116]

Third, as we have seen, the CJEU in *Pringle* adopted a narrow view of monetary policy to find that EU Member States could establish the ESM by way of Treaty. Yet such a narrow conception of 'monetary policy' presents a risk for financial stability. The Court defined monetary policy purely by reference to measures that serve directly the primary objective of maintaining price stability.[117] It distinguished the provision of financial assistance as aiming at the stability of the euro area as a whole, which is distinct from the price stability objective. It found—without much reasoning—that the grant of financial assistance to a Member State falls outside the category of 'monetary policy'. It then pointed out that such assistance complements the EU's economic policy, which is intended to consolidate macroeconomic stability and the sustainability of public finances. That policy is largely preventive, whereas the ESM envisaged by Article 136(3) TFEU concerns the management of financial crises. That amendment therefore concerns economic, and not monetary policy.[118] The restrictive interpretation by the Court of the scope of

[108] Hinarejos, above n 76 at 575.
[109] Craig and Markakis, above n 56 at 17.
[110] ibid.
[111] ibid.
[112] ibid.
[113] ibid.
[114] ibid.
[115] ibid at 181.
[116] ibid.
[117] Case C-370/12 *Thomas Pringle v Government of Ireland*, Judgment of 27 November 2012.
[118] ibid paras 54–60.

the EU's monetary policy leads to its finding that Article 136(3) TFEU is within the sphere of economic policy. The Court here emphasises that the EU's role is restricted, under Articles 2(3) and 5(1) TFEU, to adopting coordinating measures (para 64). It further establishes that no Treaty provision confers on the EU the competence to establish a permanent stability mechanism.[119] In contrast with the Advocate General, the Court does not dwell on the nature of the EU's competence in matters of economic policy, though it seems to endorse the Advocate General's view according to which the EU's competence is not shared (let alone exclusive), but of a lesser nature: mere coordination.[120] Importantly, had Member States not been able to agree on the ESM in 2011, the ECB may not have been able—due to the narrow conception of monetary policy—to fulfil a core function of most central banks—namely to maintain financial stability.

Neither the TFEU nor the ECB Statute refers expressly to 'financial stability' as an objective, or task of the ECB. That said, fundamental financial instability is likely—at least in the medium run—to undermine price stability, the ECB's primary objective under Article 127(1) TFEU, and put at risk the support that the ECB ought to provide to the general economic policies of the Union. The ECB divides its functions into (1) basic tasks (monetary policy, foreign exchange operations, management of reserves and the operation of the payment system); and (2) further tasks (issuance of banknotes, collection of statistics, financial stability and supervision and international and European co-operation).[121] In terms of the mandate and the governing instruments, financial stability thus appears to play a lesser role.

This seemingly narrow view of 'monetary policy' risks boxing the euro area into a competence straightjacket that does not allow the Eurosystem with the ECB at its helm to perform essential functions of modern central banking—to preserve financial stability—in fighting financial crises.[122] More broadly, a very deep crisis can put the survival of the European Monetary Union (EMU) as such at risk, or risk the exclusion of one (or more) Eurozone members from the currency union, such as Greece.

IS MONETARY POLICY A GENUINELY EXCLUSIVE COMPETENCE?

In formal terms, Article 3 TFEU states unambiguously that '[t]he Union shall have exclusive competence [for] monetary policy for the Member States whose currency is the euro'. Yet this formal allocation of competence to the Union tells us little about the balance of power for the conduct in monetary policy. If exclusive competence at bottom means that Member States have (formally) no say in

[119] ibid paras 64–67.
[120] Opinion of AG Kokott, C-370/12, *Pringle*, para 93.
[121] See www.ecb.europa.eu/ecb/tasks/html/index.en html.
[122] See further Louis and Lastra, above n 38 at 134–39.

devising policy, then monetary policy, even in formal terms, is not genuinely an exclusive competence. Instead, the chapter contends that monetary policy is, to a significant extent, an exclusive competence of the Eurozone in name only. At the very least, the position is far more nuanced than the label of exclusive competence suggests at first sight.

Monetary policy is an exclusive competence of the Union in name only for three reasons: (1) the Treaties confer such competence for monetary policy on the Eurosystem, an independent entity insulated from executives, legislatures and, to a significant degree, judiciaries at the national and EU level; (2) the Eurosystem—the monetary authority for the Eurozone—is composed both of a unique EU organisation (the ECB) and presently 19 national central banks;[123] (3) the ECB is not exclusively responsible for specific tasks that are often considered to be part of monetary policy.

First, competence for monetary policy does not vest in the 'Union' as such. In the terms of Article 2 TFEU, the Treaties do not 'confer on the Union exclusive competence' for monetary policy. Rather, according to Article 282 TEU, the competence for monetary policy vests in the Eurosystem.[124] Within the Eurosystem the ECB plays the lead role. It is an 'unparalleled organization' with separate legal personality, internally and externally, rather than a 'mere' Union institution such as the Council or the Commission.[125] The Treaties and the Statute ensure that this organisation, as well as national central banks, enjoy a high degree of independence from the political branches at EU and at national level.[126] Each of the 20 institutions that make up the Eurosystem has to be independent from the executives and legislatures at Member State and EU level. In sum, it is not the Union that it empowered to act through legislation and binding legal act, but the Eurosystem, an independent and unique entity.

Second, the Eurosystem is a hybrid European-national entity. A unique feature of monetary policy in the EMU is the very substantial involvement of national institutions—namely national central banks (NCBs). The main decision-making body for monetary policy is the ECB's Governing Council, composed of six Executive Board Members headed by the President of the ECB and currently 19 national central bank governors.[127] The ECB's other decision-making body, the Executive

[123] By contrast, the ESCB comprises the ECB and the NCBs of all 28 Member States, even those that have retained their own currency for the time being.

[124] Art 282(1) TEU.

[125] C Zilioli and M Selmayr, 'The Constitutional Status of the European Central Bank' (2007) 44 *Common Market Law Review* 355, 346.

[126] Arts 30–31 TEU; Art 7 Statute of the European System of Central Bank and of the European Central Bank. The ECB is functionally, institutionally, personally and financially independent, see Convergence Report, European Central Bank 21 (2012). For example, the shareholders of the ECB are national central banks, rather than EU Member States. See generally F Amtenbrink and K Van Duin, 'The European Central Bank before the European Parliament: theory and practice after ten years of monetary dialogue' (2009) 34 *European Law Review* 561.

[127] Art 12 ECB Statute.

Board, is responsible for the implementation of monetary policy as decided by the Governing Council. Importantly, pursuant to Article 10 of the Statute, the Executive Board members account for only 28 per cent of total voting rights in the Governing Council, whereas NCB governors account for 72 per cent. The balance of voting rights is thus heavily weighted towards Member States, rather than European decision makers. The allocation of the preponderance of voting rights to officials of Member State institutions, albeit independent, has important implications for where the balance of power for the conduct of monetary policy lies in practice.[128]

The experience of central banking in the United States is instructive in this respect. Up to the Great Depression, the US central bank was similarly decentralised as the contemporary Eurosystem. The Banking Act of 1935, one of the major reforms of the New Deal, ushered in much stronger central control by the centre, where the Federal Reserve Board—as opposed to the 12 regional Federal Reserve Banks—took the lead in devising monetary policy. For the first time, the Board had the majority of votes on the central monetary policy committee, the Federal Open Market Committee.[129] As we have seen, ECB monetary policy makers are currently in the minority on the Governing Council.

Third, the Statute adopts a narrow notion of 'monetary policy'[130] and formally confers exclusive competence on the ECB only with respect to monetary policy so defined. Article 12.1 of the ECB Statute contains an illustrative list of measures that fall under monetary policy, namely 'decisions relating to intermediate monetary objectives, key interest rates and the supply of reserves in the ESCB'. While NCBs are bound to follow the instructions with respect to these measures, they are free to carry out other functions under Article 14(4) of the Statute of the ESCB and the ECB—unless the Governing Council finds with a two-thirds majority that these 'interfere with the objectives and tasks of the ESCB'.[131]

[128] For example, tensions emerged between German Bundesbank President Jens Weidmann and other members of the Governing Council concerning outright monetary transactions and the Greek programme. See P Blustein, *Laid low: The IMF, the Euro Zone and the First Rescue of Greece* (CIGI Papers, 2015) 342; 'Europe's monetary opposition,' 6 October 2012 available at www.economist.com/node/21564245, 'Weidmann isolated as ECB plan approved', 6 September 2012 available at www.ft.com/content/3651b028-f846-11e1-b0e1-00144feabdc0 and 'Special Report: Inside Mario Draghi's euro rescue plan', 26 September 2012, available at www.reuters.com/article/us-ecb-draghi-plan-idUSBRE88O09A20120926.

[129] Banking Act of 1935, Title II, Amendments to the Federal Reserve Act; BS Bernanke, 'A Century of US Central Banking: Goals, Frameworks, Accountability' (2013) 27 *The Journal of Economic Perspectives* 3, 8; HH Preston, 'The Banking Act of 1935' (1935) 43 *Journal of Political Economy* 743, 753–54; FA Bradford, 'The Banking Act of 1935' (1935) 25 *The American Economic Review* 661, 665; AD Gayer, 'The Banking Act of 1935' (1935) 50 *The Quarterly Journal of Economics* 97.

[130] Narrow compared to modern central banks around the world.

[131] Art 14.4 of the Statute of the European System of Central Banks and the European Central Bank provides that: 'NCBs may perform functions other than those specified in this Statute unless the Governing Council finds, by a majority of two thirds of the votes cast, that these interfere with the objectives and tasks of the ESCB. Such functions shall be performed on the responsibility and liability of national central banks and shall not be regarded as being part of the functions of the ESCB.' Further on Art 14.4 see BC Scouteris and PL Athanassiou (forthcoming), 'National central bank tasks and the

In practice, the most important other function is lender of last resort lending, specifically in the form of emergency liquidity assistance (ELA). ELA is a central feature of modern central banking, which refers to lending to illiquid but solvent financial institutions and states.[132] Recipient financial institutions must be solvent, albeit in temporary need of liquidity, and provide adequate collateral.[133] If these two conditions are met, central banks should lend without limit[134] although they typically lend only on a discretionary basis, without spelling out hard and fast rules ex ante.[135]

ELA, as an alternative to central bank money, has played a crucial role in sustaining the financial systems of several EU Member States. In 2012, 10 per cent of all liquidity supplied to Eurozone banks constituted ELA and without it, the financial systems of Cyprus, Greece, Ireland and also the United Kingdom would probably have collapsed in the wake of the euro crisis.[136]

We can distinguish between 'classic' lender of last resort assistance to specific, individual institutions, and general, system-wide liquidity providing operations to financial institutions at large.[137] Traditionally, individual ELA fell outside the ESCB's responsibilities and was in practice left to NCBs. The Eurosystem did not want responsibility for such individual ELA, as evidenced by the silence of the Treaties on the Eurosystem's lender of last resort responsibility.[138]

The ECB has traditionally stipulated that liability for individual ELA rests with NCBs.[139] ELA loans are provided by and at the discretion of NCBs; they appear on NCB balance sheets; loss pooling is prohibited;[140] and ECB opinions and public

boundaries of the ECB Governing Council's powers under Article 14.4 of the Statute: State of play and future prospects', Commemorative Volume in memory of Professor Dr Leonidas Georgakopoulos (Bank of Greece's Centre for Culture, Research and Documentation).

[132] WH Buiter and E Rahbari, 'The European Central Bank as a lender of last resort for sovereigns in the Eurozone' (2012) 50 JCMS Annual Review Lecture; I Jack and T Cassels, 'Cyprus: an analysis of the impact of the resolution methodology on stakeholders' claims including the emergency liquidity assistance' (2013) 8 *Capital Markets Law Journal* 450, 459.

[133] W Bagehot, *Lombard Street: A Description of the Money Market* (New York, Scribner, 1873) 197; A Steinbach, 'The Lender of Last Resort in the Eurozone' 53 *Common Market Law Review* 361, 363–64.

[134] Bagehot, above n 133; Steinbach, above n 133 at 364.

[135] ibid.

[136] See eg 'ECB's emergency loan lifeline for Greek banks', 1 July 2015, available at www.ft.com/content/3fa39a3e-2006-11e5-aa5a-398b2169cf79; 'Irish central bank boosts emergency liquidity', 16 January 2011, available at www.ft.com/content/8796eb78-1fea-11e0-b458-00144feab49a; and I Plenderleith, 'Review of the Bank of England's provision of emergency liquidity assistance in 2008–09' (2012) Report presented to the Court of the Bank of England available at www.bankofengland.co.uk/publications/Documents/news/2012/cr1plenderleith.pdf.

[137] Steinbach, above n 133.

[138] Borger, above n 60 at 149.

[139] ECB Financial Stability Review (2006) available at www.ecb.europa.eu/pub/pdf/other/financialstabilityreview200612en.pdf?eeb9342332f4cd3127e55b523c51c9ff. See also ECB Annual Report (1999) available at www.ecb.europa.eu/pub/pdf/annrep/ar1999en.pdf, 109: 'The main guiding principle is that the competent NCB takes the decision concerning the provision of ELA to an institution operating in its jurisdiction. This would take place under the responsibility and at the cost of the NCB in question'.

[140] ECB Annual Report (1999), above n 139.

statements emphasise that ELA is not a Eurosystem function. Rather, the 'competent NCB takes the decision concerning the provision of ELA to an institution operating in its jurisdiction'.[141] However, although ELA is primarily an NCB function, the ECB oversees the provision of ELA. The ECB's Governing Council may, with a two-thirds majority vote, object to ELA that a NCB plans to extend.[142]

However, simply because the Union Treaties are silent as to any lender of last resort role for the ESCB does not mean that it can never perform that function, particularly in the case of general liquidity support to the financial system at large warranted by financial stability considerations. ECB President Draghi, when discussing whether ELA should be treated as senior to unsecured deposits and senior debts of Cypriot bank Laiki, described ELA as part of 'ECB' operations: 'if you want to remain as a counterparty in the ECB's monetary policy operations, it should certainly be treated as such.'[143] Further, in responding to criticism that the ECB had political motives, he asserted: '[w]e acted exactly within our mandate … We would have been acting politically if we had not done this.'[144]

Especially since the Eurozone crisis, it is increasingly questioned whether NCBs remain exclusively competent for system-wide ELA. According to one school of thought, system-wide emergency liquidity assistance is an inherent part of monetary policy and inheres in the ESCB's responsibility for financial stability for the whole Eurozone.[145] Accordingly, some argue that the ESCB's contribution to financial stability was not limited to giving advice under Article 25.2 of the ECB Statute, and that the ESCB could also use its powers under Article 18.1 of the ECB Statute for last resort assistance in case of a general lack of liquidity. This view gained ground during the Eurozone crisis, but remains controversial. The ESCB regards itself[146] competent for 'enhanced credit support' to financial institutions if the Eurozone's financial stability is at risk.[147]

There is a lack of clarity as to how the Eurozone's ELA system functions.[148] And importantly for present purposes, the competences of the ECB and NCBs are not clearly delineated. Moreover, it is unclear whether ELA, in the absence of state guarantees, constitutes monetary or fiscal policy. When ELA is conditional upon prior state guarantees to avoid the risk of the ECB becoming liable, it is more likely

[141] ibid.

[142] Art 14.4 of the Statute of the European System of Central Banks and the European Central Bank.

[143] Transcript of the Introductory Statement to the press conference held at Frankfurt am Main with Mario Draghi and Vitor Constâncio (4 April 2013), available at www.ecb.int/press/pressconf/2013/html/is130404.en.html4.

[144] ibid.

[145] Whether the ECSB has responsibility for 'financial stability' has been controversial, particularly since the Eurozone crisis.

[146] Borger, above n 600, 150; Case C-62/14, *Peter Gauweiler and others v Deutscher Bundestag*, Judgment of 16 June 2015.

[147] Steinbach, above n 1333 at 368. Art 18.1 ECB Statute also provided the legal basis for the programme on outright monetary transactions, examined in *Gauweiler* below.

[148] At least to some extent, this lack of clarity may be by design.

to qualify as fiscal policy.[149] But as argued elsewhere in this chapter, delineating monetary and economic/fiscal policy is often difficult.

ELA in the Eurozone has also been controversial. A leading example is the provision of €9.2 billion ELA by the Cypriot central bank to Laiki Bank. The Bank of Cyprus subsequently inherited this ELA liability.[150] Critics have accused the Cypriot central bank for lending to a bank that was likely insolvent, making it extremely unlikely that Laiki would ever be able to repay the loan.[151] Cypriot President Anastasiades noted that Laiki Bank had received ELA "under very questionable circumstances"'[152] and requested that EU leaders 'unwind' Cyprus' restructuring and the partial merger of Laiki and Bank of Cyprus.

It is part of a broader debate on the scope of 'monetary policy', in particular the weight that the ECB should give to financial stability considerations. 'Tellingly, a draft Statute of the ESCB and ECB, drawn up by the Committee of Central Bank Governors, initially envisaged giving the ESCB a greater responsibility for financial stability and listing it among its "basic" tasks instead of placing it in a separate provision. Several States opposed the proposal, and it did not make it into the final Treaty text.'[153]

CONCLUSION

From the standpoint of competence, the question of whether a measure qualifies as monetary or as economic policy is sometimes of crucial importance—as manifested in the two key crisis cases that reached the CJEU (*Pringle* and *Gauweiler*). Whereas the Treaties formally assign exclusive competence to the Eurosystem for monetary policy, the EU only has a coordinating competence for economic policy.

[149] W Buiter, J Michels and E Rahbari, 'ELA: An Emperor Without Clothes?' (21 January 2011) Citi Economics, Global Economics View, which suggests that balance-sheet exposure of NCBs through ELA should be covered by state guarantees in order to ensure compliance with the concept of financial independence of the ECB and NCBs; Belgium has in place legislation requiring any ELA granted by the NCB to be underwritten by explicit state guarantees; ECB opinions endorse such an approach: see Opinion of the European Central Bank at the request of the Belgian Ministry of Finance on a preliminary draft law on measures promoting financial stability and in particular establishing a State guarantee for the provision of credit in the context of financial stability (CON/2008/46): 'In order for emergency liquidity assistance provided with a State guarantee as collateral, as provided for in the draft law, to comply with the monetary financing prohibition, the following criteria should be met … there must be no doubts as to the legal validity and enforceability of the State guarantee under Belgian law. In this respect, the ECB welcomes the fact that the establishment of the State guarantee is enshrined in the draft law.'

[150] Jack and Cassels, above n 132 at 451.

[151] ibid.

[152] ibid at 459.

[153] See Art 3 of the Draft Statute of the ESCB and ECB (Europe Documents, No 1669/1670, 8 December 1990). For a discussion of this draft see R Smits, *The European Central Bank: institutional aspects* (The Hague, Kluwer Law International, 1997) 336–38. See also R Lastra, 'The governance structure for financial regulation and supervision in Europe' (2003) 10 *Columbia Journal of European Law* 49, 56.

This chapter has showed that the EU's formally exclusive monetary policy competence defies categorisation—neither in formal nor in substantive terms is it a genuine exclusive competence. But not only is it difficult to draw a bright line between exclusive and shared competence. The boundary between economic and monetary policy is also porous, and not particularly meaningful in economic terms. As this chapter has also shown, built into the Eurosystem is a high degree of subsidiarity, in contrast to the formally exclusive competence for monetary policy.

The important policy question is whether the governance of economic and monetary union as currently configured has struck the right balance between the supranational and national, between the centre and the periphery. In the monetary and economic policy arenas, both too little and too much European integration can lead to crisis, particularly if integration across the economic/monetary policy divide is asymmetric, with integration of monetary policy proceeding at a faster pace than integration of economic policy.[154]

One prominent diagnosis is that the Eurozone is stuck in an unstable equilibrium, and that Member States face a choice: progress towards a genuine economic and monetary union, or disintegration.[155] In theory, monetary policy competence could be repatriated, especially in case of a break-up of European monetary union.[156] Speculation about such break-up reached fever pitch at the height of the Greek debt crisis and has periodically resurfaced.[157] The worst for EMU is if neither national central banks nor the ECB can effectively act as lender of last resort in crises. But the more likely outcome is a move towards deeper economic integration, with more centralisation of macroeconomic policy and a broader understanding of monetary policy (including a financial stability mandate for the Eurosystem and lender of last resort function).[158]

[154] E Chiti, AJ Menéndez and PG Teixeira (eds), *The European Rescue of the European Union?* (ARENA Report No 3/12 2012) 2; Hinarejos, above n 10 at ch 1; S Dahan, O Fuchs and M Layus, 'Whatever It Takes? Regarding the OMT Ruling of the German Federal Constitutional Court' (2015) 18 *Journal of International Economic Law* 137, 148.

[155] European Commission (2012), 'A blueprint for a deep and genuine economic and monetary union Launching a European Debate' COM(2012)777 final/2; H Van Rompuy and others (2012), 'Towards a Genuine Economic and Monetary Union'; T Cesaroni and R de Santis, *Current Account 'Core-Periphery Dualism' in the EMU* (CEPS Working Document, 2015). See generally J von Hagen and B Eichengreen, 'Federalism, Fiscal Restraints, and European Monetary Union' (1996) 86(2) *American Economic Review* 134–38 and J Rodden, *Hamilton's paradox: the promise and peril of fiscal federalism* (Cambridge, Cambridge University Press, 2006).

[156] MD Bordo and L Jonung, 'The Future of EMU: What Does the History of Monetary Union Tell Us?' (1999) Working Paper 7365; KH O'Rourke and AM Taylor, 'Cross of Euros' (2013) 27 The *Journal of Economic Perspectives* 167–91.

[157] eg S Deo, P Donovan and L Hatheway, 'A brief history of break-ups' (2011) *Global Economic Perspectives*; S Fiedler, 'A Greek Euro-Zone Exit Could be a Tragedy' (2011) *Wall Street Journal*, 4–6 November 2011; Allen and Overy, 'The Euro and Currency Unions' (2011) Global Law Intelligence Unit. Most recently, Ted Malloch, a contender to become the new US ambassador to the European Union, called into question the sustainability the Eurozone: H Smith, 'Trump envoy says Greece is now more likely to leave the euro', *The Guardian*, 8 February 2017.

[158] A greater focus on financial stability and the ECB's lender of last resort function was the natural, if in some quarters controversial, outgrowth of the Eurozone crisis; see P Praet, 'The ECB and its role as lender of last resort during the crisis, Committee on Capital Markets Regulation conference

When the Eurozone, and Greece in particular, faced the prospect of a currency union without a lender of last resort, the ECB devised the OMT programme. Thereby, it took its responsibility for financial stability and its lender of last resort function seriously.[159] The OMT programme has achieved parts of its stated aims, secured the Eurozone's financial stability in the short run and decreased yield spreads on the sovereign debt of Eurozone Member States.[160] The Banking Union, and the upward migration of supervisory responsibilities to the ECB,[161] may contribute to enlarging the monetary policy competence in practice and impact the provision of ELA to financial institutions.

on The lender of last resort—an international perspective', Washington DC, 10 February 2016, available at www.ecb.europa.eu/press/key/date/2016/html/sp160210.en.html. A formal change of the ECB's mandate is both extremely unlikely and almost certainly unnecessary. See generally T Linzertand and F Smets, 'Monetary policy in a banking union' in F Ester and others (eds), *Financial Regulation: A Transatlantic Perspective* (Cambridge, Cambridge University Press, 2015).

[159] P De Grauwe, 'The European Central Bank as Lender of Last Resort in the Government Bond Markets' (2013) 59 *CESifo Economic Studies* 520.

[160] C Altavilla, D Giannone and M Lenza, 'The Financial and Macroeconomic Effects of OMT Announcements', ECB Working Paper Series No 1707, August 2014; N Cassola and J Jorge, 'The ECB's OMTs: A tale of governments, investors, and the central bank' (2016) 65 *Journal of International Money and Finance* 94–116; European Parliament, Effectiveness of the ECB programme of asset purchases: Where Do We Stand?, Monetary Dialogue 21 June 2016, Compilation of Notes. The macroeconomic effects of predecessor programmes, the ECB's Securities Market Programme and two Covered Bond Purchase Programmes from 2009 to 2012 were also significant; HD Gibson, SG Hall and GS Tavlas (2016), 'The effectiveness of the ECB's asset purchase programs of 2009 to 2012' 47 *Journal of Macroeconomics* 45–57. Strong criticism has also been voiced; see eg H-W Sinn, *The Euro trap: on bursting bubbles, budgets, and beliefs* (Oxford, Oxford University Press, 2014) 280–93. The OMT programme may have inflated asset prizes unsustainably and may had have an important redistributive impact.

[161] Council Regulation (EU) No 1024/2013 of 15 October 2013 conferring specific tasks on the European Central Bank concerning policies relating to the prudential supervision of credit institutions, OJ 2013 L 287/63; D Howarth and L Quaglia, 'Banking Union as Holy Grail: Rebuilding the Single Market in Financial Services, Stabilizing Europe's Banks and "Completing" Economic and Monetary Union' (2013) 51 *Journal of Common Market Studies* 103–23.

7

The EU's Exclusive Competence in Competition Law

PABLO IBÁÑEZ COLOMO*

INTRODUCTION

ARTICLE 3(1)(B) TFEU lists competition[1] as one of the areas in which the EU enjoys an exclusive competence. Compared to other areas, there is something peculiar about this provision. This peculiarity results, first, from the way in which the scope of exclusivity is defined. Pursuant to Article 3(1)(b) TFEU, the EU shall have a competence insofar as it is 'necessary for the functioning of the internal market'. This qualification is intended to clarify that EU competition law can co-exist and overlap—as it co-exists and overlaps in practice—with national systems.[2] The growth and development of national competition regimes is in fact a tangible manifestation of the influence of EU law on Member States' legal systems. By and large, the substantive aspects of these regimes are modelled upon the TFEU provisions, which form the core of the EU system for the protection of competition.

The second peculiarity is explained by the substantive and institutional aspects of the discipline. Article 3(1)(b) further qualifies the exclusive competence of the Union, in the sense that it confines it to the 'establishing' of 'rules'. This qualification seeks to distinguish between the adoption of legislation on the one hand and its implementation on the other. The divide is important in EU competition law, and captures an important feature of enforcement in the field. The exercise

* Pablo Ibáñez Colomo is Associate Professor of Law at the Department of Law, London School of Economics and Political Science, email P.Ibanez-Colomo@lse.ac.uk.

[1] Competition is understood by reference to the scope of Chapter 1 ('Rules on Competition') in Title VII of the Treaty. Chapter 1 comprises Arts 101 to 109 TFEU, which address competition between undertakings—including the rules that apply to public undertakings and undertakings entrusted with the operation of a service of general economic interest—and aids granted by Member States. See in this sense Joined Cases C-274/11 and C-295/11 *Spain and Italy v Commission* EU:C:2012:782. See, for a similar position, P Craig, *The Lisbon Treaty Law, Politics, and Treaty Reform* (Oxford, Oxford University Press, 2010) 159–61.

[2] Early on, the Court of Justice was asked to deal with the relationship between EU competition law and its national equivalents. See in this sense Case 14/68 *Walt Wilhelm and others v Bundeskartellamt* EU:C:1969:4.

of an exclusive competence is often intuitively associated with the adoption of harmonisation measures via general and abstract legislation. This intuition, which would faithfully reflect the reality of many EU policies, is not an accurate depiction of the functioning of competition law regimes. Contrary to what is true of other areas, the substantive principles of (EU) competition law are not necessarily (in fact, not even primarily) defined in legislative and quasi-legislative instruments. Articles 101, 102 and 107(1) TFEU can apply meaningfully to concrete factual scenarios without an implementing measure. Typically, the question in competition law cases is, for instance, whether a given practice amounts to a restriction of competition within the meaning of Article 101(1) TFEU or to an abuse of a dominant position under Article 102 TFEU.

Legislative (and quasi-legislative) instruments serve two main purposes in EU competition law. First, they provide the institutional and procedural framework in which the relevant provisions are to be applied. Regulation 1/2003,[3] which concerns the enforcement of Articles 101 and 102 TFEU, is a prime example in this regard. It defines the range of acts that authorities (including the Commission) and national courts may adopt as well as the procedural devices that may be relied upon to preserve effective competition. As the Court held in *AKZO v Commission*, such rules comprise the power of the Commission to conduct inspections.[4] Second, legislative and quasi-legislative instruments can ease the administrability of a competition law system.[5] In particular, they allow authorities to make a more efficient use of their resources. The so-called block exemption regulations and the accompanying soft law have acquired a prominent role in the context of Articles 101 and 102 TFEU[6] and in the field of EU State aid law (Articles 107 and 108 TFEU).[7] These instruments identify broad categories of practices that are deemed compatible with the Treaty provisions. In this sense, they provide legal certainty to stakeholders.

[3] Council Regulation (EC) No 1/2003 of 16 December 2002 on the implementation of the rules on competition laid down in Articles 81 and 82 of the Treaty OJ 2003 L 1/1.

[4] Case C-550/07 *Akzo Nobel Chemicals Ltd and Akcros Chemicals Ltd v Commission* EU:C:2010:512 para 116.

[5] Pursuant to Art 103(2)(b) TFEU, the Council is entitled to adopt directives or regulations designed 'to lay down detailed rules for the application of Article 101(3), taking into account the need to ensure effective supervision on the one hand, and to simplify administration to the greatest possible extent on the other'.

[6] See in particular Commission Regulation (EU) No 330/2010 of 20 April 2010 on the application of Article 101(3) of the Treaty on the Functioning of the European Union to categories of vertical agreements and concerted practices OJ 2010 L 102/1; Commission Regulation (EU) No 1217/2010 of 14 December 2010 on the application of Article 101(3) of the Treaty on the Functioning of the European Union to certain categories of research and development agreements OJ 2010 L 335/36; Commission Regulation (EU) No 1218/2010 of 14 December 2010 on the application of Article 101(3) of the Treaty on the Functioning of the European Union to certain categories of specialisation agreements OJ 2010 L 335/43; and Commission Regulation (EU) No 316/2014 of 21 March 2014 on the application of Article 101(3) of the Treaty on the Functioning of the European Union to categories of technology transfer agreements OJ 2014 L 93/17.

[7] See in particular Commission Regulation (EU) No 651/2014 of 17 June 2014 declaring certain categories of aid compatible with the internal market in application of Articles 107 and 108 of the Treaty OJ 2014 L 187/1.

The distinction between the adoption of rules and their implementation is important in a different sense. While the former is an exclusive competence of the EU, the latter is decentralised. Thus, Articles 101 and 102 TFEU are applied by national competition authorities (NCAs) and national courts. The Commission has in fact reported that, in the current context, the majority of administrative decisions concerning the two provisions is now adopted by NCAs.[8] Similarly, national courts can verify whether State aid has been granted in breach of the stand-still obligation set out in Article 108(3) TFEU and draw all the necessary consequences of the failure of a Member State to notify the measure.[9] Insofar as it is necessary to examine whether Article 108(3) TFEU has been breached, it may be necessary for national courts to interpret the notion of aid as laid down in Article 107(1) TFEU.[10]

This background gives an idea of the sort of controversies to which the exercise of the exclusive competence of the EU in the area of competition may give rise in practice. These controversies relate in part to the open-textured nature of EU competition law. A provision like Article 101(1) TFEU—pursuant to which agreements that have as their object or their effect the restriction of competition are prohibited—does not have a finite scope of application defined ex ante. It can be enforced in a very broad range of practices, and this, in a wide range of scenarios. Substantive overlaps with other fields of law are thus inevitable. For instance, overlaps (and occasional tensions) with intellectual property law and with network industries regulation have been noted and abundantly discussed in the literature. Some of these fields of law are harmonised at the EU level, others may be close to some areas that are part of the core of Member States' competencies. As a consequence, a given matter may be regulated through the ordinary legislative procedure or indirectly by the Commission through the use of its powers to enforce EU competition law. In such circumstances, concerns have been raised about the legitimacy of action by the latter.

The substantive and institutional interface between EU and national competition law is another potential source of tension. From an institutional standpoint, the shared powers between the Commission and national courts and authorities requires the development of an apparatus to co-ordinate the activities between them and ensure the consistent and effective enforcement of EU competition law. The experience of more than a decade of enforcement under Regulation 1/2003 suggests that the process of substantive decentralisation may inevitably lead to the progressive harmonisation of procedural and institutional matters relating directly or indirectly to the enforcement of EU competition law. In 2014, the European Parliament and the Council adopted a Directive concerning actions for damages

[8] Communication from the Commission to the European Parliament and the Council, Ten Years of Antitrust Enforcement under Regulation 1/2003: Achievements and Future Perspectives COM(2014) 453, 3–5 (hereinafter, the 'Ten Years Communication').

[9] See eg Case C-199/06 *Centre d'exportation du livre français (CELF) and Ministre de la Culture et de la Communication v Société internationale de diffusion et d'édition (SIDE)* EU:C:2008:79.

[10] Commission notice on the enforcement of State aid law by national courts OJ [2009] C 85/1.

(hereinafter, the 'Damages Directive'), which led to the adoption of some common rules on issues such as access to evidence and the interface between the public and the private enforcement of EU competition law.[11] At the time of writing this chapter, the Commission had launched a consultation on the need to harmonise the powers of NCAs to ensure that they become effective enforcers.[12]

From a substantive standpoint, the interface between EU and national competition law may give rise to questions about the appropriate boundaries of the discipline. The application of EU competition law to a given practice typically has consequences for the application of national rules and on the exercise by national authorities of their powers. NCAs are required to apply Article 101(1) TFEU to agreements that have an effect on trade between Member States. The practical consequence is that national competition law will have to be brought in line with the EU system. When an agreement falls within the scope of Article 101(1) TFEU, moreover, NCAs will be bound by a set of obligations relating to the allocation of cases and the consistency of enforcement. By analogy, mergers with a 'Union dimension' are examined on competition law grounds by the Commission alone in accordance with the 'one stop shop' principle.

These two distinct sources of controversy about the application of EU competition law can be broken down into two distinct issues, which are examined below. One issue is 'horizontal' in nature, in the sense that it relates to the relationship between EU competition law and other fields, whether regulated at the EU and/or national level. While concerns with the legitimacy of Commission intervention have been raised in some cases, EU courts have consistently taken the view that the friction between disciplines is one that can be addressed through the default mechanisms available in EU law—primacy and judicial review of administrative action. The second issue is 'vertical' in nature, in the sense that it relates to the relationship between the Commission and national authorities and courts concerning the application of (EU) competition law and the institutional and substantive boundaries of the discipline.

SUBSTANTIVE OVERLAPS AND THE LEGITIMACY OF INTERVENTION IN EU COMPETITION LAW

The Features of Competition Law Provisions

EU competition law provisions are very versatile instruments. They are worded in broad and vague terms. For instance, Article 101(1) TFEU fails to define what

[11] Directive 2014/104/EU of the European Parliament and of the Council of 26 November 2014 on certain rules governing actions for damages under national law for infringements of the competition law provisions of the Member States and of the European Union Text with EEA relevance OJ 2014 L 349/1.

[12] Commission, 'Antitrust: Commission consults on boosting enforcement powers of national competition authorities' (Brussels, 4 November 2015).

amounts to a restriction of competition. At most, the letter of the Treaty provides a non-exhaustive list of behaviours that are prima facie in breach of the provision.[13] Similarly, Article 107(1) TFEU is not explicit about the notion of 'aid', or about what it means to favour 'certain undertakings or the production of certain goods'.[14] As a result of this choice, the scope of enforcement is not confined to a pre-defined set of practices. EU competition law provisions cover a virtually limitless set of potential scenarios. For instance, for a pharmaceutical company to supply misleading information to a patent office may amount to an abuse of a dominant position under Article 102 TFEU.[15] The manifest inability of a dominant firm to satisfy demand may also amount to a breach of the same provision when read in conjunction with Article 106 TFEU.[16]

The versatility of EU competition law has allowed courts and authorities to bring an answer to challenges that were difficult—if not impossible—to envisage when the relevant provisions were enacted. These provisions can apply even though they were conceived in a markedly different economic and legal reality. For instance, Article 101 TFEU has been seamlessly enforced to tackle agreements concerning the distribution of goods and services via the internet.[17] Similarly, contentious issues that have emerged in high-technology industries—such as the theory of patent hold-up,[18] or issues relating to the status of online platforms[19]—have been addressed under Article 102 TFEU. In this regard, the provisions on State aid are not fundamentally different from Articles 101 and 102 TFEU. From the very early judgments, the Court refused to define the scope of the notion of aid in a formal way. Thus, the instrument by which the aid is granted is not a relevant factor in the assessment, provided that it has the effect of favouring some firms or sectors of the economy.[20]

[13] Art 101(1) TFEU, for instance, provides the following non-exhaustive list of practices: '(a) directly or indirectly fix purchase or selling prices or any other trading conditions; (b) limit or control production, markets, technical development, or investment; (c) share markets or sources of supply; (d) apply dissimilar conditions to equivalent transactions with other trading parties, thereby placing them at a competitive disadvantage; (e) make the conclusion of contracts subject to acceptance by the other parties of supplementary obligations which, by their nature or according to commercial usage, have no connection with the subject of such contracts'.

[14] Art 107(1) TFEU reads as follows: 'Save as otherwise provided in the Treaties, any aid granted by a Member State or through State resources in any form whatsoever which distorts or threatens to distort competition by favouring certain undertakings or the production of certain goods shall, in so far as it affects trade between Member States, be incompatible with the internal market'.

[15] Case C-457/10 P *AstraZeneca AB and AstraZeneca plc v Commission* EU:C:2012:770.

[16] Case C-41/90 *Klaus Höfner and Fritz Elser v Macrotron GmbH* EU:C:1991:161.

[17] Guidelines on vertical restraints 2010 C 130/1 paras 52/54; and Case C-439/09 *Pierre Fabre Dermo-Cosmétique SAS v Président de l'Autorité de la concurrence and Ministre de l'Économie, de l'Industrie et de l'Emploi* EU:C:2011:649.

[18] See M Lemley and C Shapiro, 'Patent Holdup and Royalty Stacking' (2007) 85 *Texas Law Review* 1991; and Case C-170/13 *Huawei Technologies Co Ltd v ZTE Corp and ZTE Deutschland GmbH* EU:C:2015:477.

[19] Commission, 'Online Platforms and the Digital Single Market Opportunities and Challenges for Europe' COM(2016) 288 final; and Commission, 'Antitrust: Commission sends Statement of Objections to Google on comparison shopping service; opens separate formal investigation on Android' (Brussels, 15 April 2015).

[20] Case 30/59 *De Gezamenlijke Steenkolenmijnen in Limburg v High Authority* EU:C:1961:2.

The flexibility of EU competition law is not reflected only in the range of scenarios to which it can potentially apply, but in the range of remedies that can be adopted to bring infringements to an end. Treaty provisions such as Articles 101 and 102 TFEU are worded as general prohibitions. Similarly, Article 107(1) TFEU lays down a principle of incompatibility of State aid with the internal market. It is now undisputed that this negative wording has no bearing on the nature of the remedies that can be required by courts and authorities. Remedies need not be negative in nature, in the sense that they need not take the form of a (one-off) cease-and-desist order. Competition authorities may impose positive obligations on firms. For instance, it is possible to bring an end to an infringement by requiring a dominant firm to license its intellectual property rights to its downstream competitors.[21] Similarly, the approval of a merger may be made conditional on the parties committing to give access to their facilities to downstream rivals for a given period.[22]

In the same way that remedies in EU competition law may be positive or negative in nature, they may be structural or behavioural. A behavioural remedy is one that seeks to address the concern by changing the behaviour of the firms under investigation. A structural remedy, on the other hand, is one that results in a change in the structure of the market. Thus, a firm may be required to sell some assets to a rival so that a new competitive force is created, or to remove the ability of a firm to engage in a particular line of conduct. For instance, an energy company may be required to sell its assets relating to the transmission of electricity in order to address concerns with its ability and incentive to foreclose competition on related markets.[23] Similarly, the parties to a merger may be required to sell some production capacity to third parties to preserve competition on the relevant market.[24]

Enforcement Instruments in Competition Law

Competition law can be enforced using a variety of instruments. In this sense, individual decisions concluding, for instance, that a provision has been infringed, or that a transaction is incompatible with the internal market, capture only partially the ways in which the Commission, as a competition authority, can influence the behaviour of firms and stakeholders. Soft law instruments have become

[21] Joined Cases C-241/91 and C-242/91 *Radio Telefis Eireann and Independent Television Publications Ltd v Commission* EU:C:1995:98.

[22] Commission notice on remedies acceptable under Council Regulation (EC) No 139/2004 and under Commission Regulation (EC) No 802/2004 OJ 2008 C 267/1 paras 62–66 (hereinafter, the 'Remedies Notice'). See also, as an example, *Intel/McAfee* (Case COMP/M.5984) Commission Decision of 26 January 2011.

[23] See eg *German Electricity Wholesale Market and German Electricity Balancing Market* (Joined Cases COMP/39.388 and COMP/39/389) Commission Decision of 26 November 2008 OJ 2009 C 36/8.

[24] See the Remedies Notice, above n 22 paras 23–46. See eg *Nestlé/Perrier* (Case IV/M.190) Commission Decision 92/553/EEC 1992 L 356/1.

very prominent in the practice of the Commission (and national competition authorities). These instruments make it possible to provide indications about the stance of an authority in relation to broad categories of practices and/or scenarios. By clarifying its position, the Commission is able to refocus its resources on the most problematic of infringements without sacrificing the effectiveness of the system across the board.

Among quasi-legislative instruments, Guidelines are the most frequently used in practice. They have allowed the Commission to define the instances in which some agreements (including vertical agreements and horizontal co-operation agreements) are likely to be deemed compatible with Article 101 TFEU, whether because they are not restrictive of competition or because they fulfil the conditions set out in Article 101(3) TFEU.[25] Guidelines and similar instruments, including the so-called Frameworks, also dominate the enforcement of EU State aid law. They allow the Commission to set out the conditions under which horizontal or sector-specific measures—including regional, rescue and restructuring and environmental aid—is to be deemed compatible with Article 107(3) TFEU.[26]

In the practice of the Commission, other instruments have served a similar role. Following the adoption of Regulation 1/2003, sector inquiries have been conducted relatively frequently. These inquiries—which are conducted in accordance with Article 17 of Regulation 1/2003[27]—are a means for the Commission to gain an understanding of the functioning of certain industries or activities, including energy,[28] pharmaceuticals[29] and e-commerce.[30] It has become customary for the Commission to issue reports in the context of a sector inquiry. These reports provide indications about the practices that the authority perceives to be problematic, and about the remedies that firms may adopt to bring an end to potential

[25] See in this sense the Guidelines on vertical restraints, above n 17; the Guidelines on the applicability of Article 101 of the Treaty on the Functioning of the European Union to horizontal co-operation agreements OJ 2001 C 11/1; and Guidelines on the application of Article 101 of the Treaty on the Functioning of the European Union to technology transfer agreements OJ 2014 C 89/3.

[26] See in particular Guidelines on regional State aid for 2014–2020 OJ 2013 C 209/1; Guidelines on State aid for rescuing and restructuring non-financial undertakings in difficulty OJ 2014 C 249/1; and Guidelines on State aid for environmental protection and energy 2014–2020 OJ 2014 C 200/1.

[27] Pursuant to Art 17(1) of Regulation 1/2003: 'Where the trend of trade between Member States, the rigidity of prices or other circumstances suggest that competition may be restricted or distorted within the common market, the Commission may conduct its inquiry into a particular sector of the economy or into a particular type of agreements across various sectors. In the course of that inquiry, the Commission may request the undertakings or associations of undertakings concerned to supply the information necessary for giving effect to Articles 81 and 82 of the Treaty and may carry out any inspections necessary for that purpose'. It is also possible to conduct sector inquiries in EU State aid law. See Art 25 of Council Regulation (EU) 2015/1589 of 13 July 2015 laying down detailed rules for the application of Article 108 of the Treaty on the Functioning of the European Union OJ 2015 L 248/9.

[28] Commission, 'Competition: Commission energy sector inquiry confirms serious competition problems' (Brussels, 10 January 2007).

[29] Commission, 'Antitrust: shortcomings in pharmaceutical sector require further action' (Brussels, 8 July 2009).

[30] Commission, 'Antitrust: Commission launches e-commerce sector inquiry' (Brussels, 6 May 2015).

infringements.[31] In practice, they may influence firm behaviour in the same way Guidelines and other soft law instruments.[32]

Competition Law as a Tool to Mimic, Replace and Refine Legislation

In theory, there is an important difference between intervention under EU competition law and the adoption of legislation. The former is understood to intervene on a case-by-case basis and the latter is based on general and abstract provisions. In practice, the difference is not as marked as it may seem. The development of a body of case law and/or administrative practice can have the same impact as a regulatory instrument applying to all firms in an industry. Operators that are in a comparable factual and legal situation will typically adapt their behaviour to conform to the principles underlying previous cases. Soft law instruments, by their very nature, are intended to apply at a higher level of generality. This fact, together with the versatility of the provisions, means that EU competition law can mimic a wide range of regulatory instruments.

For instance, EU competition law can mimic a sector-specific regime applying to the network industries. These sector-specific regimes often provide for an obligation on the incumbent operator to supply access to its infrastructure (typically, the segments that cannot be easily duplicated) on regulated terms and conditions (which include, in particular, a non-discrimination obligation). Article 102 TFEU can be—and has been[33]—relied upon to achieve a similar outcome in practice. Because the Commission has the power to impose relatively heavy fines on firms, one or several prohibition decisions can have a strong deterrent effect on the same—or comparable—behaviour. In practice, Article 102 TFEU can become self-enforcing in relation to certain infringements. Quasi-legislative instruments outlining the potential infringements and identifying remedies can have the same impact on firm behaviour.

EU competition law mimicking a legislative instrument can either anticipate, or overlap with, a regulatory regime. First, it can provide a template for subsequent legislation. The Commission has in fact relied upon its powers to enforce Article 106 TFEU in combination with Articles 101 and 102 TFEU to advance the liberalisation of some sectors of the economy.[34] More generally, there are several

[31] See in this sense Commission, 'Inquiry pursuant to Article 17 of Regulation (EC) No 1/2003 into the European gas and electricity sectors' COM(2006) 851 final.

[32] This point was identified early on by some commentators. See in this sense N Petit and M Rato, 'From Hard to Soft Enforcement of EC Competition Law—A Bestiary of "Sunshine" Enforcement Instruments' in C Gheur and N Petit (eds), *Alternative enforcement techniques in EC competition law: Settlements, commitments and other novel instruments* (Bruylant, 2009).

[33] See in particular *Telekomunikacja Polska* (Case COMP/39.525) Commission Decision of 22 June 2011 OJ 2011 C 324/7; and *Slovak Telekom* (Case AT.39523) Commission Decision of 15 October 2014 OJ 2015 C 314/7.

[34] For an overview of the activity of the Commission throughout the 1990s, see JL Buendía Sierra, *Exclusive Rights and State Monopolies under EC Law: Article 86 (former Article 90) of the EC Treaty* (Oxford University Press, 2000).

examples of measures that have been introduced in the context of competition law proceedings and that have been subsequently enshrined in legislation. The regulation of payment systems is one such example.[35] An EU Regulation was adopted following a series of Commission decisions concerning Visa and MasterCard.[36] Second, EU competition law can overlap with a regulatory regime in place. In such instances, it can emerge as an alternative avenue to achieve the objectives of the said regime. For instance, the enforcement of Articles 101 and 102 TFEU in the telecommunications sector can contribute to the preservation of effective competition in liberalised markets.[37] Where there is a substantive overlap between EU competition law and a legislative instrument, the former can be used to refine the latter. This may be the case where a legislative instrument has substantive gaps, or where it lacks the necessary enforcement tools to achieve its objectives. EU competition law can also be used to replace an existing legislative instrument. This situation may arise where the enforcement of EU competition law provisions contradicts or conflicts with an existing regulatory regime.

The Interaction between EU Competition Law and EU Policies

The phenomenon of interaction of EU competition law with other policies can be observed at the EU and at the national levels. At the EU level, EU competition law has overlapped and anticipated harmonisation measures adopted in accordance with Article 114 TFEU. This overlap is remarkable due to the institutional implications that it has. First, intervention under EU competition law allows the Commission to reach the preferred outcome without involving the Parliament and the Council. In this sense, the scope of the Commission powers is broader than under Article 114 TFEU, where it only has the power of initiative. The Commission may indeed be able to achieve a policy objective without it being necessary to resort to the ordinary legislative procedure. If it is not in a position to persuade the Parliament and the Council to endorse some of its proposals, it may choose to rely on its powers to enforce competition rules. In the context of the liberalisation of the electricity and gas industries, for instance, the Commission, as the institution with the power of initiative, expressed a preference for the unbundling of the ownership of transmission activities.[38] However, the final version of the regulatory package

[35] Regulation (EU) 2015/751 of the European Parliament and of the Council of 29 April 2015 on interchange fees for card-based payment transactions 2015 L 123/1.

[36] See in particular *Visa International—Multilateral Interchange Fee* (Case No COMP/29.373): Commission Decision 2002/914/EC OJ 2002 L 318/17; *Visa MIF* (Case AT.39398) Commission Decision of 26 February 2014 OJ 2014 C 147/7 and *MasterCard, Eurocommerce* and *Commercial Cards* (Joined Cases COMP/34.579, 36.518 and 38.580) Commission Decision of 19 December 2007.

[37] This is particularly apparent in cases aimed at preventing the exclusion of new entrants in recently liberalised markets. See in particular Case C-280/08 P *Deutsche Telekom AG v Commission* EU:C:2010:603; and Case C-52/09 *Konkurrensverket v TeliaSonera Sverige AB* EU:C:2011:83.

[38] P Lowe, 'The Liberalisation of EU Energy Markets', The Beesley Lectures, London, 9 November 2006.

did not mandate this option, and provided for alternatives.[39] The Commission, however, was able to achieve the preferred outcome by means of the enforcement of EU competition law in individual cases.[40]

Second, the Commission often enjoys a dual role in instances in which EU competition law mimics, or overlaps with, legislation adopted at the EU level. In addition to its power of initiative, the Commission may be given enforcement and/or supervision powers under the regime in question. For instance, it may have the power to ensure the consistent interpretation of the relevant legislation at the national level, or it may be involved in the decision-making powers of national authorities. The telecommunications industry is one in which the Commission is entrusted with such tasks in accordance with the principles set out in the Regulatory Framework for electronic communications.[41] The Commission has the power to oversee the interpretation and application of the Framework by the national regulatory authorities (NRAs).[42] However extensive, this power is not comparable to its status in the context of Articles 101 and 102 TFEU, both from a procedural and a substantive standpoint. Indeed, the NRAs—not the Commission—are in charge of the implementation of the Regulatory Framework. In the context of EU competition law, by contrast, the Commission not only has decision-making powers but is entitled to require the necessary behavioural and/or structural remedies and to levy fines.[43] Given this asymmetry of powers, it may be more effective for the Commission to rely upon competition law to achieve the objectives of the regulatory regime, or to overrule the NRAs through the enforcement of Articles 101 and 102 TFEU.

Against this background, it is easy to make sense of the enforcement of Article 102 TFEU to the practices implemented by incumbent telecommunications operators. In fact, some of the landmark cases in this area can be rationalised as a reaction against the failure of NRAs to properly apply the Regulatory Framework for electronic communications. In *Deutsche Telekom*, for instance, the anticompetitive outcome against which the Commission reacted could indeed have been avoided if the German NRA had set the relevant rates at a level allowing

[39] Directive 2009/72/EC of the European Parliament and of the Council of 13 July 2009 concerning common rules for the internal market in electricity and repealing Directive 2003/54/EC OJ 2009 L 211/55; and Directive 2009/73/EC of the European Parliament and of the Council of 13 July 2009 concerning common rules for the internal market in natural gas and repealing Directive 2003/55/EC OJ 2009 L 211/94.

[40] See eg *E.On/MOL* (Case COMP/M.3696) Commission Decision of 21 December 2005 OJ 2006 L 253/20; *German Electricity Wholesale Market and German Electricity Balancing Market*, above n 23; and *RWE Gas Foreclosure* (Case COMP/39.402) Commission Decision of 18 March 2009.

[41] See in particular Directive 2002/21/EC of the European Parliament and of the Council of 7 March 2002 on a common regulatory framework for electronic communications networks and services as amended by Directive 2009/140/EC and Regulation 544/2009 OJ 2002 L 108/33 (hereinafter, the 'Framework Directive').

[42] ibid, Arts 7, 7a and 7b.

[43] See in this sense Arts 7–10 and 17–24 of Regulation 1/2003.

new entrants to compete.[44] In fact, one of the contentious aspects of the case related to whether the exclusionary effects were attributable to the behaviour of the incumbent operator or to the regulatory authority in the end.[45] Intervention under Article 102 TFEU in that case allowed the Commission to signal to NRAs that it was committed to the liberalisation process and that there were alternative avenues to ensure its success.

The Interaction between EU Competition Law and National Legislation

Due to its versatile and transversal nature, EU competition law can influence national policies. In this sense, it is not fundamentally different from harmonisation measures adopted in accordance with Article 114 TFEU, or from free movement provisions.[46] In practice, the features of EU competition law provisions are particularly interesting where they interfere with areas in which the adoption of harmonisation measures is not possible and/or realistic in the short run. In such circumstances, the enforcement of EU competition law provisions allows the Commission to refine or replace some aspects of national legislation that may be perceived to be an obstacle for the achievement of the objectives of the EU Treaties and that might not otherwise have been possible. These ideas may be illustrated by reference to two examples: the tension between intellectual property and the internal market on the one hand, and the application of EU State aid rules to corporate taxation on the other.

There is a mismatch between most intellectual property systems, which are national in scope, and the ambition of creating an EU-wide internal market. Tensions between the two are inevitable and were readily identified in the 1960s.[47] These tensions have only been partially tackled through negative and positive integration. In accordance with the doctrine of exhaustion, introduced by the Court in the 1970s, intellectual property rights cannot be invoked to prevent the circulation within the EU of goods that have been put on the internal market by the right holder or with its consent.[48] The doctrine of exhaustion, however, does not

[44] See in this sense P Larouche, 'Contrasting Legal Solutions and the Comparability of EU and US Experiences' in F Lévêque and H Shelanski (eds), *Antitrust and Regulation in the EU and US: Legal and Economic Perspectives* (Elgar, 2009).

[45] See in this sense *Deutsche Telekom*, above n 37 paras 56–96.

[46] For an analysis of this question, see G Davies, 'Democracy and Legitimacy in the Shadow of Purposive Competence' (2015) 21 *European Law Journal* 2.

[47] See in this sense W Alexander, 'L'établissement du Marché commun et le problème des brevets parallèles' (1968) *Revue trimestrielle de droit européen* 513 and P Demaret, *Patents, Territorial Restrictions, and EEC Law: A Legal and Economic Analysis* (Verlag Chemie, 1978).

[48] See in particular Case 78/70 *Deutsche Grammophon Gesellschaft mbH v Metro-SB-Großmärkte GmbH & Co KG* EU:C:1971:59; and Case 15/74 *Centrafarm BV and Adriaan de Peijper v Sterling Drug Inc* EU:C:1974:114. For an analysis of the question, see Demaret, above n 47 and D Keeling, *Intellectual Property Rights in EU Law, vol 1: Free Movement and Competition Law* (Oxford, Oxford University Press, 2003). See also Case 78/70 *Deutsche Grammophon Gesellschaft mbH v Metro-SB-Großmärkte GmbH & Co KG* EU:C:1971:59; and Case 15/74 *Centrafarm BV and Adriaan de Peijper v Sterling Drug Inc* EU:C:1974:114.

apply to instances in which intellectual property rights are exploited in an intangible manner, as in the form of a broadcast.[49] Thus, absent harmonisation measures addressing the question, copyright may be invoked to prevent the cross-border transmission of, inter alia, television services. This is a question with which the Commission has struggled since the 1980s. In relation to satellite services, the issue was addressed through a harmonisation measure that introduced the 'country of origin' principle. Thus, a satellite transmission is deemed to occur only in the country in which the uplink of the signal takes place.[50] For other services—most notably, those provided via the internet—copyright can still be validly invoked in every country in which it is received. As a result, copyright can be relied upon to prevent the cross-border provision of services.[51] This reality is an obstacle to the achievement of the so-called Digital Single Market, which has emerged as one of the priorities of the Commission as an institution.[52]

In these circumstances, EU competition law can be relied upon as an alternative instrument to achieve the objectives of the Digital Single Market. In relation to online transmissions, the Commission sent a Statement of Objections to the Hollywood major studios and to Sky UK, the leading pay TV broadcaster in the UK and Ireland.[53] This case, which is pending at the time of writing, is based on the idea that agreements that require broadcasters to block access to online content from countries in which they do not enjoy the rights are contrary to Article 101(1) TFEU. This case, if pursued to its logical consequences, would alter the nature and operation of copyright in the online world. Paramount, which proposed a set of remedies to put an end to the proceedings, committed—in essence—not to enforce copyright against breaches resulting from the cross-border provision of online services.[54] The outcome would thus not be fundamentally different from the outcome that was achieved through the harmonisation of the copyright regime applying to satellite transmissions.

The interaction between EU State aid law and national tax systems is not always an easy one. Taxation is an area that is close to the core of Member States' competences, and action at the EU level is circumscribed to certain issues. In particular, the TFEU does not provide for any rules concerning direct business taxation. As a result, any EU initiatives in the field make it necessary to rely upon Article 115

[49] Case 62/79 *SA Compagnie générale pour la diffusion de la télévision, Coditel, and others v Ciné Vog Films and others* EU:C:1980:84.

[50] Council Directive 93/83/EEC of 27 September 1993 on the coordination of certain rules concerning copyright and rights related to copyright applicable to satellite broadcasting and cable retransmission OJ 1993 L 248/15.

[51] *IFPI 'Simulcasting'* (Case No COMP/C2/38.014) Commission Decision 2003/300/EC OJ 2003 L 107/58.

[52] See in this sense Commission, 'A Digital Single Market Strategy for Europe' COM(2015) 192 final.

[53] Commission, 'Antitrust: Commission sends Statement of Objections on cross-border provision of pay-TV services available in UK and Ireland' (Brussels, 23 July 2015).

[54] Commission, 'Antitrust: Commission accepts commitments by Paramount on cross-border pay-TV services' (Brussels, 26 July 2016).

TFEU, which requires unanimity among Member States. Even though some progress has been made in discrete areas,[55] and some ambitious initiatives are on the table, the idea of harmonising direct business taxation looks like a distant prospect at the time of writing this piece. These cumbersome procedures stand in stark contrast with the ability of the Commission to interfere with the tax regimes of Member States through the enforcement of Articles 107 and 108 TFEU.

It is clear from the case law that these provisions can be relied upon to question the design of tax systems. In *Gibraltar*, for instance, the Court validated the analysis of the Commission, which concluded that the corporate tax regime applied by the British overseas territory was selective and, as such, that it was caught by Article 107(1) TFEU.[56] It is also clear from the case law that EU State aid rules may be relied upon to question the scope of a tax. In other words, Article 107(1) TFEU may be triggered not only where the tax regime provides for a derogation, but also where it is designed in a way that it does not cover certain firms or activities. In *British Aggregates*, for instance, the Court ruled that Member States are not free, in the absence of EU-wide harmonisation measures, to decide which activities to tax.[57] Thus, it is possible to conclude, on the basis of Article 107(1) TFEU, that certain activities should have been subject to a measure. In *Laboratoires Boiron*, the Court concluded that the application of a tax on direct sales to some firms but not to others may amount to State aid.[58]

The extent to which EU State aid law can interfere with national tax systems has been explored in a series of cases relating to the award of tax rulings by some Member States. These cases—which include action against Apple,[59] Fiat,[60] McDonald's[61] and Starbucks[62]—cannot be understood without considering the broader context of corporate taxation. The taxation of multinationals is a complex issue that may give rise to opportunistic behaviour on the part of firms.[63] As a consequence, several initiatives have been taken internationally, particularly at the

[55] Several initiatives have been adopted in recent years, including Council Directive 2014/107/EU of 9 December 2014 amending Directive 2011/16/EU as regards mandatory automatic exchange of information in the field of taxation OJ 2014 L 359/1; and Council Directive (EU) 2015/2376 of 8 December 2015 amending Directive 2011/16/EU as regards mandatory automatic exchange of information in the field of taxation OJ 2015 L 332/1. The legal basis for these two Directives was Art 115 TFEU.

[56] Joined cases C-106/09 P and C-107/09 P *Gibraltar and United Kingdom v Commission* EU:C:2011:732.

[57] Case C-487/06 P *British Aggregates Association v Commission* EU:C:2008:757.

[58] Case C-526/04 *Laboratoires Boiron SA v Union de recouvrement des cotisations de sécurité sociale et d'allocations familiales de Lyon* EU:C:2006:528.

[59] Commission, 'State aid: Ireland gave illegal tax benefits to Apple worth up to €13 billion' (Brussels, 30 August 2016).

[60] *State aid which Luxembourg granted to Fiat* (Case SA.38375), Commission Decision of 21 October 2015.

[61] *Alleged aid to McDonald's* (Case SA.38945), Commission Decision of 3 December 2015.

[62] *State aid implemented by the Netherlands to Starbucks* (Case SA.38374), Commission Decision of 21 October 2015.

[63] For an overview of the issue, from the perspective of State aid, see W Haslehner, 'Double Taxation Relief, Transfer Pricing Adjustments and State Aid Law', in I Richelle, W Schon and E Traversa (eds), *State Aid Law and Business Taxation* (Springer, 2016).

level of the OECD, in order to minimise this sort of conduct.[64] However, these initiatives are typically based on soft law instruments and thus depend on governments' willingness to conform to them. In this broader context, EU State aid can become a useful tool to 'give teeth' to these instruments—or, if one prefers, turn them into hard law. The cases mentioned above are based on the idea that the key principle in international taxation—the so-called arm's length principle[65]—is an integral element of Article 107(1) TFEU.[66] These cases, which advanced an interpretation of EU State aid law provisions that many commentators perceive to be controversial,[67] are currently pending before the GC.[68]

The Legitimacy of Intervention under EU Competition Law

The legitimacy of intervention under EU competition law in the instances described above has been called into question by stakeholders and commentators.[69] It is often argued that the application of EU competition law provisions in such instances is questionable insofar as it is a means to circumvent the requisite legislative procedures (and thus the democratic safeguards embedded in such procedures). The alleged circumvention would be particularly problematic insofar as it would allow the Commission to achieve the outcomes that it would not otherwise have been able to achieve. Similarly, it has been argued that intervention in this sense is questionable because it affords the Commission to take action in areas—such as direct business taxation—in which it has no competence.[70] The use of soft law instruments has also attracted criticism. These are perceived as forms of

[64] See in particular the initiatives taken at the level of the OECD. OECD, 'Transfer Pricing Guidelines for Multinational Enterprises and Tax Administrations 2010' (16 August 2010). In 2015, the organisation concluded its work on Base Erosion and Profit Shifting strategies by multinationals. See OECD, 'G20 Base Erosion and Profit Shifting Project—2015 Final Reports—Executive Summaries', available at www.oecd.org/ctp/beps-reports-2015-executive-summaries.pdf.

[65] See in this sense Art 9 of OECD, Model Convention with respect to taxes on income and on capital, pursuant to which where 'conditions are made or imposed between the two enterprises in their commercial or financial relations which differ from those which would be made between independent enterprises, then any profits which would, but for those conditions, have accrued to one of the enterprises, but, by reason of those conditions, have not so accrued, may be included in the profits of that enterprise and taxed accordingly'.

[66] Commission Notice on the notion of State aid as referred to in Art 107(1) of the Treaty on the Functioning of the European Union 2016 C 262/1 para 174.

[67] For a recent discussion, see P Nicolaides, 'State Aid Rules and Tax Rulings' (2016) 15 *European State Aid Law Quarterly* 416. For a different perspective, see R Lyal, 'Transfer Pricing Rules and State Aid' (2015) 38 *Fordham International Law Journal* 1017.

[68] Case T-759/15 *Fiat Chrysler Finance Europe v Commission*, pending; Case T-636/16 *Starbucks and Starbucks Manufacturing Emea v Commission*, pending; and Case T-778/16 *Ireland v Commission*, pending.

[69] For an overview of the arguments, see N Dunne, 'Commitment Decisions in EU Competition Law (2014) 10 *Journal of Competition Law & Economics* 399.

[70] See eg T Webb, 'Kroes hits out at DG Comp tax probes', *Global Competition Review* (London, 1 September 2016).

quasi-legislation that not only circumvent the requisite procedures but also have the effect of depriving firms of a due process of law.[71]

An analysis of the case law suggests that these criticisms do not seem justified from a legal standpoint. The EU courts have consistently refused to draw artificial boundaries to intervention under EU competition law. Thus, the letter of the provisions—as interpreted by the Court—is the only meaningful limit to enforcement by the Commission. So long as enforcement is based on a sound understanding of the substantive limits of these provisions, intervention is (legally speaking) unproblematic. This argument was made explicit by the GC in a challenge brought by EDP—a Portuguese incumbent in the energy sector—against a decision declaring a concentration to be incompatible with the internal market. EDP argued, inter alia, that the decision had to be annulled as being ultra vires. According to the firm, the Commission had used the merger control regime to advance the liberalisation of energy markets in the EU—as opposed to the protection of the competitive process.[72] This argument was rejected by the GC. According to the judgment, the fact that the remedies required in the case would not have been justified under the Merger Regulation would not in itself suggest that the Commission had misused its powers. It would simply mean that the decision was vitiated by an error of law.[73]

The Court followed a similar approach in *Deutsche Telekom*. It was argued in the case that the breach of Article 102 TFEU was not attributable to the dominant firm (the incumbent telecommunications operator in the country), but to the behaviour of the regulator, which had set the relevant wholesale access prices that were at the origin of the infringement. From this perspective, it could be argued that the case sought to address a regulatory problem—the lack of commitment to liberalisation on the part of the authority—as opposed to a competition law one. The Court did not follow the incumbent operator on this point. In line with the relevant case law, it ruled that firms—including those that are subject to sector-specific regulation—can only escape the application of EU competition law provisions where national legislation does not leave any scope for manoeuvre.[74] Thus, Article 102 TFEU remained applicable in the case insofar as the firm had the ability to set the relevant retail prices—and thus to avoid abusing its dominant position.[75]

[71] Petit and Rato, above n 32, speak of 'sunshine enforcement'.

[72] Case T-87/05 *Energias de Portugal, SA v Commission* EU:T:2015:333 para 86 ('[t]he applicant claims, essentially, that the Commission misunderstood the powers conferred on it by the Merger Regulation by requiring that the commitments should be aimed at the liberalisation of the electricity and gas markets').

[73] ibid para 93: 'Even on the assumption, and this question will be examined below, that the finding that one of the proposed commitments is insufficient or that the Commission's requirement of a particular commitment should be considered excessive by reference to the resolution of the competition concerns identified by the Commission in the contested decision, such an error would constitute a breach of Article 2(3) of the Merger Regulation and not a misuse of powers'.

[74] *Deutsche Telekom*, above n 37 paras 80–84.

[75] ibid para 86, where the Court noted that Deutsche Telekom 'was able to make applications to RegTP for authorisation to adjust its retail prices for end-user access services, specifically retail prices for narrowband access services for the period between 1 January 1998 and 31 December 2001, and retail prices for broadband access services for the period from 1 January 2002'.

Under the approach followed by the Court, if a breach of Article 102 TFEU can be established, it is irrelevant that the issue under examination is, in addition to a competition law problem, the expression of a regulatory failure. In this regard, the Court adopted a position that is markedly different from that of the US Supreme Court. In *Trinko*, the US Supreme Court suggested that US antitrust has a limited role to play where there is a regime in place with which antitrust intervention would overlap.[76] The ECJ, on the other hand, did not see any obstacle in the concurrent application of EU competition law alongside telecommunications regulation, and thus in the use of competition law as something akin to an alternative avenue to address concerns with the sector-specific regime. If anything, the primacy of Treaty provisions over secondary EU law and national law would mean that the enforcement of EU competition law is required.

The controversial application of EU State aid rules to some issues relating to direct business taxation, or to copyright, will be examined in accordance with the same principles. Thus, arguments that Article 107(1) TFEU is being relied upon to induce the harmonisation of corporate tax within the EU, or that Article 101(1) TFEU is a mechanism to achieve copyright reform, will not be successful. In the two cases, the question would revolve around whether the interpretation of the relevant provisions is in line with the applicable case law. In relation to tax rulings, the question will be whether they provide a selective advantage within the meaning of Article 107(1) TFEU. In relation to copyright and geo-blocking, the question is instead whether the agreements in question amount to a restriction of competition within the meaning of Article 101(1) TFEU.

It has been mentioned above that soft law instruments such as Guidelines can be relied upon as subtle devices to steer the behaviour of firms and public authorities. Their legitimacy could thus be questioned if they are understood to be indirect means to introduce (quasi-)legislative measures. The Court, however, has refused to attach binding effects to soft law. This question was addressed explicitly in *Kotnik*.[77] The case concerned the legal status of the 2013 Banking Communication.[78] In this document, the Commission identified the conditions under which it considers State aid granted to banks to be compatible with the internal market. The Slovenian Constitutional Court asked whether, considering the exclusive competence of the EU in the field, the Communication was legally binding on Member States.[79] In his Opinion, AG Wahl noted that the Commission has no 'general legislative power' in the field of State aid.[80] As a

[76] *Verizon Communications v Law Offices of Curtis V Trinko*, LLP, 540 US 398 (2004).

[77] Case C-526/14 *Tadej Kotnik and Others v Državni zbor Republike Slovenije* EU:C:2016:570.

[78] Communication from the Commission on the application, from 1 August 2013, of State aid rules to support measures in favour of banks in the context of the financial crisis ('Banking Communication') OJ 2013 C 216/1.

[79] *Kotnik*, above n 77 para 30.

[80] Case C-526/14 *Tadej Kotnik and Others v Državni zbor Republike Slovenije*, Opinion of AG Wahl EU:C:2016:102 paras 36–37. In para 37, AG Wahl notes that 'the Commission is not empowered to

result, it would be incorrect to treat the 2013 Banking Communication as such. On the other hand, there is nothing preventing the Commission from issuing soft law instruments as a means to provide legal certainty and achieve consistency. Considering the wide discretion enjoyed by the Commission when considering the compatibility of State aid under Article 107(3) TFEU, soft law instruments in the field work in practice in a way that is not fundamentally different from a legislative instrument.[81]

THE RELATIONSHIP WITH NATIONAL COMPETITION LAW AND NCAs

The Concurrent Application of EU Competition Law and National Regimes

It has been mentioned in the introduction that the exclusive competence of the EU in competition law matters is confined to what is necessary for the functioning of the internal market. Thus, the EU competition law system coexists with national regimes dealing with agreements, unilateral practices and mergers. Regulation 1/2003 provides for the terms of the coexistence between Articles 101 and 102 TFEU and their national counterparts. Pursuant to Article 3(1) of the Regulation, NCAs must apply EU competition law to agreements and unilateral practices that have an effect on trade between Member States. More importantly, Article 3(2) provides that the enforcement of national competition law may not lead to the prohibition of agreements that would not have as their object or effect the restriction of competition or that would satisfy the conditions of Article 101(3) TFEU.[82] Put differently, Article 3(2) requires that national law be interpreted in line with Article 101 TFEU when agreements are capable of affecting trade between Member States. Accordingly, EU competition law can be said to influence the substantive interpretation of national law falling outside the scope of the exclusive competence of the EU.

As can be seen, the influence of EU competition law—that is, whether national law is to be interpreted in line with Article 101 TFEU—depends on whether the agreement under consideration is capable of affecting trade between Member

lay down general and abstract binding rules governing, for example, the situations in which aid may be considered compatible because it is aimed at remedying a serious disturbance in the economy of a Member State under Article 107(3)(b) TFEU. Any such body of binding rules would be null and void.'

[81] A Bouchagiar, 'The Binding Effects of Guidelines on the Compatibility of State Aid: How Hard is the Commission's Soft Law?' (2016) *Journal of European Competition Law & Practice*, forthcoming.

[82] In accordance with Art 3(2) of Regulation 1/2003, '[t]he application of national competition law may not lead to the prohibition of agreements, decisions by associations of undertakings or concerted practices which may affect trade between Member States but which do not restrict competition within the meaning of Article 81(1) of the Treaty, or which fulfil the conditions of Article 81(3) of the Treaty or which are covered by a Regulation for the application of Article 81(3) of the Treaty. Member States shall not under this Regulation be precluded from adopting and applying on their territory stricter national laws which prohibit or sanction unilateral conduct engaged in by undertakings'.

States. By definition, this question is to be established on a case-by-case basis by NCAs evaluating whether Article 101 TFEU applies in a given scenario. As in other areas, however, the Commission has made use of quasi-legislation to advance its own interpretation of the notion. When Regulation 1/2003 was issued, it published a set of Guidelines assisting national courts and NCAs when examining whether agreement have an effect on trade between Member States.[83] It is not surprising that the Guidelines were considered to lean towards a broad understanding of the notion.[84] This understanding, however, is not fundamentally at odds with the relevant case law, under which the threshold to establish an effect on trade between Member States is relatively low.[85]

Against this background, one could have expected, as some commentators did, that Article 101 TFEU could come very close to replacing national regimes in practice.[86] The reality of enforcement at the national level after 10 years suggests that a different picture is emerging. The influence of Article 101 TFEU on national competition law depends on the willingness of NCAs to endorse the approach of the Commission on their case-by-case analysis of whether the agreements they examine are capable of affecting trade between Member States. In this regard, an analysis of the activity of NCAs suggests that the interpretation they have offered of this notion has not been a uniform one. A statistical overview of the proportion of cases in which the agreement under consideration has been found to be capable of affecting cross-border trade shows important variations across Member States. In some of them, the percentage of cases that are found to have a potential cross-border impact is remarkably low.[87] In the same vein, an analysis of the interpretation of the notion in specific cases reveals that some NCA decisions appear to be at odds with the principles set out in the case law.[88] The Commission, in turn, appears to show flexibility towards the approach displayed by NCAs.[89]

Because the exclusive competence of the EU does not extend to the application of competition rules that are necessary for the functioning of the internal market, NCAs and national courts are empowered to apply Articles 101 and 102 TFEU.

[83] Guidelines on the effect on trade concept contained in Articles 81 and 82 of the Treaty, OJ 2004 C 101/81.

[84] See in this sense I Forrester, 'Modernisation: an Extension of the Powers of the Commission?' in D Geradin (ed), *Modernisation and Enlargement: Two Major Challenges for EC Competition Law* (Intersentia, 2004).

[85] For an analysis of the relevant case law, see J Faull and A Nikpay (eds), *The EC Law of Competition* (Oxford University Press, 2014) paras 3.385–3.435.

[86] See eg A Riley, 'EC Antitrust Modernisation: The Commission Does Very Nicely—Thank You! Part One: Regulation 1 and the Notification Burden' (2003) 24 *European Competition Law Review* 604.

[87] See in this sense M Botta, A Svetlicinii, M Bernatt, 'The assessment of the effect on trade by the national competition authorities of the "new" Member States: Another legal partition of the Internal Market?' (2015) 52 *Common Market Law Review* 1247.

[88] ibid.

[89] See in this sense the Commission, 'Ten Years of Antitrust Enforcement under Regulation 1/2003' SWD (2014) 230/2 (hereinafter, the 'Staff Working Document'), where the Commission does not seem to raise any concerns in this regard.

In fact, one of the primary objectives of Regulation 1/2003 was to decentralise the enforcement of the two provisions.[90] The Regulation safeguards the pre-eminence of the Commission by introducing a hierarchy among competition authorities. In accordance with Article 11(6) of Regulation 1/2003, the opening of proceedings by the Commission in a competition case shall relieve NCAs of their competence to apply Articles 101 and 102 TFEU in that case. This provision looks like a reasonable, if not necessary, means to ensure that EU competition law is applied consistently and that clear principles of allocation of cases exist within the network of competition authorities.[91] On the other hand, Article 11(6) expands the influence of the Commission beyond the substantive aspects of Articles 101 and 102 TFEU.

The reality of enforcement under Regulation 1/2003 gives the impression that different, more flexible forms of co-operation within the network of competition authorities have emerged. In this sense, it is difficult to argue that the Commission has expanded the exclusive competence of the EU to the application of competition rules. It seems clear that the Commission has respected the role of NCAs, and has not taken active steps to relieve them of their competence in accordance with Article 11(6) of the Regulation. In the Working Document issued by the Commission 10 years after the entry into force of Regulation 1/2003, it explained that it had never made use of these powers.[92] The observed behaviour of the Commission does not appear to be due to the conservative attitude of NCAs, or to the fact that they focus on cases with limited pan-European interest. There have been some high-profile cases where it would have been natural for the Commission to become involved, but chose not to do so. One clear example concerns the practices implemented by the so-called online platforms, which raised novel issues of law. Even though there were several NCAs examining the same practices, the Commission chose not to interfere and claim the cases.[93]

The Decentralised Enforcement of EU Competition Law

Regulation 1/2003 was predicated on the idea that it was possible to decentralise the enforcement of Articles 101 and 102 TFEU while preserving the autonomy

[90] For an extensive analysis, see W Wils, 'Regulation 1/2003: A Reminder of the Main Issues' in D Geradin (ed), *Modernisation and Enlargement: Two Major Challenges for EC Competition Law* (Intersentia, 2004).

[91] For an analysis of the provision, see E Gippini Fournier, 'The Modernisation of European Competition Law: First Experiences with Regulation 1/2003' in HF Koeck and MM Karollus (eds), *The Modernisation of European Competition Law: Initial Experiences with Regulation 1/2003: Fide XXIII Congress Linz 2008—Congress Publications* Vol 2 (Nomos, 2008).

[92] See Staff Working Document: '[t]o date, the Commission has not used the power to initiate proceedings after the reception of an envisaged decision pursuant to Article 11(4) over the entire period of application of Regulation 1/2003, essentially for the reason that case practice in the ECN has developed in a broadly coherent manner and more upstream means of interaction have been preferred as being more efficient'.

[93] For an overview, see FE Gonzalez-Diaz and M Bennett, 'The law and economics of most-favoured nation clauses' (2015) 1 *Competition Law & Policy Debate* 26.

of national courts and authorities. The experience of more than a decade seems to contradict this view. It suggests that the decentralised application of EU law eventually leads to some coordination at the institutional and procedural levels. In practice, the substantive aspects of a discipline do not seem easy to disentangle from its non-substantive dimension. This is so, in particular, in a field like EU competition law, the objectives of which cannot be meaningfully achieved without an effective procedural and institutional apparatus. Effective deterrence of infringements, for instance, may require the application of fines and effective access to courts by firms and consumers. At the same time, the experience that has followed the application of Regulation 1/2003 is valuable for other areas of EU law.

Action by the EU in procedural and institutional matters concerns two particular issues. In 2014, the Parliament and the Council adopted a Directive on damages actions for breaches of competition law provisions.[94] The impetus for this initiative comes from the perception that the public enforcement of EU competition law needs to be complemented by a system of private enforcement before courts.[95] In the context of the assessment of the first ten years of enforcement under Regulation 1/2003, the Commission advanced the idea of taking action to preserve the independence of NCAs and to ensure that they have the means to enforce Articles 101 and 102 TFEU.[96] The Commission identified disparities in the powers enjoyed by NCAs. For instance, some of them lacked the ability to conduct inspections from non-business premises. Others lacked an effective leniency programme. The method for the calculation of fines, for instance, has emerged as another contentious issue. In a Staff Working Document, for instance, the Commission refers to the approach to the calculation of fines favoured by the German Federal Supreme Court, which departs from that followed by the Commission in accordance with its Guidelines.[97]

These initiatives differ from Regulation 1/2003 in that they are not only based on Article 103 TFEU, pursuant to which the Council can adopt the 'appropriate regulations or directives to give effect to the principles set out in Articles 101 and 102'. Article 114 TFEU has also been relied upon. In its proposal for the Directive on damages actions, the Commission explained that the legislation pursued a dual

[94] Damages Directive, above n 11.

[95] See in this sense Commission, 'Proposal for a Directive of the European Parliament and of the Council on certain rules governing actions for damages under national law for infringements of the competition law provisions of the Member States and of the European Union' COM(2013) 404 final 2: 'Compliance with the EU competition rules is thus ensured through the strong public enforcement of these rules by the Commission and the NCAs, in combination with private enforcement by national courts'.

[96] See in this sense the Ten Years Communication, para 27: 'To ensure the effective enforcement of the EU competition rules, NCAs should be independent when exercising their functions and should have adequate resources. Challenges in this regard still persist, in particular concerning the autonomy of NCAs *vis-à-vis* their respective governments, and appointments and dismissals of NCA management or decision-makers.'

[97] See in this sense Commission Staff Working Document, Enhancing competition enforcement by the Member States' competition authorities: institutional and procedural issues' SWD(2014) 231/2, para 75.

objective: to give effect to Articles 101 and 102 TFEU and to create a level playing field for firms offering their goods and services in the internal market and for consumers seeking compensation for EU competition law infringements.[98] The same is true in relation to the initiatives aimed at strengthening the powers of NCAs and their independence. In the Inception Impact Assessment, the Commission took the view that a dual legal basis would relied upon in legislation.[99] Thus, from a formal standpoint, Article 103 TFEU has not been stretched outside of its boundaries. From a substantive standpoint, on the other hand, EU competition law has expanded beyond Article 3(1)(b) TFEU.

CONCLUSIONS

An overview of the exercise of the exclusive competence in the field of competition provides valuable lessons for EU law-wide discussions. To begin with, the activity of the Commission is a useful reminder that some areas of EU competence are transversal in nature. It seems difficult to define any clear ex ante boundaries to intervention in such areas. Intervention by the Commission in the exercise of its competition law powers may overlap (as it has overlapped in the past) with legislation adopted pursuant to, inter alia, Article 114 TFEU. For instance, remedies in a competition law case may mimic the outcomes that would result from the application of a sector-specific regime. To the extent that Commission action is based on a sound interpretation of the relevant provision on which it is based, it is difficult to argue that it is illegitimate, or that it amounts to a circumvention of the legislative procedures. These are issues that the EU courts have consistently emphasised.

Second, EU competition law provides a prime example of the decentralised application of EU law. While the 'establishing' of rules necessary for the operation of the internal market is an exclusive competence of the EU, NCAs and national courts play a major role in the application of Articles 101 and 102 TFEU, as well as—in the case of national courts—in the context of EU State aid law. More than a decade after the adoption of Regulation 1/2003, it would seem that the decentralisation of the implementation of an EU policy tends to lead to the harmonisation of related procedural and institutional matters over which Member States enjoy autonomy—at least in principle. In the case of EU competition law, it has become clear that the success of the policy depends on the effectiveness of some mechanisms to ensure the effective detection and deterrence of infringements and which appear to require an alignment with the approach of the Commission.

[98] Commission Proposal, above n 95 at 8.

[99] Inception Impact Assessment, 'Enhancing competition in the EU for the benefit of businesses and consumers—Reinforcement of the application of EU competition law by national competition authorities, available at http://ec.europa.eu/smart-regulation/roadmaps/docs/2017_comp_001_iia_ecn_project_en.pdf.

8

EU External Competence—Rationales for Exclusivity

MARISE CREMONA*

INTRODUCTION: FOUNDATIONS FOR EXTERNAL COMPETENCE

THE AIM OF this chapter is to offer a reflection on the rationales for determining that EU external competence should be exclusive, as developed first by the Court of Justice and later by the EU Treaties. In doing so it explores the differences between express and implied competences, the implications of these differences for exclusivity, as well as assessing recent institutional practice.

The terms express and implied external competences are hallowed by long usage and are readily understood. They go back to the first decades in the life of the European (Economic) Community when the Treaty of Rome, despite including a general procedural provision on treaty-making, explicitly provided for only two types of international agreement: association agreements and trade agreements.[1] The Court of Justice, as we know, held that external powers could also be derived from provisions establishing other policy competences, such as transport or fisheries, the implied external treaty-making power complementing the explicit internal law-making power.[2] In its *AETR* judgment the Court used the Community's legal personality as a basis for reasoning that 'in its external relations the Community enjoys the capacity to establish contractual links with third countries over the whole field of objectives defined in Part One of the Treaty'.[3] Whether this capacity translates into a power in a specific case depends on an examination not only of the external competences granted explicitly by the Treaty but also 'other Treaty provisions' and measures adopted on the basis of those provisions by the Community's institutions.

* Marise Cremona is Professor of European Law and Co-Director of the Academy of European Law at the European University Institute in Florence.

[1] These were supplemented by the use of what is now Art 352 TFEU, normally in conjunction with one of the express competences: for example, the Framework Agreement for commercial and economic co-operation between the European Communities and Canada, based on Arts 113 and 235 EEC (now as amended Arts 207 and 352 TFEU), Council Regulation 2300/76/EEC, OJ 1976 L 260/1.

[2] Case 22/70 *Commission v Council* EU:C:1971:32; Joined Cases 3, 4 and 6-76 *Cornelis Kramer and others* EU:C:1976:114.

[3] Case 22/70, above n 2 at para 14.

The line of case law since *AETR* establishes two foundations for implying external powers.[4] The first, derived from *AETR* itself, is based on the existence of internal legislation whether or not adopted within the framework of a common policy,[5] and is founded on pre-emption, the occupation of the field by existing Community or Union law. The enactment in 1969 of a Regulation which harmonised social legislation relating to road transport, 'necessarily vested in the Community power to enter into any agreements with third countries relating to the subject-matter governed by that regulation'.[6]

The second foundation is the existence of an objective established by the Treaty, for the attainment of which Treaty-based internal powers may be complemented by external powers, whether or not expressly referred to. This rationale is based on the principle of *effet utile*, the implication of powers necessary to achieve an expressly defined objective. Thus in *Kramer*, in 1976, the Court held that the Community possessed external powers in the field of fisheries conservation despite the fact that internal measures had not yet been adopted:

> [T]he Community has at its disposal, on the internal level, the power to take any measures for the conservation of the biological resources of the sea ... The only way to ensure the conservation of the biological resources of the sea both effectively and equitably is through a system of rules binding on all the States concerned, including non-member countries. In these circumstances it follows from the very duties and powers which Community law has established and assigned to the institutions of the Community on the internal level that the Community has authority to enter into international commitments for the conservation of the resources of the sea.[7]

Or as recently expressed more generally by the Court,

> [W]henever EU law creates for those institutions powers within its internal system for the purpose of attaining a specific objective the EU has authority to undertake international commitments necessary for the attainment of that objective even in the absence of an express provision to that effect.[8]

Both these rationales are based on a complementarity between internal and external powers and the link between these powers and the purpose for which the Community (and now Union) has been given a policy competence. They differ, as we shall see, in their relation to internal legislation and consequently in their implications for exclusivity.

Since the foundational cases of the 1970s, Treaty revisions have added many new explicit external competences (such as development co-operation) and have included provisions on external relations in new sectoral competences (such as

[4] A Dashwood and J Heliskoski, 'The Classic Authorities Revisited' in A Dashwood and C Hillion (eds), *The General Law of EC External Relations* (London, Sweet & Maxwell, 2000).

[5] Case 22/70, above n 23; Opinion 2/91 EU:C:1993:106.

[6] Case 22/70, above n 2 at para 28.

[7] Joined Cases 3, 4 and 6-76, above n 2 at paras 30–33.

[8] Opinion 1/13 EU:C:2014:2303 para 67, citing also Opinion 1/03 EU:C:2006:81 para 114.

environment and asylum policy). The restructuring of the Treaties by the Lisbon Treaty in 2009 included a provision establishing the general conditions under which external treaty-making powers may be identified. Article 216(1) TFEU provides:

> The Union may conclude an agreement with one or more third countries or international organisations where the Treaties so provide or where the conclusion of an agreement is necessary in order to achieve, within the framework of the Union's policies, one of the objectives referred to in the Treaties, or is provided for in a legally binding Union act or is likely to affect common rules or alter their scope.

In this provision we find first a reference to express external powers ('where the Treaties so provide'), then to the *effet utile* rationale ('where the conclusion of an agreement is necessary in order to achieve, within the framework of the Union's policies, one of the objectives referred to in the Treaties'), and finally to the *AETR* rationale ('where the conclusion of an agreement … is provided for in a legally binding Union act or is likely to affect common rules or alter their scope'). It seems clear that Article 216(1) is intended to reflect the case law on implied external powers, and does not create a new independent or self-standing legal basis for the conclusion of international agreements. As Advocate General Kokott rightly says,

> Article 216(1) TFEU must not be confused with a general conferral of powers on the Union institutions for external action. On the contrary, an external competence can only ever be inferred from that rule in conjunction with the provisions of the Treaties, objectives of the Union, legal acts and rules of Union law mentioned in it.[9]

So—in addition to a reference to Article 218 TFEU, which is the procedural legal basis for concluding international agreements—a substantive policy provision in the Treaties is still required as a legal basis for an agreement based on implied powers. Indeed, although AG Kokott has proposed that in such cases Article 216(1) TFEU should now be included as a legal basis alongside the substantive legal basis (the internal competence-conferring provision) so as to demonstrate clearly the link between the internal competence and the implied external power, neither the practice of the institutions nor the judgments of the Court have (so far) followed this approach, preferring to keep to pre-Lisbon practice.[10] Thus agreements in the field of environmental policy have been concluded simply on the basis of the internal environmental policy competence; the concluding decision may mention that the agreement 'contributes to the achievement of the objectives of the environmental policy of the Union', reflecting the terms of Article 216(1) TFEU, but that provision is not included among its legal bases.[11]

[9] Case C-81/13 *UK v Council*, opinion of AG Kokott EU:C:2014:2114 para 102.

[10] For the Advocate General's views on this point, which this author finds convincing, see C-81/13, above n 9 at para 104; Case C-431/11 *United Kingdom v Council*, opinion of AG Kokott EU:C:2013:187 paras 64–70; Case C-263/14 *European Parliament v Council*, opinion of AG Kokott EU:C:2015:729 para 58.

[11] See eg Council Decision 2013/86/EU of 12 February 2013 on the conclusion on behalf of the European Union of the Nagoya-Kuala Lumpur Supplementary Protocol on Liability and Redress to the

The inclusion of Article 216(1) in the TFEU means that it is now probably more accurate to refer not to express and implied external powers, but rather to distinguish between competences which are explicitly part of the Union's external action (including common foreign, security and defence policies, common commercial policy, development co-operation, humanitarian aid, association and co-operation with third countries) and competences which are described as the 'external aspects of [the Union's] other policies',[12] including environment, transport, social policy, migration, data protection and police co-operation. It is this distinction which helps us to identify the different rationales for exclusive competence.

The Lisbon Treaty also codified existing case law on exclusive external competences. As a result we have a group of policies which are explicitly exclusive, listed in Article 3(1) TFEU. These include one external action policy (the common commercial policy) and several other policy fields which may have 'external aspects' (competition policy, conservation of fisheries, monetary policy). Here, exclusivity attaches to the policy field itself and does not depend on further conditions. It may be said to be *a priori* exclusivity.[13] In addition the Treaties now provide that exclusive competence to conclude international agreements will arise under certain conditions. Under Article 3(2) TFEU: The Union shall also have exclusive competence for the conclusion of an international agreement when its conclusion is provided for in a legislative act of the Union or is necessary to enable the Union to exercise its internal competence, or in so far as its conclusion may affect common rules or alter their scope.

The similarity between Articles 216(1) TFEU and 3(2) TFEU is striking, but they are neither identical nor coterminous. In what follows we will turn to the rationales for exclusivity, first as developed for explicitly external policy competences, and then for the external dimension of other policies, or 'implied powers', governed by Article 3(2).

EXCLUSIVITY AND EXPRESS EXTERNAL POWERS

Only one of the EU's express external action competences is defined as an exclusive policy field: the Common Commercial Policy (CCP). The Common Foreign and Security Policy is defined as neither exclusive nor shared competence but its

Cartagena Protocol on Biosafety, OJ 2013 L 46/1. See also Council Decision 2013/5/EU of 17 December 2012 on the accession of the European Union to the Protocol for the Protection of the Mediterranean Sea against pollution resulting from exploration and exploitation of the continental shelf and the seabed and its subsoil, OJ 2013 L 4/13.

[12] Art 21(3) TEU.

[13] A Dashwood, 'The Relationship between the Member States and the European Union/European Community' (2004) 41 *Common Market Law Review* 355 at 369; R Schütze, 'Dual Federalism Constitutionalised: The Emergence of Exclusive Competences in the EC legal order' (2007) 32 *European Law Review* 3 at 5.

provisions assume that the Member States will continue to conduct their own national foreign policies, albeit subject to an obligation of loyalty to Union policy positions and actions.[14] Development co-operation and humanitarian aid are shared competences expressly stated to be non-pre-emptive in effect, with a strong emphasis placed on coherence between Union and Member State action.[15] Association and co-operation agreements are matters of shared competence but also of an atypical kind. For some time, Association agreements have been concluded as mixed agreements, and all Association agreements now in force are mixed; however, this is a competence which must be exercised either by the EU alone or by the EU together with its Member States in a mixed agreement: an agreement establishing an Association between the EU and a third country, with the institutional relationship that entails,[16] could not be concluded by one or more Member States acting alone without the EU. Co-operation agreements cover different degrees of co-operation, either wide-ranging or concerning a specific field of co-operation; they may be mixed or concluded by the EU alone.[17] An EU co-operation agreement with a third country would not necessarily preclude a Member State concluding a co-operation agreement with the same third country; this would depend on the type of co-operation and the level of commitment envisaged.

The CCP, on the other hand, may be said to be paradigmatic of exclusive external competence. The CCP is exclusive as a result of Article 3(1) TFEU, as a policy field. This *a priori* exclusivity was developed by the Court of Justice in the 1970s (alongside its development of implied external powers) and it is to those judgments that we need to look to find its rationale. The unity of the common market (and now the internal market) is protected by a common commercial policy based on 'uniform principles'.[18] The establishment of a customs union requires a common external tariff. A common external tariff precludes the Member States

[14] eg Arts 24(2) and (3) and 32 TEU; Declarations 13 and 14 concerning the common foreign and security policy.

[15] Arts 208(1), 210 and 211 TFEU. Under Art 4(4) TFEU 'the exercise of [the Union's] competence shall not result in Member States being prevented from exercising theirs'. On EU–Member State coordination see the Joint Statement by the Council and the Representatives of the Governments of the Member States meeting within the Council, the European Parliament and the Commission on European Union Development Policy, 'The European Consensus', 22 November 2005, Council doc 14820/05.

[16] Art 217 TFEU.

[17] The EU's Framework Agreement with the Republic of Korea (a wide-ranging co-operation agreement) is mixed: Framework Agreement between the European Union and its Member States, on the one part, and the Republic of Korea, on the other part, OJ 2013 L 20/2. The Protocols to the Euro-Mediterranean Association Agreements (themselves mixed) establishing Framework agreements on the participation of the Associated states in EU programmes have been concluded by the EU alone: see eg Protocol to the Euro-Mediterranean Agreement establishing an Association between the European Community and its Member States, of the one part, and the People's Democratic Republic of Algeria, of the other part, on a Framework Agreement between the European Union and the People's Democratic Republic of Algeria on the general principles for the participation of the People's Democratic Republic of Algeria in Union programmes, OJ 2015 L 148/3.

[18] Art 207(1) TFEU.

from setting their own external tariffs and from legislating in areas which affect its operation, such as classification of goods,[19] or the imposition of charges of equivalent effect.[20] During the mid-1970s the principle of exclusivity was applied both to the conclusion of international agreements[21] and the adoption of autonomous measures.[22] The rationale for exclusivity presented by the Court in these cases has both an internal and an external dimension. It is based first on the distortions that would result to the *internal* market were Member States permitted to adopt unilateral trade measures. Thus, in *Donckerwolcke*, the emphasis is on the need for goods in free circulation to be 'assimilated' to Community-origin goods in order to achieve full free movement of goods within the customs union.[23] In *Opinion 1/75* distortions of competition between Community undertakings, it was argued, may result from divergent national policies.[24] The reasoning adopted in these cases, although based on the needs of the common (internal) market, does not base exclusivity on the adoption of Community legislation or the completion of the common market or common commercial policy. In *Opinion 1/75* the Court describes how exclusive competence to enter into an international agreement on credit guarantees does not depend on the pre-existence of a detailed body of Community rules on the matter, but that internal legislation and international agreements will 'combine gradually' to form a body of rules making up the CCP.[25] In *Donckerwolcke* the Court insisted that although full freedom of movement for goods in free circulation would depend on the completion of the CCP, which had not yet taken place, any national measure required specific Community authorisation.[26]

The degree of unity required in external trade relations is linked to the depth of internal integration. A customs union of the type envisaged by Article XXIV:8(a) GATT 1994 may not require full uniformity as long as restrictions on external trade are substantially the same.[27] However, the greater the economic integration within the internal market—the closer it becomes to a single market—the greater the need for common rules in relation to external trade. Hence the completion

[19] Case 40/69 *Hauptzollamt Hamburg-Oberelbe v Firma Paul G Bollmann* EU:C:1970:12 paras 4 and 9.

[20] Joined Cases 37 and 38-73 *Sociaal Fonds voor de Diamantarbeiders v NV Indiamex et Association de fait De Belder* EU:C:1973:165 para 13.

[21] Opinion 1/75 EU:C:1975:145.

[22] Case 41/76 *Donckerwolcke and Schou* EU:C:1976:182.

[23] Case 41/76, above n 22 at paras 26–32.

[24] Opinion 1/75, above n 21 at 1364.

[25] Opinion 1/75, above n 21 at 1363.

[26] Case 41/76, above n 22 at para 32. See also Joined Cases 37 and 38-73, above n 20, in which the Court held that the adjustment (equalisation or elimination) of national charges of equivalent effect to customs duties which predated the introduction of the common external tariff fell within the exclusive jurisdiction of the Community institutions.

[27] The WTO's Appellate Body has held, in fact, that Art XXIV may not provide protection for a more complete alignment of restrictions if this cannot be justified as necessary to the customs union: Turkey—Restrictions on Imports of Textile and Clothing Products, Appellate Body Report WT/DS34/AB/R, 22 October 1999.

of the internal market required—in addition to the common customs tariff—the completion of the common commercial policy: the removal of differential national policies on non-tariff barriers which might justify internal frontier controls, to be replaced where necessary by Community-level restrictions.[28]

The second rationale for exclusivity put forward in *Opinion 1/75* is the need to preserve the unity of the Community position with respect to third states, and to defend the 'common interests' of the Community. The Court used strong language: the exercise of concurrent powers by the Community and Member States is 'impossible':

> [it] would amount to recognizing that, in relations with third countries, Member States may adopt positions which differ from those which the Community intends to adopt, and would thereby distort the institutional framework, call into question the mutual trust within the Community and prevent the latter from fulfilling its task in the defence of the common interest.[29]

The first rationale for the exclusivity of the CCP is designed to protect the internal unity of the common market, a policy goal established by the Treaty. The second rationale, in contrast, is based on the external unity of the Community as an international actor and negotiator, a unity needed to allow the Community institutions to develop and defend its policies at an international level. They both lead to the conclusion that the exclusivity of the CCP is *a priori* in the sense that it does not depend on a case-by-case examination of the content of legislation or the character of specific policy choices.

This *a priori* exclusivity has now been enshrined in the Treaties by Article 3(1) TFEU, but to what extent do these two original rationales still apply? Although the requirements of internal unity are still present, it is the external dimension which is more apparent in both institutional practice and the case law of the Court of Justice. The CCP in its initial decades was primarily concerned with establishing the (uniform) conditions under which goods could enter the internal market, including tariff and non-tariff barriers, trade defence and preferential agreements, especially for developing countries. More recently, although these aspects have certainly not disappeared, attention has also turned to measures designed to help open up third country markets to EU exporters and to supporting and influencing bilateral, regional and multilateral regulatory initiatives.[30] Modern trade agreements include services and a substantial regulatory component, as well as provisions on investment. Increasingly, the CCP is seen to entail important regulatory policy-making, with internal as well as external impact, and its exclusive nature

[28] M Cremona, 'The Completion of the Internal Market and the Incomplete Commercial Policy of the European Community' (1990) *European Law Review* 283. See eg Case C-150/94 *UK v Council* EU:C:1998:547.

[29] Opinion 1/75, above n 21 at 1364.

[30] European Commission, 'Trade, Growth and World Affairs: Trade Policy as a Core Component of the EU's 2020 Strategy', 9 November 2010, COM(2010)612; European Commission, 'Trade for all—Towards a more responsible trade and investment policy', 14 October 2015, COM(2015)497.

creates a tension with the shared competence and multi-level governance characteristic of internal market regulation. As a result, we see challenges to the scope of the CCP (how widely drawn should the exclusive competence be?) and even, in practice, to its exclusivity.

On the one hand the extended scope of the CCP may be said to reflect a need for external unity, especially within the context of the WTO. The WTO agreements were concluded under shared competence as mixed agreements: in *Opinion 1/94* the Court had held that only certain aspects of intellectual property protection and trade in services could be brought under the existing CCP, and the remainder did not fall within exclusive implied powers. Over a series of Treaty revisions culminating in the Lisbon Treaty, the CCP has been extended to include the commercial aspects of intellectual property, trade in services and foreign direct investment, and earlier limitations on exclusive competence in certain fields have now been abandoned.[31] In the new Article 207 TFEU, as interpreted by the Court of Justice, unity as regards external trade is emphasised, and is separated from internal legislative competence which may well be shared. In *Daiichi Sankyo*, for example, the Court held that the TRIPS (the WTO agreement on trade-related intellectual property rights) as a whole now falls within the scope of the CCP. The CCP, the Court said, was concerned with trade with third countries, not trade between Member States. An act falls within the common commercial policy 'if it relates specifically to international trade in that it is essentially intended to promote, facilitate or govern trade and has direct and immediate effects on trade'.[32] The objective of the rules in TRIPS, it says, is the liberalisation of international trade and not the harmonisation of Member State laws. Crucially, since by no means all TRIPS obligations are the subject of EU legislation, exclusive competence over the TRIPS as an international instrument does not translate into an a priori exclusive *internal* competence over the fields covered by TRIPS rules. Future internal EU legislation on the harmonisation of intellectual property rights would be based on internal shared competences, carried out in conformity with the EU's obligations under TRIPS. Thus the CCP is defined broadly to cover all rules which specifically relate to international trade, but this does not displace the operation of the (shared) internal market competence where rules are adopted within the EU.

A similar approach is evidenced in the first case in which the Court addressed the application of the revised CCP to trade in services, although here internal legislation covering the field had already been adopted. In *Conditional Access Services*,[33] the issue was the appropriate legal basis for the conclusion of an international agreement which was intended essentially to extend aspects of the EU *acquis* to third countries within the framework of the Council of Europe.

[31] In some cases, while competence is exclusive, decisions must be adopted by unanimity in the Council: see Art 207(4) TFEU.

[32] Case C-414/11 *Daiichi Sankyo Co Ltd, Sanofi-Aventis Deutschland GmbH v DEMO Anonimos Viomikhaniki kai Emporiki Etairia Farmakon* EU:C:2013:520 para 51.

[33] Case C-137/12 *Commission v Council* EU:C:2013:675.

The internal EU legislation has an internal market legal basis but this does not imply that the same provision should provide an implied external legal basis for the international agreement. On the contrary: the fact that internal legislation had already been adopted was evidence that the predominant aim of the agreement was not internal harmonisation but international trade in services between Member States and third countries.

In both these cases we can see reflected a conception of the CCP which builds upon the external unity rationale found in *Opinion 1/75*. The external orientation of the CCP is emphasised and its exclusivity is concerned with EU policy-making towards external markets; it does not affect the allocation of internal legislative competence. External action taken by the EU (exclusively) on the basis of Article 207 does not inevitably entail that future internal legislation in the field must be adopted at EU level. As Article 207(6) TFEU says, 'The exercise of the competences conferred by this Article in the field of the common commercial policy shall not affect the delimitation of competences between the Union and the Member States'. Against this background it is significant that the current trend in EU trade agreements is to exclude the possibility of direct effect, sometimes even in the text of the agreement itself.[34] As a result, although the Union is of course bound by agreements it concludes under Article 207, policy choices as to how these external commitments are implemented are reserved for internal legislative procedures, and will not be pre-empted by direct enforcement in the courts.

These cases illustrate the tension over the extension of the CCP and the reaffirmation of its exclusive nature by the Lisbon Treaty. This picture they present, of a broader and clearly exclusive CCP covering all trade agreements, must, however, be nuanced.

First, there are still outstanding debates over the precise scope of the CCP. The most important of these concerns the scope of 'foreign direct investment', and in particular whether Article 207 includes post-establishment investor protection, including non-discrimination, fair and equitable treatment and protection against expropriation. There are hopes that this will be clarified in the pending Opinion on the EU's free trade agreement with Singapore, but it is hard to predict how and where the Court will draw the line.[35] In any event it seems clear that some issues normally covered by investment agreements, and included in the new generation of deep free trade agreements, including portfolio investment, will fall outside the CCP.[36]

[34] See eg Trade Agreement between the European Union and its Member States, of the one part, and Colombia and Peru, of the other part, OJ 2012 L 354/3, Art 336. See further A Semertzi, 'The Preclusion of Direct Effect in the Recently Concluded EU Free Trade Agreements' (2014) 51 *Common Market Law Review* 1125; M Cremona, 'A Quiet Revolution: The Common Commercial Policy Six Years after the Treaty of Lisbon', SIEPS Policy Paper, SIEPS 2017:2.

[35] A request for an opinion concerning the EU's competence to conclude the proposed Free Trade Agreement with Singapore has been submitted by the Commission under Art 218(11) TFEU: Opinion 2/15, pending.

[36] In Opinion 2/15, pending, the Commission has argued that those elements of the agreement which fall outside the CCP nevertheless fall within exclusive competence on the basis of Art 3(2) TFEU.

There is also the rather overlooked but potentially important exclusion of international agreements 'in the field of transport' from the CCP.[37] Transport agreements are covered by Articles 90–100 TFEU, a shared competence to conduct a common transport policy. This express exclusion from the CCP may make it difficult to claim that the inclusion of transport services within trade agreements is 'merely ancillary' and therefore should not affect an exclusive Article 207 TFEU legal basis.[38] A number of trade agreements will thus require an additional transport legal basis, a competence which is shared, though subject to the possibility of exclusivity on the basis of Article 3(2) TFEU.

Second, important trade agreements are in practice increasingly concluded as mixed agreements. They may be embedded in Association agreements, which have come to be accepted as mixed agreements given their political importance (the Deep and Comprehensive Free Trade Agreement with Ukraine is an example). There is a growing political pressure that major trade agreements which include a strong regulatory and investment component such as the CETA with Canada or the TTIP with the USA should also be concluded as mixed agreements.

And third, the move to exclusive external competence over foreign direct investment created potentially serious problems for the many hundreds of bilateral investment treaties (BITs) concluded by the Member States. As a transitional measure the Member States have been authorised, under certain conditions, to maintain and conclude BITs with third countries.[39] This is a particular example of a wider point: that the EU may choose to authorise the Member States to act in cases of exclusive competence.[40]

What we see, then, is that the CCP is an a priori exclusive competence which seems to have been reaffirmed and strengthened by the Lisbon Treaty and the post-Lisbon judgments of the Court of Justice (at least so far). However, the scope of the CCP is contested, and we also see pressure towards greater political acceptance of mixity for important trade agreements despite the difficulties this poses for ratification. Somewhat paradoxically, the strengthening of the CCP competence in the Lisbon Treaty together with changing trade policy priorities, including an increased emphasis on international regulatory engagement, may make what I have called the 'external unity' rationale for exclusivity more difficult to sustain in practice.

To conclude this section, we should briefly turn back to the EU's other *non-exclusive* express external action competences, such as development co-operation.

[37] Art 207(5) TFEU.

[38] In Opinion 1/08 EU:C:2009:739, the Court rejected an argument that the predecessor to Art 207(5) TFEU was applicable only to agreements which were exclusively or predominantly concerned with transport.

[39] Regulation 1219/2012/EU establishing transitional arrangements for bilateral investment agreements between Member States and third countries, OJ 2012 L 351/40.

[40] M Cremona, 'EU External Relations: Unity and Conferral of Powers' in L Azoulai (ed), *The Question of Competence in the European Union* (Oxford, Oxford University Press, 2014).

Why shouldn't the external unity rationale for exclusivity, which is based on the need of the EU to project its own policies and to defend its common interests, also apply in these cases? A simple answer would be that the Member States have chosen, when including new external competences in the Treaties, to ensure that they are not exclusive, at least *a priori*. But this is not necessarily at the expense of external unity. It is in the nature of trade policy that it establishes a set of rules applicable to imports and exports of goods and services; external unity cannot coexist with overlapping and potentially divergent sets of rules. The same is not the case with other types of EU external action, such as development co-operation, humanitarian aid or the common foreign and security policy. An EU development programme can co-exist with the national development programmes of the Member States. In these policy fields the external unity rationale does indeed apply, but in a different way: there is a need for coordination and co-operation to ensure that Union policy choices are defended and not undermined by the Member States, and that EU and Member State actions are complementary; a number of Treaty provisions are designed to ensure this.[41] Just as exclusivity was originally derived from the loyalty obligation now contained in Article 4(3), the Court has used the same provision to develop a duty of co-operation applicable in cases of shared competence, linking this to the requirement of unity in international representation.[42]

EXCLUSIVITY AND THE EXTERNAL DIMENSION OF INTERNAL POLICIES

The projection of the Union's international presence, its defined policies and common interests, manifested by the emphasis on external unity, is not surprisingly central to those Union competences which are expressly defined in terms of external action. When we turn to those policy fields which are not defined in external terms, but which may have an external dimension, we find a different emphasis.[43] Just as the existence of these external powers is linked to the existence of internal legislation and the need for external action to support 'internal' objectives, so too is the requirement of exclusivity. Indeed, in *AETR* we see a conflation between the existence of an implied external power, predicated on the exercise of an internal competence through the enactment of common rules, and its exclusive nature: 'As and when such common rules come into being, the Community alone

[41] eg Arts 4(3) and 24(3) TEU; Arts 208(1), 210 and 211 TFEU.

[42] Case C-246/07 *Commission v Sweden* EU:C:2010:203 para 104. See further M Cremona, 'Defending the Community Interest: the Duties of Cooperation and Compliance' in M Cremona and B De Witte (eds), *EU Foreign Relations Law—Constitutional Fundamentals* (Oxford, Hart Publishing, 2008).

[43] For recent discussion see A Rosas, 'Exclusive, shared and national competence in the context of EU external relations: do such distinctions matter?' in I Govaere, P Van Elsuwege, S Adam and E Lannon (eds), *The EU in the World: Essays in Honour of Marc Maresceau* (Leiden, Brill, 2013); I Govaere, '"Setting the International Scene": EU External Competence and Procedures Post-Lisbon Revisited in the Light of ECJ Opinion 1/13' (2015) 52 *Common Market Law Review* 1277 at 1286–95.

is in a position to assume and carry out contractual obligations towards third countries affecting the whole sphere of application of the Community legal system'.[44] Exclusivity is a necessary result of the adoption of 'common rules' because it is necessary to protect the *acquis*. Later cases accepted that the *acquis* does not necessarily require to be protected by an exclusive external competence, as for example where the internal EU legislation does not have a pre-emptive character. An analysis has to be carried out in each case to see whether exclusivity is justified:

> any competence, especially where it is exclusive and not expressly conferred by the Treaty, must have its basis in conclusions drawn from a specific analysis of the relationship between the agreement envisaged and the Community law in force and from which it is clear that the conclusion of such an agreement is capable of affecting the Community rules.[45]

Opinion 1/94 provides us with a striking example of the different rationales at work. Insofar as the WTO agreements fell outside the CCP (as it stood in 1994) and within implied external powers, the arguments for exclusive competence failed in the absence of internal legislation which would have been affected by the international action:

> the Member States, whether acting individually or collectively, only lose their right to assume obligations with non-member countries as and when common rules which could be affected by those obligations come into being. Only in so far as common rules have been established at internal level does the external competence of the Community become exclusive.[46]

To alternative arguments that exclusivity was justified since shared competence to conclude the WTO agreements would mean that '[t]he Community's unity of action vis-à-vis the rest of the world will thus be undermined and its negotiating power greatly weakened' (in other words, an external unity argument for exclusivity), the Court replied that although these concerns were legitimate, they did not in themselves justify an extension of exclusive competence. The solution lay in the duty of co-operation between Community and Member States in the management of the mixed agreement.

In determining the exclusivity of these external powers the starting point must of course be the characterisation of the underlying internal competence. In a few cases this is in itself defined as exclusive by Article 3(1) TFEU and will therefore be exclusive also in its external manifestation. But most internal competences are not a priori exclusive; they are shared and subject to pre-emption. This includes competences which expressly envisage the conclusion of international agreements,

[44] Case 22/70, above n 2 at para 18.

[45] Opinion 1/03, above n 8 at para 124; this passage is cited verbatim in Case C-114/12 *Commission v Council* EU:C:2014:2151 at para 74.

[46] Opinion 1/94 EU:C:1994:384 para 77.

such as the provision for readmission agreements[47] or agreements in the field of environmental protection,[48] and other competences, such as transport and energy, which make no specific mention of external action but where it may be implied on the basis of Article 216(1) TFEU. In such cases, exclusivity is determined according to the criteria established in Article 3(2) TFEU. Pre-emption in fields of shared competence is mentioned in Article 2(2) TFEU: Member States 'shall exercise their competence to the extent that the Union has not exercised its competence'. The precise relation between this provision and Article 3(2) is not spelled out in the Treaties; however, it appears that when dealing with exclusivity in the context of the conclusion of an international agreement, the Court will turn to Article 3(2) rather than Article 2(2). In the *Broadcasting Convention* case,[49] the Commission had referred to both Articles 2(2) and 3(2) TFEU in support of exclusivity. In response to an argument proposed by some of the intervening Member States the Court declared Protocol 25 on shared competence to be irrelevant on the ground that it refers only to Article 2(2) and 'seeks to define the scope of the exercise by the European Union of a shared competence with the Member States which was conferred on it by the Treaties, and not to limit the scope of the exclusive external competence of the European Union in the cases referred to in Article 3(2) TFEU'. The implication is that it is Article 3(2) and not Article 2(2) that is applicable to the case.

Article 3(2) sets out three alternative grounds for exclusivity: (i) the conclusion of the agreement is provided for in a legislative act of the Union; (ii) its conclusion is necessary to enable the Union to exercise its internal competence; (iii) in so far as its conclusion may affect common rules or alter their scope. These all derive from earlier case law, including *AETR*, *Opinion 1/94* and the *Open Skies* cases.[50] The logic of the first and third derive from *AETR*, although they are also mentioned in *Open Skies*;[51] it is a pre-emptive logic: the Union acquires exclusive competence in the fields covered by the internal legislative act, either through an explicit reference in that act to the power to negotiate with third countries, or because the legislation establishes 'common rules' which may be affected if the Member States were to retain the power to act.[52] The second ground seems to be derived from *Opinion 1/76*[53] and has an obvious link with the *effet utile* foundation for implied external powers. In some subsequent cases the Court treated this

[47] Art 79(3) TFEU.

[48] Art 191(4) TFEU.

[49] C-114/12, above n 45.

[50] Opinion 1/94, above n 46; Case C-476/98 *Commission v Germany* EU:C:2002:631.

[51] C-476/98, above n 50 para 109, citing also inter alia Opinion 1/94, above n 46 para 95.

[52] It should be noted that the final phrase of Art 3(2) TFEU is worded oddly; it refers to the possibility that conclusion of the agreement *by the Union* would affect common rules or alter their scope. In fact, the test as developed by the Court's case law requires that if the agreement were to be concluded *by the Member States* it would affect the Union's common rules, and this is the way the test has been applied in the post-Lisbon cases.

[53] Opinion 1/76 EU:C:1977:63.

as a potential ground for exclusive competence,[54] which is presumably why it is included in Article 3(2), but it has never formed the basis of a successful exclusivity claim. If we compare Articles 3(2) and 216(1) we see that whereas external powers may be exercised where necessary to achieve a Treaty objective, they will only be exclusive where the external agreement is a necessary precondition for the exercise of the internal power. As the Court expressed it in *Opinion 1/03*,

> the situation envisaged in *Opinion 1/76* is that in which internal competence may be effectively exercised only at the same time as external competence … the conclusion of the international agreement being thus necessary in order to attain objectives of the Treaty that cannot be attained by establishing autonomous rules.[55]

Several authors have convincingly argued that in fact *Opinion 1/76* should be seen as referring to the existence of competence rather than its exclusivity.[56] Perhaps this ground of exclusivity as expressed in Article 3(2) is best seen as referring to cases where the common rules which require protection are defined not in prior legislation but by the adoption of the international agreement itself. In any event, the case law since the Lisbon Treaty has not suggested that this principle will play a greater role as a result of its inclusion in the Treaties.

The post-Lisbon case law of the Court so far has turned on the final phrase of Article 3(2) TFEU, whereby the Union shall have exclusive competence for the conclusion of an international agreement 'insofar as its conclusion may affect common rules or alter their scope'. The Court has explicitly linked this phrase to *AETR* and the case law following and developing that judgment;[57] it has shown no inclination to use the recasting of its case law in the Treaties as an opportunity to recalibrate its approach,[58] nor has it shown any reluctance towards reaching a finding of exclusive competence. In two cases since the Lisbon Treaty the Court has explicitly addressed the application of Article 3(2) TFEU;[59] in a third case a finding of exclusivity was not required but the Court uses language which evokes Article 3(2) TFEU.[60] The emphasis of the Court, in finding that Union powers are exclusive, has been on 'the uniform and consistent application of the EU rules and the proper functioning of the system which they establish'.[61] Each of these cases is also characterised by a close connection between EU law and the

[54] eg Opinion 1/94, above n 46 para 89; C-476/98, above n 50 para 82.

[55] Opinion 1/03, above n 8 para 115.

[56] P Eeckhout, *External Relations of the European Union, Legal and Constitutional Foundations* (Oxford, Oxford University Press, 2004) 68; A Dashwood and J Heliskoski, above n 4 at 13–14.

[57] C-114/12, above n 45 paras 66–67.

[58] For example it was argued in Opinion 1/13, above n 8 para 63, by the Council and intervening Member States that since Art 3(2) TFEU uses the 'common rules' formula of *AETR* without mentioning later formulations which refer to a field covered 'to a large extent' by common rules, these later formulations should now be disregarded. The Court impliedly dismisses this argument by referring to post-*AETR* case law.

[59] C-114/12, above n 45 and Opinion 1/13, above n 8.

[60] Case C-399/12 *Germany v Council* EU:C:2014:2258.

[61] Opinion 1/13, above n 8 para 74.

international rules, a connection that may be established by the EU legislation itself and which results in 'a unitary body of rules'[62] or 'a harmonised legal framework'.[63]

In the *Broadcasting Convention* case[64] the issue was EU competence to negotiate a Council of Europe Convention which is based on the existing EU *acquis*. The Commission argued that competence is exclusive on the basis of Articles 2(2) and 3(2) TFEU.[65] The Court's judgment goes into considerable detail, analysing the likely scope of the Convention in the light of the existing body of EU legislation, and concluding that although aspects of the Convention may go beyond existing EU law, it 'falls within an area covered to a large extent by common EU rules and that those negotiations may affect common EU rules or alter their scope'.[66] The reasoning addresses in a combined way both the overlap between the two sets of rules and the potential effect of the international rules on the EU regime.[67]

Opinion 1/13 concerned the acceptance of the accession of third States to the 1980 Hague Convention on the civil aspects of international child abduction: the Court decided that this acceptance falls within the EU's exclusive competence, based on the third ground in Article 3(2) TFEU. First the Court assessed the relative scope of the Convention and the relevant EU legislation,[68] concluding that the Convention commitments are covered 'to a large extent' by the EU's common rules.[69] Indeed, the Regulation refers expressly to the Convention, providing that in relations between Member States the Regulation shall take precedence over the Hague Convention but that in matters not governed by the Regulation, the Hague Convention will continue to apply.[70] As the Court says, the provisions of the Regulation are either 'based on the rules of the 1980 Hague Convention or establish the consequences that are to follow when those rules are applied'.[71] The Court then examines whether it would affect the common rules of the EU system if the Member States were to take individual decisions on the acceptance of new State parties. The Court's affirmative finding is based on the fact that the Convention applies between an acceding State and only those existing parties that have accepted its adherence. If, in a case involving two or more Member States and a third State, the EU Member States were to be in different positions as to the application of the

[62] Opinion 1/13, above n 8 para 78.

[63] C-114/12, above n 45 para 79.

[64] C-114/12, above n 45.

[65] No reference to a putative substantive legal basis is made either in the Council decision authorising the negotiation or in the arguments before the Court as set out in the judgment, but since Art 2(2) and 3(2) TFEU are referred to in argument, the substantive legal basis under consideration would have been shared competence (eg Art 114 TFEU).

[66] C-114/12, above n 45 para 102.

[67] eg C-114/12, above n 45 paras 87, 92 and 98.

[68] Regulation No 2201/2003/EC concerning jurisdiction and the recognition and enforcement of judgments in matrimonial matters OJ 2003 L 338/1.

[69] Opinion 1/13, above n 8 para 73.

[70] Regulation No 2201/2003/EC, above n 68 Arts 60 and 62.

[71] Opinion 1/13, above n 8 para 78.

Convention in their relations with that third State, 'there would be a risk of undermining the uniform and consistent application of Regulation No 2201/2003 and, in particular, the rules concerning co-operation between the authorities of the Member States'.[72] Although not as such a formal source of Union law (the EU is not a party) the Convention has, as a result of the explicit reference in the Regulation, become closely integrated with the EU legal regime and consequently subject to the need for uniform application by the Member States.

One striking aspect of this case is the fact that the exclusive competence of the EU operates in a context where the EU itself cannot (at least at present) become a party to the Convention in question, and its competence must be exercised through the Member States. The Member States act on behalf, and in the interests, of the EU.[73] This scenario (that is, the EU being constrained to act through its Member States) was also present in the third case we will consider here, *Germany v Council (OIV)*.[74] The case concerned a Council decision establishing the position to be adopted on the Union's behalf within the International Organisation for Vine and Wine (OIV), which had been adopted on the procedural legal basis of Article 218(9) TFEU.[75] The EU is not a party to the OIV Agreement but the recommendations adopted within the framework of the agreement are implemented into EU legislation. Although the parties disagreed on the issue of exclusivity[76] the Court did not need to address this point directly since the Council, by adopting a decision, had already decided to exercise EU competence; the issue before the Court was the appropriate legal basis for that decision given that the EU is not a member of the OIV. It found that the EU had the competence to act: 'the European Union, while not a party to the OIV Agreement, is entitled to establish a position to be adopted on its behalf with regard to those recommendations, in view of their direct impact on the European Union's acquis in that area'.[77] And Article 218(9) TFEU provided the correct legal basis for a Council decision, insofar as the decision relates to a 'position of the Union' whether or not the EU is a party to the agreement.[78]

[72] Opinion 1/13, above n 8 para 89. For an argument that the Court did not satisfactorily justify the existence of an *AETR*-effect, see P Beaumont, 'A Critical Analysis of the Judicial Activism of the Court of Justice of the European Union in Opinion 1/13', University of Aberdeen Centre for Private International Law, Working Paper 2015/1. On the implication of the case more generally see P Franzina (ed), *The External Dimension of EU Private International Law after Opinion 1/13* (Cambridge, Intersentia, 2016).

[73] Case C-45/07 *Commission v Greece* EU:C:2009:81 paras 30–31; Opinion 2/91, above n 5 para 5.

[74] C-399/12, above n 60.

[75] Art 218(9) provides that 'The Council, on a proposal from the Commission or the High Representative of the Union for Foreign Affairs and Security Policy, shall adopt a decision … establishing the positions to be adopted on the Union's behalf in a body set up by an agreement, when that body is called upon to adopt acts having legal effects'.

[76] Germany claimed that the action fell within the scope of the agricultural policy, a shared competence, C-399/12, above n 60 para 34; the Council argued that Art 3(2) applied given that the OIV recommendations 'will serve as a basis for drawing up EU legislation or will be rendered applicable by such legislation', C-399/12, above n 60 para 43.

[77] C-399/12, above n 60 para 64.

[78] C-399/12, above n 60 para 49.

Article 218(9) only applies where the acts to be adopted by the international regime will have 'legal effect', and it is therefore natural for the Court to frame the discussion in terms that recall Article 3(2) TFEU. It emphasises the impact of the OIV recommendations on the EU *acquis*, finding that they 'are capable of decisively influencing the content of the legislation adopted by the EU legislature',[79] and that although not binding on the EU they have legal effects for the purpose of Article 218(9) 'by reason of their incorporation into EU law' through the relevant regulations.[80]

In each of these cases we can identify a close connection between the international agreement and internal EU law: in one case the agreement was to take EU law as its inspiration, in others the internal EU law built on, supplemented and/or implemented the international agreement. These close connections—explicitly or implicitly—enable an '*AETR*-effect' to be established for the purposes of Article 3(2) TFEU. Where the interconnection is not so close, the 'effect' on common rules may be harder to establish and the burden of proof—'in accordance with the principle of conferral'—is with the party seeking to establish exclusivity.[81] I would argue, however, that the presence of an *AETR*-effect in these cases is not a coincidence. It is precisely in such cases involving the interaction between EU and international regulatory regimes that these sectoral implied external powers are likely to be used.

CONCLUSION

Exclusivity thus carries different connotations in the case of express and implied external powers. In the case of powers expressly granted for the purpose of external action (in particular the CCP, the common foreign and security policy, development co-operation and association agreements), the breadth and open-ended nature of these powers mean that competence carries with it the power to shape external policy, to define the scope of EU international action. In most cases this is not a power which excludes the Member States, but when it does (in the case of the CCP) its boundaries will of course be contested. The exclusivity of the CCP is externally oriented (that is, it is about shaping the external policy of the EU) and does not impinge on the internal division of competence (Article 207(6) TFEU). Defining the limits of the post-Lisbon CCP, as the Court has been asked to do in *Opinion 2/15*, becomes crucial. The post-Lisbon extension of the CCP, which the Court has (so far) furthered, has been accompanied by increased attention to the ways in which the Member States may continue to act internationally via authorisation, or exclusions—an unsurprising but seemingly ironic result given that the

[79] C-399/12, above n 60 para 63.
[80] C-399/12, above n 60 para 64.
[81] C-114/12, above n 45 para 75.

Lisbon Treaty deliberately removed the areas of shared competence in the CCP that had been introduced by the Nice Treaty.

Where implied external powers are linked to internal policy fields they need to demonstrate either the *AETR* or the *effet utile* rationale, as now expressed in Article 216(1) TFEU, and will tend to be sectoral in nature, tied to the Treaty-based objectives of those specific policies. In such cases exclusivity is internally oriented; it is linked to the need to preserve the integrity and functioning of the internal *acquis*. External powers are there to serve internal policy goals and exclusivity ensures that control over international commitments which impact on internal legislation lies with the EU. It is not surprising that it is the *AETR* rationale—in the form of the conditions for exclusivity found in Article 3(2) TFEU—that has given rise to disputes before the Court in the cases since the Lisbon Treaty, notably in the *Broadcasting Convention* case and *Opinion 1/13*. These cases involved scenarios where internal EU law and the international regime are closely interconnected and where the Court was in fact not so much concerned with who should be acting at the international level (competence) as with ensuring control over the integrity of the Union's internal regime, with managing the ways in which international law interacts with EU law. Strikingly, this method has been used even in cases where the international commitments are those of the Member States and where the EU itself cannot exercise its powers except indirectly through them.

The choice between express and implied external powers does not therefore represent a straightforward choice between less or more exclusivity. But it does imply a difference in the rationale for, and implications of, exclusivity. And when external powers are justified by the existence of a body of EU legislation, the interactions between external and internal regimes mean that exclusivity is in turn likely to be required.

9

Competence, Human Rights, and Asylum: What Price Mutual Recognition?

TAKIS TRIDIMAS*

THE PURPOSE OF this chapter is to discuss selected issues of EU competence in the field of fundamental rights, with special reference to the case law on the interaction between fundamental rights protection and mutual recognition in the field of asylum. After some reflections on the post-Lisbon competence landscape and the evolving role of fundamental rights in EU policy and law-making, the chapter makes brief reference to recent developments in migration and asylum law and focuses on the case law of the ECJ on mutual recognition in the field of asylum.

COMPETENCE CLARITY IN THE POST-LISBON LANDSCAPE: AN UNACHIEVABLE OBJECTIVE?

One of the avowed objectives of the Treaty of Lisbon was to provide greater clarity on the division of competences between the EU and its Member States.[1] Nonetheless, some six years after its coming into force, the scope of both internal and external EU competence continues to create political tensions and give rise to some intractable legal problems. This is not a failure of the Lisbon Treaty. The inclusion of general rules outlining the areas where the EU may act, the types of competence that it enjoys, and the rules governing its exercise, was a welcome development. Competence rules are of constitutional importance. Their formalisation in Treaty text enhances constitutional identity, provides a key reference point for institutional actors and citizens, and contributes to legal certainty. But it could not be expected to provide finality or bright lines the quest for which, in a polity such

* Takis Tridimas is Professor of European Law at King's College London and Visiting Professor at the College of Europe.

[1] For a discussion, see, among others, P Craig, *The Lisbon Treaty: Law, Politics, and Treaty Reform* (Oxford, Oxford University Press, 2010) 155–92; T Tridimas, 'Competence after Lisbon: The Elusive Search for Bright Lines' in D Ashiagbor, N Countouris, I Lianos (eds), *The European Union after the Treaty of Lisbon* (Cambridge, Cambridge University Press, 2012) 47–76; LS Rossi, 'Does the Treaty of Lisbon Provide a Clearer Separation of Competences between the EU and Member States?' in A Biondi, P Eeckhout and S Ripley (eds), *EU law After Lisbon* (Oxford, Oxford University Press, 2012) 85–106.

as the EU, is elusive. Many reasons account for this. First, in common with many constitutional norms, the rules defining EU competence are often open-textured and leave ample room for interpretation. Second, the scope of EU competence, as it results from the accumulation of specific Treaty provisions that provide legal bases for action, is very wide. Treaty provisions also grant the EU legislature wide discretion.[2] Such a broad remit, coupled with the urge of institutions to expand their own power and the multiplicity of EU and national actors involved in decision making, make tensions inevitable. Third, post Lisbon, the EU has been hit by successive crises of wide-ranging economic and political repercussions. The Eurozone crisis posed an existentialist threat to economic and monetary union, whilst the migration crisis strained Schengen and tested EU solidarity. The EU found itself less prepared in terms of legal powers than a meaningful response would require, leading to improvisation and normative experimentation of an unprecedented degree. This is particularly evident in the field of Eurozone governance where there has been heavy reliance on international agreements concluded between the Eurozone Member States, outside the strict framework of EU law.[3]

It is a constitutional irony that, although the Lisbon Treaty did away with Article 293 EC, which provided for the conclusion of international agreements by Member States in certain areas, the use of such agreements to complement EU law has since intensified. In short, following the competence formalisation that occurred through Lisbon, the division of constitutional space between the Union and the Member States looks, perhaps, more confused, more fragile, and characterised by greater entropy.

RESPECT FOR FUNDAMENTAL RIGHTS: FROM CONSTRAINING FORCE TO POLICY

In the EU polity, the protection of fundamental rights has traditionally been conceived not as an independent, self-standing policy but as a fundamental value, a transversal underlying objective, and a constraining force. This is because the European Communities were not conceived as a human rights organisation. The protection of fundamental rights was, first and foremost, a judge-made development seeking to provide legitimacy and constitutional grounding to the integration

[2] This is, for example, the case in relation to Art 114 TFEU, which provides the EU with ample discretion at two levels: It grants the EU a transversal harmonisation power spanning all sectors of the economy and is also, to a good extent, value-neutral in relation to the substantive content of the harmonisation measures. Although Art 114(3) requires the EU institutions to seek to achieve a high level of protection in relation to health, safety, the environment and consumers, the EU legislature enjoys a large amount of discretion in setting the level of protection and prioritising conflicting objectives.

[3] See, in particular, the Fiscal Compact Treaty, the European Stability Mechanism (ESM) Treaty and the Inter-Governmental Agreement on the Transfer and Mutualisation of Contributions to the Single Resolution Fund which supplements the Single Resolution Mechanism as the second pillar of Banking Union.

construct. Even though the Treaty of Lisbon granted the Charter binding effect, Article 6 TEU recognises multiple, overlapping sources for the protection of fundamental rights by referring to the Convention and the general principles of law, thus paying homage to the national constitutional traditions. It may be said that fundamental rights operate as normative forces at different levels. By virtue of Article 2 TEU, they are an overarching value of defining importance to the constitutional identity of the Union. Furthermore, they are a *sine qua non* for the legality of EU and Member State action that falls within the scope of EU law. As such, their primary function has been that of a constitutional constraint. In the competence discourse, fundamental rights protection has been understood as setting limits rather than empowering the EU to take positive action. In fact, an important concern of the Member States has been to contain the Charter–competence dynamic and the conception of EU fundamental rights as an autonomous force of competence generation.[4] The emphasis on the function of fundamental rights as marking the boundaries of legality has, in turn, elevated the definition of the scope of application of the Charter to an important aspect of the division of competence between the EU and the Member States. The determination of the scope of application of the Charter is important both for practical and theoretical reasons. In practical terms, it is necessary to know in what kind of situations the Charter may be invoked. This is particularly so to the extent that its scope of application or the level of protection that it offers is broader or narrower than other sources of fundamental rights provided by national law. In theoretical terms, it raises issues pertaining to the objectives and effect of the EU constitutional model and its relationship with the national constitutions. The broader the scope of application of the Charter, the more the EU asserts its own autonomous constitutional space and the more the Charter can be seen as a replacement of, rather than a complement to, national constitutional norms.

This model, which gives prevalence to fundamental rights as a force of negative integration, has been challenged in many ways. First, in the field of external relations, the EU is committed to advancing democracy, the rule of law and the universality and indivisibility of human rights.[5] This somewhat messianic objective has an important bearing on the EU's external relations policy. Second, on the strength of Article 7 TEU, the Commission has been more activist in pursuing a rule of law agenda concretising and raising the standards that Member

[4] Both the TEU and the Charter stress that the latter is not intended to extend the competences of the Union as defined in the Treaties; see Art 6(1) TEU; Art 51(2) of the Charter. The same principle is repeated in Declaration 31 accompanying the Treaty of Lisbon (OJ 2010 C 83/335), which received judicial acknowledgment in Case C-339/10 *Asparuhov Estov and Others* [2010] ECR I-11465, para 12. In *Dereci* the Court heeded to the limitation of Art 51(2) by separating the application of fundamental rights from the definition of the substantive rights emanating from EU citizenship: see Case C-256/11 *Dereci v Bundesministerium für Inneres*, judgment of 15 November 2011, paras 71–72.

[5] Art 21(1) TEU. The EU has also pursued a strong human rights policy as part of accession negotiations: see the Copenhagen criteria established by the Copenhagen European Council in 1993 and strengthened by the Madrid European Council in 1995.

States are expected to fulfil.[6] Third, the field of equality is one where, on the basis of Article 19 TFEU, the EU has pursued a broad legislative agenda for combatting non-discrimination and promoting inclusiveness.[7] A similar tendency is now noticeable in relation to the protection of personal data.[8] Finally, fundamental rights standards are an integral part of measures adopted in the area of freedom, security and justice.[9] In that field, owing to the areas covered, fundamental rights are not merely a constraining force but shape the content of EU harmonisation initiatives and may themselves form the subject-matter of harmonisation.[10] The above developments illustrate that it is possible to refer to the development of concrete fundamental rights EU policies in selected spheres. This does not necessarily mean higher or better protection. The concretisation of constitutional principles by statutory rules may, in fact, circumscribe the judicial inquiry, legitimise restrictions on grounds of majoritarian choice and ultimately serve to limit the content of rights. Some tendencies to this effect are, for example, noticeable in the law of free movement of persons where the case law suggests that proportionality analysis and the need for an overall evaluation may be displaced by specific legislative dispositions.[11]

[6] See Communication from the Commission to the European Parliament and the Council, A new EU Framework to strengthen the Rule of Law, COM(2014) 158 final, Strasbourg, 11.3.2014, and the Council Conclusions on ensuring respect for the rule of law, 16 December 2014. The Commission has since undertaken a number of initiatives including the adoption on 27 July 2016 of a Recommendation regarding the rule of law in Poland, http://ec.europa.eu/justice/effective-justice/files/recommendation-rule-of-law-poland-20160727_en.pdf/. For a discussion of this area, see C Closa and D Kochenov (eds), *Reinforcing Rule of Law Oversight in the European Union* (Cambridge, Cambridge University Press, 2016).

[7] See Directive 2000/43 implementing the principle of equal treatment between persons irrespective of racial or ethnic origin, OJ 2000, L 180/22; Directive 2000/78 establishing a general framework for equal treatment in employment and occupation, OJ 2000, L 303/16; and see also the recast Directive 2006/54 on the implementation of the principle of equal opportunities and equal treatment of men and women in matters of employment and occupation, OJ 2006 L 204/23.

[8] See Art 16 TFEU and the reform brought about by Regulation 2016/679, OJ 2016 L 119/1 and Directive 2016/680, OJ 2016 L 119/89.

[9] Measures in this area, as indeed in other areas of EU law, tend to incorporate a fundamental rights compatibility clause in their preamble. See, to give but few examples, Regulation 810/2009 (the EU Visa Code), OJ 2009 L 243/1, preamble, recital 29; Framework Decision on the European Arrest Warrant, OJ 2002, L 190/1, preamble, recital 12, and the measures listed in footnotes 15 to 19 (cf Directive 2001/55/EC on minimum standards for giving temporary protection in the event of a mass influx of displaced persons, OJ 2001 L 212/12); Needless to say, the evocative declaration of respect for fundamental rights by no means predetermines actual compliance.

[10] See the directives adopted under Article 82(2) TFEU on the right to a fair trial: Directive 2010/64/EU on the right to interpretation and translation in criminal proceedings, OJ 2010, L 280/1; Directive 2012/13 on the right to information in criminal proceedings, OJ 2012, L 142/1; Directive 2013/48/EU on the right of access to a lawyer in criminal proceedings, OJ 2013 L 294/1.

[11] Following Case C-333/13 *Dano* EU:C:2014:2358, in Case C-67/14 *Alimanovich* EU:C:2015:597, the ECJ gave preference to legislation over primary law refusing to interpret the Citizenship Directive in the light of the Charter and suggesting that Treaty rights are exhausted in legislation. It also rejected the need for an individual assessment viewing the provisions of the Citizenship Directive as the defining and inclusive source of rights. This was followed in *Vestische Arbeit Jobcenter Kreis Recklinghausen v Jovanna García-Nieto*, C-299/14, EU:C:2016:114.

MIGRATION AND ASYLUM: SELECTED DEVELOPMENTS

The pursuance of common asylum and immigration policies is an integral part of the Union's area of freedom, security and justice which falls within the EU's shared competence. In fact, this is an area where the Member States play a particularly important role, legislative and operational planning being expressly made subject to the European Council's strategic guidelines.[12] Asylum and immigration policies are governed by the overarching principles of solidarity and fairness. Although the precise meaning of those principles is not easy to pin down, they are not merely aspirational in character. They are justiciable and create binding legal effects. Concrete measures may be assessed for compatibility with them. Fairness has both an internal and an external dimension referring to the fair sharing of responsibility among Member States[13] and also the fair treatment of third country nationals.[14]

As it currently stands, the framework of EU and migration law is defined by the Dublin III Regulation,[15] the Qualification,[16] Procedures,[17] and Reception[18] Directives, and supplemented by the Eurodac Regulation,[19] the Temporary Protection,[20] and the Return Directive.[21] A European Asylum Support Office (EASO) has also been established.[22] This legislative package represents the third generation of EU measures in the area following the Dublin Convention.

The leitmotif of the common asylum system is the principle of mutual recognition. In the wider area of freedom, security and justice, that principle presents distinct advantages. It has the merit of efficiency as it facilitates the Europeanisation of sensitive policy areas, including asylum, immigration and criminal law,

[12] Art 68 TFEU.

[13] Art 80 TFEU.

[14] Arts 67(2) and 79(1) TFEU.

[15] Regulation (EU) No 604/2013 establishing the criteria and mechanisms for determining the Member State responsible for examining an application for international protection lodged in one of the Member States by a third-country national or a stateless person (recast), OJ 2013 L 180/31. This regulation replaced the Dublin II Regulation: Regulation No 343/2003.

[16] Directive 2011/95/EU on standards for the qualification of third-country nationals or stateless persons as beneficiaries of international protection, for a uniform status for refugees or for persons eligible for subsidiary protection, and for the content of the protection granted, OJ 2011 L 337/9. This directive replaced Council Directive 2004/83/EC of 29 April 2004 (OJ 2004 L 304, p 12).

[17] Directive 2013/32/EU on common procedures for granting and withdrawing international protection (recast) OJ 2013 L 180/60; the Directive replaced Council Directive 2005/85/EC (OJ 2005 L 326, p 13).

[18] Directive 2013/33/EU laying down standards for the reception of applicants for international protection (recast), OJ 2013 L 180/96, replacing Council Directive 2003/9/ (OJ 2003 L 31, p 18).

[19] Regulation (EU) No 603/2013, OJ 2013 L 180/1 replacing Council Regulation (EC) No 2725/2000 of 11 December 2000 concerning the establishment of 'Eurodac' for the comparison of fingerprints for the effective application of the Dublin Convention (OJ 2000 L 316, p 1).

[20] Council Directive 2001/55/EC on minimum standards for giving temporary protection in the event of a mass influx of displaced persons and on measures promoting a balance of efforts between Member States in receiving such persons and bearing the consequences thereof, OJ 2001 L 212/12.

[21] Directive 2008/115/EC on common standards and procedures in Member States for returning illegally staying third-country nationals, OJ 2008 L 348/98: Art 63(3)(b) now: 79(2)(c).

[22] Regulation (EU) No 439/2010 establishing a European Asylum Support Office, OJ 2010 L.132/11.

without first having to undergo the time-consuming and burdensome process of coordinating substantive national laws. It also fosters institutional collaboration of national agencies, and has the potential to lead to gradual convergence which is not superimposed by ex ante normative harmonisation but arises ex post with the benefit of experience. Nevertheless, mutual recognition also suffers from fundamental weaknesses. Relying on commitment to, rather than compliance with, values and standards, it assumes equivalence of national laws and state practices in circumstances where such equivalence cannot necessarily be ensured. It can thus act as a Trojan horse undermining national constitutional standards and transferring the burdens of integration to the citizen. Measures adopted by the EU in the field of asylum and international protection tend to contain fundamental rights compliance declarations.[23] This high rhetoric, however, is not necessarily accompanied by a high degree of protection in legislative or judicial outcomes.

In response to the migration crisis, on 13 May 2015 the Commission presented a comprehensive European Agenda on Migration[24] outlining short-term crisis management measures and long-term plans for the reform of migration law. The crisis was by all accounts unprecedented.[25] The Agenda stressed the exceptional pressure placed on frontline Member States owing to the influx of large numbers of refugees and led, inter alia, to the adoption by the Council of decisions suspending the application of the Dublin Regulation to Greece and Italy. Those decisions were adopted on the basis of the emergency response mechanism envisaged in Article 78(3) TFEU, one of the few provisions of the Treaties which provides specific legal authority for dealing with emergency situations.[26] The decisions provided for the relocation to other Member States of applicants who apply for international protection in Italy or in Greece and for whom those States would otherwise be responsible pursuant to the criteria provided by Dublin III. The number of those that would be relocated was established by reference to the percentage of the persons who were in clear need of international protection from the overall number of third country nationals who had entered Italy or Greece irregularly over a previous period.[27] The number to be relocated

[23] See above, n 9.

[24] COM(2015) 240 final, 13.5.2015.

[25] According to Frontex data, the central and eastern Mediterranean routes were the main irregular border crossings in 2014 and 2015. In 2014, those routes represented more than 75% of the EU total irregular border crossing. In that year, more than 170 000 migrants arrived irregularly in Italy, representing an increase of 277% compared to 2013. Greece witnessed an increase of 153% compared to 2013. In the first six months of 2015, Greece witnessed a six-fold increase over the corresponding period of 2014. See Council Decision 2015/1523 establishing provisional measures in the area of international protection for the benefit of Italy and Greece, OJ 2015 L 239/146, preamble, recital 10.

[26] Art 78(3) is part of the common asylum policy and empowers the Council, after consulting the European Parliament, to adopt provisional measures for the benefit of Member States confronted with an emergency situation characterised by a sudden inflow of nationals of third countries.

[27] Relocation was to be applied only in respect of an applicant belonging to a nationality for which the proportion of decisions granting international protection among decisions taken at first instance on applications for international protection as referred to in Chapter III of Directive 2013/32 (the common procedures Directive) was, according to the latest available updated quarterly Union-wide

was first determined at 40,000[28] and subsequently increased by another 120,000.[29] The temporary suspension was envisaged for a period of two years.[30]

A further initiative was undertaken in the international plain. On 18 March 2016, in a public statement, the EU and Turkey agreed on a number of action points including a resettlement plan under which for every Syrian being returned to Turkey from Greek islands, another Syrian will be resettled from Turkey to the EU taking into account the UN vulnerability criteria from Turkey to the Member States, within the framework of the existing commitments.[31] The EU–Turkey agreement has proved politically controversial and gives rise to a number of issues from the point of view of its compatibility with fundamental rights.[32] An attempt to challenge it proved unsuccessful. The General Court held that, 'notwithstanding the regrettably ambiguous terms of the EU-Turkey statement' and irrespective of whether it might have binding force, it was not attributable to the European Council as an EU institution but the Governments of the Member States.[33] The formalistic reasoning of the judgment is unpersuasive. It is unsatisfactory that the General Court focused on the subjective intentions of the authors of the statement without examining the allocation of competences in the field of asylum. More broadly, the capacity of the same actors to act either as EU institutions or *qua* representatives of sovereign States operates in a constitutional vacuum which practically forecloses access to justice and falls well short of rule of law standards.

The Commission has also put forward extensive proposals for broader law reform. In its Communication of 6 April 2016, it identified several weaknesses

average Eurostat data, 75 % or higher. See Article 3(2) of Council Decision 2015/1523, op cit., n 25 and Article 3(2) of Council Decision (EU) 2015/1601, infra, n 29.

[28] See Council Decision (EU) 2015/1523 of 14 September 2015 establishing provisional measures in the area of international protection for the benefit of Italy and of Greece, OJ 2015 L 239/146.

[29] Council Decision (EU) 2015/1601 of 22 September 2015 establishing provisional measures in the area of international protection for the benefit of Italy and Greece, OJ 2015 L 248/80, and see amendments made by Council Decision (EU) 2016/1754 of 29 September 2016 amending Decision (EU) 2015/1601, OJ 2015 L 268/82, following the action points agreed between the EU and Turkey. See further Council Implementing Decision (EU) 2016/408 of 10 March 2016 on the temporary suspension of the relocation of 30% of applicants allocated to Austria under Decision (EU) 2015/1601 establishing provisional measures in the area of international protection for the benefit of Italy and Greece OJ 2016 L 74/36.

[30] In relation to the 40,000 refugees relocated by Decision 2015/1523, the specific distribution of refugees to each of the other Member States by numbers was agreed by resolution of the Member States meeting within the Council: see Resolution of 22 July 2015, 11131/15, ASIM 63, and see also the Conclusions of the representatives of the Member States meeting within the Council on resettling 20,000 persons in need of international protection, see outcome of the 3405th Council meeting Justice and Home Affairs, 11097/15, Brussels 20 July 2015. In relation to the 120,000 refugees relocated by Decision 2015/1601, the specific distribution was included in the annex to that decision.

[31] See the EU–Turkey Statement of 18 March 2016, International Summit EU Press Release, 144/16, 18/03/2016.

[32] See S Peers, "The final EU/Turkey refugee deal: a legal assessment", EU Legal Analysis Blog, http://eulawanalysis.blogspot.co.uk/2016/03/the-final-euturkey-refugee-deal-legal.html, last visited on 1 February 2017.

[33] Case T-257/16 *NM v European Council*, EU:T:2017:130, para 65.

in the Common European Asylum System and outlined policy proposals for the long-term management of migration flows.[34] The migration crisis exposed several design limitations, structural weaknesses, and implementation shortcomings in the Common European Asylum System. The system was not designed to cope with the mass influx of refugees. The central criterion of irregular entry for allocating responsibility for an asylum claim has a burden bias against frontier Member States along established migratory routes. It also suffers from inherent limitations: effective management of migration requires not only internal EU policies but also external action through co-operation with third countries. The system ignores a fact of economic life, namely, that some Member States are viewed as more desirable destinations than others thereby leading to secondary movements.[35] Perhaps one of the most important weaknesses of the current system is that it places a disproportionate responsibility on certain Member States and encourages uncontrolled and irregular migratory flows[36] In its Communication, the Commission identified five priority areas for improving the European Asylum System: establishing a sustainable and fair system for determining the Member State responsible for asylum seekers; reinforcing the Eurodac system; achieving greater convergence in the EU asylum system; preventing secondary movements within the EU; and providing a new mandate for the EU's asylum agency.[37] The Communication was followed by a comprehensive package for the reform of the main instruments governing EU asylum policy.[38] The Commission's proposals bear some of the hallmarks of its reaction to other crises faced by the EU. There is a clear trajectory towards the expansion of EU competence, more centralisation, a higher degree of harmonisation, and a greater role for EU agencies.

FUNDAMENTAL RIGHTS AND MUTUAL RECOGNITION: *NS* AND ITS AFTERMATH

As already stated, the principle of mutual co-operation defines the integration paradigm in the area of freedom, security, and justice.[39] It is closely linked to the

[34] Communication from the Commission to the European Parliament and the Council Towards a Reform of the Common European Asylum System and Enhancing Avenues to Europe, COM(2016) 197 final, 6 April 2016.

[35] ibid p 4.

[36] ibid p 2.

[37] ibid p 6.

[38] See Commission Proposal for a new Dublin Regulation COM(2016) 270 final, Brussels, 4.5.2016; a new Qualification Regulation replacing the Qualification Directive, COM(2016) 466, Brussels, 13.7.2016; a proposal replacing the Asylum Procedures Directive with a Regulation, COM(2016) 467 final, Brussels, 13.7.2016; a proposal revising the Reception Conditions Directive, COM(2016) 465 final, Brussels, 13.7.2016; a proposal establishing a Union Resettlement Framework and amending Regulation (EU) No 516/2014, COM(2016) 468 final, Brussels, 13.7.2016; and a new Eurodac Regulation, COM(2016) 272 final, Brussels, 4.5.2016; and a proposal for a new Regulation governing the European Union Agency for Asylum, COM(2016) 271 final, Brussels, 4.5.2016.

[39] For a comprehensive assessment, see, among others, C Janssens, *The Principle of Mutual Recognition in EU law* (Oxford, Oxford University Press, 2014).

concept of mutual trust, the latter being a *sine qua non* of the former. A key issue is the extent to which mutual recognition and mutual trust must give way to the protection of fundamental rights. Should those principles be upheld even where the standards for the protection of fundamental rights differ in Member States? If so, what level of variation can be tolerated and under what conditions? The problems arising pertain not only to the conflict between substantive principles of law but also the division of competences. In particular, the question arises whether Member States may subject the application of EU measures founded on mutual recognition on national standards of fundamental rights protection.

Despite its nebulous content, the Court has held that the principle of mutual trust between Member States is of fundamental importance.[40] In the area of freedom, security and justice, that principle imposes two obligations on Member States. First, when implementing EU law, Member States may be required to presume that fundamental rights have been observed by the other Member States, so that they may not demand a higher level of national protection than that provided by EU law.[41] Second, save in exceptional cases, they may not check whether another Member State has actually, in a specific case, observed the fundamental rights guaranteed by the EU.[42] The first obligation is the corollary of the mutual recognition model and accords to EU law a maximalist effect. If a Member State could require another to comply with standards above those which are required by EU law, mutual recognition would be undermined and become hostage to national constitutional standards. In cross-border situations, the national human rights standard is displaced by the EU standard. A prime illustration of this is provided by *Melloni*,[43] where the Court projected an inclusive, centralised approach to the protection of fundamental rights placing the Charter at the apex of the edifice. The second obligation differs from the first in that it does not pertain to the level of protection but competence to verify whether that level is observed. It also differs in that it is casted in less absolute terms, being applicable 'save in exceptional circumstances'.[44]

In the field of asylum, the issue came to the fore in *NS*,[45] which concerned Regulation No 343/2003 (Dublin II),[46] the predecessor to Dublin III.[47] Dublin II, as Dublin III, is based on the principle that an application of asylum must be examined by a single Member State and lays down criteria for determining the Member State responsible for examining an application. In general, subject to specific rules, responsibility lies with the Member State of first entry. Article 3(2) of Dublin II

[40] Opinion 2/13 *on the draft agreement on the Accession of the European Union to the European Convention for the Protection of Human Rights and Fundamental Freedoms*, EU:C:2014:2454, para 191.

[41] Op 2/13, para 192.

[42] ibid.

[43] Case C-399/11 *Melloni v Ministerio Fiscal*, EU:C:2013:107.

[44] ibid.

[45] Joined Cases C-411/10 and C-493/10 *NS v Secretary of State for the Home Department*, EU:C:2011:865.

[46] Council Regulation (EC) No 343/2003 of 18 February 2003 (OJ 2003 L 50/1).

[47] Council Regulation (EU) No 604/2013 of 26 June 2013 (OJ 2013 L 180/31).

states that, by way of derogation, each Member State may examine an application for asylum lodged with it even if such examination is not its responsibility.[48] In *NS*, the applicants had sought asylum in the UK or Ireland having first entered the EU via Greece. They argued that the procedures and conditions for asylum seekers in Greece were inadequate and that the UK or Ireland were required to exercise their power under Article 3(2) to accept responsibility for deciding on their asylum claims.

The key issue raised in *NS* was, essentially, whether a Member State should send back an asylum seeker to the Member State responsible for examining his application if such return exposed him to inhuman or degrading treatment. The Court reasoned as follows. It pointed out that the EU measures which establish the Common European Asylum System were conceived in a context making it possible to assume that all the participating states observe fundamental rights. The Dublin II Regulation was adopted precisely because of the principle of mutual confidence in order to rationalise the treatment of asylum claims. In those circumstances, it had to be assumed that the treatment of asylum seekers in all Member States complied with the requirements of the Charter, the Geneva Convention, and the ECHR.[49] Nevertheless, it was not inconceivable that that system may, in practice, experience major operational problems in a given Member State, meaning that there is a substantial risk that asylum seekers may, when transferred to that Member State, be treated in a manner incompatible with their fundamental rights.[50] However, it does not follow that any infringement of a fundamental right will affect the obligations of the other Member States to comply with the provisions of Dublin II.[51] That would be the case only where there are substantial grounds for believing that there are 'systemic flaws' in the asylum procedure and reception conditions for asylum applicants in the Member State responsible, resulting in inhuman or degrading treatment within the meaning of Article 4 of the Charter.[52]

The Court, thus, drew a distinction between, on the one hand, mere infringements of fundamental rights by the Member State responsible for examining an asylum application, and, on the other hand, systemic flaws in the asylum procedure and reception conditions resulting in inhuman or degrading treatment. Only where there is a substantial risk of such an infringement occurring can the principle of mutual recognition be displaced.[53]

The judgment came in the aftermath of *MSS*,[54] where the ECtHR had found that, in light of deficiencies in asylum procedures in Greece, by returning the applicant there, the Belgian authorities had exposed him to detention and living

[48] The corresponding provision in force now is that of Art 17(1) of Dublin III.
[49] *NS*, ibid paras 78–80.
[50] ibid para 81.
[51] para 82.
[52] para 86.
[53] Confirmed in Case C-4/11 *Puid* EU:C:2013:740, para 30.
[54] *MSS v Belgium and Greece* (2011) 53 EHRR 28.

conditions that were in breach of Article 3 of the Convention. *NS* confirms that the principle of mutual recognition does not create a conclusive presumption that the Member State of return complies with fundamental rights. Nevertheless, the test of 'systemic flaws' is far too stringent. It tolerates a violation of fundamental rights in the interests of upholding the integrity of the European asylum system evincing a near-dogmatic adherence to the principle of mutual respect. The threshold of 'systemic flaws' does not exist under the Convention.[55] *NS* introduces a threshold that 'exists nowhere else in refugee law'[56] pointing to a doctrine of EU exceptionalism.

The Court reasoned by reference to the objectives and the wording of EU asylum measures pointing out that it would be incompatible with the aims of the Dublin II Regulation if the slightest infringement of the directives governing international protection[57] were sufficient to prevent the transfer of an asylum seeker to the Member State primarily responsible.[58] If the mandatory consequence of any such infringement was to prevent transfer, that would add to the criteria for determining the Member State responsible set out in Chapter III of Dublin II another exclusionary criterion which is not stated therein. Such a result would deprive those obligations of their substance and endanger the realisation of the objective of quickly designating the Member State responsible for examining an asylum claim lodged in the European Union.[59] The Court found the solution in the internal logic of the mutual recognition system as exemplified in the EU measures governing asylum, elevating the issue to an existentialist one, bringing to the fore 'the raison d'être of the European Union and the creation of an area of freedom, security and justice and, in particular, the Common European Asylum System.'[60]

NS exposes, perhaps, not so much a flaw in the reasoning of the Court as in the mutual recognition principle which is aspirational in character and relies on commitment to fundamental rights protection rather than compliance with them. But the formalistic approach of *NS* does not withstand a Convention-based analysis. The Strasbourg case law has emphasised time and again that the Convention is intended to guarantee rights that are practical and effective and not merely illusory and the ECtHR will look behind the formal appearance and investigate 'the realities of the situation complained of'.[61] Seen in that light, *NS* not only gives preference to the principle of mutual recognition over the protection of fundamental rights but also over the principle of effective protection of fundamental rights.

[55] According to the judgment in *Soering v United Kingdom* (1989) 11 EHRR 439, the removal of a person from a Member State of the Council of Europe to another country is forbidden if it is shown that there is a real risk that the person transferred will suffer treatment contrary to Art 3 of ECHR.

[56] See EM, para 39, per Lord Kerr.

[57] Namely, Directives 2003/9, 2004/83 and 2005/85.

[58] para 84.

[59] para 85.

[60] para 83.

[61] *Sporrong and Lönnroth v Sweden*, Application No 7151/75, Judgment 23 September 1982, para 63.

Following *NS*, the UK Supreme Court made a valiant effort to procure a Convention-compatible interpretation of the ECJ's judgment. In *EM*,[62] the appellants were Iranian and Eritrean nationals who had come to the UK via Italy. They complained that, if they were returned to Italy, they would be exposed to inhuman or degrading treatment contrary to Article 3 of the Convention. In the light of *NS*, the Court of Appeal had identified a difference of standards. Under the case law of the ECtHR, return had to be declined if there was a risk that it would lead to a breach of the applicant's human rights. By contrast, the ECJ case law required risk of a systemic breach. The Court of Appeal felt bound to give precedence to the ECJ case law but the Supreme Court avoided the conflict by interpreting *NS* as not requiring the existence of a systemic risk. In its view, the meaning of *NS* was that a risk of systemic deficiencies was sufficient rather than a *sine qua non* for the refusal to return.[63]

The judgment of the Supreme Court is a fascinating exercise in turning necessity into virtue. Lord Kerr pointed out that an exclusionary rule based only on systemic failures would be arbitrary both in conception and in practice, and run counter to Article 3 ECHR.[64] It is, however, doubtful whether the meaning attributed to *NS* by the Supreme Court was its intended meaning. Lord Kerr gave precedence to the parts of the ECJ judgment dealing with the application in the concrete case of the principles laid down therein, rather the parts of the judgment where the principles themselves were laid down.[65] The tenor of the judgment appears to be that systemic deficiencies must exist to displace the application of the rules laid down in Dublin II. In any event, the meaning attributed to *NS* by the Supreme Court could not possibly be said to be *acte clair* given also that the Court of Appeal had taken the opposite view. In terms of EU orthodoxy, therefore, the issue merited a new reference to the ECJ.

As a matter of substance, it is difficult to disagree with the Supreme Court. As Lord Kerr observed, a violation of Article 3 'is not intrinsically dependent on the failure of a system'.[66] Also, as a matter of practical experience, gross violations of Article 3 rights can occur without there being any systemic failure.[67] *NS* denies the individual character of fundamental rights protection and runs counter to a fundamental tenet of asylum law. It results in the odd situation that a person will have to be returned to a Member State even though he proves that there is a real risk that he will be subjected to inhuman or degrading treatment simply because he cannot prove that there are systemic breaches of human rights.[68]

[62] *R (on the application of EM (Eritrea)) v Secretary of State for the Home Department* [2014] UKSC 12.

[63] para 56 per Lord Kerr.

[64] para 48.

[65] Lord Kerr read paras 85–86 in the light of para 94 of the judgment rather than the other way around.

[66] ibid para 42.

[67] ibid.

[68] *R (on the application of EM (Eritrea)) v Secretary of State for the Home Department* [2014] UKSC 12, at para 37 per Lord Kerr.

In *Tarakhel*, the Strasbourg Court held that, in transfers under the Dublin Regulation system, "a thorough and individualized examination of the situation of the person concerned"[69] must be carried out and the national authorities must make an overall evaluation taking into account the overall situation with regard to the reception arrangements for asylum seekers in the Member State concerned and the specific situation of the applicants with a view to determining whether there are substantial grounds for believing that the applicant would be at risk of inhuman and degrading treatment. In short, under the case law of the ECtHR, the assessment must be individualised and entails the exercise of close scrutiny.[70]

Although practical considerations and the need to uphold the integrity of the asylum system countenance the view that not every violation may justify departure from the rules of the Regulation, the ECJ places the bar too high. *NS* prioritised respect for the principle of mutual recognition above respect for fundamental rights creating a significant gap in legal protection. It sacrificed fundamental rights protection to the dogma of mutual recognition. The judgment sought to draw a balance between, on the one hand, the protection of fundamental rights and, on the other hand, the need to uphold the principle of mutual recognition as the linchpin of the EU model on freedom security and justice. The criterion of systematic breach appeared to provide the furthest possible concession for fear that, if further concessions were made, the application of the common asylum system would become too porous allowing national human rights standards to trump compliance with EU requirements.

The ECJ's finding in *NS* has been incorporated in the amended Dublin III Regulation.[71] Article 3(2) states that, where it is impossible to transfer an applicant to the Member State responsible because there are substantial grounds for believing that there are systemic flaws in the asylum procedure and in the reception conditions, resulting in a risk of inhuman or degrading treatment, the determining Member State must continue to examine the criteria set out in the regulation in order to establish whether another Member State can be designated as responsible. Strictly speaking, the amendment does not deal with the situation where the determining Member State considers that there is a risk of inhuman or degrading treatment for the specific applicant which does not result from systemic flaws. In such a case, the issue remains open whether it must abstain from returning the applicant to that Member State. It is submitted that it should do so as this is the only interpretation compatible with the requirements of Article 4 of the Charter and Article 3 of the Convention. Furthermore, the term 'systemic flaws' is in itself ambiguous and should receive a very wide interpretation so as to bring it closer to the Strasbourg requirements.[72]

[69] *Tarakhel v Switzerland* (App 29217/12) at para 104.

[70] ibid paras 105 and 126.

[71] Regulation (EU) No 604/2013 establishing the criteria and mechanisms for determining the Member State responsible for examining an application for international protection lodged in one of the Member States by a third-country national or a stateless person (recast), OJ 2013 L180/31.

[72] It has been suggested that that the ECJ and the ECtHR may be much closer than they appear since in all cases examined by the ECJ (*NS, Puid,* Case C-4/11 EU:C:2013:740) and *Abdullahi* Case

A number of consequential issues arise from *NS*. On what basis may a Member State determine whether there is a systemic deficiency in the asylum procedures of another Member State? Also, is a Member State entitled or indeed required not to return an asylum seeker where there is a real risk that he would be subjected to a violation of a right other than the right to inhuman and degrading treatment? In relation to the first question, it appears that Member States may evaluate the existence of a systemic risk on the basis of previous findings of the ECtHR, objective reports or official documents of international non-governmental organisations[73] or, especially, EU official reports and documents.[74] The second question remains open. It is correct that the right against inhuman and degrading treatment is an absolute one but it would be difficult to defend a restriction of the exception on that ground. There is no reason why a substantial risk of systemic flaws which may result in the violation of other rights, for example the right to judicial protection, should be treated differently.[75]

SPILL-OVER AND RETREAT

In *Abdullahi*,[76] the systemic flaws principle spilled over to the field of remedies. The case concerned a Somali national who had entered Greece illegally and after passing through non-EU States and Hungary, was arrested and claimed asylum in Austria. In accordance with Article 10(1) of Dublin II, Hungary agreed to take charge of her as the Member State of irregular entry. Ms Abdullahi claimed that the Member State responsible for her asylum application was not Hungary but

C-394/12, EU:C:2013:813) systemic flaws were taken for granted and that, even though the ECtHR did not use that caveat in *MSS*, its analysis in that case suggested that such systemic flaws were present. See ELRev October 2015 editorial, p. 3. No head on collision has therefore occurred and there is scope for pragmatic convergence: on the one hand, the requirement of systemic flaws may not be as strict as it appears since the ECJ has not had the opportunity to interpret it and, on the other hand, the requirement to carry out an individualized assessment under the Strasbourg case law may be less exacting: op.cit. p. 3. There is much merit in the above analysis. Still, the divergent approaches reveal more than mere judicial posturing. Strasbourg and Luxembourg have different priorities and, under *NS* (and now Dublin III), the condition of systemic flaws appears to be a condition that must be satisfied. See now *C.K., H.F., A.S. v Republica Slovenija*, Case C-578/16 PPU, EU:C:2017:127, discussed below.

[73] In *MSS* the ECtHR referred to the correspondence sent by the United Nations High Commissioner for Refugees (UNHCR) to the Belgian minister responsible, and also the Commission reports on the evaluation of the Dublin system and the proposals for recasting Regulation No 343/2003 in order to improve the efficiency of the system and the effective protection of fundamental rights (*MSS v Belgium and Greece*, paras 347–50).

[74] See *NS* para 92 and *Aranyosi*, Joined Cases C-404/15 and C-659/15 PPU EU:C:2016:198, para 89, discussed below.

[75] Support for this view may be derived from *Aranyosi*, where, in the context of the European Arrest Warrant, it was held that the court of the executing Member State must assess the risk of a violation of the right against inhuman or degrading treatment in the issuing Member State having regard to the standard of protection of fundamental rights guaranteed by EU law, 'in particular, by Art 4 of the Charter': see para 88 and below. This suggests that the judicial authority of the executing State must also assess, where necessary, possible violation of other rights.

[76] Case C-394/12 *Abdullahi v Bundesasylamt* EU:C:2013:813.

Greece and that, given Greece's poor record, it was for Austria to examine her application. The key question was whether Dublin II provided an asylum applicant with the right to request a review of the determination of the Member State responsible on the grounds that the criteria laid down in the regulation had been misapplied. The Court took a restrictive view holding that, where a Member State has agreed to take charge of an asylum seeker as the state of the applicant's first entry into the EU, the only way in which the applicant could call into question that decision was by pleading systemic deficiencies in the asylum procedure and the reception conditions in that Member State, which posed a real risk of inhuman or degrading treatment.[77] *Abdullahi* took a restrictive view of the right to judicial remedies under Dublin II. The Court held essentially that Article 19(2) of the Regulation, which provides for an appeal against a decision to transfer an asylum seeker to another Member State, does not enable him to question in general the application of the criteria determining the Member State responsible. The only way in which an applicant can call into question the decision to transfer him to the Member State which has accepted responsibility for examining his application as the first state of illegal entry is by pleading systemic deficiencies. It is in effect not open to the applicant to claim that the Member State that has accepted to deal with his application is not the first state of illegal entry. The Court found justification for this restrictive view on the need to uphold the principle of mutual recognition and the system established by Dublin II. A general right to question transfer on the basis that the Member State which has accepted responsibility is not the Member State responsible under the regulation would be incompatible with the organisational rules governing the relations between the Member States and the ample discretion left to them under Dublin II.

This restrictive view however proved short-lived and, in a change spearheaded by AG Sharpston, the pendulum swung in *Ghezelbash*[78] and *Karim*.[79] Both cases concerned applicants who challenged return decisions in circumstances where another Member State had agreed to take them back. The crucial difference was that, in contrast to *Abdullahi*, those cases were decided under Dublin III. In *Ghezelbash* the Court held that under Dublin III, an asylum seeker is entitled to plead, in an appeal against a decision to transfer him, the incorrect application of one of the criteria for determining responsibility laid down in the regulation. The Court pointed out that Dublin III enhanced the legal protection of asylum seekers providing for a remedy of greater scope and more specific mechanisms and processes. Article 27(1) provides that the asylum seeker is to have the right to an effective remedy in the form of an appeal or a review, on points of fact and law, against a transfer decision before a court or tribunal. A systematic interpretation of Dublin III and its 'general thrust'[80] suggested that it no longer provided merely

[77] para 60.
[78] Case C-63/15*Ghezelbash v Staatssecretaris van Veiligheid en Justitie* EU:C:2016:409.
[79] Case C-155/15 *Karim v Migrationsverke* EU:C:2016:410.
[80] para 45.

for organisational rules governing relations between Member States but turned the asylum process from a dialogue between state actors to a tripartite relationship granting a voice to the individuals concerned. In *Karim*, the Court spelt out the demise of *Abdullahi* stating that Dublin III provides an asylum applicant with an effective remedy against a transfer decision, which may result in a Member State's responsibility being called into question even where there are no systemic deficiencies in the asylum process or in the reception conditions for asylum applicants in that Member State, resulting in a risk of inhuman or degrading treatment.[81]

Although these developments have caused some disquiet among Member States at a sensitive time in migration, they are fully in conformity with the changes made by Dublin III, the right to an effective legal remedy, and the rights of defence. In that respect, they bring the interpretation of the Dublin system closer to the remedies applicable under the Qualification Directive.[82] Desirable restrictions on migration cannot be made by restricting process rights but by establishing a meaningful and workable system of rules.Even though *Ghezelbash* and *Karim* decouple the systemic flaws requirement from the right to seek a remedy, they do not interfere with the substantive scope of *NS*. Indeed, as stated above, express reference to systemic flaws is made in Dublin III and in *Ghezelbash* the Court sought to ring-fence the principle of mutual trust from the right to challenge the return decision. It held that if, in reviewing the decision to return the applicant, it was established that an error had been made, that would not affect the principle of mutual trust, as such a finding would simply mean that the Member State to which the applicant was to be transferred was not the Member State responsible within the meaning of the criteria.[83]

It thus now appears to be established that an asylum seeker has the right to challenge the determination of the Member State responsible with a view to ensuring that that determination has been made in accordance with the criteria laid down in Chapter III of the Dublin III Regulation.

The Court was faced with a similar conflict between mutual recognition and fundamental rights in the field of the European Arrest Warrant in *Aranyosi*.[84] The case concerned the execution in Germany of EAWs issued by Hungary and Romania. The ECtHR had found that, for reasons of overcrowding, the conditions of prisons in those countries were in violation of Article 3 of the Convention. Those findings led the referring court in *Aranyosi* to consider that, in the event of surrender, the individuals concerned might be subject to conditions of detention that were in breach of EU fundamental rights. The questions raised were whether the Framework Decision on the EAW must be interpreted as meaning that, where there is solid evidence that detention conditions in the issuing Member State are incompatible with Article 4 of the Charter, the executing judicial authority may

[81] para 22.
[82] See eg Case C-277/11 *M.M.* EU:C:2012:744.
[83] para 55.
[84] Joined Cases C-404/15 and C-659/15 PPU *Aranyosi* EU:C:2016:198.

or must refuse to execute an EAW or whether it may or must make surrender conditional on there being obtained from the issuing Member State information enabling it to be satisfied that those detention conditions are compatible with fundamental rights.

The ECJ introduced a two-step approach reminiscent of that of *NS*. It held that, where the judicial authority of the executing Member State is in possession of evidence of a real risk of inhuman or degrading treatment, it must assess the existence of that risk. The consequence of the execution of an EAW must not be that the individual suffers such treatment.[85] The court of the executing Member State must assess the risk of a violation of the right against inhuman or degrading treatment having regard to the standard of protection of fundamental rights guaranteed by EU law and not the (possibly higher) standard applicable under its national law.[86] To that end, the executing judicial authority must rely on information that is objective, reliable, and specific and demonstrates that 'there are deficiencies, which may be systemic or generalised, or which may affect certain groups of people, or which may affect certain places of detention'.[87] That information may be obtained, inter alia, from judgments of international courts, the ECtHR, judgments of courts of the issuing Member State, and also decisions, reports and other documents produced by bodies of the Council of Europe or under the aegis of the UN.[88]

However, a finding that there is a real risk of inhuman or degrading treatment by virtue of general conditions of detention in the issuing Member State cannot lead, in itself, to the refusal to execute an EAW.[89] The court must make a further assessment, specific and precise, of whether there are substantial grounds to believe that the individual concerned will be exposed to that risk because of the conditions for his detention.[90]

Aranyosi is more nuanced than *NS* and receptive to a narrow interpretation. First, it makes no reference to *NS*. Second, the reason why the Court answers by reference to a two-limb test is because of the circumstances giving rise to the reference. The referring court questioned whether surrender would be compatible with EU law because there was probative evidence that the conditions of prisoners in the issuing states were in general below the requisite standard of protection. If the persons concerned therefore were surrendered, there was a risk that they would suffer inhuman or degrading treatment not because of circumstances specific to themselves but as a result of the general conditions prevailing in the prison system of Hungary and Romania. In other words, the Court did not examine the possibility that an exception to the principle of mutual recognition and the surrender

[85] *Aranyosi*, para 88.

[86] *Aranyosi*, para 88; Case C-399/11*Melloni* EU:C:2013:107, paras 59 and 63, and Opinion 2/13, EU:C:2014:2454, para 192.

[87] para 89.

[88] para 89.

[89] para 91.

[90] para 92.

of a person pursuant to an EAW would be justified in exceptional circumstances if there was probative evidence to suggest that there was a real risk that a person may be subjected to inhuman or degrading treatment for reasons pertaining specifically to that person. Third, the language of the judgment is indeterminate. The Court refers to deficiencies that *may* be systemic or generalised and not to deficiencies that must have those attributes.[91] In that respect, the tenor of *Aranyosi* is different from that of *NS*.[92] *Aranyosi* therefore is compatible with the proposition that the executing judicial authority must refuse surrender where there is objective evidence to suggest a real risk that the fundamental rights of the person concerned may be violated in the issuing Member State. This view is also dictated by the Court's declaration that Article 3 ECHR imposes, on the authorities of the state on whose territory an individual is detained, a positive obligation to ensure that *any* prisoner is detained in conditions which guarantee respect for human dignity.[93] Furthermore, given the overarching character of fundamental rights and the express commitment of the Framework Decision that it must not have the effect of modifying the obligation to respect fundamental rights as enshrined in Article 6 TEU,[94] it should be accepted that the same obligation ensues if there is evidence that there is a risk not only of inhuman and degrading treatment but also other fundamental rights.

In *Aranyosi*, the ECJ also gave some guidelines on the way the executing court is to perform the second step, namely, determine if there is evidence of risk of violation in the issuing Member State. The steps provided by the ECJ are the following: The executing judicial authority must, pursuant to Article 15(2) of the Framework Decision, request of the judicial authority of the issuing Member State that there be provided all necessary supplementary information on the conditions in which it is envisaged that the individual concerned will be detained in that Member State.[95] That request may also relate to the existence, in the issuing Member State, of any national or international procedures and mechanisms for monitoring detention conditions.[96] The issuing judicial authority is obliged to provide the requested information.[97] If, in the light of the information provided and any other information that may be available to the executing judicial authority, that authority finds that there exists a real risk of inhuman or degrading treatment, the execution of the EAW must be postponed but cannot be abandoned.[98] Those practical steps, however, may be unrealistic in that the judicial authority of the issuing Member State may lack the requisite information, the power to obtain it, or the power to make the evaluation it is asked to make. Even though national

[91] See para 89.
[92] Compare para 89 of *Aranyosi* with para 86 of *NS*.
[93] See para 90.
[94] See Art 1(3) of the Framework Decision.
[95] para 95.
[96] para 96.
[97] para 97.
[98] para 98.

law must make those powers available in order to comply with EU law, this may not be the case. The articulation of specific obligations by the case law can be expected to lead to the gradual convergence of national requirements but such convergence cannot currently be taken for granted. The ECJ, however, did state that the presumption of innocence must be respected and that, in accordance with Article 6 of the Charter, the executing judicial authority may decide to hold the person concerned in custody only in so far as the procedure for the execution of the European arrest warrant has been carried out in a sufficiently diligent manner and the duration of the detention is not excessive.[99]

In the very recent judgment in *CK*,[100] a five member chamber made a volte face holding that, under Dublin III, the transfer of an asylum seeker to the Member State responsible for examining her application cannot take place where there is a real risk of her suffering inhuman or degrading treatment. The Court departed from the systemic flaws requirement. It held that, where the transfer of an asylum seeker with a particularly serious mental or physical illness would result in a real and proven risk of a significant and permanent deterioration in her state of health, that transfer would constitute inhuman and degrading treatment. The authorities of the Member State were therefore under an obligation to examine the medical evidence and refuse the transfer if it would lead to a violation of Article 4 of the Charter. The judgment is characterized by a rights-based rationale, which is absent in the previous judgments of the Grand Chamber,[101] and close adherence to the Strasbourg case law. In *CK*, the Court founded its reasoning on the absolute nature of the right against inhuman and degrading treatment. Notably, it rejected the Commission's argument that, under Article 3(2) of Dublin III, only the existence of systemic flaws is capable of affecting the obligation to transfer. It held that such a reading would be irreconcilable with the general character of Article 4, which prohibits inhuman or degrading treatment in all its forms, and manifestly incompatible with its absolute nature.[102] Although the Court stressed that Dublin III differed in essential respects from Dublin II, the truth is that the text of the regulation is indeterminate.[103] In essence, the Court recognized that, where it comes to the protection of fundamental human rights, the statutory dispositions are less important, the emphasis being on the constitutional commands, in *casu*, Article 4 of the Charter. The judgment provides a welcome and long overdue rebalancing of the case law.

[99] See *Aranyosi*, paras 99–100 and C-237/15 PPU *Lanigan* EU:C:2015:474, paras 58–60.

[100] *CK, HF, AS v Republica Slovenija*, Case C-578/16 PPU, EU:C:2017:127.

[101] The judgments in *N.S. Abdullahi, Ghezelbash, Karim, Aranyosi,* discussed above, were all judgments of the Grand Chamber.

[102] See para 93.

[103] See above.

CONCLUSIONS

This chapter sought to highlight selected aspects of the interaction between EU competence and fundamental rights protection with particular reference to the principle of mutual recognition in the field of asylum. The following conclusions may be derived from this analysis. First, despite the formalisation of competence rules in the Treaty of Lisbon, the division of competences between the Union and its Member States remains uncertain, fragile and characterised by a significant degree of entropy. Second, although in the post-Lisbon era the protection of fundamental rights can be perceived not only as a constraining force but a positive EU policy, the express enshrinement of rights in legislative dispositions may not necessarily lead to a higher level of protection. Finally, the case law on mutual recognition is characterised by ambivalence. The *NS* line of case law subjects the individuality of rights to the dogma of mutual recognition although subsequent developments may signal a strategic retreat on the part of the Court. *CK* is a welcome rebalancing of the principles of mutual recognition and respect for fundamental rights which should be embraced by the Grand Chamber.

Part III

Practical Perspectives

10

The Exclusive Competences of the European Union: Some Random Jottings

KIERAN BRADLEY*

INTRODUCTION: LAEKEN, LISBON AND THE REBRANDING OF CONFERRAL

AS IS WELL known, the European Union, like the European Communities before it,[1] is based on the principle of conferral, that is, that 'the Union shall act only within the limits of the competences conferred on it by the Member States [and that c]ompetences not conferred on the Union in the Treaties remain with the Member States'.[2] While this was generally understood to be the case, it was not spelt out *expressis verbis* in the founding Community Treaties; for long, it was considered enough that each institution was enjoined to 'act within the limits of the powers conferred upon it by th[e] Treaty', while the Maastricht Treaty extended the same injunction to the Community itself.[3] At the same time, the Maastricht Treaty introduced the idea of the 'exclusive competence' of the Community, without providing any indication of what exactly was intended, nor indeed defining the concept of 'competence' itself.

All changed, changed utterly, with the Treaty of Lisbon; the principle of conferral is now explicitly set down, and repeated several times, in the early titles of the Treaty on the European Union, while the Treaty on the Functioning of the European Union has as one of its two principal *raisons d'être* that of 'determin[ing] the areas,

* Special Advisor to the CJEU, and former judge of the EU Civil Service Tribunal. The views expressed are purely personal and may not be attributed to any institution with which the author is or has been associated.

[1] For the purposes of the present chapter, the term 'Union' will be used throughout, even where this is anachronistic, except where it is necessary to distinguish between this and the European Community/ies.

[2] Art 5(2) TEU.

[3] eg Art 4(1), 2nd subpara, EEC, later Art 7(1), 2nd subpara, EC Treaty; Art 5, 1st subpara, EC.

delimitation of and arrangements for exercising [the] competences' of the Union. Title I of the TFEU sets out 'Categories and Areas of Union Competence'. To this end, Articles 2–6 TFEU list different 'areas' of exclusive, shared and ancillary competences, as well as indicating areas of Union activity which apparently do not fall into any of these categories.

The motivation behind the rebranding of conferral is to be found in the Laeken Declaration of December 2001, in which the European Council give it as its view that '[c]itizens ... sometimes have the impression that the Union takes on too much in areas where its involvement is not essential ... the important thing is to clarify, simplify and adjust the division of competences between the Union and the Member States in the light of the new challenges facing the Union'.[4] Amongst the measures suggested at Laeken in the name of transparency was the introduction of 'a clearer distinction between three types of competence', being 'the exclusive competence of the Union, the competence of the Member States and the shared competence of the Union and the Member States'. This scheme was only partly taken up by the Treaty of Lisbon, which provides for a variety of exclusive, shared and ancillary Union competences. Though the Member States enjoy by default any competences not conferred upon the Union,[5] the Treaties do not seek to identify the categories of Member State competence as such; the European Convention 'bravely attempted to identify areas within the exclusive competence of the Member States, but [the] listed matters ... [were] simply not wholly and inevitably immune from the reach of the EU'.[6] They do, however, enjoin the Union to respect, inter alia, the national identities of the Member States 'inherent in their fundamental structures, political and constitutional' and 'their essential State functions, including ... territorial integrity ... maintaining law and order and safeguarding national security'.[7] This may have been intended at last to institute a 'nucleus of sovereignty which the Member States can invoke' whose inexistence Lenaerts so memorably declared a generation ago.[8]

In line with the invitation of the editors of this volume, the present chapter addresses the question whether the Lisbon reforms have made the division of competences 'clearer, more coherent and better at containing European integration', in respect particularly of competences listed as 'exclusive' in Article 3 TFEU.

[4] Presidency Conclusions, European Council Meeting in Laeken, 14 and 15 December 2001, SN 300/1/01 REV 1, Annex I, page 21.

[5] Art 4(1) TEU.

[6] S Weatherill, 'Competence Creep and Competence Control' (2004) 23 *Yearbook of European Law* 1, 23. This article provides an invaluable guide to the background of the Lisbon Treaty provisions on competences.

[7] Art 4(2) TEU.

[8] K Lenaerts, 'Constitutionalism and the Many Faces of Federalism' (1990) 38 *The American Journal of Comparative Law* 205, 220.

WHY CLASSIFY COMPETENCES?

The classification of legislative[9] competences as exclusive or non-exclusive is a relatively common feature of federal and federal-type constitutions; typically, one level of government has exclusive powers over a list of matters, while sharing power with the other level. Thus in Australia, for example, it is the federal government that is vested with exclusive powers, while in Canada exclusive competence on various matters is held by the provincial legislatures, with the federal government being vested with the residual powers not conferred on the provinces. In the European Union's largest and most influential federal state, the German federal government enjoys exclusive legislative powers in a long list of areas; in these areas, 'the *Länder* shall have power to legislate only when and to the extent they are expressly authorised to do so by a federal law'.[10] A second list indicates the concurrent powers, which the *Länder* may exercise 'so long as and to the extent that the Federation has not exercised its legislative power by enacting a law'; the *Länder* also enjoy the default power to legislate on any matter on which the Basic Law does not confer legislative power on the Federation.[11] In the Belgian variant, each level of government is vested with exclusive powers over different matters.[12]

It has been suggested that 'different types of competence pitch the *relative degree of responsibility of public authorities* within a material policy field' and that 'different competence types must transmit different genetic constitutional codes to "their" legal acts'.[13] The public authorities in question refer essentially to those of the central government and of the constituent states, and it becomes important to be able to distinguish between types of competence in order to know who does what. The classification of the legislative competences of the European Union, and the identification of some of these as 'exclusive', were not foreseen in the original Treaties. In discussing the first reference to a possible classification of competences in the Maastricht Treaty, one author fulminated that the distinction between 'exclusive' and 'non-exclusive' competences was 'totally alien to, and contradicts the logic of, the structure and actual wording of the original EEC Treaty and the jurisprudence of the Court of Justice'.[14] Even in the early days, however,

[9] The present chapter will not examine the question of 'administrative competence', that is the power to implement Union law, which falls in principle to the Member States, subject to certain exceptions (see Arts 290 and 291 TFEU).

[10] Arts 71 and 73, German Basic Law.

[11] Arts 72 and 70, German Basic Law.

[12] See eg P Popelier et al, *Social Federalism—How is a Multi-level Welfare State Best Organised?* (Re-Bel e-book, 9 February 2011).

[13] R Schütze, 'The European Community's Federal Order of Competences—A Retrospective Analysis' in M Dougan and S Currie, *50 Years of the European Treaties* (Oxford, Hart Publishing, 2009) 63, 71 (emphasis in original).

[14] AG Toth, 'A Legal Analysis of Subsidiarity' in D O'Keeffe and P Twomey, *Legal Issues of the Maastricht Treaty* (Chichester, Chancery Law, 1994) 37, 39.

an alternative view, that the Union's competences were in the nature of shared powers, was held in some quarters.[15]

EXCLUSIVE EU COMPETENCES

Origins and Overview

Exclusive competences, which are 'constitutionally guaranteed monopolies' in that '[o]nly one governmental level is entitled to act autonomously',[16] are presumptively the strongest form of power the particular government enjoys. In many systems, the exclusive character of legislative powers may not be presumed. On the grounds that the federal government of the United States enjoyed enumerated rather than plenary powers, for example, its powers were deemed to be exclusive only in three circumstances: where the Constitution expressly so provided, where the states were prohibited from exercising an authority bestowed on the Union not so described, and where the Union was granted an authority 'to which a similar authority in the States would be absolutely and totally contradictory and repugnant'.[17] An exclusive competence 'puts the European [Union] in a very comfortable position and, at the same time, makes the Member States very dependent on it'.[18]

The Court of Justice first introduced the idea of exclusivity into Union law; it did so very sparingly, often without any elaborate explanation of its characterisation of the power in question. In *ERTA*, for example, the Court based its finding on the exclusive character of the Union's competence to conclude an international agreement on road transport on the idea that 'the unity of the Common Market and the uniform application of [Union] law' would be undermined by any autonomous Member State action in this area.[19] Similarly, a concurrent power of the Member States in the area of the common commercial policy would, the Court held in Opinion 1/75, 'risk ... compromising the effective defence of the common interests of the [Union]'.[20] It is unclear if these general considerations could in principle have been extrapolated to render other Union competences exclusive.

The Court's classification, in the *UK Fisheries* case,[21] of the power to regulate the 'conservation of marine biological resources under the common fisheries policy', on the other hand, appears to have been based on a specific Treaty provision, Article 102 of the 1972 Act of Accession. From the indication that after a given

[15] R Schütze, above n 13 at 70–71.

[16] ibid 72.

[17] A Hamilton in I. Kramnick (ed), The Federalist Papers (London, Penguin, 1987) 220.

[18] R Van Ooik, 'The European Court of Justice and the Division of Competences in the European Union' in D Obradovic, and N Lavranos (eds), *Interface between EU Law and National Law* (Groningen, Europa Law Publishing, 2007).

[19] Case 22/70 *Commission v Council* EU:C:1971:32, paras 20, 21 and 31.

[20] Opinion 1/75 *OECD Understanding on a Low Cost Standard* EU:C:1975:145, 1364.

[21] Case 804/79 *Commission v United Kingdom* EU:C:1981:93.

deadline, 'the Council ... shall determine conditions for fishing with a view to ensuring ... conservation of the biological resources of the sea', the Court deduced that 'the power to adopt [such] measures ... belonged fully and definitively to the [Union]'.[22] The mere fact of the expiry of a deadline, if that was indeed the basis of the Court's assessment, seems a somewhat thin reason for claiming exclusivity; in its original version, the EEC Treaty was replete with injunctions to the Council to regulate matters within a given deadline,[23] without the Court's finding that the expiry of the deadline sufficed to render other competences exclusive.

From the point of view of transparency, the term 'exclusive competence' poses three sets of questions: the first concerns the notion of 'competence'; the second concerns the notion of exclusivity; and the third the identification of EU exclusive competences.

What 'Competences' Are We Talking About?

Article 2(1) TFEU defines the notion of 'competence' for the purposes of the application of the Treaties as being the power 'to legislate and adopt legally binding acts', while Articles 3–6 provide lists of categories of competence; the list of exclusive competences set out in Article 3 TFEU is in effect exhaustive, in that any Union competence not listed in any other category is shared, under the default rule of Article 4(1) TFEU.

The list of competences is not even half the story, however; the powers of the Union are not couched in terms of grants of material competence, as are those of the German federal government, for example. They are instead, in Davies' felicitous phrase, 'purposive competences' and not sector-specific competences; the Union thus enjoys 'a power to take measures to achieve a particular goal' rather than being 'defined in terms of a particular field to be regulated'.[24] Of fundamental importance in this regard is the stipulation in Article 2(6) TFEU that '[t]he scope of and arrangements for exercising the Union's competences shall be determined by the provisions of the Treaties relating to each area'. The provisions in question are the specific—or in some cases less specific—legal bases for Union action in a given field of activity.[25] It follows from Article 2(6) TFEU that the Union does not enjoy the plenitude of legislative powers in a given area such as is described in the lists of Articles 3–6 TFEU; instead its competences comprise the aggregate of the powers conferred on the Union by the individual legal bases, which powers

[22] ibid para 17.

[23] As strikingly illustrated in the *Common Transport Policy* case, 13/83, *Parliament v Council* EU:C:1985:220, paras 64–68.

[24] G Davies, 'Democracy and Legitimacy in the Shadow of Purposive Competence' (2015) 21 *European Law Journal* 2, 2.

[25] See eg K Bradley, 'Powers and Procedures in the EU Constitution: Legal Bases and the Court' in P Craig and G de Búrca (eds), *The Evolution of EU Law*, 2nd edn (Oxford, Oxford University Press, 2011) 85–109.

may only be exercised in accordance with the limits, and in conformity with the principles and rules, there provided, as well as any with any general requirements as are applicable, such as proportionality and, except for competences deemed exclusive, subsidiarity.

The situation is therefore different from that which obtains in principle under most familiar national constitutions. Thus when the German Basic Law provides, for example, that 'the Federation shall have exclusive legislative power with respect to … statistics for federal purposes', in principle this provision means what it says: the Basic Law does not provide other material limitations on the scope of the legislative power.[26] However, when Article 3(1)(b) TFEU provides the Union with the exclusive competence for 'the establishment of competition rules necessary for the functioning of the internal market', it does not mean that the Union can adopt all and any such rules, but rather that it may adopt the rules in this area provided for in the relevant Treaty provisions. Thus under Article 103 TFEU, the Union may, indeed must, adopt '[t]he appropriate regulations or directives to give effect to the principles' governing the prohibition of certain anti-competitive behaviour imposed by Articles 101 and 102 TFEU, while Article 109 TFEU provides the equivalent authority for regulations for the application of Articles 107 and 108 TFEU on state aids. While certainly wide, and probably as wide as is required for its purposes, the Union's competence in respect of 'competition rules necessary for the functioning of the internal market' is not necessarily co-extensive with the formulation in Article 3(1)(b) TFEU. Where the Union wishes to adopt rules to eliminate appreciable distortions of the conditions of competition in order to ensure the proper functioning of the internal market, for example, it acts under Article 114 TFEU, which is a shared, not an exclusive, competence, in accordance with Article 4(2) TFEU.[27]

While the exclusive character of a competence is clearly determinative of the possibility of a Member State to legislate autonomously in the given field (that is, none, unless so authorised by the Union),[28] in the European Union constellation the Member States in their capacity as Union institutional actors both individually and collectively in the Council play a major role in determining the content of a Union measure which falls within the category of the Union's exclusive competence, a role which varies in function of the legal basis of the legislative act and the resulting legislative procedure. In the case of monetary policy for the Member States in the Eurozone, for example, this influence goes from the Council acting unanimously at one end of the spectrum, to the ECB acting under its autonomous powers at the other, with other variants in between (ordinary legislative procedure, Council acting by a qualified majority with only an opinion of the European

[26] Art 73(1)11, German Basic Law; the list of exclusive federal competences is in turn subject to the proviso that some are shared by the European Union, but the point is that the *Länder* may not exercise these competences.

[27] Case C-376/98 *Germany v Parliament and Council ('Tobacco Advertising I')* EU:C:2000:544.

[28] See below.

Parliament). In other words, the exclusive character of a Union competence in no way precludes far-reaching influence by the Member States, or indeed a single one of them, on the content of the specific measure.

What Sort of Exclusivity?

As well as defining competence, Article 2(1) TFEU defines the notion of exclusivity as meaning that 'only the Union may exercise that competence', 'the Member States being able to do so themselves only if so empowered by the Union or for the implementation of Union acts'. As Lenaerts and Van Nuffel would have it, exclusive competences are 'those which have been definitively and irreversibly forfeited by the Member States by reason of their straightforward transfer to the Union'.[29] It is important to distinguish this 'constitutional' exclusivity from the pre-emption of the exercise of national power which arises from the exercise by the Union of its legislative powers: '[i]n the context of non-exclusive competences, the constitutional principles of primacy, direct effect, and loyal cooperation … preclude national measures insofar as common rules exist that can conflict with those measures'.[30] Constitutional exclusivity is also different from the restriction on the exercise by the Member States of their competences which arise from their duties under Union law, as illustrated, for example, by the *Rottmann* ruling.[31] In line with relatively well-established case law, the Court here held that 'the fact that a matter falls within the competence of the Member States does not alter the fact that, in situations covered by European Union law, the national rules concerned must have due regard to the latter'.[32] The peculiarity in this case was that Mr Rottmann's situation appears to have been 'covered by European Union law' solely by virtue of his once having had Austrian nationality, which he had lost by committing an act of deception on the authorities of another Member State. Clearly, the notion of 'situations covered by European Union law' is very broad indeed.

Why Are Some Competences Exclusive?

The Treaties do not provide any clear guideline as to the criteria which applied for classifying competences as exclusive or otherwise. In the absence of such a guideline, one would normally look for a pattern in the list of competences actually listed as 'exclusive'. It is generally agreed, however, that the competences listed in

[29] K Lenaerts and Piet Van Nuffel, *European Union Law*, 3rd edn (London, Sweet & Maxwell, 2011) para 7-021, 125.

[30] A Arena, 'Exercise of EU Competence and Pre-emption of Member States' Powers in the Internal Market and the External Sphere: Towards "Grand Unification"?', 35 *Yearbook of European Law* 28, 33; see Art 2(2) TFEU.

[31] Case C-135/08 *Rottmann v Freistaat Bayern* EU:C:2010:104.

[32] ibid para 41.

Article 3(1) TFEU, which are those operating primarily within the internal plane rather than in the domain of external relations, are 'a rather odd assortment of areas'.[33] The necessarily exclusive character of some of these is relatively obvious and uncontested, such as monetary policy for the Eurozone Member States, the common commercial policy and the conservation of marine biological resources under the common fisheries policy. A priori, the customs union between the Member States of the Union is less a grant of legislative power than a fundamental feature of the Union which was originally established by Title I of Part 2 of the EEC Treaty, which prohibited customs duties on imports and exports on intra-Union trade, some of the provisions of which famously had direct effect.[34] In this regard, the Member States had already exercised, in the Treaty itself, their joint competence regarding the setting up of a customs union.[35] The only measures which the customs union chapter now charges the legislature to adopt concern the fixing of the common customs tariffs and measures to strengthen customs co-operation between the Member States amongst themselves and between the Member States and the Commission.

Some commentators have expressed surprise at the classification of 'the establishment of competition rules necessary for the functioning of the internal market' as an exclusive competence, given that it 'found no support in the previous case law of the Court of Justice'.[36] More precisely, according to Dougan, '[i]nsofar as [Article 3 TFEU] purports to represent a statement of the [pre-Lisbon] law, it is surely incorrect … [as] the Court had held in *Walt Wilhelm* that [Articles 102 and 103 TFEU] are areas of shared competence in which [Union] and national competition laws co-exist', and the reference to competition law should be deleted from this provision.[37] Under another view, however, the restriction to rules which are necessary for the internal market leaves the Member States free to take legislative action themselves with respect to situations that fall outside 'competition rules necessary for the functioning of the internal market and also 'to implement the Union rules on competition'.[38] In any event, the Court of Justice took the first opportunity to confirm the exclusive character of this competence, albeit that it did so by merely citing Article 3(1)(b) TFEU.[39]

One matter which merits special mention, not least because of its topicality, amongst the Union's exclusive competences is that to conclude an agreement whereby a Member State leaves the European Union, in accordance with Article 50 TEU. In the case of accession, the decision to admit a new Member State is taken by

[33] S Weatherill, *Law and Values in the European Union* (Oxford, Oxford University Press, 2016) 25.

[34] See in particular Case 26/62 *Van Gend en Loos* EU:C:1963:1.

[35] See also Arts 10–20 EEC, and now Art 30 TFEU.

[36] LS Rossi, 'Does the Lisbon Treaty Provide a Clearer Separation of Competences between EU and Member States?' in A Biondi et al, *EU Law after Lisbon* (Oxford, Oxford University Press, 2012) 85, 99.

[37] M Dougan, 'The Convention's draft Constitutional Treaty: bringing Europe closer to its lawyers?' (2003) *European Law Review* 763, 771.

[38] K Lenaerts and Pieter Van Nuffel, above n 29, para 7-021, 126.

[39] Case C-550/07 P *AkzoNobel Chemicals and Akcros Chemicals v Commission* EU:C:2010:512, para 116.

the Council, acting unanimously, while the agreement setting out the conditions of admission and the necessary adjustments to the Treaties is concluded between the existing Member States and the acceding state and is subject to national ratification. Conversely, the agreement laying down the arrangements for a Member State's withdrawal from the Union is concluded exclusively by the Union, 'in accordance with Article 218(3) TFEU',[40] and is not subject to national ratification, notwithstanding its constitutional character and wide-ranging repercussions. While such an agreement might be said to 'affect common rules or alter their scope' in the sense of the third limb of Article 3(2) TFEU, right up to the moment this agreement comes into force, it is an act of Union law, being an agreement between the Union and a Member State, rather than a pure international agreement between the Union and a third State or another international organisation. The 'framework for [the] future relationship' between the Union and the exiting Member State is, on the other hand, an 'ordinary' international agreement with what will by then be a third State.

HAVE THE LAEKEN GOALS BEEN ACHIEVED?

Transparency

The question under this heading is whether the new division of competences is clearer, that is, more transparent for the citizen, as was intended by the authors of the Laeken Declaration. In practice, the competences listed in Article 3 TFEU appear to be 'exclusive' in the same way as a 'secret' is something that you tell one other person.

In the first place, having given with one hand by defining exclusivity, Article 2(1) TFEU takes away with the other, by providing that the Union may empower the Member States to legislate and adopt legal acts in areas of so-called exclusive competence; Article 3 competences thus only enjoy a qualified exclusivity. This is not entirely new and may in many circumstances be justified as being preferable to a doctrinaire prevention of the adoption of any regulatory action at all. One of the best examples is the *UK Fisheries* case, where the Court first held that the Union enjoyed exclusive competence to lay down fishing quotas as part of the common fisheries policy.[41] However, the Union had in fact been unable to adopt the necessary measures because of the United Kingdom's stubborn opposition to the Commission's proposals, combined with the Council's inability to shake off the shackles of the Luxembourg Compromise and its own dependence on the habit of unanimity. The Court rejected any suggestion that the powers might

[40] Opinion is divided on whether Art 218 TFEU as a whole applies to the negotiation of this agreement, except for those matters specifically regulated in Art 50 TEU, or whether Art 218(3) TFEU is the only provision which applies, leaving the institutions free to make other arrangements.

[41] Case 804/79, above n 21.

revert to the Member States even in part, holding that the Union must 'retain in all circumstances its capacity to comply with its responsibilities, subject to the observance of the essential balances intended by the Treaty'.[42] Given the objective urgency of some conservation measures, it did, however, allow that Member States could act, but only 'as trustees of the common interest' and under the close supervision of the Commission.[43]

In more modern times, Council Regulation (EC) No 664/2009 provides a less dramatic, and more sweeping, example of the Member States being authorised to act in an area of the Union's exclusive competences.[44] It allows the Member States to amend existing international agreements with third States, or conclude new agreements, relating to matters such as jurisdiction and choice of law in a number of family law matters; as noted in the preamble, '[s]uch agreements, of which there is a large number, often respect special ties between a Member State and a third country and are intended to provide an adequate legal framework to meet specific needs of the parties concerned'.[45] It is also clear that the conclusion of agreements at the Union level with the individual third States concerned was not necessarily a priority, especially given the large number of states concerned. It is interesting to note that the Regulation was adopted some months before the Lisbon Treaty formalised this possibility in a provision of primary law.

Second, the Union's exclusive competence to conclude international agreements under Article 3(2) TFEU only arises under certain conditions, some of which at least require quite an effort of interpretation on the part of the institutions. Thus, for example, it will not always be obvious to the citizen whether and to what extent the Union is justified in claiming exclusive competence to conclude an agreement on the grounds that it is 'necessary to enable [it] to exercise its internal competence' or that the conclusion of such an agreement 'may affect common rules or alter their scope'. Such questions regularly generate sophisticated, and no doubt well-justified, debates amongst lawyers and judges; for the informed citizen, however, these exclusive competences must appear both conditional and qualified.

But it gets worse: the European Commission on occasion gives the impression that the classification of the Union's competences is a matter of choice rather than resulting from the application of Treaty rules. Such was the case in particular of the Comprehensive Economic and Trade Agreement with Canada or 'CETA', which was originally touted, and indeed negotiated, as being a matter of the Union's exclusive competence. In July 2016, however, the Commission underwent a Pauline conversion, sort of. In a press release, the Commissioner responsible, Mrs Maelström, stated that '[f]rom a strict legal standpoint, the Commission considers this agreement to fall under exclusive EU competence. However, the

[42] ibid para 23.
[43] ibid para 30.
[44] OJ 2009 L200/46.
[45] Preamble to Regulation (EC) No 664/2009, para 2.

political situation in the Council is clear, and we understand the need for proposing it as a "mixed" agreement, in order to allow for a speedy signature'.[46] While the political, and even legal,[47] reasons behind the Commission's flip-flop might be sound, the citizen might be forgiven for thinking that the exclusive character of some of the Union's competences is qualified, conditional and optional.

Finally, while it may be more a theoretical than a real risk, there is still room for a clash between the exercise of exclusive competences and the requirement in Article 4(2) TEU that the Union respect the national identities of the Member States 'inherent in their fundamental [governmental] structures' and their essential State functions. This provision has on occasion been relied upon in the case law as a curb on the application of the *Rottmann* doctrine to the exercise of Member States competences, but it could also be employed as a limitation on the exercise, or possibly even to challenge the existence, of an exclusive Union competence to regulate a given matter.[48]

Beyond the Treaty provisions, the citizen's comprehension of 'exclusive competence' may be made even more difficult by the practice of the institutions in other areas. Thus the Union sometimes exercises non-exclusive competences acting on its own, for example, in the fields of development co-operation and even the CFSP, as if these were for all intents and purposes exclusive.[49] Then there are circumstances where a Member State may not, for reasons pertaining to its obligations under EU law, exercise its competences in an area of shared competence, even though the Union has not exercised its share of the competence. One striking example is *Commission v Sweden*,[50] where Sweden had proposed the listing of a particular chemical under an international convention on organic pollutants, at a time when the Union had not yet exercised its competence to make such a proposal. The Court held that where competence to conclude a given agreement was shared, 'it is essential to ensure close cooperation between the Member States and the [Union] institutions … [t]hat obligation to cooperate flows from the requirement of unity in the international representation of the Union'.[51] Sweden was found to have dissociated itself from a 'concerted common strategy within the Council' in relation to the listing of the chemicals concerned and thereby to have breached its general duty of Union solidarity.[52]

The contribution to transparency of the categorisation of competences may be further mitigated in practice by the necessity to adopt a measure which falls within two distinct categories of competence at the same time, for reasons pertaining to

[46] 'European Commission proposes signature and conclusion of EU-Canada trade deal', Strasbourg, 5 July 2016.

[47] See Opinion 2/15, *EU-Singapore Free Trade Agreement*, EU:C:2017:376.

[48] eg T Konstadinides, *Dealing with Parallel Universes: Antinomies of Sovereignty and the Protection of National Identity in European Judicial Discourse* (2015) 34 *Yearbook of European Law* 127.

[49] M Cremona, 'EU External Competences', this volume, Chapter 8.

[50] Case C-246/07, EU:C:2010:203.

[51] ibid para 73.

[52] Then under Art 10 EC, and now in a slightly modified form, Art 4(3), 2nd and 3rd paras, TEU.

the choice of legal basis. According to the established case law, where a measure 'simultaneously pursues a number of objectives, or has several components, which are inextricably linked without one being incidental to the other, such that various provisions of the Treaty are applicable, such a measure will have to be founded on the various legal bases corresponding to those components'.[53]

One example is Directive 2014/104/EU, which lays down rules to facilitate the recovery in the Member States' courts, in particular by private parties, of damages for breaches of national and Union competition law.[54] At first blush, this might be considered a measure within the Union's exclusive competence *par excellence*, as it indubitably contains 'competition rules necessary for the functioning of the internal market'. As noted in the preamble to the Directive, the proper enforcement of these rules is 'a matter of public policy … in order to ensure that competition in the internal market is not distorted'; their harmonisation is justified by the need to avoid 'the divergence of applicable rules, which could jeopardise the proper functioning of the internal market'.[55] However, because the content of the Directive goes beyond merely giving effect to the principles of the Treaty rules on private sector competition (cartels and abuse of a dominant position), for instance by modifying national rules concerning the right to claim damages, the legislature felt obliged—very plausibly[56]—to base the directive on both Article 103 TFEU (exclusive competence) and Article 114 TFEU (shared competence). At the end of the day, it is the legal basis of a measure, rather than the categorisation of competences in Articles 2 to 6 TFEU, which indicates its real character.

Coherence[57]

The list of so-called 'exclusive competences' set out exhaustively in Article 3 TFEU reflects partly the case law of the Court of Justice and partly the imagination of the authors of the Lisbon Treaty. Given that the criterion of 'exclusivity' is the dividing line between the application of the subsidiarity principle and all that that entails, to say nothing of the technique of enhanced co-operation, the absence from the list of certain matters which a priori might be considered exclusive raises the question of the coherence of the exercise of putting competences into little boxes labelled 'exclusive', 'shared' or ancillary, with some competences which do not fit in any box.

[53] Case C-263/14 *Parliament v Council ('Tanzania Agreement')* EU:C:2016:435, para 44.

[54] OJ 2014 L349/1.

[55] Preamble to Directive 2014/104, recitals 1 and 6 respectively.

[56] The Commission's justification for proposing the double legal basis is set out in some detail in COM(2013) 404 final, 11 June 2013, section 3.1, 8–10.

[57] Some of the problems discussed under 'transparency' above result from a certain lack of coherence in the Treaty scheme.

To take one example, the division of jurisdiction between the Court of Justice and the General Court, and the reform of the European Union judicature generally,[58] do not come within the four corners of Article 3(1) TFEU, despite falling within what Schütze has called 'the spectrum of naturally exclusive ... organisational powers of an international organisation'.[59] It is difficult to see how the Member States could achieve the Union objectives of Court reform other than by Union action, or how the national parliaments can usefully consider whether the objectives of the reform of the Union courts 'cannot be sufficiently achieved by the Member States'. The application of enhanced co-operation to modify the provisions governing the functioning of an institution which serves the common good of the Union is even more anomalous to contemplate.

Competence Creep

It has been suggested that while the Lisbon division of competences was designed to 'contain European integration', the establishment in primary law of a list of exclusive competences could be responsible for further competence creep. This term has been compared[60] with its military equivalent, mission creep, which may be defined as 'the expansion of a project or mission beyond its original goals, often after initial successes. Mission creep is usually considered undesirable due to the dangerous path of each success breeding more ambitious attempts, only stopping when a final, often catastrophic, failure occurs.' It might well be conceded that success has bred ambition in the context of the European Union; that said, however, it would be difficult to pinpoint how the expansion of its competences, including its exclusive competences, has been responsible for any 'final catastrophic failures'. Indeed, some of the current failures of the Union might well arise because of its lack of competence, or its possible failure to exercise competences it has, in certain areas, such as economic policy, or in relation to the migration crisis. Even the planned withdrawal of the United Kingdom from the European Union was not in any significant sense motivated by a deep-seated rejection of the expansion of the Union's competences; well before the referendum, the United Kingdom government conducted a thorough examination of the state of the Union's competences which apply to that Member State and concluded that, for the most part, the correct balance had been struck.[61]

While is true that the idea of 'containment' was present in the minds of the authors of the Lisbon Treaty, the Laeken Declaration balanced the need to 'ensure

[58] Art 281(2) TFEU.

[59] R Schütze, 'Dual federalism constitutionalised: the emergence of exclusive competences in the EC legal order' (2007) *European Law Review* 3, 5.

[60] M Accetto, 'In and Out of Sight: On Uncultivated Growth of EU Competences', Lisbon 2016, 9.

[61] See www.gov.uk/government/news/final-reports-in-review-of-eu-balance-of-competences-published.

that a redefined division of competence does not lead to a creeping expansion of the competence of the Union' and the objective of 'ensur[ing] at the same time that the European dynamic does not come to a halt'. In this sense, 'the Laeken Declaration launched a judicious enquiry, not a witch-hunt'.[62] Moreover, as has been noted, much of the debate concerning the competence problem is based on the 'inarticulate premise that the shift in power [towards the Union] is the result primarily of some unwarranted arrogation of power by the EU institutions to the detriment of States' rights'. This premise is in fact quite erroneous; the expansion of Union competences is largely due to the 'conscious decision of the Member States', as well as the purposive interpretation by the institutions of the competences they were granted.[63]

Arguably, however, the success of the Union—such as it is—is to a very large extent due to its dynamism. The ideas of progress, improvement, development and expansion, or in a slogan, an 'ever closer Europe', were built into the Union's DNA, going back as far as the preamble to the EEC Treaty and its repeated appeals to these and similar notions of dynamism. The extent to which the Court of Justice was, or should have been, faithful to the traditional rules of Treaty interpretation when it laid down the constitutional foundations of the Union, is a matter of argument. But it seems tolerably clear that had the Court gone the other way—no direct effect of Treaty provisions, no primacy of EU law, no implied powers or exclusive competence—its judgments on these matters could quickly have consigned the Treaty of Rome to the dustbin of history.

CONCLUSION: A QUESTION PERPETUALLY ARISING?

So, has the 'competence question' finally been resolved?

In the first place, the jury is still out on the question of whether the ossification of the categories of Union competences, particularly in relation to those deemed exclusive, is necessarily a good thing. Arguably the Court only recognised the exclusive character of a small number of, albeit important, competences on the basis of a perceived need to preclude Member State action, where this would render Union action ineffective.[64] Should such a need arise in the future, the Lisbon scheme would prevent any re-classification of a shared or ancillary competence as 'exclusive'.

Moreover, the approach of the Lisbon Treaty to clarification, coherence and, especially, containment of competences appears to be based primarily on the proliferation of legal principles and rules. However, these principles and rules will be applied by the same institutional actors as are held to be responsible for the

[62] S Weatherill, above n 6.

[63] P Craig, *The Treaty of Lisbon* (Oxford, Oxford University Press, 2010) 156.

[64] J-P Jacqué, *Droit institutionnel de l'Union européenne*, 7th edn (Paris, Dalloz, 2012) para 23.

problem in relation to the extent and implementation of the Union's competences in the first place, to wit, the Member States acting in the Council, even unanimously,[65] and the other Union institutions, including the Court of Justice. In respect of the implementation of exclusive competences, even the limited safeguard of the subsidiarity mechanism wielded by the national parliaments does not apply. It is not, however, clear that the vesting in the Union of a small range of exclusive competences constitutes a major problem. Even the German Federal Constitutional Court—not noted for its enthusiasm for competence creep—has shown a certain tolerance for the Union's 'tendency of political self-enhancement', for example, via reliance on implied powers.[66]

At the end of the day, perhaps we are obliged to fall back on the enduring wisdom of Chief Justice John Marshall in *M'Culloch v Maryland*, a judgment of the US Supreme Court handed down almost two centuries ago:

> [t]his government is acknowledged by all to be one of enumerated powers ... the question concerning the extent of the powers actually granted, is perpetually arising, and will probably continue to arise, as long as our system continues to exist.[67]

The idea is not that we should give up trying to solve the competence question, but that we should be suitably modest in our expectations of succeeding.

[65] Weatherill, above n 6.

[66] Decision of 30 June 2009, 2 BvE 2/08, quoted in K Reuter, 'Competence Creep via the Duty of Loyalty', doctoral thesis, European University Institute, Florence, May 2013, 53.

[67] 4 Wheat 316, 4 L Ed 579 (1819).

11

The Lisbon Treaty's Competence Arrangement Viewed from European Commission Practice

KAREN BANKS*

ISSUES OF EXCLUSIVE or shared competence—and indeed the question whether the EU has any competence at all over a given matter—figure largely in the daily work of the Commission. From fisheries to public health matters, from disputes with Member States over whether a proposed international agreement is covered by the exclusive EU competence for trade matters, to the question whether and how the EU can step back from full harmonisation of a sector in order to restore a competence to the Member States, questions touching on competence arise constantly, and are the subject matter of vigorous debates both internally and with the other institutions.

EXCLUSIVE COMPETENCE

Two areas of exclusive EU competence which the Commission constantly seeks to safeguard are those relating to trade and the conservation of marine biological resources under the common fisheries policy.

As regards trade, the EU has built up a consolidated practice, based on its exclusive competence for the common commercial policy as set out in Article 3(1)(e) TFEU, of negotiating and concluding international trade agreements as a bloc. This exclusive competence implies that Member States are not free to act independently of the EU in negotiating any trade agreement on their own behalf. The fact that the EU has no agreement in place with a given third country does not entitle a Member State to act in that area. The enormous benefits accruing from negotiating with one voice on behalf of a 28-member Union have generally led the Member States to respect this exclusive competence. However, it regularly happens that what is essentially a trade agreement also contains certain non-trade dimensions,

* Karen Banks is Deputy Director-General in the Legal Service of the European Commission, in charge of "Quality of Legislation, Infringements and Information". The views presented in this article are those of the author alone and do not represent an official position of the European Commission.

such as provisions on research or technological development, or else provisions concerning the enforcement of the agreement through the adoption of measures such as seizure and confiscation of goods. Member States frequently insist that such provisions warrant national (Member State) participation since they are allegedly not covered by the common commercial policy, but rather pertain to retained national competences. The implications are serious, since in such cases the agreement will be considered 'mixed' and Member States will not allow the EU to conclude the agreement in question alone. Rather, they will insist that they too, as sovereign States, must ratify it in parallel. Long discussions inevitably ensue as to whether the matters in question are really independent aims of the agreement or whether they are rather auxiliary or instrumental to the main (trade) purpose being pursued. Where no agreement is arrived at, the matter may end up in court.

For instance, in Case C-137/12, the Commission sued the Council because the latter had refused to accept the trade legal basis (Article 207(4) TFEU in combination with Article 218(5) TFEU) as the appropriate one for the decision on the signing of the European Convention on the legal protection of services based on, or consisting of, conditional access.[1] The aim of the Convention was to ensure a similar minimum level of protection of the services concerned across Europe. The EU already had harmonised rules ensuring such protection on its territory, and its purpose in signing the Convention was to extend the application of similar provisions across the European continent, with a view to promoting the supply of such services beyond its borders by EU service providers. In spite of the clear connection with international trade in services, the Council and a number of intervening Member States took the view that the Convention was designed to prevent the export of illicit devices to the EU from other European countries in order to ensure the proper functioning of the internal market, and that therefore the proper legal basis was Article 114 TFEU. The Court rejected this approach, pointing out that such an objective fell, by its very nature, within the ambit of the common commercial policy. It also rejected the argument that provisions of the Convention relating to seizure and confiscation measures were matters justifying Member State competence, since those provisions were purely instrumental to the main objective of the Convention, and did not constitute separate aims in themselves. The Court concluded that the contested decision pursued a primary aim connected to the common commercial policy whereas the improvement of conditions for the functioning of the internal market was an ancillary objective which provided no justification for Article 114 as a legal basis. It also confirmed that the signing of the Convention on behalf of the EU fell within the exclusive competence of the EU.

Occasionally, the Commission asks the Court for an opinion pursuant to Article 218(11) TFEU in order to ascertain whether a given agreement can be concluded by the EU alone. It has done so quite recently in relation to the proposed Free Trade Agreement with Singapore.[2] There are a number of provisions in that

[1] Case C-137/12 *European Commission v Council of the European Union* [2013] 275.
[2] Case A-2/15.

agreement, for instance those relating to portfolio investments, in relation to which the Commission takes the view that they fall within the ambit of the common commercial policy, but the Member States do not agree and insist that the agreement should be concluded both on behalf of the EU and by the Member States.

Contention as to whether an agreement is to be qualified as 'mixed', with the resulting requirement for Member State participation, is not limited to situations where the substance of the agreement straddles both matters of exclusive Union competence and (allegedly) retained national competence. Recourse to a 'mixed' agreement may also be advocated by Member States on political grounds where an agreement includes matters of shared competence, such as transport. In legal terms, nothing would prevent the Union from concluding the agreement in question, since it has a (shared) competence for transport which it could exercise by concluding the agreement. However, Member States are generally reluctant to accept that the EU can exercise a competence on the international level unless it has already done so very thoroughly in an internal EU context (ie by legislating at EU level).[3] They will thus insist that, as soon as matters of shared competence are included in an agreement, the agreement in question must be ratified by them as well as by the EU. This of course leads to very considerable delay in the coming into force of the agreement under consideration.

As for the exclusive EU competence for fisheries matters provided for in Article 3(1)(d) TFEU, this exclusive competence is of long standing. In Joined Cases 3, 4 and 6/76 *Kraemer and others*[4] the Court said:

> The only way to ensure the conservation of the biological resources of the sea both effectively and equitably is through a system of rules binding on all the States concerned, including non-member countries. In these circumstances it follows from the very duties and powers which Community law has established and assigned to the institutions of the Community on the internal level that the Community has authority to enter into international commitments for the conservation of the resources of the sea.

The Court went on to make it clear that the existence of the common fisheries policy led to an obligation for the Member States to take all action necessary to ensure that the Community (as it then was) could accede to any international fisheries agreement which was of strategic interest for it.

Since then, the Commission has negotiated on behalf of the EU a myriad of bilateral fisheries agreements with different third countries. The EU is a member of 14 different regional fisheries management organisations covering the principal oceans of the world, and it generally exercises considerable influence in those organisations thanks to the effect of speaking with one voice on behalf of the

[3] For an example of the Court's approach to assessing whether a provision of an international agreement falls within the scope of Union competence (namely Art 33 of the TRIPs Agreement), see Case C-431/05 *Merck Genéricos—Produtos Farmacêuticos L^{da} v Merck & Co Inc and Merck Sharp & Dohme L^{da}* EU:C:2007:496 paras 34–48.

[4] Joined Cases 3, 4 and 6/76 *Cornelis Kramer and others* [1976] 114.

whole EU. However, over the years the importance of environmental policy has been growing, and the conservation of natural resources is of course at the heart of that policy. This makes for controversy as regards the conservation of marine biological resources: are they to be protected, as they traditionally have been, under the common fisheries policy, implying a balance between conservation and the preservation of the livelihoods of fishermen, or are they now to be seen as part of the natural heritage of the world, to be protected for their own sake?

Member States make regular efforts to argue that a given international agreement aiming at the conservation of marine biological resources falls under environmental rather than fisheries policy, thus enabling them to put forward initiatives within the framework of that agreement, on the basis that environmental matters come within the area of competences shared between them and the EU. For instance, in the context of whaling, Member States have insisted on the use of the environmental legal basis rather than the fisheries one for the establishment of positions to be adopted by the Union in the framework of the International Whaling Commission. Moreover, even though the EU—wearing its 'fisheries' hat, and acting on the basis of Article 43 TFEU—is a member of the International Commission for the Conservation of Atlantic Tunas (ICCAT)—Germany chose last year to sponsor a recommendation on blue fin tuna in the context of the Convention for the Protection of the Marine Environment of the North East Atlantic, an environmental organisation.

Needless to say, this raised eyebrows in ICCAT, and risked creating doubt as to the commitment of the EU to that organisation. Such initiatives not only result in massive energy having to be invested in protesting with the offending Member State, making representations to other Member States as to the lack of wisdom and legality of such demarches, and diplomatic efforts behind the scenes in order to limit the effects of the initiative in question, such activities on the part of Member States naturally also undermine the united image which it is desirable for the Union to have in international regional fisheries organisations in order to enable it to defend EU interests in the most effective way.

The effects of the exclusive EU competence for the conservation of marine biological resources in the framework of the common fisheries policy are also felt on the internal level. Pursuant to Article 2(1) TFEU, Member States are prohibited from legislating or adopting legally binding acts in areas of exclusive EU competence, unless they are empowered to do so by the Union or they do so in order to implement EU acts. Thus, when the United Kingdom wanted to protect a coral reef in its territorial waters by banning fishing activities in that area, it had to request the Commission to propose the necessary measures. In the same vein, in order to allow Member States some freedom to adopt fisheries measures in their 12-mile zones, the basic fisheries regulation has traditionally provided for this. Article 5(2) of Regulation 1380/2013[5] (the current Basic Regulation) allows the Member States to impose certain restrictions on access to those waters.

[5] Regulation (EU) No 1380/2013 of the European Parliament and of the Council of 11 December 2013 on the Common Fisheries Policy, amending Council Regulations (EC) No 1954/2003 and (EC)

Another area of exclusive EU competence is that of monetary policy for the Member States whose currency is the euro (Article 3(1)(c) TFEU). The constraints this exclusivity implies for independent Member State action—including joint action outside the mechanisms provided for by the Treaty—came into focus in the context of the Treaty establishing the European Stability Mechanism (ESM). This Treaty, under which the Member States having the euro as their currency established an international financial institution with the purpose of mobilising funding and providing stability support under strict conditionality for the benefit of euro area Member States experiencing, or threatened by, severe financial difficulties, was challenged in the *Pringle* case.[6] Mr Pringle also attacked the decision amending Article 136 TFEU, the purpose of the amendment being to confirm the possibility for euro area Member States to set up a mechanism such as the ESM 'if indispensable to safeguard the stability of the euro area as a whole'. In its intervention before the Court, the Commission insisted that neither the amendment to Article 136 nor the ESM Treaty itself encroached on the EU competence for monetary policy. As for the area of economic policy, the Treaties do not provide for an exclusive competence for the setting up of a permanent mechanism such as the ESM. The Court had already established in the past[7] that, in the absence of an exclusive EU competence, the Member States were free to exercise their own retained competences collectively, outside the Treaty structures. The Court maintained that line in Pringle, only insisting—as the Commission had done—that, in so acting, the Member States must comply with EU law, that is, they must not exercise their competence in contradiction with EU rules. It is clear from para 52 of the Court's judgment that, had the Court considered that the amendment of Article 136 granted the Member States a competence in the area of monetary policy, that would have encroached on the Union's exclusive competence as laid down in Article 3(1)(c) TFEU and could not have been adopted via the simplified procedure provided for Article 48(6) TEU.

SHARED COMPETENCES

In the areas of shared competence, the controversies which arise obviously do not concern the question whether Member States are in principle free to act, but rather whether their action is, *in concreto*, compatible with EU law. Two agricultural cases may serve to illustrate the point. In Case C-47/09,[8] the Commission sued Italy

No 1224/2009 and repealing Council Regulations (EC) No 2371/2002 and (EC) No 639/2004 and Council Decision 2004/585/EC (OJ L 354, 28 December 2013, 22).

[6] Case C-370/12 *Thomas Pringle v Government of Ireland, Ireland and The Attorney General* [2012] 756.

[7] Joined Cases C-181/91 and C-248/91 *European Parliament v Council of the European Communities and Commission of the European Communities* (Bangladesh Case) [1993] 271; Case C-316/91 *European Parliament v Council of the European Union* (EDF case) [1994] 76.

[8] Case C-47/09 *European Commission v Italian Republic* [2010] 714.

for permitting the expression 'pure chocolate' to be used to describe chocolate produced using only cocoa butter by way of vegetable fat, whereas the relevant EU legislation had harmonised the permissible sales names for chocolate in such a way that the addition of the word 'pure' was not allowed. The Court upheld the Commission's position. In Case C-333/14,[9] on the other hand, in the context of a national regime imposing a minimum unit price for the retail selling of wines in view of reducing consumption, the Court found that, while such a regime ran counter to the philosophy of the free formation of prices which characterised the common market organisation (CMO) for wine, a Member State was nevertheless free to pursue an objective relating to the general interest other than those aimed at by the CMO. The objective of protecting human life and health could thus justify a measure which undermined the system, on which the CMO for wine is founded, of free formation of prices in conditions of effective competition, subject of course to respect for the principle of proportionality. A Member State must thus weigh the objectives of the CMO against the purpose pursued by the national legislation, in order to strike a fair balance.

Another issue which has arisen in the context of shared competences is the possibility for the Union to undo an existing harmonisation of legislation, in order to restore competence to Member States in a given area. Article 2(2) TFEU indicates that this must be possible, since it provides that 'Member States shall again exercise their competence to the extent that the Union has decided to cease exercising its competence'.

However, the first attempt by the Commission to restore competence to Member States pursuant to this provision showed how difficult such an exercise can be.

Considerable controversy had arisen surrounding the EU regime for the authorisation of genetically modified organisms (GMOs). Directive 2001/18/EC of the European Parliament and of the Council of 12 March 2001 on the deliberate release into the environment of genetically modified organisms and repealing Council Directive 90/220/EEC[10] and Regulation (EC) No 1829/2003 of the European Parliament and of the Council of 22 September 2003 on genetically modified food and feed[11] establish a comprehensive legal framework for the authorisation of GMOs, which was fully applicable to GMOs to be used for cultivation purposes throughout the EU as seeds or other plant-propagating material. Under this set of legislation, GMOs for cultivation undergo an individual risk assessment before being authorised to be placed on the Union market. The aim of this authorisation procedure is to ensure a high level of protection of human life and health, animal health and welfare, the environment and consumer interests, whilst ensuring the effective functioning of the internal market.

[9] Case C-333/14 *Scotch Whisky Association and Others v The Lord Advocate and The Advocate General for Scotland* [2015] 845.

[10] OJ L 106, 17 April 2001, 1.

[11] OJ L 268, 18 October 2003, 1.

Once a GMO is authorised for cultivation purposes in accordance with the EU legislative framework on GMOs and complies, as regards the variety that is to be placed on the market, with the requirements of EU legislation on the marketing of seed and plant-propagating material, Member States are not authorised to prohibit, restrict or impede its free circulation within their territory, except under the conditions defined by EU legislation. Obviously, a ban on cultivating GMOs would have qualified as such a restriction.

The problem was that a considerable number of Member States did not want to allow the cultivation of GMOs on their territory. However, the only possibility they had to prevent this, once a GMO had been authorised under the EU legislation, was to invoke a provision which allowed them to adopt emergency measures where an authorised GMO was likely to constitute a serious risk to human health, animal health or the environment.[12] The Court clarified in Joined Cases C-58/10 and C-68/10 *Monsanto*[13] that this provision could only be relied on where new evidence (that is, evidence discovered after the EU harmonisation) based on reliable scientific data showed that there was a significant risk which clearly jeopardised human health, animal health or the environment. In spite of these rules, a number of Member States adopted emergency measures without sufficient evidence to justify them. The Commission's efforts to have such measures revoked were rejected by the Council under the then-existing comitology procedure. Subsequently, a group of 13 Member States called on the Commission to prepare proposals to give freedom to Member States to decide on cultivation of GMOs.[14] Meanwhile, the authorisation process for GMOs was in difficulty, as the Member States were divided in their philosophies on the matter, so that it was impossible to obtain a qualified majority vote one way or the other.

In July 2010, the Commission made a proposal to amend Directive 2001/18/EC by inserting a provision which would have allowed Member States to restrict or prohibit the cultivation on their territories of GMOs which had been authorised at EU level, but only on grounds other than those of health or the environment, since these would have been fully considered in the EU authorisation process. The idea was to leave the EU-level marketing authorisation intact, and simply to expand the possibilities for Member States to prevent the cultivation of GMOs on their territories.

Since the directive being amended was based on Article 95 EC, the new proposal was based on the corresponding provision following the entry into force of the Lisbon Treaty, namely Article 114 TFEU. The Commission took the view that, since the text 'resulting' from the amendment proposed would clearly benefit the

[12] Some Member States also relied on Art 114(5) TFEU, which similarly allows a Member State to notify the Commission of measures which it deems it necessary to introduce on duly justified scientific grounds, due to a problem specific to that Member State arising after the adoption of a harmonisation measure.

[13] Joined Cases C-58/10 and C-68/10 *Monsanto SAS and Others v Ministre de l'Agriculture et de la Pêche* [2011] 553.

[14] This took place in Council discussions from March to June 2009.

functioning of the internal market, its recourse to Article 114 TFEU as legal basis was fully justified. It also explained, in the Explanatory Memorandum accompanying the proposal, that it was the fact that Member States had no margin of appreciation on cultivation of GMOs which had led several of them to vote against authorisation on non-scientific grounds, and which had caused a number of them to invoke available safeguard clauses, or to use the special notification procedure provided for in Article 114(5) TFEU, as ways to prohibit the cultivation of GMOs at national level. The Council Legal Service, however, took the view that this was insufficient to warrant the use of Article 114 as legal basis. It first raised the interesting question as to whether the legislator is entitled to use Article 114 TFEU in order to reduce the level of harmonisation already achieved. Without insisting on this point, it went on to consider that, in any event, Article 114 could only be used if the purpose of the amendment was to 'improve' the functioning of the internal market, and apparently it did not consider the issues of difficulties in obtaining approvals of GMOs, and the repeated adoption of unjustified emergency measures by Member States, to be problems for the internal market which could be remedied by the proposal under consideration.

Needless to say, the Commission did not accept this position. In a Staff Working Document,[15] its services explained that the theory of parallelism of forms justifies using the legal basis of the act being modified in order to modify it. It further pointed out that requiring a measure which seeks to hand back competence to Member States to fulfil in itself the requirements normally associated with a given legal basis could actually make it excessively difficult to fulfil the intention of the authors of the Lisbon Treaty as expressed in Article 2(2) TFEU, last sentence, that the Union should be able to decide to cease exercising a competence, and to leave the terrain in question free for occupation by the Member States. Since the intention to 'undo' legislation is in principle the contrary of the purpose expressed to be the aim of most legal bases, too demanding an approach would risk making it impossible to find an appropriate legal basis for many acts of 'handing back competence'. If Article 352 had to be used, unanimity would be required. Since Article 2(2) does not provide a legal basis for the EU to act, it seems reasonable to suppose that, where the EU legislator decides to cease exercising a competence, it is intended to do so on the basis of the very provision which formed the legal basis of the harmonisation it now seeks to undo.

In any event, the Commission was willing to add further recitals to its proposal in order to spell out its argument that, *pace* the lack of need to show that the proposed amendment fulfilled in itself the requirements of Article 114 TFEU, as a matter of fact allowing Member States more flexibility as regards cultivation of GMOs on their territory would help to smooth the process of authorisation of GMOs and prevent the adoption of unjustified emergency measures, all of which would facilitate the smooth functioning of the internal market. In the outcome,

[15] SEC(2010) 1454 final.

not only this sort of reasoning was added to the proposal, but in addition a much more sophisticated mechanism was provided for than had originally been proposed, according to which during the authorisation procedure a Member State could demand that all or part of its territory be excluded from cultivation, and the applicant could adjust the geographical scope of its application accordingly. Where that did not happen, and an authorisation covered (also) the territory of a given Member State, the latter could nevertheless adopt measures restricting or prohibiting the cultivation on all or part of its territory of a GMO, or a group of GMOs, 'provided that such measures are in conformity with Union law, reasoned, proportional and non-discriminatory and, in addition, are based on compelling grounds'. A series of illustrative grounds is then provided, including 'environmental policy objectives'. However, it is specified that the grounds relied on must not conflict with the environmental risk assessment carried out for the purposes of the EU authorisation procedure. In other words, a Member State may have an environmental policy objective which implies avoiding GMO crops, but it may not base itself on a reasoning of environmental risk which has been excluded during the authorisation process.

We thus now have a fully EU-level system of marketing authorisations for GMOs,[16] while the Member States are free to make their own decisions on the cultivation of GMO crops on their territories, so long as they have serious reasons for the measures they take, and provided they observe general principles of EU law and do not contradict actual findings made at EU level. It took nearly six years to achieve this result. It will be interesting to see whether the next proposal to repatriate competences to the Member States will go more smoothly.

'SUPPORTING' COMPETENCE

Finally, in the areas in which the EU's competence is restricted to supporting, coordinating or supplementing the actions of the Member States, the problem can be to find an effective way to advance a policy aim. Sometimes the Commission's services are not content to propose an action plan or a funding programme, but want to propose binding rules. In the area of public health, this is possible only in a very limited number of areas. Article 168(4) TFEU allows for harmonisation of national laws as regards setting high standards of quality and safety of organs and substances of human origin, blood and blood derivatives; setting such standards for medicinal products and devices for medical use; and measures in the veterinary and phytosanitary fields which directly aim at the protection of public health. Beyond those areas, EU action is restricted to incentive measures, recommendations, and general supporting and coordinating activities. Some years ago,

[16] Directive (EU) 2015/412 of the European Parliament and of the Council of 11 March 2015 amending Directive 2001/18/EC as regards the possibility for the Member States to restrict or prohibit the cultivation of genetically modified organisms (GMOs) in their territory (OJ L 68, 13 March 2015, 1).

the competent services of the Commission were convinced that there was a need for binding EU rules on smoking in public places. However, after examination of all possibilities, it was concluded that the most they could propose was a Council Recommendation. This resulted in Council Recommendation[17] of 30 November 2009 on smoke-free environments.[18]

CONCLUSION

It will be clear from the foregoing that a good deal of the Commission's time is spent in considering issues of EU competence, whether in suing a Member State which has taken an initiative in the international arena in an area of exclusive EU competence, discussing internally as to whether a given international agreement should be proposed as an 'EU-only' agreement, or arguing over the possibility of proposing harmonisation measures on the internal level. More broadly, in the area of the fundamental freedoms, there are frequent discussions as to whether to accept a Member State's arguments in favour of a restriction it imposes. At heart, this is also a discussion about competences: how broadly should we construe the rules on free movement, and correspondingly how much room should we leave for Member States to pursue public interest objectives, thereby exercising their own competences? These kinds of questions are the daily bread of the Commission and are likely to remain for a long time at the centre of discussions about the nature of the Union we are constructing.

[17] This Recommendation was based on Art 152(4) EC, but the outcome would be no different under the terms of Art 168 TFEU.

[18] OJ C 296, 5 December 2009, 4.

12

The Lisbon Treaty's Competence Arrangement Viewed by the European Parliament

MARÍA JOSÉ MARTÍNEZ IGLESIAS*

THE CHANGES INTRODUCED by the Treaty of Lisbon did not alter the fundamental obligation of the institutions of the Union to respect the Treaties and the system of allocation of competences established in them. In the same way as before the entry into force of the Treaty of Lisbon, the Union institutions involved in the decision-making process remain the primary guarantee of respect for the distribution of competences between the Union and the Member States. The first check on the respect of the distribution of competences is that exercised by the institutions when adopting decisions or legislating.

The principles of conferral, subsidiarity and proportionality remain the pillars of the system of delimitation of competences. By focusing on these three principles we can better understand the view and the practice of the European Parliament in relation to the competences system of the Treaties.

THE PRINCIPLE OF CONFERRAL

The Lisbon Treaty has in fact brought very limited changes to the system of distribution of competences between the Union and Member States. The system continues to revolve around the principle of conferral[1] and the legal basis. As stated in Article 2(6) TFEU, 'the scope of and arrangements for exercising the Union's competences shall be determined by the provisions of the Treaties relating to each area', in other words, the legal bases.

* María José Martínez Iglesias is the Director for Legislative Affairs in the Legal Service of the European Parliament. The views presented in this article are those of the author alone and do not represent an official position of the Legal Service of the European Parliament.

[1] After stating that 'the limits of Union competences are governed by the principle of conferral', para 2 of Art 5 TEU provides a definition of the principle: 'Under the principle of conferral, the Union shall act only within the limits of the competences conferred upon it by the Member States in the Treaties to attain the objectives set out therein.'

This provision serves to quell any uncertainty over the nature of the main new feature of the Treaty of Lisbon, which is the title of the TFEU concerning the categories and areas of Union competence. This title aims to provide a concise and easy-to-read catalogue of the Union's competences. It complements but does not replace the system of legal bases as the real clauses of conferral of competences. Indeed, the previous system, which consisted of the enunciation of the principle of conferral together with the provisions for each policy with case-by-case enabling clauses, has remained unchanged. However, it has been superposed by this doctrinal and jurisprudential origin explanation, which clarifies the nature of each category of competence and its consequences.

In fact, case law makes the legal basis a constitutional feature, determining first and foremost the legality of an act. The choice of an incorrect legal basis may therefore justify the annulment of the act in question. Hence the seriousness with which the institutions approach the choice of the legal basis.

The essential function of a legal basis is to enable the institutions to exercise a competence through the procedures for the adoption of the legal acts of the Union. In fact, we find a formulation of the principle of conferral directly related to the institutions in Article 13(2) TEU: 'Each institution shall act within the limits of the powers conferred on it in the Treaties, and in conformity with the procedures, conditions and objectives set out in them.'[2]

The choice of legal basis therefore has important consequences, both in terms of the content of the legal acts for which it serves as a foundation, and also in terms of (horizontal) distribution of competences between the institutions. So it is no surprise that the institutions, in particular the legislative triangle composed by the Commission, Council and Parliament, take the determination of legal bases very seriously. The very fact that the lack of agreement between the institutions on the choice of a legal basis is a constant and fertile source of interinstitutional disputes, demonstrates the significance of this issue.

Actually, the reason why the European Parliament pays such a close attention to the choice of legal bases is to defend its own prerogatives.

Since well before the Lisbon Treaty, the European Parliament has used a specific internal procedure for the verification of the legal bases for legislative proposals and 'other documents of a legislative nature'. Rule 39 of its Rules of Procedure establishes a complex procedure, whose objective is primarily to guarantee that the question of legal basis is settled in full knowledge of the facts, and attributes this verification function to a specialised committee, the Committee on Legal Affairs. This committee, which carries out specialised horizontal tasks within the Parliament, and which is also competent for litigation before the Courts, ensures that a measured deliberation precedes any decision aimed at modifying the legal basis proposed by the Commission and which could ultimately lead

[2] The procedures for the adoption of EU legal acts are also an element of the delimitation of competences. Decision making by unanimity or qualified majority, whether based on the Ordinary Legislative Procedure or not, has always been perceived by Member States as an important aspect of the transfer of competences to the Union.

to an interinstitutional conflict, whether political or judicial. The opinion of the Committee on Legal Affairs is compulsory but not binding.

In fact, when the Parliament initiates working on a legislative procedure, the committee responsible for the subject matter must first analyse the legal basis of the proposal. This analysis is not only a check on the suitability of the legal basis in relation to the content of the proposal, but also an assessment of the respect to the principles of conferral, subsidiarity and proportionality set out in Article 5 TEU. It functions, therefore, as a real check on the distribution of competences enshrined in the Treaties.

In the event that the main parliamentary committee in the procedure decides to contest the validity of the proposed legal basis, it must seek the opinion of the Committee on Legal Affairs. This latter committee may also issue an own-initiative opinion on the legal basis of a proposal. If the Committee on Legal Affairs decides, anyhow, to contest the validity of a legal basis, its opinion is put to a vote in the Parliament plenary before the vote on the proposal itself.

The fact that amendments tabled to the Parliament plenary with the aim of changing a proposal's legal basis are inadmissible if the validity of that legal basis has not been challenged by the Committee on Legal Affairs or the committee responsible for the matter, is a measure of the importance the Parliament attaches to the examination of legal bases. Even the committee responsible is not allowed to submit any amendment to the legal basis if the Committee on Legal Affairs has not ruled on it.

Under its Rules of Procedure, the Parliament may examine the legal bases of all proposals on which it is consulted, not just those on which it is co-legislator, to be sure its prerogatives are respected.

The expression 'other documents of a legislative nature', used in Rule 42, refers to all kinds of acts, not necessarily acts of the Union, which may have implications for the competences of the Union and, in particular, for Parliament's prerogatives. This category encompasses international agreements that would require the approval or the consultation of the Parliament, international agreements between Member States of the Union (such as the Stability Treaty or the Bank Resolution Fund) or acts of the so-called 'soft law' (which could jeopardise the prerogatives of the legislator by avoiding the adoption of a formal act of the Union).

The legal bases of legislative proposals initiating from the Parliament, based on Article 225 TEU, are also submitted to a detailed examination. The President of the Parliament has the power to declare legislative initiatives by members inadmissible, if the Committee on Legal Affairs considers the legal basis of the proposal invalid.

The procedure for the verification of legal bases is used very frequently. Since the entry into force of the Lisbon Treaty, the Committee on Legal Affairs has issued 75 formal opinions on the legal bases of legislative proposals.[3]

[3] But the list of legal acts whose legal basis has been discussed by the Parliament do not end here. For example, this does not include all opinions requested by the parliamentary committees to the Legal Service, which are much more numerous.

As mentioned above, legal bases are the cause of numerous disputes between the institutions. Following the entry into force of the Treaty of Lisbon, some of the legal bases modified by the Treaty have proved particularly controversial.

This is the case of Article 43 TFEU concerning agricultural and fisheries policy, and in particular the distinction between the scope of paragraphs 2 and 3. Paragraph 2 provides for the Ordinary Legislative Procedure to adopt legislative acts while paragraph 3 provides for a non-legislative procedure, in which the decision rests with the Council after a non-binding opinion from the Parliament. The action for annulment[4] brought by the Parliament against Decision 2014/19/EU on the bilateral agreement with Venezuela on the authorisation of surplus fish catches allowed the Court to delimit, in its judgment of 26 November 2014, the scope of the two paragraphs of Article 43 TFEU. The action for annulment brought by the Parliament against Regulation (EU) No 1243/2012 on the long-term plan for cod stocks concerned the same question.[5]

To illustrate the issue at hand, it is also relevant to mention the actions for annulment[6] against several legal acts concerning amendments to the status of Mayotte with regard to the European Union, presented by the Parliament. The Council adopted several acts aimed at adapting various acts of the Union to the specific conditions of Mayotte as a result of its change of status to become a French overseas department, and thus a fully fledged EU territory. The Court judgment clarified the delimitation of the scope of application of the legal basis included in Article 349 TFEU, relating to the outermost regions. As in the case of Article 43 TFEU, the legal bases considered provide for substantially different levels of implication of the Parliament in the decision-making procedure. In fact, Article 349 TFEU provides for the adoption of the act by the Council after a simple opinion of the Parliament, while the relevant sectoral legal bases, upheld by the Parliament, provide for the Ordinary Legislative Procedure.

Another example of such contentious interinstitutional activity resulting from a conflict over a legal basis is the action for annulment brought by the Parliament against the Council Decision 2011/853/EU on the European Convention on the legal protection of services based on, or consisting of, conditional access. The conflict in this case concerned the choice between Articles 207 and 114 TFEU.[7] Obviously, in all those cases the action before the Court was founded on grounds or inadequacy of the legal basis to the content or objectives of the legal act in question. The procedure applicable constitutes a consequence of the choice of the legal basis and not a condition for such a choice. Nevertheless, it acts as a strong incentive to contest the legal basis.

It is worth mentioning that, in the litigation against the Council on legal basis, Parliament finds itself always (alone or together with the Commission) in the

[4] Case C-103/12 *Parliament and Commission v Council* EU:C:2014:334.
[5] Joined Cases C-124/13 and C-125/13 *Parliament v Council* EU:C:2015:790.
[6] Joined Cases C-132/14 to C-136/14 *Parliament v Council* EU:C:2015:813.
[7] Case C-137/12 *Commission v Council* EU:C:2013:675.

position of the complainant. There are still in the Treaties many legal bases which attribute the decision-making responsibility to the Council alone in the framework of legislative or non-legislative procedures. This means that, even against a Parliament or Commission position, the Council can adopt the controversial act which would eventually be contested. The European Parliament has not such a prerogative and thus cannot find itself in the position of defendant.

Sometimes the controversy about the legal basis does not result in a dispute before the Court of Justice, but in conflicts of a political nature, which can be extremely time-consuming. It is worth mentioning the conflict between the Council and the Parliament on the legal basis of the Schengen evaluation mechanism,[8] which was the reason why the 'Schengen' legislative package was blocked for more than a year.

It is no surprise, then, that the new interinstitutional agreement on 'Better Law Making'[9] provides, in paragraph 25,[10] a mechanism to prevent interinstitutional conflicts over the legal bases ending up in court. It is simply a case of facilitating discussions between the three institutions when a change in the Commission's proposed legal basis is foreseen.

THE PRINCIPLE OF SUBSIDIARITY

The principle of subsidiarity complements the principle of conferral and is conceived as a criterion for the exercise of competences attributed to the Union.

First of all, it must be remembered that each institution is bound to act with full respect to the principles of subsidiarity and proportionality. In fact, every legislative proposal of the Commission[11] includes in its explanatory statement a reasoned justification with respect to the two principles in accordance with Article 5 of the Protocol. The Rules of Procedure of the Council[12] and the Rules of Procedure of the European Parliament take into account the respect of subsidiarity in the framework of the legislative procedures.

[8] Council Regulation (EU) No 1053/2013 of 7 October 2013 establishing a monitoring and evaluation mechanism to verify the application of the Schengen acquis is established, and repeals the Decision of the Executive Committee of 16 September 1998 on the establishment of a Standing Committee on the evaluation and implementation of Schengen.

[9] OJ L 123, 12 May 2016.

[10] 'If a modification of the legal basis entailing a change from the ordinary legislative procedure to a special legislative procedure or a non-legislative procedure is envisaged, the three Institutions will exchange views thereon. The three Institutions agree that the choice of legal basis is a legal determination that must be made on objective grounds which are amenable to judicial review. The Commission shall continue to fully play its institutional role to ensure that the Treaties and the case-law of the Court of Justice of the European Union are respected.'

[11] The Protocol also applies to 'draft legislative acts' originated by other institutions or by groups of Member States which occasionally exercise the legislative initiative. This is the reason why the Protocol uses the term 'draft legislative act' instead of 'proposal', a term that the Treaties reserve to the Commission initiatives.

[12] Art 3 provides for the respect of the deadline of eight weeks for the National Parliament to react to a legislative proposal.

Since the entry into force of the Maastricht Treaty, the European Parliament has committed to a careful verification of both the principles of subsidiarity and proportionality through its Rules of Procedure. In particular, Rule 42 charges a particular committee with the task of performing these verifications. The Committee on Legal Affairs can, on its own initiative, address recommendations on the respect of the subsidiarity principle to the committee responsible for the subject matter. However, this procedure has been used only once, in a very recent case related to the legislative initiative by the European Parliament on the modalities of its right of inquiry, as we will see later.

The only real innovation of the Lisbon Treaty in relation to the subsidiarity principle is a procedural one. Protocol 2 on the application of the principles of subsidiarity and proportionality confers a central role in assuring the compliance of legislative acts with the principle of subsidiarity on national parliaments, mainly through two early warning procedures.

It should be noted that the subsidiarity check exclusively concerns legislative acts, as defined in Article 189 TFEU.[13] Though it comes as a surprise that many non-legislative legal bases are excluded from the subsidiarity check due to this limitation, there is no special, more extensive meaning of 'legislative acts' in the Protocol. There is, in fact, a link between the legislative 'material' and the role of the national parliaments. This role derives from the competences being transferred from them to the Union. This is how the European Parliament itself views the subsidiarity check. In its Resolution of 16 April 2014 on relations between the European Parliament and the national parliaments, it affirmed

> that the monitoring of compliance with the subsidiarity principle by the national parliaments and the European institutions should be seen not as an undue restriction, but as a mechanism for guaranteeing the competences of the national parliaments.

The fact that the subsidiarity check exclusively concerns legislative acts means that the European Parliament is always involved in the decision-making procedure, be it as co-legislator in the Ordinary Legislative Procedure, or by giving its consent or through an opinion in the case of the special legislative procedures.

After the entry into force of the Lisbon Treaty, the European Parliament adapted its Rules of Procedure to allow for an adequate reaction to the subsidiarity check in a very 'national parliaments-friendly' way. Rule 42, which establishes the internal procedure to apply when a national parliament or one of its chambers sends a reasoned opinion to the President of the institution,[14] goes beyond what is required by the Protocol. The document is referred to the committee competent for the subject matter and sent merely for information to the committee specialised in subsidiarity, the Committee on Legal Affairs. From a legal point of view, the

[13] The 'orange card' procedure is exclusively restricted to acts adopted by the Ordinary Legislative Procedure.

[14] According to Art 6 of Protocol 2, Reasoned opinions by National Parliaments are to be sent to the Presidents of the Commission, Council and Parliament.

eight-week[15] deadline granted to national parliaments by Article 6 of Protocol 2 implies that the legislative act is not adopted by the relevant institution during this period. Rule 42 goes beyond that guarantee. Except in urgent cases, the parliamentary committee responsible for the preparatory phase of procedure will not adopt its report on the proposal under examination before a period of eight weeks has expired. By applying the deadline to the preparatory body of the Parliament (well before the vote by the plenary), Rule 42 endeavours to ensure that reasoned opinions are taken into consideration from the very first step of the procedure.

In the case of the so called 'yellow card', the draft must be reviewed by the Commission (or the authors of the proposal if others). In this case, the European Parliament commits in Rule 42 to delaying any decision on the draft until the author of the proposal has stated how it intends to proceed.

In the case of the so called 'orange card', the proposal must be reviewed by the Commission and then, if the Commission chooses to maintain the proposal, the legislators must consider the specific question of whether the proposal is or is not compatible with the principle of subsidiarity. In this case, Rule 42 provides for a specific vote in the plenary about subsidiarity before the vote on the proposal itself. Furthermore, if the Commission intends to maintain its proposal, the committee responsible for the matter must ask for an opinion from the Committee on Legal Affairs (this opinion is compulsory but not binding). The main committee will make a proposal to the plenary on the specific question of the respect of the principle of subsidiarity. If a recommendation to reject the proposal on grounds of non-respect of the principle of subsidiarity is adopted by a simple majority (of the votes cast), the legislative procedure will be declared closed. Unlike the yellow card procedure, no orange card procedure has ever been triggered.

It is important to highlight that the subsidiarity check does not allow national parliaments to interfere directly with the legislative procedures of the Union. Indeed, given that governments (which are the components of the Council) are usually supported by a majority in their national parliaments, a proposal that is shown the orange card would probably have no chance of passing through the legislative procedure. Nevertheless, the subsidiarity check has made a decidedly positive contribution to the dialogue between the different levels of legislators.

Indeed, the subsidiarity check operates within the general framework of the so-called political dialogue, which not only concerns compliance with the principle of subsidiarity, but also—and more generally—all aspects of the documents transmitted to national parliaments, beyond merely legislative proposals. Thus, for the sake of clarity and legal certainty, the Commission has asked national parliaments to distinguish between reasoned opinions (opposition to an act on the grounds that it does not respect the subsidiarity principle) and contributions (observations or comments on the substance of a proposal or on subsidiarity aspects, but not

[15] This period should not be confused with the eight-week deadline provided for in Art 4 of Protocol 1 on the Role of National Parliaments, for a legislative proposal to be placed on a provisional agenda of the Council for its adoption. In this case, which also applies to exclusive competences, the deadline is aimed at facilitating the scrutiny of governments sitting in the Council by their respective Parliaments.

opposing the act).[16] This differentiation is not straightforward and some national parliaments have continued to send 'contributions' under the heading 'reasoned opinion'. The resulting confusion is a serious matter, as the treatment of reasoned opinions, which must respect the provisions of Protocol 2, could result in litigation before the Court of Justice and jeopardise legal certainty.

The treatment of these two kinds of documents within the European Parliament is very different. Reasoned opinions are considered part of the legislative procedure. They are distributed like any other document of the procedure and translated into all the Union's languages in order to allow Members of the European Parliament to effectively 'take them into account' when deliberating and deciding on a legislative proposal, as required by Protocol 2. On the other hand, contributions are not translated and are only actively distributed to selected members. Instead, they are available for all members to view on a dedicated page on the European Parliament's website.

As for the practical relevance of the subsidiarity check, from the entry into force of the Lisbon Treaty to 2016, national parliaments have submitted 2,017 documents with comments on a total of 526 draft legislative acts. Among them, 311 were reasoned opinions, following the definition given in Protocol 2, and 1,706 were contributions.

The yellow card procedure has so far been triggered three times. The first two cases, both in 2012, concerned a proposal for a Council regulation on the exercise of the right to take collective action within the context of the freedom of establishment and the freedom to provide services[17] and a proposal for a Council regulation on the establishment of the European Public Prosecutor's Office (EPPO).[18] In the first case—the draft regulation on the exercise of the right to take collective action—the Commission did not find that the principle of subsidiarity had been breached. However, taking into account the views expressed and the state of the discussions between relevant stakeholders, the Commission decided, on 26 September 2012, to withdraw the proposal. In the second case—the draft regulation on the establishment of the EPPO—the Commission adopted a Communication[19] on 27 November 2013, in which it concluded that the proposal complied with the subsidiarity principle and decided to maintain the proposal.

The third, and more recent, case of the yellow card procedure concerned the proposal for a Directive amending the Posting of Workers Directive.[20] Fourteen parliamentary chambers of 11 Member States issued reasoned opinions.

[16] See the letter from President Barroso and Vice-president Wallström of 1 December 2009 including the *Practical arrangements for the operation of the Subsidiarity Control Mechanism* in http://ec.europa.eu/dgs/secretariat_general/relations/relations_other/npo/docs/letter_en.pdf.

[17] COM(2012) 130. The following Parliaments or chambers sent reasoned opinions: DK, LV, FI, PT, PL1, FR2, BE1, NL1, SE, LU, MT, UK1.

[18] COM(2013) 534. The following Parliaments or chambers sent reasoned opinions: CZ2, NL1, NL2, UK1, UK2, IE, HU, RO1, SI1, FR2, CY, MT, SE.

[19] COM(2013) 851 final.

[20] COM(2016) 128 final. The following Parliaments or chambers sent reasoned opinions: RO1, RO2, CZ1, CZ2, PO1, PO2, LI1, DA, CR, LA, BU, HU, ES and SK.

It is worth noting that, in addition, six national parliaments[21] sent contributions as part of the political dialogue, mainly considering the proposal to be compatible with the principle of subsidiarity. The geopolitical cleavage shows that the problem here concerns more the content of the proposal than the subsidiarity principle. The Commission adopted a Communication[22] in which it concluded that its proposal complied with the principle of subsidiarity and that the withdrawal or amendment of the proposal was not required.

In all these cases, the European Parliament entered into an intense dialogue with the national parliaments involved in the procedures.

As was mentioned before,[23] Protocol 2 submits initiatives from the European Parliament, the Court of Justice, the European Central Bank and a group of Member States to the subsidiarity check. However, many of the legal bases of the Treaties, which provide for the legislative initiative to be exercised by institutions other than the Commission, correspond to exclusive competences of the Union, to which, according to Article 5 TEU, the subsidiarity principle does not apply.

This perplexing situation derives from the fact that, according to Article 4(1) TFEU,[24] the list of exclusive competences in Article 3 TFEU is deemed to be exhaustive. But nevertheless, the Treaties lay down an array of legal bases that enable the Union's institutions to adopt acts of great consequence, without expressly including them in the catalogue of competences provided for in Articles 3–6 TFEU, nor thus in the list of exclusive competences. These are mainly provisions of an institutional or political nature.

Examples include the legislative legal bases for which the European Parliament has the right of initiative: the uniform procedure for elections to the European Parliament (Article 223 TFEU), the Statute for Members of the European Parliament (Article 223 TFEU), the provisions governing the exercise of the right of inquiry (Article 226 TFEU) and the Statute of the European Ombudsman (Article 228 TFEU). But also the composition of the European Parliament (Article 14 TEU), even though this last act has no legislative nature.[25] Without claiming to be exhaustive, other examples of this category of acts include the Statute for European Political Parties (Article 224 TFEU), the Staff Regulations of Officials of the European Union (Article 336 TFEU), the amendment of the Statute of the Court of Justice of the European Union according to the ordinary legislative procedure (Article 281 TFEU), the conferral on the Court of Justice of the competence to adjudicate in matters relating to intellectual property rights (Article 262 TFEU), the establishment of specialised courts (Article 257 TFEU) and the citizens' initiative (Article 24 TFEU).

[21] ES, IT, PT, UK1, FR2.

[22] COM(2016) 505 final.

[23] See above n 11.

[24] 'The Union shall share competence with the Member States where the Treaties confer on it a competence which does not relate to the areas referred to in Arts 3 and 6.'

[25] And consequently it would not in any case be submitted to the early warning mechanism laid down in Protocol 2.

These legal bases correspond to a particular kind of Union competence which we might define as competences of 'self-organisation'. If the list of exclusive competences was really exhaustive, then these competences of self-organisation should be regarded as shared competences. However, the actual nature of these competences runs against the definition of shared competences provided in Article 2(2) TEU, which states that 'the Union and the Member States may legislate and adopt legally binding acts in that area', and that 'the Member States shall exercise their competence to the extent that the Union has decided to cease exercising its competence'. Logic dictates that in all those areas it is inconceivable that Member States may adopt binding legal acts. Only the Union may do so. In these legal bases related to 'self-organisation', the existence of separate national standards would be unthinkable. One therefore must conclude that these are exclusive competences, to which the subsidiarity principle does not apply.

This issue has been the subject of intense and controversial debate in relation to the draft legislative proposal on the detailed provisions governing the exercise of the European Parliament's right of inquiry,[26] between various national parliaments on the one hand, which would tend to consider that the list of exclusive competences is exhaustive, and the European Parliament on the other. The controversy is still on-going, now in relation to the draft legislative act concerning the uniform electoral rules. In this last case, after its adoption by the EU institutions, the legislative act has to be ratified by national parliaments, which makes them a part of the decision-making process.

THE PRINCIPLE OF PROPORTIONALITY

The European Parliament's Rule of Procedure 42 also commits it to paying particular attention to the principle of proportionality in the framework of the legislative procedures. According to Article 5(4) TEU, 'under the principle of proportionality, the content and form of Union action shall not exceed what is necessary to achieve the objectives of the Treaties'. Proportionality is about the intensity of the action of the Union and above all about the type of legal acts the Union may use.[27] Many legal bases indicate what kind of binding legal act—directives, regulations or decisions—must be used in each case. But other legal bases, under terms like 'measures' or 'actions', allow the legislator the choice. It is this choice that must be guided above all by the principle of proportionality.[28]

[26] P7_TA(2012)0219.

[27] Art 296 TFEU states that, 'where the Treaties do not specify the type of act to be adopted, the institutions shall select it on a case-by-case basis, in compliance with the applicable procedures and with the *principle of proportionality*'.

[28] Para 6 of the former Protocol 30 established a preference for directives.

Furthermore, under the respect of the proportionality principle and within the framework of the statement of reasons of legal acts, Article 5 of Protocol 2 requires an assessment of a proposal's

> financial impact and, in the case of a directive, of its implications for the rules to be put in place by Member States, including, where necessary, the regional legislation. The reasons for concluding that a Union objective can be better achieved at Union level shall be substantiated by qualitative and, wherever possible, quantitative indicators. Draft legislative acts shall take account of the need for any burden, whether financial or administrative, falling upon the Union, national governments, regional or local authorities, economic operators and citizens, to be minimised and commensurate with the objective to be achieved.

The European Parliament, the Council and the Commission have just reached a new inter-institutional Agreement (IIA) on Better Law-making,[29] which develops in detail all the above elements and more, as did the old one. One of the main elements of the new IIA is the improvement of the use of impact assessments as a tool for well-informed political decisions. It sets out the elements that impact assessments should cover: economic, environmental and social impacts, the 'cost of non-Europe', potential impacts on competitiveness and administrative burdens, with particular regard to SMEs, digital aspects and territorial impacts. The Parliament and Council must perform impact assessments on their own substantial amendments.

Other important elements considered and regulated by the IIA constitute also a kind of proportionality check: the justification by the Commission of its choice of legislative instrument, public and stakeholder consultations, ex-post evaluations, monitoring and reporting requirements in legislation and the systematic consideration of the use of review clauses and sunset clauses. In an effort to simplify procedures, the three institutions also agreed to cooperate in order to reduce burdens, including for SMEs, while ensuring that the objectives of the legislation are met. In this context, the Commission must undertake an annual burden survey and must also, wherever possible, quantify the possible burden-reduction or savings potential of initiatives.

The new IIA could be interpreted as evidence of the commitment of the EU institutions to a set of principles that assure the sound use of the EU's competences. However, as with the legal bases, the content of the new IIA essentially addresses potential interinstitutional conflicts. This could undoubtedly help the efficiency of the management of the procedures, even reduce deadlines; however, one cannot but express scepticism about its vocation to improve the content of the legal acts of the Union from the point of view of proportionality in the very large meaning provided for by Protocol 2.

[29] OJ L 123, 12 June 2016 at 1–14.

As for the Parliament itself, its Rules of Procedure provide for a financial verification of the legislative proposal (Rule 41), which is the task of the Committee on Budgets, and also for a verification of respect for the Charter of Fundamental Rights, to be performed by the Committee on Civil Liberties (Rule 38). Even if this latter rule has never been used, the European Parliament pays special attention to fundamental rights issues, as proved by its contentious activity.

As a conclusion, I will come back to my first assertion: Union institutions are the first and main guarantee of the respect of the system of distribution of competences when exercising their own powers. The European Parliament is not an exception to that rule, the defence of its own prerogatives being a strong incentive for deep consideration of all the requirements of Treaties in relation to the system of competences.

13

The Institutional Politics of Objective Choice: Competence as a Framework for Argumentation

PÄIVI LEINO*

RULES OF THE GAME

THAT THE CHOICE of legal basis of an EU legal act 'may not depend simply on an institution's conviction as to the objective pursued but must be based on objective factors which are amenable to judicial review'[1] is considered one of the most foundational doctrines of EU law among EU lawyers. A basic search in the Court's database Curia on the key elements of 'legal basis', 'objective factors' and 'amenable to judicial review' results in numerous hits covering key jurisprudence concerning not only interinstitutional relations but also all EU policy fields. If this case law is anything to go by, the objectivity of legal basis choices should by now be beyond doubt. The Court has justified the need to maintain the objectivity of the choices relating to legal basis with reference to institutional balance.[2] In its view, the prerogatives of institutions

> are one of the elements in the institutional balance created by the Treaties. The Treaties set up a system for distributing powers among the different Community institutions, assigning to each institution its own role in the institutional structure of the Community and the accomplishment of the tasks entrusted to the Community. Observance of the institutional balance means that each of the institutions must exercise its powers with due regard for the powers of the other institutions.[3]

* Päivi Leino is Professor of International and EU Law, University of Eastern Finland; Academy of Finland Research Fellow, Visiting fellow, EUI Law Department. I thank the legal advisers who agreed to being interviewed, Emilia Korkea-aho for comments on an earlier draft and Daniel Wyatt for research assistance.

[1] Case C-70/88 *European Parliament v Council* EU:C:1990:217 para 9; see eg Case C-411/06 *Commission v Parliament and Council* EU:C:2009:518 para 45.

[2] Case C-70/88 *Parliament v Council* EU:C:1990:217 paras 21–22. See eg J-P Jacqué, 'The principle of institutional balance' (2004) 41 *Common Market Law Review* 383; U O'Dwyer, 'La dynamique historique des relations interinstitutionelles. Le point de vue d'un praticien sur l'évolution de la procédure de codécision' (2010) 3 *Revue du Droit de l'Union Européenne* 487.

[3] Case C-70/88 *Parliament v Council* EU:C:1990:217 paras 21–22.

The role of law in European integration is further elaborated in its jurisprudence, including in *Les Verts*. This case introduced the slogan referring to the Union as 'a Community based on the rule of law'.[4] The maxim was justified by reference to how the law and the EU Founding Treaties subject the EU measures to constitutional review. 'Law' is linked to the legitimacy of the EU. It appeals to those wishing to limit power politics, integrationist ambitions and institutional discretion. Therefore, law has a 'powerfully symbolic dimension, an important aspect of which entails the invocation of a claim to legitimacy'.[5] The legal basis of an act thus serves a guarantee function, ultimately intended to protect individuals from *ultra vires* acts by the EU institutions.[6] The role of law in the process of political integration is not only to empower or compel political actors to pursue certain ends by using particular means, but also serves as a constraining force, limiting the actions or policies of these actors.[7] The legal bases in the Treaty not only specify, in more or less general terms, what can be done on their basis, but also how—following what procedure—this is to be done.[8]

Questions concerning competence and legal basis are routinely treated as a domain reserved for lawyers, as if they were—as the quote above suggests—indeed objective in nature, and as such somehow separate from policy making. EU lawyers frequently address questions relating to the EU competence to act and what kind of measures it can take. When working as a legal advisor for a Member State government and solving competence problems before national parliamentary committees, I was often faced with the difficulty of giving a clear-cut answer to a legal basis question. Outcomes of EU discussions on the choice of legal basis were hard to anticipate, no matter how objective they were claimed to be. Equally difficult was it to identify absolute national competence reserves. These difficulties are reflected in academic discussion, which suggests that the current competence constellation in the EU does not necessarily contain integration in areas of Member State competence.[9] These discussions suggest that the matter of legal basis might not be quite as straightforward and objective as the above quote indicates. The choice of legal basis has vast political and interinstitutional dimensions. It also has implications for both the various stages of the legislative procedure and the related power structures, but ultimately also for its substantive outcome. While the Court's jurisprudence consistently highlights the objectivity of the choices relating

[4] Case 294/83 *Les Verts v Parliament* EU:C:1986:166 para 23.

[5] G de Búrca, 'Rethinking Law in Neofunctionalist Theory' (2005) 12 *Journal of European Public Policy* 310 at 319–20.

[6] R Barents, 'The Internal Market Unlimited: Some Observations on the Legal Basis of Community Legislation' (1993) 30 *Common Market Law Review* 85 at 92.

[7] G de Búrca, above n 5 at 319–20.

[8] *cf* Art 16 TFEU and Art 8 of the Charter for Fundamental Rights. While both concern the protection of personal data, only the former establishes a legal basis for the adoption of rules concerning the matter. The fact that the Charter cannot be used as a basis for competence to act is also specifically confirmed by Art 51(2) of the Charter.

[9] S Garben, 'Confronting the Competence Conundrum: democratising the European Union through an expansion of its legislative powers' (2015) 35 *Oxford Journal of Legal Studies* 55.

to legal basis, it largely relates to and reflects the political, substantive and procedural implications of these choices. Against this background, that the legal rules concerning EU decision making—created for restraining EU powers to limits that are acceptable for the Member States as the 'Masters of the Treaties'—are instrumentalised to promote particular institutional, national or otherwise political objectives is something of an oxymoron. This finding is of course ill at ease with the traditional understanding of the role of law in European integration.

Questions relating to the role of law constraining decision making are of a particular interest in the context of EU law making. The Treaties establish only the main building blocks of the EU legislative procedure. In this context, formal rules are relatively few and leave space for institutional discretion. The current framework for the adoption of EU legal acts builds on interinstitutional agreements, informal arrangements and flexibility.[10] The skeleton of the ordinary and special legislative procedure provided by Articles 289 and 294 TFEU is in practice fleshed out with informal interinstitutional negotiations, in particular trilogues. These informal negotiations aim at efficient law making through the identification of joint ground on the substance of the act, whenever possible in a fast-track procedure, through a first reading solution.[11] Trilogues are increasingly taking over as the main legislative deal-making forum between the three institutions.[12] In 2009–2014, 89 per cent of Commission proposals fell under legal bases that were adopted in co-decision. Over 1,500 trilogues on approximately 350 co-decision files were held under the seventh legislative term.[13] The broad use of informal means of finding agreement turns the formal Treaty rules on three readings—parliamentary plenary and Council ministerial meetings with specified voting rules—into provisions that have lesser practical relevance. Instead, the crystallisation of interinstitutional compromise as early as possible in the procedure is what counts.

This is not to say that in making these compromises the EU legislature would be unbound. Instead, while the legal rules regulating law making in the EU set some limits to institutional imagination, they also leave much leeway for political bargaining. From within the process, law operates as 'a common language understood and shared by all'.[14] The rules of decision-making affect political choices and arguments used to defend them. Power relations are affected by how well acquainted

[10] I have explained this in detail in P Leino, 'The Politics of Efficient Compromise in the Adoption of EU Legal Acts' in M Cremona (ed), *EU Legal Acts: Challenges and Transformations, Collected Courses of the Academy of European Law* (Oxford, Oxford University Press, forthcoming 2017).

[11] On this, see D Curtin and P Leino, 'Back to the future', forthcoming in *Common Market Law Review* (2017).

[12] See eg 'Shifting EU Institutional Reform into High Gear: Report of the CEPS High-level Group' at 1–24, Report available at www.ceps.eu/book/shifting-eu-institutional-reform-high-gear-report-ceps-high-level-group.

[13] European Parliament Activity Report on Codecision and Conciliation, 14 July 2009—30 June 2014, DV 1031024EN.doc at 8.

[14] J-P Jacqué, 'The Role of Legal Services in the Elaboration of European Legislation' in A Vauchez and B De Witte (eds), *Lawyering Europe. European Law as a Transnational Social Field* (Oxford, Hart Publishing, 2013) at 43.

the key players are with the rules of law making, which also increases the role of legal advisers in decision making. Law and politics rely heavily on each other in the process of integration.

Integration is fundamentally a political process: whether to engage in it, its pace, shape, success and failure are largely determined by political actors and political will. But the law has a vital role to play in the process. It defines many of the political actors and the framework within which they operate, controlling and limiting their actions and relations and determining, at least partially, the effects and effectiveness of their acts.[15]

Formal and informal rules form the language of discussions, the 'rules of the game'. This is likened to how

> Legal doctrine not only does not, but also cannot, generate determinate results in concrete cases. Law is not so much a rational enterprise as a vast exercise in rationalization. Legal doctrine can be manipulated to justify an almost infinite spectrum of possible outcomes. Moreover, a plausible argument can be made that any such outcome has been derived from the dominant legal conceptions. Legal doctrine is nothing more than a sophisticated vocabulary and repertoire of manipulative techniques for categorizing, describing, organizing, and comparing: it is not a methodology for reaching substantive outcomes.[16]

I was asked to provide some practical views on how competence is used to frame legal argumentation both within the civil service and before the courts, relying on my experiences as a Member State legal adviser.[17] This is what I intend to do in this chapter, without much of an attempt to theorise the matter or claim that I have invoked a particular research method. However, to a certain extent I will also rely on interview material collected in the context of my current research project, which focuses on the role of legal rules and legal advice in EU law making.[18] I will first discuss the function of the legal basis requirement in the political process against the background of the ultimate aim of finding compromise on the legal act among and within the institutions. I refer to two legislative files that illustrate the role of political considerations in competence discussions particularly well: the Single Resolution Mechanism and Fund and the EU Fundamental Rights Agency. I will then consider what happens if no sustainable compromise acceptable to all parties can be identified and the process leads to litigation. But keeping the two stages—negotiation and litigation—separate is largely artificial. And as I will demonstrate, the most significant function of judicial review might in fact

[15] M Cappelletti, M Seccombe and J Weiler (eds), *Integration Through Law* (Berlin, De Gruyter, 1986) book 1 vol 1 ch 2.

[16] A Hutchinson and PJ Monahan, 'Law, Politics and Critical Legal Scholars: The Unfolding Drama of American Legal Thought' (1984) 36 *Stanford Law Review* 199 at 206.

[17] I worked in 1999–2000 and 2005–2015 as a legal advisor for several departments of the Finnish Government focusing on constitutional and institutional EU law and competence questions, and participated in various EU negotiations, including those leading to the conclusion of the Treaty of Lisbon.

[18] The data currently consists of 23 interviews with legal advisers and policy makers working for the EU institutions or Member States, conducted between February and July 2016. All interviews are on file with the author. In selecting the interviewees I have invoked the snowball effect.

be in the knowledge of its existence during the negotiation process—the shadow of hierarchy—than in its actual outcomes, which are ultimately few and usually limited in their effect. Both negotiation and litigation also demonstrate how competence considerations mainly serve to create a framework for argumentation instead of fixing clearly settled limits or no-go areas.

LEGAL BASIS IN THE POLITICAL PROCESS: CRYSTALLISATION OF A COMPROMISE

According to settled case law, the choice of the legal basis for a Union measure must rest on objective factors amenable to judicial review, including in particular the aim and the content of the measure.[19] But since the legal basis determines the position of each of the institutions and the Member States in the legislative process, it is 'inevitable that the interpretation of these provisions by each of the actors involved is influenced by their political interests'.[20] Politics are difficult to exclude when giving legal advice. The Council Legal Service (CLS) mission statement allows ample space for creativity by defining that the office

> assists the European Council, the Council and its preparatory bodies, the Presidency and the General Secretariat, in order to ensure the legality and the drafting quality. It contributes, by taking a creative approach where appropriate, to identifying legally correct and politically acceptable solutions, in cooperation with other Council departments. To that end, it gives opinions in complete impartiality—orally or in writing, at the request of the Council or on its own initiative—on any question of a legal nature.[21]

In the Parliament, questions relating to the verification of legal basis are defined as falling under a political body, the legal affairs (JURI) Committee, which may issue opinions either at the request of other committees or on its own initiative.[22] And the Commission Legal Service falls directly under the authority of its President, who has been open about his mission to run his Commission much more towards the political: 'The Commission is political. And I want it to be more political. Indeed, it will be highly political.'[23]

The Council referred specifically to the political implications of legal basis choices in the context of access to documents litigation as a reason why

[19] See Case C-411/06 *Commission v Parliament and Council* EU:C:2009:518 para 45; Case C-178/03 *Commission v Parliament and Council* EU:C:2006:4 para 41; Case C-155/07 *Parliament v Council* EU:C:2008:605 para 34.

[20] Barents, above n 6 at 89.

[21] Dated 5 September 2013, SN 3320/13.

[22] Rule 39, Rules of Procedure of the European Parliament, 8th parliamentary term—September 2015.

[23] See J-C Juncker, 'A New Start for Europe: My Agenda for Jobs, Growth, Fairness and Democratic Change—Political Guidelines for the next European Commission', Opening Statement in the European Parliament Plenary Session, Candidate for President of the European Commission, Strasbourg, 15 July 2014 at 16.

competence-related debates and disagreement between the institutions should remain confidential:

> According to the Council, since the legal basis of an EU act determines the decision-making procedure that applies, it necessarily affects the balance of powers between the institutions as well. Disputes concerning the applicable legal basis therefore remain, by their very nature, of very great political significance and are potentially highly contentious.[24]

For the Council, the disclosure of debates relating to legal basis 'could shift the focus of the debates by diverting it to a specific element of the decision-making process', which the Court has rejected with a reference to how 'the question of the legal basis is an essential question in the legislative process and does not shift the focus of debates, but is an essential part thereof'; therefore,

> a proposal is designed to be debated, in particular as regards the choice of legal basis. Moreover, … in the light of the importance of the choice of legal basis of a legislative act, the transparency of the choice does not weaken the decision-making process, but strengthens it.[25]

The Court therefore seems to accept that while the choice of legal basis is an objective question, this does not exclude it from being subject to political debate.

This is well justified when considering the consequences of this choice. Sometimes the choice of legal basis settles the nature of competence that the Union exercises,[26] and what effect Union action has on future Member State choices.[27] Moreover, the choice of legal basis may also have consequences for the discretion of the legislature in selecting the applicable legislative instrument,[28] the extent to which the measure can be used to harmonise national legislation,[29] or the way in which harmonisation can be done.[30] In addition, the choice of legal basis affects the right of initiative, which usually is with the Commission, but can under some

[24] Case C-350/12 *Council v Sophie in't Veld* EU:C:2014:2039 para 29. The Council essentially argued that following this, legal basis argumentation should remain confidential. The Court rejected this view with reference to how the existence of a divergence of views among the institutions as to the appropriate legal basis could not in itself undermine public interest (para 56). The Court pointed out how 'it is the Treaty itself which lays down a judicial procedure concerning the legal issues that may be linked to the legal basis … and which is public', para 59.

[25] Case T-395/13 *Miettinen v Council* EU:C:2015:648 paras 68–70.

[26] See eg Art 168 TFEU on public health: while public health in general falls under supportive competence, para 4 establishes a legal basis that falls under shared competence.

[27] See eg Case C-370/07 *Commission v Council* EU:C:2009:590.

[28] See eg Art 207(2) TFEU, which refers to the use of regulations defining the framework for implementing the common commercial policy, or Art 82(2) TFEU, which establishes that directives can be used to facilitate mutual recognition of judgments and judicial decisions and police and judicial co-operation in criminal matters having a cross-border dimension.

[29] On this, see Art 82(2) TFEU, which refers to the adoption of 'minimum rules [which] shall not prevent Member States from maintaining or introducing a higher level of protection for individuals'. See also Art 168(5) TFEU, which specifically excludes 'any harmonisation of the laws and regulations of the Member States'.

[30] On the interpretation of Art 114 TFEU in this respect, see Case C-270/12 *United Kingdom v Parliament and Council* EU:C:2014:18 (ESMA) para 102 et seq.

legal bases be reserved to a group of Member States, the CJEU or the ECB.[31] The relevant legal basis may also involve the European Council through the operation of emergency brakes, applicable in some policy areas and which may result in a swift move to enhanced co-operation.[32] In addition, the choice of legal basis may also affect the geographical scope of application of the instrument.[33]

Keeping in mind the very general formulation of many of the Union objectives in the Treaties, the implementation of these objectives, and thus also Union competence to act, cannot take place without the attribution of a significant degree of discretionary powers.[34] The way of formulating many of the EU's legal bases in terms of purposes to be achieved in practice entails that their use is not constrained in its subject matter or the breadth of its impact.[35] This enhances the political dimension of the choices among them. The legal basis of an act is selected based on the principal objective or 'centre of gravity', that is, what in the view of the institution concerned constitutes the principal objective of the measure in question. Therefore, the method of selecting the legal basis already 'offers a considerable flexibility for subjecting the choice of a legal basis to the political preferences of the institution concerned', which is at odds with the guarantee function of a legal basis.[36] To put it simply, if a choice is this subjective, can it also be objective at the same time?

The formal rules concerning the choice of legal basis are complemented by a number of practices informed by what can be best described as 'politics of competence'. In practice, the Commission is likely to lean towards the use of a legal basis that enables qualified majority voting in the Council. This strengthens its own position, since the Council can only amend the Commission proposal by unanimity (Article 293 TFEU). One could also envisage the Commission making choices in favour of Treaty Articles which enable the exercise of exclusive or shared competence at the expense of those relating to supportive action, since this simultaneously buttresses its own role.[37] And since it is the Commission that authors a proposal, it has all the opportunities to formulate its objectives in a manner that supports such a choice. The Parliament naturally argues for legal bases that

[31] See Art 289(4) TFEU, Art 76 TFEU (Member States), Art 281 TFEU (CJEU) and Art 129(4) (ECB).

[32] See eg Art 86(1) TFEU.

[33] This has been topical for horizontal international agreements with some provisions falling under justice and home affairs. See eg the Partnership and Cooperation Agreement between the European Union and its Member States, of the one part, and the Republic of Iraq, of the other part OJ 2012 L 204/20. See also Case C-137/12 *Commission v Council* EU:C:2013:675 paras 73–74. These protocols were not of any relevance, since they do not relate to common commercial policy. See also Case C-44/14 *Spain v Parliament and Council* EU:C:2015:554, which concerns the application of the Schengen Protocol and Case C-202/13 *McCarthy* EU:C:2014:2450.

[34] See eg Barents, above n 6 at 89.

[35] G Davies, 'Democracy and Legitimacy in the Shadow of Purposive Competence' (2013) 21 *European Law Journal* 2. For similar views 20 years earlier, see Barents, above n 6.

[36] Barents, above n 6 at 101–02.

[37] See eg Decision No 1082/2013/EU on serious cross-border threats to health and repealing Decision No 2119/98/EC OJ 2013 L 293/1, which is based on Art 168(5) TFEU.

support its own position,[38] in particular the use of co-decision at the expense of special legislative procedures. The Council defends its own institutional role[39] and its right to legislate alone in the existence of conditions that enable such a conclusion, and the rights of Member States and their competence reserves. Therefore, the objective nature of these choices is often quite relative.

Since the legal basis defines the institutional roles and the nature and delimitation of competence between the Union and its Member States,[40] this choice also affects the outcome of the legislative process in fundamental ways. A Member State deputy permanent representative with years of insight into EU legislative work explains how most legislative files are non-problematic from a legal basis point of view. Yet approximately every tenth file—often those that are politically sensitive or otherwise particularly significant—contain legal issues that remain contested until the end of the legislative process, and sometimes beyond it.[41] Therefore, there would seem to be a clear linkage between competence questions and political desirability. Legal debates concerning these choices have a natural tendency to turn into political debates conducted in legal language. Jean-Paul Jacqué describes how

> Law is a natural instrument of the political debate, since states prefer to oppose a measure through legal arguments that give an objective appearance to their political preferences rather than openly displaying a political position that is purely based on national interests.[42]

In this debate, the legal services of the three institutions—Commission, Council and the European Parliament—play a central role. In Jacqué's view, it is the Member States in particular that 'have the knack of transforming their political misgivings about a matter into legal objections'; with their attempts to do so usually leaving the lawyer 'to decompose the legal arguments to show that this is not a legal debate but a political issue that must be dealt with by the political authorities'.[43] The way in which Member States deal with questions relating to EU competence varies: in some Member States, legal questions are systematically scrutinised very early in the legislative process, immediately after the adoption of a Commission proposal.[44] In others the approach is more reactive, with the exception of files that are politically particularly contested.[45]

In particular in the Council, where formal votes are seldom taken and matters are instead settled by consensus, argumentation is greatly strengthened by an

[38] Case C-130/10 *Parliament v Council* EU:C:2012:472.

[39] See eg Case C-130/10 *Parliament v Council* EU:C:2012:472.

[40] For a discussion of these effects, see eg the CITES case, Case C-370/07 *Commission v Council* EU:C:2009:590.

[41] Interview with a Deputy Permanent Representative (Respondent 15).

[42] Jacqué, above n 14 at 43.

[43] ibid 50.

[44] Such countries include, eg, the UK and Finland, where questions of competence and legal basis fall under normal parliamentary scrutiny and their analysis is subject to tight deadlines.

[45] Interview with a legal adviser at a Member State Permanent Representation (Respondent 23).

ample knowledge of one's legal limitations. Negotiation results are highly dependent on how you dress your arguments and proper timing for presenting them in the procedure. Many legal basis and competence questions are questions of interpretation. Therefore, legal advice largely operates as 'risk assessment'. Legal advice offered by the institutions' legal services often consists of 'our best assessment is that this is the safest option', and while 'very often pushed to give a clearer answer, but whether you can or not depends on the circumstances of each individual case, and often you can't.'[46] And 'if the politicians wish to ignore or override such advice, it is their prerogative to do so (at their peril)'.[47]

Most of the time, the limits of competence are settled in the political process: in the European Council, in the context of Commission preparation, in the Council preparatory bodies or in trilogues. The recent decision to set up the Single Resolution Mechanism and Fund on the basis of Article 114 TFEU illustrates these developments. First, the European Council paved the way for the mechanism by underlining how 'a fully effective [Single Supervisory Mechanism] requires a Single Resolution Mechanism (SRM)', and encouraging the Commission to put forward a proposal establishing an SRM, 'with a view to reaching agreement in the Council by the end of the year so that it can be adopted before the end of the current parliamentary term'.[48] It is evident that in the absence of a specific legal basis for the establishment of a banking union, such a conclusion was also intended to clear any doubts as to the existence of this competence. The Conclusions were soon followed up by a Commission proposal for a regulation. Its legal basis was Article 114 TFEU, which in the view of the Commission, constituted its 'appropriate legal base' since the proposal aimed to 'preserve the integrity and enhance the functioning of the internal market'[49]—irrespective of the fact that it was only to cover the banks operating in the euro area, and not the internal market as a whole. The Council general approach, adopted on 18 December 2013, however, built on a compromise consisting of two instruments: a draft regulation and a decision by euro-area Member States committing them to negotiate, by March 2014, an intergovernmental agreement (IGA) on the functioning of the Single Resolution fund.[50] The latter was to cover those issues that were believed to have fiscal and budgetary implications and thus, in the eyes of many Member States, reached beyond EU competence. The Commission was quick to comment that it did 'not agree on every point in the general approach, but real progress has been made

[46] Interview with a Member of Council Legal Service (Respondent 6).

[47] Interview with a Member of the Legal Service of the European Parliament (Respondent 19).

[48] Council, 'Conclusions—27/28 June 2013', Brussels, 28 June 2013, EUCO 104/2/13 REV 2.

[49] Proposal for a regulation of the European Parliament and of the Council establishing uniform rules and a uniform procedure for the resolution of credit institutions and certain investment firms in the framework of a Single Resolution Mechanism and a Single Bank Resolution Fund and amending Regulation (EU) No 1093/2010 of the European Parliament and of the Council COM(2013) 520 final section 3.1.

[50] Council, 'Council agrees general approach on Single Resolution Mechanism', Brussels, 18 December 2013, 17602/13.

in very little time'.[51] The Parliament—which saw its rights of participation being limited to questions that were considered to fall under EU competence—was opposed to the division of the instrument into an EU and intergovernmental part: 'The legal framework on which to base the mechanism and fund is the Regulation. As such all issues must be open to discussion within the trilogues.'[52]

Competence issues therefore resulted in a clear split between the Member States, on the one hand, and between the institutions, on the other. Finding a sustainable compromise on both the substantive and legal aspects of the file was in the interests of all parties. There was widespread agreement on the need to create EU-level tools for bank resolution. Legal uncertainty and possible litigation were considered particularly unwanted in the case of economically significant decisions relating to such decisions.

Following trilogues on the division of the substance between the Regulation and the IGA, a deal was finally identified, building on the rapid mutualisation of the national compartments of the fund. Since the existence of national compartments was something that the European Parliament objected to as a matter of principle, a swift timetable for their disappearance was 'a key issue MEPs wanted settled before the intergovernmental chapter could be given a green light'.[53] There was sufficient conviction among the Member States about the substance of the IGA falling under Member State competence; therefore the European Parliament in fact formally had no say as far as its substance was concerned. Yet it was evident that the whole package was ultimately settled in trilogues. The final deal was based on the dual instrument of an EU regulation based on Article 114 TFEU, applied to states participating in the Single Supervisory Mechanism (euro states), and the IGA concluded between them. This choice is explained in the preamble of the Regulation in the following terms:

> The Fund should be financed by bank contributions raised at national level and should be pooled at Union level in accordance with an intergovernmental agreement on the transfer and progressive mutualisation of those contributions (the 'Agreement'), thus increasing financial stability and limiting the link between the perceived fiscal position of individual Member States and the funding costs of banks and undertakings operating in those Member States. To further break that link, decisions taken within the SRM should not impinge on the fiscal responsibilities of the Member States. In that regard, only extraordinary public financial support should be considered to be an impingement on the budgetary sovereignty and fiscal responsibilities of the Member States. In particular,

[51] Commissioner Michel Barnier's remarks at the ECOFIN Council press conference, Brussels, 19 December 2013, available at http://europa.eu/rapid/press-release_MEMO-13-1186_en.htm?locale=en.

[52] European Parliament, 'Single bank resolution mechanism and fund: Key principles for successful negotiations', ECON Press release—Economic and monetary affairs, 17 February 2014, available at www.europarl.europa.eu/news/en/news-room/20140217IPR36239/Single-resolution-mechanism-and-fund-Key-principles-for-successful-negotiations.

[53] European Parliament, 'Parliament negotiators rescue seriously damaged bank resolution system', ECON Press release—Economic and monetary affairs—20 March 2014, available at www.europarl.europa.eu/news/en/news-room/20140319IPR39310/Parliament-negotiators-rescue-seriously-damaged-bank-resolution-system.

decisions that require the use of the Fund or of a deposit guarantee scheme should not be considered to impinge on the budgetary sovereignty or fiscal responsibilities of the Member States.[54]

Since the deal has not been challenged before the Court, the division of competence remains unsettled. The plans related to the future development of the Economic and Monetary Union include a reference to bringing the IGA under Union competence, but it is not specified whether this would require Treaty amendment or not.[55]

The choice of legal basis often has consequences for how—following which procedure—the relevant decision will be taken. The ambiguity of the legal framework provides opportunities to engage in what Jupille has described as 'procedural politics',[56] and which may significantly affect the outcome of the political law-making process. The Court has consistently held that decision-making rules do not fall under Member States' or institutional discretion, but that such rules are established by the Treaties alone.[57] However, there is still some leeway for procedural imagination—in case the institutions agree on the need to use it. Again, identifying a compromise is of the essence. The introduction of 'reverse qualified majority voting' under the procedures relating to economic governance is one example of such imagination.[58] Since all the relevant institutions agreed on the need to streamline decision making, the compatibility of the procedures with the Treaties has not been addressed by the Court.[59]

Another example of procedural imagination relates to the EU Fundamental Rights Agency, which was set up following many years of uncertainty as to the scope and nature of EU competence relating to fundamental rights in particular as regards monitoring the Member States—therefore a highly political file. The negotiations were preceded by Conclusions by Member States' representatives

[54] Regulation (EU) No 806/2014 of 15 July 2014 establishing uniform rules and a uniform procedure for the resolution of credit institutions and certain investment firms in the framework of a Single Resolution Mechanism and a Single Resolution Fund and amending Regulation (EU) No 1093/2010 OJ 2014 L 225/1 preamble para 19.

[55] *The Five Presidents' Report: Completing Europe's Economic and Monetary Union*, 22 June 2015, at 20, where the integration into the framework of EU law of the relevant parts of the Intergovernmental Agreement on the Single Resolution Fund is mentioned as one of the immediate steps of Stage 1, to be completed before 30 June 2017.

[56] J Jupille, *Procedural Politics. Issues, Influence, and Institutional Choice in the European Union* (Cambridge, Cambridge University Press, 2004).

[57] See eg Case C-540/13 *Parliament v Council* EU:C:2015:224 para 32.

[58] For a discussion of this choice and its earlier use in trade policy, see P Leino and J Salminen, 'Going "Belt and Braces"—Domestic Effects of Euro-crisis Law', *EUI Working Papers LAW* 2015/15; R Palmsdorfer, 'The Reverse Majority Voting under the "Six Pack": A Bad Turn for the Union?' (2014) 20 *European Law Journal* 186. The use of RQMV has since expanded to new policy areas, see eg Regulation 1303/2013 laying down common provisions on the European Regional Development Fund, etc OJ 2013 L 347/320 Art 23(10).

[59] The Court addressed a Council decision-making procedure with a similar character in *Eurocoton*, but this decision predates the Treaty of Lisbon and relates to competition law, where institutional roles and competence are different from those applicable in economic policy. See Case C-76/01 P *Comité des industries du coton et des fibres connexes de l'Union européenne (Eurocoton) and Others v Council of the European Union* [2003] 511.

meeting in the European Council, agreeing 'to build upon the existing European Monitoring Centre on Racism and Xenophobia and to extend its mandate to make it a Human Rights Agency to that effect'—something that the Commission agreed to and indicated its intention of submitting the relevant proposal.[60] The doubts relating to the existence of competence—linked with the mandate of the future agency to scrutinise Member State action—were, however, not cleared away with the Conclusions. The three institutions disagreed on whether the Regulation establishing the Agency was to be set up on the basis of a combination of legal bases, in particular relating to discrimination, presuming co-decision,[61] or ex-Article 308 TEC building on unanimity in the Council and consultation of the Parliament. The Commission proposal built on the latter with reference to how

> It is a general objective of the Community to ensure that its own action fully respects fundamental rights. The Agency's establishment will further that objective, without there being specific powers provided for in the Treaty to that end.[62]

The legislative procedure that was informally agreed to build upon 'quasi-codecision', which involved informal trilogues, familiar from the co-decision procedure and deemed efficient in forging interinstitutional compromise, among the three institutions combined with the ex-Article 308 TEC procedure. The Parliament's willingness to engage in such a procedure was presumably linked to it being the institution most strongly behind the establishment of the Agency. During the trilogues, a shared position between the three institutions was found, to which the Parliament then formally gave its approval in the consultation procedure. Gaining the Parliament's agreement on the file—and allowing it to influence the outcome much more than a normal consultation procedure would have allowed—was deemed necessary to prevent the Parliament from challenging the legal basis, which was considered to be somewhat uncertain, before the Court. The innovative interpretation of Union competence and the applicable procedure was never addressed by the Court, since the three institutions agreed on the arrangement enabling the Agency to be set up.[63] The political message included in its

[60] Conclusions of the Representatives of the Member States meeting at head of state or government level in Brussels on 13 December 2003, available at www.consilium.europa.eu/en/european-council/conclusions/pdf-1993-2003/BRUSSELS-EUROPEAN-COUNCIL---12-AND-13-DECEMBER-2003---PRESIDENCY-CONCLUSIONS/.

[61] See the draft European Parliament legislative resolution on the proposal for a Council regulation on establishing a European Union Agency for Fundamental Rights, available in the legislative observatory at www.europarl.europa.eu/sides/getDoc.do?type=REPORT&mode=XML&reference=A6-2006-306&language=EN.

[62] Proposal for a Council Regulation establishing a European Union Agency for Fundamental Rights COM(2005) 280 final.

[63] See Council Regulation (EC) No 168/2007 of 15 February 2007 establishing a European Union Agency for Fundamental Rights OJ 2007 L 53/1. In the preamble, the choice of legal basis is described as follows: 'The contribution made by the Agency to ensuring full respect of fundamental rights in the framework of Community law is likely to help achieve the Community's objectives. With regard to the adoption of this Regulation, the Treaty does not provide for powers other than those set out in Article 308.'

establishment weighed heavier than the one relating to its modest mandate. But the compromise deal on setting up the Agency did not include the adoption of the Commission's separate proposal to extend its mandate to act under the former third pillar (police and judicial co-operation in criminal matters), where its input might have been more urgently needed than in the areas of fisheries or agriculture. And even though the third pillar is now history, the competence consideration—which at the time was presented as a mere technical issue relating to the way in which the Treaties were then constructed[64]—has not been overcome.

Thus, the legislature ultimately has a great deal of discretion with respect to legal basis and the applicable procedure. The increased use of the ordinary legislative procedure, especially after the Treaty of Lisbon entered into force, means that even when different options exist as to the most appropriate legal basis, these choices might not affect the applicable legislative procedure. Recourse to special legislative procedures with atypical institutional roles is made less often. The fact that the ordinary legislative procedure has indeed become routine seems to have brought with it a presumption that recourse to a special procedure presumes particular justification, and therefore is more or less destined to result in interinstitutional debates and package deals.[65] In its jurisprudence, the Court has demonstrated a specific concern for the prerogatives of the European Parliament,[66] which has also been reflected in the discussion on incompatible legal bases.[67] But the Court has established that even when the choice of legal basis has consequences for the Parliament's position, this fact could not determine the choice of legal basis.[68]

[64] See para 32 of the Preamble of Council Regulation (EC) No 168/2007: 'Nothing in this Regulation should be interpreted in such a way as to prejudice the question of whether the remit of the Agency may be extended to cover the areas of police cooperation and judicial cooperation in criminal matters.' The declarations adopted by the Council and individual Member States at the time of the conclusion of the FRA regulation can be found at http://fra.europa.eu/sites/default/files/st06396-ad01.en07.pdf and include several relating to competence.

[65] See eg the package deal consisting of Council Regulation (EU) No 1024/2013 conferring specific tasks on the European Central Bank concerning policies relating to the prudential supervision of credit institution OJ 2013 L 287/63 and Regulation (EU) No 1022/2013 of the European Parliament and of the Council of 22 October 2013 amending Regulation (EU) No 1093/2010 establishing a European Supervisory Authority (European Banking Authority) as regards the conferral of specific tasks on the European Central Bank pursuant to Council Regulation (EU) No 1024/2013 OJ 2013 L 287/5, which the European Parliament voted upon as a package even though the first is based on Article 127(6) TFEU presuming the use of a special legislative procedure, and the latter is based on Article 114 TFEU and the ordinary legislative procedure.

[66] On the Parliament's right to intervene in proceedings, see Case C-138/79 *Roquette Frères v Council* EU:C:1980:249 para 20; on the EP's right to be consulted, see Case C-408/95 *Eurotunnel* EU:C:1997:532 paras 45–46. In the latter, the Court confirmed that under the consultation procedure, the Parliament needs to be 'consulted again whenever the text finally adopted, taken as a whole, differs in essence from the text on which the Parliament has already been consulted, except in cases in which the amendments substantially correspond to the wishes of the Parliament itself' (para 46). On the Parliament's right to bring an action of annulment, see Case 302/87 *Parliament v Council* EU:C:1988:461.

[67] Case C-155/07 *Parliament v Council* EU:C:2008:605 (loans to the EIB) para 78.

[68] Case C-130/10 *Parliament v Council* EU:C:2012:472. In greater detail, see P Leino, 'In principle the full review—what justice for Mr Kadi?' in R Liivoja and J Petman (eds), *International Law-making. Essays in Honour of Jan Klabbers* (London, Routledge, 2013) at 225.

While the Court accepted that the participation of the Parliament reflects the principle of democracy at Union level, the difference in the degree of Parliament's involvement under the Treaty Articles[69] 'is the result of the choice made by the framers of the Treaty of Lisbon conferring a more limited role on the Parliament with regard to the Union's action under the CFSP'.[70]

The points raised above demonstrate the significance of reaching interinstitutional compromises. Legal questions are no exception. And yet, legal voices are never weaker than at the point when a compromise deal between the three institutions is about to emerge. A Council Legal Service representative explains how 'sometimes at the end of Presidencies you reach deals late at night that we find are illegal, and that many Member States opposed for that reason'.[71] A European Parliament Legal Service representative tells how 'in my impression the moments when we have difficulties, real difficulties, to have our opinion followed, is the moment of compromise emerges with the Council' (sic). Is there a possibility of saying at that moment that the solution is illegal? 'Never, never, never with this work, and never in a trilogue.'[72] Often ambiguity acts as a legislative technique enabling such compromises to be made. A Member of the CLS explains how

> [s]ometimes for to compromise an agreement you sacrifice the clarity and our capacity of influence there at the Legal Service is minimal ... Sometimes we are the perpetrators of the obscurity.[73]

Various choices can be maintained in Court by invoking the right legislative techniques. The politics of competence and legal basis result in the practice of using the preambles of acts as a means by which to justify the choices made by the legislature, defining the main and predominant objectives of the act.[74] As will be explained below, the Court has accepted this tactic. Once the substance of the file is settled and a deal made on the applicable legal basis, the preamble of the act will be adjusted accordingly. Most of the drafting of the preamble is done between the Presidency, the Council Legal Service and the Secretariat with the aim of 'how we can legally get these texts as waterproof as possible'.[75] These matters are seldom

[69] In this case Art 75 TFEU, which provides for the ordinary legislative procedure, and Art 215(1) TFEU, which only requires the Council to inform the Parliament.

[70] Para 82.

[71] Interview with a Member of the Council Legal Service (Respondent 7).

[72] Interview with a Member of the Legal Service of the European Parliament, 10 February 2016 (Respondent 2).

[73] Interview with a Member of the Council Legal Service (Respondent 13).

[74] Case C-411/06 *Commission v Parliament and Council* EU:C:2009:518 (shipments of waste), in which the Commission disagreed with the justifications of the European Parliament and the Council. The Court accepted the arguments of the latter, see especially paras 51–54. 'By contrast, and as observed by the Parliament and the Council, the preamble to the contested regulation does not make any reference to the pursuit of objectives falling within the common commercial policy' (para 54). See also Case C-217/04 *United Kingdom v Parliament and Council* EU:C:2006:279 (ENISA) paras 48–53 and 63.

[75] Interview with a legal adviser at a Member State Representation (Respondent 11).

discussed among the Member States.[76] These matters are perceived merely as technical choices that provoke little political passion. And yet, in the case of the validity of an act being challenged, these factors may prove decisive in ultimately settling whether the act will stand.

These examples illustrate the function of law in the political process: it structures the parameters within which courts, legislators, executives, administrators and other social actors operate.[77] Within these parameters, law leaves a certain leeway for political choices. The formal rules ultimately avail the legislature with a great deal of discretion. These rules are often indeterminate, and therefore definite or objective choices might be difficult to make. This also applies to legal debates, where compromises represent 'an important pattern of praxis regulating the crystallization of a legal argument'.[78] A legal proposal then becomes 'less about saying the right thing and more about reflecting a temporary equilibrium, which is bound to change again'.[79] Solutions build on compromises concerning both the interpretation of the rules and the substance of the legislative file. Together, they form a package deal.

LEGAL BASIS IN COMPETENCE LITIGATION

There is a great deal of case law relating to the choice of legal basis. This jurisprudence demonstrates just how relevant this issue is to institutional politics. While these debates are usually dressed in objective terms, they often relate to institutional power and roles under alternative legal bases. Legal basis litigation is

> a potentially useful tool in advancing wider political aims designed to expand, or to confirm, their own powers. As such, legal basis challenges form part of a political strategy to maximize power and influence over the legislative programme of the EC.[80]

One of the elements raised already during the legislative procedure is the prospect of interinstitutional litigation; therefore, legal advisers frequently refer in their legal opinions to the risks involved in adopting particular options, and how 'if you are taken to Court over this, in our view the chances of us successfully defending it would be low or non-existent'.[81] In some particularly contested legislative files, the Council Legal Service identifies at an early stage a particular line to follow in

[76] Interview with a legal adviser at a Member State Representation (Respondent 23).

[77] G de Búrca, above n 5 at 310, 319–20.

[78] K Sideri, 'The European Commission and the law-making process: compromise as a category of praxis' (2005) 2 *International Journal of Law in Context* 155 at 156.

[79] ibid at 174.

[80] H Cullen and A Charlesworth, 'Diplomacy by Other Means: The Use of Legal Basis Litigation as a Political Strategy by the European Parliament and Member States' (1999) 36 *Common Market Law Review* 1243 at 1243.

[81] Interview with a Member of Council Legal Service (Respondent 6).

negotiations in order to have a chance to win at Court.[82] The prospect of litigation is something that the Member States also consider already during the negotiating process:

> You will be questioning how much you actually achieve in a negotiation versus how much you could possibly achieve through litigation. But normally the priority would be to try and negotiate our concerns away. So our focus is not on taking litigation, it'll really be litigation as a last resort in the event that we haven't been able to negotiate.[83]

The prospect of litigation also affects voting behaviour in the Council:

> It never looks great if you're in court … and the court asks well how did you actually vote on this proposal and you say we voted in favour of it. So that will influence whether you abstain or you actually have a hostile vote … Quite often it will influence whether you put down a minutes statement on adoption.[84]

Negotiation and litigation are not as separate as one would think, that is, when the former ends, the latter takes over. They can also advance in parallel. Instead of being a purely legal exercise, the main function of litigation may in those cases relate to the communication of concerns to the other parties to the legislative process through the Court process.[85] Some recent examples of this can be found in the area of enhanced co-operation. In relation to the EU patent regime, two Member States brought annulment proceedings while the legislative process was still pending. The purpose of this action seems to mainly relate to a wish to stress the importance of their arguments as well as to demonstrate their willingness to continue the discussion in Court if their concerns were not sufficiently taken into account during the legislative procedure.[86] In relation to the financial transaction tax, the UK requested the Court to annul a Council Decision authorising enhanced co-operation, even though negotiations on the file are still on-going and the result, if any, remains unclear. In its application, the UK fully acknowledged that its action constituted a precautionary measure, which could be considered to be premature. In these kinds of situation the Court has been reluctant to intervene.[87]

Usually litigation formally enters the picture only after the conclusion of a negotiating process. When a compromise acceptable to all parties cannot be identified within a reasonable time, or there is no interest in looking for one, debates result in interinstitutional litigation.[88] Annulment proceedings can be brought within a two-month deadline (Article 263 TFEU). Apart from the Member State

[82] Interview with a Member of Council Legal Service (Respondent 20).

[83] Interview with a legal adviser at a Member State Representation (Respondent 22).

[84] ibid.

[85] ibid at 1268–69.

[86] Joined Cases C-274/11 and C-295/11 *Spain and Italy v Council* EU:C:2013:240. The Court dismissed the actions.

[87] See Case C-209/13 *United Kingdom v Council* EU:C:2014:283. While the Court was not convinced by the arguments raised, the proceedings created an additional channel for the UK to raise its concerns.

[88] See Cullen and Charlesworth, above n 80; K Lenaerts, 'How the ECJ thinks: A study on judicial legitimacy' (2013) 36 *Fordham International Law Journal* 1302.

appeals described above, all the three institutions involved in the legislative procedure are known to defend their institutional prerogatives in Court, most notably perhaps the Parliament.[89] Since its first successful annulment action,[90] there have been many others relating to the Parliament's rights of participation.[91] While the Parliament's legal service provides advice on whether legal proceedings are likely or not to succeed, the decision to initiate legal proceedings is 'also influenced by considerations of political opportunity'.[92] Well-known examples of successful interinstitutional litigation include environmental crimes—for example, an annulment action brought by the Commission supported by the Parliament against the Council for failure to use the first pillar legal basis for criminal penalties.[93] It is also an example of a case where the Council is known to have acted against the advice of its own legal service, the views of which were later confirmed by the CJEU. In Parliament, which is highly fractured in composition and where less legal advice circulates, the 'non-partisan advice of an independent administrative agency is generally followed, particularly as regards its analysis of the relevant Treaty and other legal provisions'.[94]

Many of the interinstitutional cases relating to institutional prerogatives and the choice of legal basis also reopen issues that have been subject to disagreement during the legislative procedure and on which no satisfactory compromise was reached.[95] But since the Parliament and Council today often act as co-legislators, the Parliament's incentive to litigate autonomously has decreased.[96] Still, there are currently several interinstitutional cases pending.[97]

Litigation is a mundane part of EU practice, and thus almost an everyday occurrence in EU institutional politics. A Member State legal adviser explains how despite this,

> We certainly don't do it lightly, and I think you experience the thought that is the Court's an unpredictable animal so you need to think about having quite good and solid arguments and you also have to think about who you're going to be challenging and what's

[89] See eg Case C-70/88 *Parliament v Council* EU:C:1990:217 para 28.

[90] Case C-295/90 *Parliament v Council* EU:C:1992:294.

[91] Case C-355/10 *Parliament v Council* EU:C:2012:516 (Schengen Borders Code).

[92] Interview with a Member of the Legal Service of the European Parliament (Respondent 19).

[93] Case C-176/03 *Commission v Council* EU:C:2005:542.

[94] Interview with a Member of the Legal Service of the European Parliament (Respondent 19).

[95] For an example, see Case C-344/04 *IATA* EU:C:2006:10 and Kieran Bradley's case note, 'A wing and a prayer' (2006) 43 *Common Market Law Review* 1101 at 1121.

[96] On this, see eg E Fahey, 'Of one shotters and repeat-hitters: a retrospective on the role of the European Parliament in the EU-US PNR litigation' in B Davies and F Nicola (eds), *EU law stories* (Cambridge, Cambridge University Press, 2015).

[97] These include cases relating to the Lisbon Agreement where the Council decision authorising the opening of negotiations acknowledges the existence of Member State competence, even if the matter in the view of the Commission falls under exclusive EU competence, Case C-389/15 *Commission v Council* OJ 2015 C 311/42, and the Commission request for *Opinion 3/15* on the existence of exclusive competence to conclude the Marrakesh Treaty. See also Commission annulment action concerning Council Conclusions on the World Radiocommunications Conference 2015, Case C-687/15 *Commission v Council* OJ 2016 C 68/24.

> the nature of the judge … [L]itigation can be a very effective tool in your armoury but you have to use it sparingly. You'd be crazy to say to a minister every time that you don't get your own what you want, go and litigate, because … [y]ou can lose, and … it has to be very well calibrated and thought through.[98]

There is also a personal dimension to this challenge. If a legislative file ends up before the Court, the same person who was in charge of the file within the institution's legal service is likely to be the one defending the choices before the Court. According to a member of the CLS,

> this makes you play careful and safe. But there are also files where you see immediately that we will lose. We're not directly frightened of the Court, but instead we like to make sure through the use of recitals and such. Court cases also take a long time. But the Court is not particularly well trusted.[99]

In its practice the Court tends to rely heavily on the thinking of the legislature, particularly as reflected in the preamble of the legislative act. The legislative choices and their relationship with the objectives of the act, and thus the appropriate legal basis, should therefore be thoroughly explained in the preamble, which logically guides interpretation in the desired direction. While some references to the Commission proposal and attached background documents can be found in Court rulings, the main emphasis of interpretation relies on the choices made by the legislature in identifying the appropriate means for promoting the objectives at which it is aiming and establishing what is necessary in a particular situation.[100] The recent *ESMA (short-selling)* ruling offers an example of this method. Following a number of quotations from the preamble indicating the intentions of the EU legislature, the Court concludes:

> It follows that the purpose of the powers provided for in Article 28 of Regulation No 236/2012 is in fact to improve the conditions for the establishment and functioning of the internal market in the financial field. It is apparent from all the foregoing considerations that Article 28 of Regulation No 236/2012 satisfies all the requirements laid down in Article 114 TFEU. The latter provision therefore constitutes an appropriate legal basis for the adoption of Article 28.[101]

[98] Interview with a legal adviser at a Member State Representation (Respondent 22).

[99] Interview with a Member of Council Legal Service (Respondent 20).

[100] See eg Case C-58/08 *Vodafone* EU:C:2010:321 paras 38–46, where following numerous references to the Preamble of Regulation No 717/2007, the Court concludes that '[s]uch a situation justified the Community legislature's seeking to protect the proper functioning of the internal market, as stated in paragraph 38 of this judgment. It follows from the foregoing that the object of Regulation No 717/2007 is indeed to improve the conditions for the functioning of the internal market and that it could be adopted on the basis of Article 95 EC', paras 47–48.

[101] Case C-270/12 *United Kingdom v Parliament and Council* EU:C:2014:18 paras 116–17. Also the German *Bundesverfassungsgericht* stressed the way in which the Court of Justice essentially relies on the objectives of the measure as indicated by the organ on review as well as on the recourse to the instrument of the purchase of government bonds enshrined in Article 18 of the ESCB Statute when qualifying the OMT programme as an instrument belonging to the field of monetary policy. *BVerfG*, OMT Judgment of 21 June 2016—2 BvR 2728/13, 2 BvR 2729/13, 2 BvR 2730/13, 2 BvR 2731/13, 2 BvE 13/13.

This technique of interpretation of course stresses the flexibility of the legislature in choosing the legal basis—if there is agreement on it between the European Parliament and (within) the Council—and adjusting the legal act accordingly. The same applies to discretion concerning the choice of appropriate measures. The ruling concerning the working time directive elegantly illustrates this point:

> the Council must be allowed a wide discretion in an area which, as here, involves the legislature in making social policy choices and requires it to carry out complex assessments. Judicial review of the exercise of that discretion must therefore be limited to examining whether it has been vitiated by manifest error or misuse of powers, or whether the institution concerned has manifestly exceeded the limits of its discretion.[102]

Since the Court primarily resorts to interpretative techniques, it has set the threshold for annulling acts relatively high:

> A measure is vitiated by misuse of powers only if it appears, on the basis of objective, relevant and consistent evidence to have been taken solely, or at the very least chiefly, for ends other than those for which the power in question was conferred or with the aim of evading a procedure specifically prescribed by the Treaty for dealing with the circumstances of the case.[103]

If drafting has been careful, the risk of annulment can be effectively fought back. The Treaty stipulates that '[i]f the action is well founded, the Court of Justice of the European Union shall declare the act concerned to be void' (Article 264 TFEU). The institutions are required to take the necessary measures to comply with the judgment (Article 266 TFEU), which often means replacing the act with another one under a different legal basis. This can of course be either a technical exercise or another opportunity for an institutional battle. But even when an act is annulled, the effects of litigation are seldom dramatic.[104] This is also known in the legal services of the institutions:

> And even when a competence or legal basis or procedural questions case is lost, the Court will usually maintain the effects, or there will only be a limited amendment through the introduction of another legal basis.[105]

In practice, the effects of annulled instruments are often maintained. The Court may also state on the effects of the ruling. It is common for the parties to request that the effects of the contested legal act be maintained until a new act has been

[102] Case C-84/94 *United Kingdom v Council* EU:C:1996:431 (Working Time Directive) para 58.

[103] Joined Cases C-274/11 and C-295/11 *Spain and Italy v Council* EU:C:2013:240 para 33.

[104] But there are also more dramatic results of interinstitutional litigation. For example, in the EU-US PNR Agreement case the Court annulled both the Council Decision concluding the EU-US Agreement on the processing and transfer of PNR data by Air Carriers to the US Department of Homeland Security and the relating Commission Decision on the adequate protection of personal data. This ruling took effect 90 days from the date of notification. This entailed in practice a need to reopen negotiations on the Agreement with the US authorities with a significant risk of disruptions in the air traffic between the EU and US had the new Agreement not been concluded on time. See Joined Cases C-317/04 and C-318/04 *Parliament v Council and Commission* EU:C:2006:346.

[105] Interview with a Member of Council Legal Service (Respondent 20).

adopted, and to rule on the effect of, for example, payments made or commitments entered into on the basis of the act, in case it is annulled,[106] with reference to the requirements of legal certainty and legitimate expectations. The Court also frequently does this, which further lowers the threshold for bringing annulment actions. Partial annulment of an act is in principle also possible.[107]

Considering the limited effects of the relatively few successful annulment cases brought against EU legal acts (especially considering the total figure of acts adopted every year), it is possible that the greatest influence of judicial review is in fact in the prospect of its existence and the possibility that an act results in an annulment action. It is likely that the institutions and Member States are mostly interested in avoiding legal certainty while the judicial process is pending, rather than in its actual outcome. The greater the uncertainty concerning the choice of correct legal basis, the greater the need to find compromise on the file, as the examples quoted in the previous section—the Single Resolution Mechanism and Fund, and the EU Fundamental Rights Agency—demonstrate.

The vagueness of formal rules emphasises the role of the CJEU in determining what ultimately counts as a proper choice of legal basis. In addition, it is felt that the Court currently suffers from an institutional bias: 'so if it's a Member State against an institution it's a pretty uphill battle'.[108] This provides additional impetus for trying to solve matters during the political process. While it is evident that the Court is also 'capable of being influenced by the political debates presented to it',[109] it is not straightforward to what extent its rulings reflect institutional or Member State positions, often mediated through written pleadings submitted to the Court, in such debates. There are numerous cases where the Member States have acted on a broad basis and in a coordinated manner to stress a particular position, and yet failed to convince the Court of this interpretation.[110] In his recent strategic analysis of 'How the CJEU thinks', Koen Lenaerts, President of the CJEU, argues that the Court is 'constantly seeking to strike the balance imposed by the rule of law

[106] The Court tends to justify maintaining the legal effects of annulled acts for a reasonable period until a new act is adopted with reference to grounds for legal certainty. See eg Case C-166/07 *Parliament v Council* EU:C:2009:499 (Community financial contributions to the International Fund for Ireland) para 70; Case C-155/07 *Parliament v Council* EU:C:2008:605 (Community guarantee to the European Investment Bank against losses under loans and loan guarantees for projects outside the Community) paras 86–89.

[107] Case C-376/98 *Germany v Parliament and Council* EU:C:2000:544 (Tobacco advertising) paras 115–18. In this case, however, the Court decided to annul the directive in its entirety.

[108] Interview with a legal adviser at a Member State Representation (Respondent 22).

[109] Cullen and Charlesworth, above n 80 at 1270.

[110] There are several cases that would offer interesting avenues for further analysis of in particular the effect of Member State positions on the Court. For example, in Case C-176/03 *Commission v Council* EU:C:2005:542 (environmental crimes), the European Parliament supported the Commission while 11 Member States intervened in support of the Council; in Case C-440/05 *Commission v Council* EU:C:2007:625 (ship-source pollution) the Parliament again supported the Commission while 19 Member States intervened in support of the Council; and in *Opinion 2/13* EU:C:2014:2454, apart from the three main institutions, 24 Member States submitted observations to the Court. In all of these cases, Member State positions proved unpersuasive.

among the different interests at stake in a multi-layered system of governance',[111] but stresses the need to draw the borderline between law and politics, which coincides with the contours of the Court's own legitimacy. Contested acts of secondary law cannot be rewritten by the Court, but it 'must avoid inter-institutional conflicts which could arise if the contested act is annulled'. The wording of secondary EU legislation must be interpreted, insofar as possible, in a manner consistent with the provisions of the Treaties so as not to affect its validity.[112] Therefore the CJEU often has recourse to 'reconciliatory interpretation', entailing that EU law is interpreted in line with primary EU law as far as it is not *contra legem*. Lenaerts also stresses the importance of compromises within the CJEU itself, where consensus-building requires bringing on board as many opinions as possible, limited to solving the legal questions that are necessary to solve the case at hand.

The insights offered by President Lenaerts demonstrate how legal basis choices and litigation not only concern institutional politics by the institutions involved in the legislative process (the Commission, the European Parliament, the Council and the Member States), but also involve choices and compromises within the Court itself. Therefore, one might wonder: where is objectivity, if even the prospect of judicial review might fail to guarantee this dimension? Or is this kind of objective a mere illusion?

CONCLUSIONS

The flexibility offered to the legislature in choosing the appropriate legal basis (and adjusting the act accordingly), and the amount of case law on this matter demonstrates that the choice of legal basis is far from the objective, neutral or non-political exercise that the Court's jurisprudence claims it should be. In practice, the rules relating to the objectivity of these choices have produced a great number of informal practices within the framework of formal rules, which stress institutional discretion and rely on compromises for their existence and application. The Treaty and Court jurisprudence set parameters within which political solutions can be made, but these rules are also easily instrumentalised. This illustrates the close relationship between these rules and legislative technique. Legal acts can be written in different ways, depending on the objectives at which they are claimed to aim. Subjective choices follow as a logical consequence of the game. Legal rules make a difference, but instead of ultimately settling any outcomes, they make us argue in a particular way.

However we try to structure the limits and requirements of the competence framework, there is a need to accept that competence is ultimately largely a political question and, for the most part, settled in the political process. In practice, if

[111] Lenaerts, above n 84 at 1304.

[112] Case C-540/13 *Parliament v Council* EU:C:2015:224.

there is agreement between the institutions, the act will stand. Interinstitutional compromises play a key function in the way in which legislative decision making operates in the EU context. The promise of judicial review—a key element of the guarantee function that a legal basis is believed to have—that brings comfort to lawyers' troubled minds has little practical relevance, presuming that all parties to the negotiations are pleased with the outcome. Finding a compromise on the substantive aspects of a legislative file, its legal basis and procedural questions relating to its adoption are intertwined and thus all form a part of the same package deal. And if there is sustainable compromise, there is unlikely to be anyone to appeal the case to the Court. The legislative act will stand, no matter how unorthodox its legal basis might be. Therefore, the promise of judicial review mainly serves as a constraining force during the negotiation process, instead of offering a systematic review of adopted EU acts and their compatibility with the EU Treaties.

While concern about the way in which legal limits will not hold has clear grounds to it, the way EU decision-making works demonstrates that most of the time they are not, in fact, supposed to hold. Legal rules are secondary to political compromise concerning their interpretation. However, the credibility of legal basis argumentation presumes that ostensibly subjective choices are not made too often,[113] and that the institutional choices made usually pass scrutiny by the CJEU. Most of the time, the key question concerning the exercise of EU competence might not be one of judicial review, which is the way in which the discussion so far has been construed, centring on the CJEU. Instead, the question of its limits is a question of political control and how it should be organised. And this is an area where much remains to be done.

[113] Lenaerts, above n 88 at 1245.

Part IV

Critical Reflections on Legitimacy and Proposals for Reform

14

Integration through Soft Law: No Competence Needed? Juridical and Bio-Power in the Realm of Soft Law

MARK DAWSON*

INTRODUCTION

WHEN CONSIDERING THE larger question of the delineation of competences in the EU, soft law's emergence began as little more than an annoyance. The Maastricht Treaty's discussions over subsidiarity conceptualised subsidiarity—and competence more broadly—in terms of hard law, and the division of legislative powers between the Community and the Member States. Even the introduction of the Open Method of Coordination (OMC) in the late 1990s seemed to do little to challenge hard law's pre-eminence. As emphasised in the 2000 Governance White Paper, the OMC was no substitute for hard law but a method to be used only where action under the Community method was impossible.[1] The academic 'rush' towards the OMC seemed, by the mid-2000s, to be running out of steam, with many commentators doubting the efficacy and wider legitimacy of soft law instruments.[2]

In spite of this, soft law has been the Rasputin of the competence debate. Each chronicle of its death foretold has been met with plenty of signs of lasting durability. The erosion for example of the social OMCs through the evolution of the Lisbon 2020 strategy[3] has been accompanied by the emergence of a far broader European Semester process, which both encompasses a larger number of policy fields and carries a wider range of instruments at its disposal to ensure compliance with its norms. Far from being an instrument confined to areas of weak EU

* Mark Dawson is Professor of European Law and Governance at the Hertie School of Governance.

[1] European Commission, 'White Paper on Governance', COM(2001) 428 final, 21.

[2] See eg M Eckhardt, 'The Open Method of Coordination on Pensions: an Economic Analysis of its Effects on Pension Reforms' (2005) 15 *Journal of European Social Policy*; M Lodge, 'Comparing Non-Hierarchical Governance in Action: The Open Method of Coordination in Pensions and Information Society' (2007) 45 *Journal of Common Market Studies* 2.

[3] M Daly and P Copeland, 'Poverty and Social Policy in Europe 2020: Ungovernable and Ungoverned?' (2014) 42 *Policy and Politics* 351.

competence, soft law is frequently used across the whole gamut of EU policy, with an increasing use of notices and guidelines to enforce EU competition rules.[4] Soft law does not seem to be receding but rather becoming a permanent element of the EU's policy-making machinery.

To what extent is this advance a challenge to the EU's system of enumerated competence? This paper will argue that soft law's emergence is a severe challenge but for different reasons than first thought. First, let us deal with the standard 'soft law challenge'. This challenge presupposes that soft law subverts the EU's competence system because of its ability to supplant or replace hard law. In doing so, soft law may mean that many of the constitutional guarantees acting under hard law imply (including respect for the system of enumerated competences itself) are evaded.[5] What if soft law is used to channel policy that should properly have been enacted via ordinary EU law, evading the EU's institutional balance in the process?[6] Part of the complaint against measures adopted during the twin euro and migration crises have been of this nature, that is that either soft law, or international agreements, are utilised to achieve goals that could have been achieved through 'normal' EU law, or competences explicitly provided by the Treaties.

While this challenge seems pressing, EU law carries some conceptual and judicial tools to meet it. There is a certain paradox implicit in soft law.[7] If soft law is really 'law' it has to carry effects of some kind. A soft law process that carried no claim to authority, or that was treated by its addressees as merely advisory, would surely not merit the label of soft *law* at all. At the same time, if soft law goes further than this: if it no longer merely steers policy but controls or coerces it, it is no longer *soft*. Soft law must be more than advisory, yet *if it is more*—if it harmonises national preferences—it cannot be accurately described as 'soft law' at all.

Faced with this conceptual paradox, the European Courts have sought a way out by examining soft law not in terms of its form but its effects. In numerous cases, the Courts have insisted that documents or letters purporting to be soft law should be treated as hard where they affect the *legal* position of states or individuals.[8] Seen from this angle, the challenge of soft law to the system of enumerated competences disappears. Soft law is only a challenge to the competence system if it carries hard effects, yet if it does, it will be treated as hard law, and thereby subject to competence control and review. The 'challenge' of soft law is thus simply one of classification—is a given instrument hard and legal or is it merely a soft policy tool

[4] See O Stefan, 'European Competition Soft Law in European Courts: A Matter of Hard Principles?' (2008) 14 *European Law Journal* 6.

[5] See G de Búrca, 'The Constitutional Challenge of New Governance in the European Union' (2003) 28 *European Law Review* 6.

[6] See the example of the Bologna process as discussed in S Garben, *EU Higher Education Law: The Bologna Process and Harmonization by Stealth* (Alphen aan den Rijn, Kluwer Law, 2011).

[7] See M Dawson, *New Governance and the Transformation of European Law* (Cambridge, Cambridge University Press, 2011) 77–83.

[8] See eg Joined Cases C-8-11/66 *Noordwijks Cement Accoord* [1967] ECR 75; C-30/95 *France and Others v Commission* [1998] ECR I-1375; Case C-322/88 *Grimaldi* [1989] ECR 4407.

(and hence simply a 'complement' to national action)? To the challenge of those who argue that the overriding of judicial redress or competence guarantees by soft law is a problem, EU law seems to have an answer: soft law can be judicially controlled but at that point at the EU or national levels where it begins to carry *legal effects*.

As this chapter will argue, this answer, while superficially appealing, is only so from a particular, and narrow, perspective. It is appealing only if one ignores the distinctive features of soft law, and particularly those features which provide it with its normative and empirical purchase. As the chapter will argue, the threat of soft law to the division of competence in the EU can only be understood once one understands the nature of power in soft law. Soft law may in fact exercise a type of power that is just as coercive and meaningful as 'hard' legal power but carries a different form. The concept of 'legal effects' does not in this sense remove soft law's challenge to the 'competence conundrum' but rather acts as a red herring, distracting us from soft law's real challenge and influence.

As the next sections will explore, the article will argue that we should understand soft law as a manifesting a type of 'bio' or disciplinary power, in a Foucauldian sense, rather than legal or juridical power of the type most classically envisaged in EU law debates. Soft law carries power but it is neither transmitted through law nor is it controlled by law, and cannot therefore be controlled by a system of enumerated competences. Soft law does not classically coerce but rather demonstrates its power through binding its addressees into a common pattern of thought and action.

The chapter will advance this argument in four steps. The first of these will introduce the Foucauldian concept of bio-power, distinguishing it from juridical power. The second will apply the concept of bio-power to current discussions over the development of soft law. The third will analyse how bio-power is framing current discussions over EU competence, particularly through one current debate: over 'Better Regulation' in the EU. Finally, the fourth will conclude by examining how bio-power, and soft law, could be used to reconsider the EU's current competence arrangements. As the chapter will argue, soft law's bio-power adds further weight to those arguing for a fundamental overhaul of the EU's current competence arrangements.

FROM JURIDICAL TO 'BIO' POWER

The work of Michel Foucault has been criticised as ignoring the legal discipline or even 'expelling' the law altogether.[9] In truth, Foucault's account of modern power has to be seen in a much more nuanced light. In Foucault's work, law is posited as one of many sources of power and authority in modern society—to this extent Foucault shares much in common with other post-structural social theories, such

[9] A Hunt, 'Foucault's Expulsion of Law: Towards a Retrieval' (1992) 17 *Law and Social Inquiry* 1.

as that of Niklas Luhmann,[10] who posited law as a self-referential or autopoetic system among other such systems of social communication (such as science, religion, economy, and so on).[11]

Law is also for Foucault often associated with a specific form of *juridical* power. Juridical power is associated by Foucault with Courts and legal institutions but also with a specific form of sovereignty prior to the advent of the French Revolution. The power of the sovereign in such a society is conceived as 'the right to decide life and death'. The sovereign provides his subjects with significant latitude over their lives but reserves for him or herself the power to act with extreme violence against those who threaten sovereign authority. As Foucault puts it in *The History of Sexuality:*

> The right which was formulated as the 'power of life and death' was in reality the right to take life or let live. Its symbol, after all, was the sword. Perhaps this juridical form must be referred to a historical type of society in which power was exercised mainly as a type of deduction (*prélèvement*), a subtraction mechanism, a right to appropriate a portion of the wealth, a tax of products, goods and services, labour and blood, levied on the subjects. Power in this instance was essentially a right of seizure: of things, time, bodies and ultimately life itself; it culminated in the privilege to seize hold of life in order to suppress it.[12]

Under the juridical account, power is something held by one person at the expense of others. Power is repressive and negative—it seeks to inhibit individuals from acting and punishes them where they traverse its commands. Finally, power is exercised via the medium of law, that is, via universal rules of conduct.

For Foucault, the *very definition* of a modern society is that it does not operate along this metric of power alone. In a functionally complex and normatively diverse modern society, the power of deduction alone cannot maintain effective social order:

> If power were never anything but repressive, do you really think one would be brought to obey it? What makes power hold good, what makes it accepted, is simply the fact that it doesn't only weigh on us as a force that says no, but that it traverses and produces things, it induces pleasure, forms knowledge, produces discourse. It needs to be considered as a productive network which runs through the whole social body, much more than as a negative instance whose function is repression.[13]

Modern power is therefore as much productive and positive as it is repressive and negative. It does not merely suppress, but reproduces, the individual, and allows them to realise their lives. Returning to the discussion on sovereignty, the

[10] On the links between the two, see P Kjaer, *Between Governing and Governance. On the Emergence, Function and Form of Europe's Post-National Constellation* (Oxford, Hart Publishing, 2010).

[11] N Luhmann, *Law as a Social System* (Oxford, Oxford University Press, 1993).

[12] M Foucault, 'Right of Death and Power over Life' in *The History of Sexuality* (Paris, Editions Gallimard, 1976) 136.

[13] M Foucault, 'Truth and Power' in C Gordon (ed), *Power/Knowledge: Selected Interviews and Other Writings* (New York, Pantheon, 1980) 119.

modern sovereign does not therefore merely allow his or her citizens a free space, conditioned by the threat of the sword. Instead, the sovereign's very existence is legitimated by their ability to improve and sustain the condition of the body politic, interfering in life repeatedly precisely to stave off death. The sovereign administers and makes possible the very life of the polity, waging war in the name of its security, providing education to maximise its potential, and building health and care services to secure its well-being. 'The old power of death that symbolized sovereign power was now carefully supplanted by the administration of bodies and the calculated management of life.'[14]

For law, this is mirrored by a shift in modern law from law to 'regulation'. The legal system operates no longer simply as a set of universal, negative rules but as a series of norms, seeking to appraise and correct behaviour, and to set out particular courses of action as just, inevitable or necessary (just as others are cast as deviant and damaging). To take an example from the field which Foucault posits as the centre of the new bio-power, sexuality, homosexuality in the mid-to-late twentieth century began to be conceptualised not as a criminal justice issue—a perversion to be punished—but as a medical issue, that is, a sickness or abnormality that reflection or therapy could 'cure' (and that was later seen as 'natural' and therefore legally institutionalised).

Modern power seeks in this sense not to punish ex post but to prevent ex ante, conditioning the individual, and society at large, to prevent behaviour deemed as undesirable from the outset (or conversely, to promote behaviour seen as conducive to society's reproduction). Power can in this sense be seen as the 'conduct of conduct'.[15] It does not force individuals to act in certain ways but defines the course and methods of their action. Our metaphors when thinking about power are shifted—from the idea of punishment encapsulated in the grisly execution to the notion of discipline offered by the micro-interventions of the school curriculum or the pre-natal classes of expecting parents.[16] It is for this reason that 'bio-power' escapes from seeing law as the central transmitter of legitimate power and authority. Law is one among other forms of power and control in modern societies, operating alongside and tandem with other power structures.

Finally, this entails that power is not 'held' in the sense of a zero-sum game. Central institutions may seek to influence others but they are also likely to be the objects of power. As individuals, we are surveyed and controlled but we also survey others. Power thus has no final resting place but is held in a 'capillary' network where each actor conditions and is conditioned by others.[17] Power does not operate *upon* us but *through* us (a radical, if unsettling, thought).

[14] *The History of Sexuality,* above n 12 at 140.

[15] M Foucault, 'The Subject and Power' in *Beyond Structuralism and Hermeneutics* (Chicago, University of Chicago Press, 1982) 220.

[16] M Foucault, *Discipline and Punish* (Paris, Editions Gallimard, 1975) 3–7.

[17] *Selected Interviews,* above n 13 at 39.

BIO-POWER AND SOFT LAW

Why is bio-power a useful concept when thinking about soft law?[18] To begin, one must acknowledge that many of those most critical of soft law have often couched their critiques in quite different terms. One could point, for example, to the coercive nature of much of soft law and its ability to tie itself to hard law and forms of financial sanction. A good example is financial conditionality in the context of the euro crisis. Memorandums of understanding drawn up by 'bail-out' states in order to receive funding from the ESM and other European funding mechanisms are in theory voluntary commitments (and have been often treated by the European Courts as such).[19] In reality, however, they are highly binding, both originating from the demands of creditors and backed up by the threat of financial catastrophe if breached.[20] In this sense, there are certainly forms of soft law that fit within what Foucault termed juridical power—the power of the sword.

It would be misleading, however, to paint all soft law with this brush. Most soft law is not repressive in nature. If the EU acts in the arena of soft law to 'complement' the activities of the Member States in the areas listed under Article 6 TFEU, it does not in any sense prohibit them from acting but often seeks to enhance their capacity to act. The classical, and perhaps most successful, example of complementary competence—the EU's Erasmus programme—is a case in point. While it is certainly an exercise in enhancing the EU's normative power, and achieving certain EU goals such as educational mobility, it is not an exercise of power at the expense of the ability of the Member States to organise their educational systems themselves. Power is exercised but not in the sense of the 'power of deduction' encapsulated by juridical power (as discussed above).

There is power nonetheless. If we compare Erasmus with other soft law processes—for example, the Bologna process outside the EU system, or the OMC process within it—they do not seek to repress the Member States but nonetheless seek to influence how the Member States see and think about their education and social systems. We see 'conduct of conduct', that is, while particular outcomes are not always mandatorily prescribed, what is demanded are a set of steps designed to change the way in which national policy is conducted and evaluated (often with just as significant effects as hard legal coercion).

This begins, first, at an ideational level. Much of soft law operates at the level of knowledge in the sense that—like bio-power—it attempts to define what is or is not 'good policy' or to inculcate particular ways of analysing and remedying

[18] Some existing scholarship attempts to consider new governance methods in light of Foucault ideas. See eg JH Haahr, 'Open Coordination as Advanced Liberal Government' (2004) 11 *Journal of European Public Policy* 2.

[19] See Cases C-128/12, *Sindicato dos Bancários do Norte and Others v BPN* [2013]; C-264/12, *Sindicato Nacional dos Profissionais de Seguros e Afins v Fidelidade Mundial* [2014].

[20] See eg C Kilpatrick, 'Are the Bailouts Immune to Social Challenge because they are not EU Law?' (2014) 10 *European Constitutional Law Review* 3.

social, economic and other problems. While in the Bologna process, the overriding goal is often one of compatibility and comparability (that is, good qualifications are those that can be easily measured and compared between states), the OMC typically also begins with a set of criteria which do not proscribe conduct, yet nonetheless attempt to create a set of standards against which good and bad policy are judged. To take an example of an OMC-like process from the human rights field, the EU's Roma Integration strategy mandates national governments to produce reform programmes. Its central reference point, however, is a set of 10 basic common principles for Roma Inclusion, that national governments should incorporate into their domestic plans.[21] The EU's assessment of those plans—and certain positive inducement such as social and cohesion funding—are then conducted according to their conformity with the common principles.

In other soft law processes, indicators and benchmarks play a similar role. In social policy, a key element of policy coordination on social inclusion is the Social Protection Performance Monitor (SSPM): a dashboard of indicators that monitors social performance and trends across both the EU as a whole and its Member States.[22] The idea of such dashboards is to allow countries—and their populations and media—to gauge their social performance, ideally placing pressure on under-performing states to improve their social policies. Once again, governance is conducted via knowledge, with 'success' and 'failure' measured within parameters set by the EU's Social Protection Committee.

For proponents of such soft law processes, their ability to assess social performance, and to enter into national political discourse certain concepts such as flexicurity or the idea of active labour markets, is often lauded as one of their lasting achievements.[23] Soft law in this way does not prohibit national conduct but attempts to *realise* it in a particular way, promising positive outcomes for those states that follow 'correct' policy paths. Through ideational and comparative tools, soft law exercises 'bio-power' in the sense that it encourages member governments to 'see the light', to 'learn', or simply to conduct policy in a manner conducive to the EU's preferences.[24] The EU in its OMC-modus does not therefore mandate particular rules for issues like social inclusion, yet nonetheless creates a paradigm for what social inclusion means and requires, that Member States must gradually internalise.[25]

[21] European Commission, *Ten Basic Common Principles on Roma Inclusion* (Brussels, Office for Official Publications of the EU, 2009).

[22] See 'Social Protection Performance Monitor (SPPM)—Methodological Report by the Indicators Sub-group of the Social Protection Committee', 17 October 2012, available at http://ec.europa.eu/social/main.jsp?catId=758.

[23] See eg J Zeitlin, 'The Open Method of Coordination and National Social and Employment Policy Reforms: Influences, Mechanisms, Effects', in M Heidenreich and J Zeitlin (eds), *Changing European Employment and Welfare Regimes* (London, Routledge, 2009).

[24] On learning under the OMC, see CM Radaelli, 'Europeanization, Policy Learning and New Modes of Governance' (2008) 10 *Journal of Comparative Policy Analysis: Research and Practice* 3.

[25] On this, see S Bernhard, 'The European Paradigm of Social Exclusion' (2007) 2 *Journal of Contemporary European Research* 1.

Second, soft law often attempts to influence the process by which national policy is conducted and evaluated at a procedural level.[26] As in the model Foucault discusses, EU intervention is not repressive and once and for all, but aspirational and regulatory, encouraging Member States to meet certain targets and allowing repeated macro-intervention by the EU institutions in order to meet those goals. The main 'hard' obligation of many soft law processes is therefore often procedural rather than substantive—to report on what you are doing and to respond to recommendations (for 'improvement').

The European Semester is a central example of this. It carries a hard law shell in the form of the EU's six- and two-pack measures. The bulk of these measures, however, are devoted to establishing a policy coordination process for national fiscal policy, including targets and benchmarks to be met, actors to be consulted, deadlines to be heeded, and cycles for the exchange of information and recommendations between the Member States and the EU institutions. Many of the obligations involved include the establishment of domestic procedures and rules to facilitate EU goals (for example, fiscal councils to audit national budgets, or balanced budget rules as demanded under the Fiscal Compact).[27] The bulk of the EU's energies are devoted not to direct demands but to 'getting under the skin' of the domestic policy-making process, encouraging states to internalise EU goals within domestic policy making, and gradually correct national policy to meet them.

Foucault once used the metaphor of the Panopticon to describe this effect.[28] Designed by Jeremy Bentham, the Panopticon was a mythical prison designed to deceive its inmates. Rather than be hemmed in by walls, the Panopticon would allow, through the use of mirrors and effects, a single guard to survey all cells. While inmates could not all be watched at once, they could always be *potentially* watched. The device's central premise was the idea of self-control: inmates would modify their own behaviour in anticipation of the possibility of observation (and ultimately, punishment). For Foucault, Bentham's Panopticon was a useful metaphor for power and surveillance in the modern state: individuals are often not directly observed by the state, but rather condition and correct themselves in the shadow of observation.

While there is some distance between Bentham and economic policy coordination, there is something of the Panopticon in the design of soft law as a procedurally heavy process. This has often been described in governance research as 'the shadow of hierarchy', that is, the guidance of policy through soft law with hard law

[26] On this procedural understanding of new governance, see *New Governance and the Transformation of EU Law*, above n 7 ch 3.

[27] On the former, see Regulation 473/2013/EU, Art 5(2); on the Fiscal Compact's balanced budget rule, see Treaty on Stability, Coordination and Governance, Art 3(2).

[28] *Discipline and Punish*, above n 16 ch 3.

present as a default or remedial option.[29] While under the six- and two-packs, for example, financial penalties are possible, they have rarely been issued. Penalties are instead conceptualised as 'dissuasive', with domestic levers encouraging governments and other national actors to *themselves* regulate their fiscal conduct to achieve EU goals, without the need for external intervention. In this sense, while the failure of the EU to act to correct excessive deficits could be conceptualised as a sign of weakness, it could also be seen as an indicator of strength, that is, of the ability of soft law to achieve corrective effects without the need for juridical or financial coercion. The Panopticon effect is another sign of soft law's (and bio-power's) complex workings.

Thirdly, the European Semester and other soft law processes speak to the nature of bio-power as a form of power operating in a network or via a feedback loop. This was another central element of Foucault's account, that is, that power in modern societies is never definitely held or exercised by one actor or from one place. Similarly, under soft law processes such as the OMC, it is not just that Member States learn from 'good practices' established at EU level but also that they influence the definition of 'good practice', conducting peer review on their neighbours based on evolving normative standards.[30] It is for this reason that some commentators have characterised soft law processes as 'reflexive':[31] they do not simply seek to transmit policy objectives from one level to another but to continuously shape and amend them according to experiences of how effective policies are when transposed at national and local levels. Norms are not just created hierarchically at the EU level and applied nationally but reformulated according to practice, with no one actor having a decisive say.

This 'networked' nature of soft law also relates to common criticisms of soft law processes. One common critique of EU economic governance is that the Eurogroup is not bound to a particular Treaty definition of its policy mandate but tends to engage in a group-thinking exercise where finance ministers influence and are influenced by the positions of their peers.[32] Governance, as we will further explore, is not conducted via defined rules but via norms of good practice that change according to changing preferences of the institutions that apply them.

[29] A Héritier and M Rhodes (eds), *New Modes of Governance in Europe: Governing in the Shadow of Hierarchy* (Houndmills, Palgrave Macmillan, 2011); W Schelkle, 'EU Fiscal Governance: Hard Law in the Shadow of Soft Law?' *Columbia Journal of European Law* (2007) 13.

[30] C Sabel and J Zeitlin, 'Learning from Difference: The New Architecture of Experimentalist Governance in the European Union', in *Experimentalist Governance in the European Union* (Oxford, Oxford University Press, 2010).

[31] S Deakin and O de Schutter, 'Reflexive Governance and the Dilemmas of Social Regulation' in *Social Rights and Market Forces: Is the Open Coordination of Employment and Social Policies the Future of Social Europe?* (Brussels, Bruylant, 2005).

[32] See, rather infamously, the critiques offered by a former Eurogroup member, Yannis Varoufakis: 'The Eurogroup Made Simple', 30 March 2016, available at https://yanisvaroufakis.eu/2016/03/30/the-eurogroup-made-simple/.

In this sense, we should not see power in soft law as 'zero-sum' but as something that operates through institutions and is never definitively held by one actor. The EU surveys its Member States but is also surveyed by them: it tries to influence national policy, but is also influenced by 'what works' and what does not work at the national level.[33] Power becomes increasingly diffuse (and difficult to identify in clear lines).

Finally, and relatedly, soft law shares with Foucault's account a preference against operating through the medium of 'law as rules'. As soft law is generally non-binding, it is rarely subject to judicial or parliamentary oversight. To give one example, country-specific recommendations (CSRs) under the European Semester do not require the approval of the European Parliament and have not yet been challenged judicially.[34] This latter aspect is unsurprising given the network effect discussed above—if soft law is challenged, it is neither clear whether it produces 'legal effects' nor at which level these effects are being created.

Instead, soft law often exists as a series of vague or unclear standards whose precise scope would be difficult for any Court to determine (creating clear conflicts with traditional conceptions of legality).[35] Indeed, soft law does not seem to require the medium of law or legal institutions to be effective, and to transmit and influence policy.[36] Early predictions that fields operating under soft law would eventually be 'hardened',[37] or that the European Semester would be communitarised, have not yet come to pass (an indication perhaps that soft law's preference for 'norms' rather than rules may also chime in with the needs of many contemporary EU decision makers).

Combining these four features together—soft law's ideational power, its procedural nature, its use of networks, and its preferences for norms over rules—there is much to connect soft law with what Foucault described as the 'bio-power' of modern states and societies. Just as Foucault urged us to 'cut off the head of the King', when thinking about sovereignty, we may need to be just as radical in conceptualising how power really functions in the EU's contemporary legal and political order.[38]

[33] On this more sinister potential framing of experimentalist ideas about new governance, see P Kjaer, 'Three Forms of Governance and Three Forms of Power' in EO Eriksen, C Joerges and F Roedl (eds), *The Unsettled Political Order of Europe* (London, Routledge, 2008).

[34] C Fasone, 'European Economic Governance and Parliamentary Representation: What Place for the European Parliament?' (2014) 20 *European Law Journal* 2.

[35] See on this question M Dawson, 'Soft Law and the Rule of Law in the European Union' in A Vauchez and B De Witte, *Lawyering Europe: European Law as a Trans-national Social Field* (Oxford, Hart Publishing, 2013).

[36] On the shift in economic governance from rules to norms or 'decisions', see D Chalmers, 'The European Redistributive State and a European Law of Struggle', 18 *European Law Journal* (2014) 5 at 682–84; A Menendez, 'Editorial: A European Union in Constitutional Mutation', 20 *European Law Journal* (2014) 2 at 136–37.

[37] See eg P Kjaer's characterisation of methods like the OMC as 'pre-integrative'. Kjaer, above n 33 at 102.

[38] *Truth and Power*, above n 13 at 121.

THE POWER OF 'BETTER' REGULATION

Why is the characterisation of bio-power as a form of soft law relevant for the discussion over competence? Part of that relevance relates to the way in which the competence debate treats power and authority in EU law. In large part, it treats power according to the juridical concept of power discussed in the second section. In this sense, the EU's competence system sees power as 'deductive', that is, as the capacity of one system to pre-empt the other, or of one actor to act in place of the other. A classic example of this is Article 2(2) TFEU—authority in different areas of EU law is to be divided, such that the exercise of authority by one level of governance deprives the other level of *its* capacity to act. Where that actor exceeds its competence, its action is to be controlled repressively, that is, subjected to judicial annulment. In this sense, the competence system seeks primarily to control legal (rather than others forms of) authority, and to do so through the mechanics of power as a deductive or 'zero sum' exercise.

The problem of soft law, and of bio-power, is that it simply does not run through these categories. As discussed, soft law often does not seek to exercise legal power, or to preclude other actors or levels of governance from acting. It nonetheless may carry highly coercive and real effects in steering their action, or precluding particular forms of action. By ignoring this form of power, the competence system ignores one of the principal dynamics of power and authority in modern societies (and with it one of the principal ways in which power can be abused).

To reinforce this point, it may be useful to develop one more example in depth.[39] The EU's recently announced package of 'Better Regulation' measures could also largely be characterised under the heading of soft law. The central arc of the package is a set of Better Regulation guidelines to be implemented by the Commission in preparing, executing and monitoring EU legislation.[40] This is accompanied by an Inter-Institutional Agreement, signed by the Union's three main political bodies.[41]

The entire agenda of 'Better Regulation' has been hardened in recent years by the demands of ex-post judicial review. Good examples are the cases of *Vodafone* and *Volker and Markus Scheke*, where the presence or lack of a Commission Impact Assessment (IA) was seen as relevant for the exercise of judicial review.[42] Others have argued that elements of 'Better Regulation' should be seen in hard law

[39] Some of the arguments brought below are also discussed in M Dawson, 'Better Regulation and the Future of EU Regulatory Law and Politics', *Common Market Law Review*, forthcoming.

[40] Commission Communication, 'Better Regulation for Better Results: An EU Agenda', COM(2015) 215. The Better Regulation Guidelines are available at http://ec.europa.eu/smart-regulation/guidelines/toc_guide_en.htm.

[41] Text of the Inter-Institutional Agreement on Better Law-making. Available at http://eur-lex.europa.eu/legal-content/EN/TXT/PDF/?uri=OJ:L:2016:123:FULL&from=EN.

[42] See the defence of judicial review in these cases via structuralist notions of judicial review advanced by the CJEU's President in K Lenaerts, 'The European Court of Justice and Process-oriented Review' (2012) *College of Europe Research Papers in Law* 1.

terms in so far as they may significantly assist the European Courts in determining whether policy makers have complied in their decision-making with overarching constitutional principles demanded by the Treaties (such as subsidiarity, proportionality and fundamental rights compliance).[43]

Better Regulation remains, however, a process guided by largely 'soft' norms. This is particularly so when one considers the law-making process. While the CJEU has increasingly begun to take IAs into consideration in its rulings, it has yet to insist on IA as a legal requirement for the legislative institutions.[44] In *Afton*, for example, mandatory limits on a fuel additive were challenged by an affected operator, who argued that the Commission's IA had demonstrated that voluntary limits could prevent the risks of additives as effectively as mandatory measures.[45] The CJEU, however, following concerns regarding institutional balance, insisted that the IA 'was not binding on either the Council or the Parliament, who, under the co-decision legislative procedure laid down by Article 251 EC, were entitled to make amendments to that proposal'.[46] In this sense, the majority of the Better Regulation agenda seems to largely escape competence control by following the very hard/soft law distinction discussed in the introduction to this chapter. Its rules and guidelines are 'soft' policy tools and are therefore not seen as fundamentally altering the balance of power between institutions, or between the EU and its Member States.

How quickly should we accept this conclusion? Another approach is to see the primary form of power exercised via Better Regulation (BR) as bio or disciplinary power; a characterisation that may better capture the significance of the Better Regulation agenda. This once again begins at an ideational level. As its architects are keen to insist, BR is not about more or less but about *better* regulation.[47] It does not therefore seek to exclude regulatory options but merely to lay down a series of overarching principles through which legislation should be formulated. Among the principles are the idea that there should be a clear added value to acting at the EU level and that disproportionate burdens on business and regulators should be avoided.[48] BR is defined largely in terms of implementing costs—'designing EU policies and laws so that they achieve their objectives at minimum cost'.[49] This relates to the way the impacts of proposals are to be assessed: 'if, and where possible, impacts should be assessed quantitatively and costs monetized'.[50] BR in this sense carries bio-power's positive promise: it promises national and other

[43] See eg A Meuwese and P Popelier, 'Legal Implications of Better Regulation: A Special Issue' (2011) 17 *European Public Law* 3.

[44] See D Keyaerts, 'The Impact of Better Regulation in the Case-law of the European Court of Justice' (2012) *European Journal of Risk Regulation* 2 at 245.

[45] Case C-343/09 *Afton Chemical Limited v Secretary of State for Transport* [2010] ECR I-07027.

[46] ibid para 57.

[47] Commission Communication, 'Better Regulation for Better Results: An EU Agenda', COM(2015) 215 at 2.

[48] ibid at 5.

[49] ibid at 4.

[50] Better Regulation Guidelines, above n 40 at 27.

actors to establish a more effective and cost-efficient set of policies, if only its regulatory tools are properly applied.

The relation between Better Regulation and bio-power continues at a procedural level. Among the procedural hurdles is the notion that legislation ought to be subject to impact assessment and cost–benefit analysis throughout the decision-making process.[51] This includes moving towards different modes of regulation and encouraging the consultation of new regulatory actors. The guidelines frequently ask officials to consider 'nonregulatory alternatives, self or co-regulation, market based solutions' and so on and to 'take the 'think small first' principle into account: are micro-enterprises excluded from the scope of any proposed legislation'?[52] The Commission's prior impact assessment board already took this set of criteria into account in rejecting a number of proposals forwarding social and environmental objectives on the grounds that options with significant compliance costs on business had not been scrutinised sufficiently closely.[53]

The difficulty of course is that process and outcome are not so easily separated. By demanding, for example, that the benefits of legislation are quantified, there is a danger that those objectives most amenable to quantification are privileged and those least amenable sidelined (how does one, for example, monetise the advantages for birds or other wildlife of a safe natural habitat?).[54] Equally, by focusing on the removal of regulatory burdens, those EU policies that impose high regulatory costs, but nonetheless do so in the aim of a key non-market objective, face a particularly high burden of justification.[55]

A useful example may be the Commission's recent decision to withdraw a proposal already endorsed via the social dialogue—the framework agreement on health and safety standards in the hairdressing sector.[56] While the Commission has always in the past forwarded to the Council as legislative proposals framework agreements adopted by the Social Partners under the procedure envisaged in Article 155(2) TFEU, the Commission has repeatedly delayed the legislative

[51] Better Regulation Communication, above n 40 at 8.

[52] ibid at 23.

[53] See eg the recent rejection of an IA on a proposal concerning positive measures for service providers to ensure equal access of the disabled on the grounds that the exclusion of micro-enterprises from the proposal had not been adequately considered. IAB Opinion of 15 May 2013. Available at http://ec.europa.eu/smart-regulation/impact/ia_carried_out/docs/ia_2015/ sec_2015_471_0.pdf.

[54] On these difficulties, see S Rose-Ackerman, 'Putting Cost-Benefit Analysis in its Place: Re-thinking Regulatory Review' (2011) 65 *University of Miami Law Review*; J Torriti, 'Impact Assessment in the EU: A Tool for Better Regulation, Less Regulation or Less Bad Regulation?' (2007) 10 *Journal of Risk Research* 2; A Renda, *Impact Assessment in the EU: The State of the Art and the Art of the State* (Brussels, Centre for European Policy Studies, 2006).

[55] The result has been the subjection of a number of social policy proposals—including those adopted under the social dialogue to 'REFIT'. See Press Release, 'REFIT—Fit for growth—Commission takes ambitious next steps to make EU law lighter', 2 October 2013. Available at http://europa.eu/rapid/press-release_IP-13-891_en.htm.

[56] See the Declaration of the European Social Partners on Health and Safety in the Hairdressing Sector, 26 April 2012. Available at http://ec.europa.eu/social/main.jsp?langId=en&catId=329&newsId=1286&furtherNews=yes.

implementation of this agreement, first on the grounds of Member State resistance, and second, on the grounds of its inconsistency with the aim of lowering regulatory burdens on SMEs.[57] In this sense, BR does not just spread a particular modus of policy but also a certain ideational paradigm about what counts as 'good' and 'bad' policy making, and a certain set of procedural hurdles that encourages other actors to discipline and censure their own policy agendas.

Finally, there is a strong idea in Better Regulation of power as networked rather than zero-sum. Via the Inter-Institutional Agreement the Commission's preferred mode of regulation is also spread to other institutions. During the legislative process, the Commission commits through the BR framework to aiding the Council and Parliament in conducting IAs on legislative amendments, using the Commission's own IA as a starting point for their work.[58] The Commission's regulatory paradigm is also spread to the Member States. Other key pledges of the Better Regulation agenda include the idea that, after the legislative process is completed, Member States and the Commission should draw up implementation plans, avoiding the 'gold-plating' of measures through the insertion at national level of higher social, environmental or regulatory standards not connected to the original EU act.[59] Lastly, existing legislation is to be assessed according to cost–benefit analysis—the so-called 'REFIT' agenda—with future EU action as much devoted to legislative simplification and withdrawal as the creation of new proposals.[60]

As in Foucault's model, power does not operate *upon* but *through* institutions. A paradigm of good and bad regulation is created that is followed and reformulated by political actors from the beginning of the decision-making process to its end. Commission action does not determine but realises and activates EU policy: nothing is foreclosed but options with prohibitive costs and unknown side effects are procedurally 'weaned out', avoided and cast as examples of 'bad practice'.

At the same time—and against the easy characterisation of Better Regulation as an institutional 'power-grab'[61]—the Commission's own ideas of BR are influenced by others. While part of this may emerge from the broader shift in social science and policy evaluation towards the quantification of public policy, others have pointed to the demands of the US government (via negotiations on TTIP) to enhance EU Impact Assessment in line with the US practice of 'notice and comment' on regulatory proposals.[62] As with Foucault's notion, power is never

[57] See eg the tying by the Commission of the hairdressing agreement with the discussion on lowering regulatory burdens in COM(2014) 368, 'Regulatory Fitness and Performance Programme (REFIT): State of Play and Outlook' at 4.

[58] Inter-Institutional Agreement, above n 41 para 15.

[59] According to the Commission, such gold-plating 'may enhance the benefits but can also add to the unnecessary costs for businesses and public authorities which are mistakenly associated with EU legislation'. Better Regulation Communication, above n 40 at 6.

[60] See eg the Commission's 2016 work agenda, which includes 27 initiatives associated with REFIT. 'Commission Work Programme 2016: No Time for Business as Usual', COM(2015) 610, Annex 2.

[61] See K Wegrich, 'Which Results? Better Regulation and Institutional Politics' (2015) *European Journal of Risk Regulation* 3 at 371.

[62] See A Alemanno, 'How Much Better is Better Regulation' (2015) *European Journal of Risk Regulation* 3 at 352.

exclusively held in one place, but passed from one actor to another. The ideas about 'better' regulation that the EU now seeks to forward are themselves adjusted and re-used versions of notions of good regulation advanced by other international institutions (such as the World Bank).[63]

It is of course too early to tell what the real impact of 'Better Regulation' will be. Notably, many elements of the 2015 package simply re-hash earlier attempts at regulatory reform (to take one example, the battle to encourage the other EU institutions to take IA seriously has been ongoing since 2003 without apparent success). Many of the key elements of the Commission's initial BR package were resisted by the other EU institutions in the process of agreeing the IIA, fearful that their rights of political amendment could be curtailed.[64]

This very resistance, however, tells its own story. If 'Better Regulation' really were simply a set of soft and voluntary guidelines and best practices it would hardly be worth resisting. The real impacts of changing regulatory paradigms have been felt well beyond the political institutions—objecting to perceptions of a de-regulatory turn via REFIT, over 50 civil society groups joined to form a 'Better Regulation watchdog' to oversee the impact of REFIT on citizen, worker and consumer rights in May 2015.[65] While Better Regulation may be implemented via 'soft law', its potential effects, while non-juridical, are also very real. The bio-power of the EU's new regulatory paradigm is likely to have significant repercussions on the Union's constitutional order: an effect to which legal scholarship must also respond.

BIO-POWER AND THE 'COMPETENCE CONUNDRUM'

How does this account of power under soft law help us address the future of the system of enumerated competences in the EU? Part of the answer is empirical—the significance of soft law seems to be spreading and is likely to spread further as political opposition to further integration heightens. Part of this could be explained by political resistance to transfers of power: the analysis above, though, suggests another element. Soft law may be chosen not always as a 'second best' but because its tools of persuasion and proceduralisation are often effective.

A second element of the answer is that attempting to control EU power via judicial and political oversight of competence allocation may be important but it does not get to the heart of how power is exercised via soft law. Competence control

[63] See eg the Better Regulation for Growth initiative co-sponsored by the World Bank and the Dutch and UK governments. Available at www.wbginvestmentclimate.org/advisory-services/regulatory-simplification/business-regulation/better-regulation-for-growth/brg.cfm.

[64] See eg the IIA's eventual provisions on Impact Assessment and particularly this statement: 'impact assessments are a tool to help the three institutions reach well informed decisions and not a substitute for political decisions within the democratic decision-making process.' Inter-Institutional Agreement, above n 41 para 12.

[65] See the founding statement of the BR Watchdog. Available at www.betterregwatch.eu/BRWN_Founding_ Statement_and_Members.pdf.

is aimed at hard, juridical power: EU action under soft law is simply not of this nature. This does not, however, obviate the normative need for control. The type of power and coercion being exercised via soft law may be just as real; it simply doesn't carry hard law's traditional repressive form.

A final element of the answer may be to think more radically about competence control. Certainly the ideas above add weight to the idea that competence control according to the categories of Articles 2–6 TFEU is largely redundant and could be abolished altogether, as Sacha Garben has recently argued.[66] It also adds weight to a related argument, that control of the exercise of power and authority in the EU are unlikely to be matters of categorical legal review but of political judgment. The counter-weight to soft law's—and better regulation's—notion of what constitute 'good' and 'bad' practice or policy, or of where the EU does or does not objectively 'add value', is to politicise these categories. The answer to the competence conundrum is in this sense to politicise and contest rules and forms of power seen as natural, neutral or objective through either EU-level or national parliamentary procedures (an idea that finds resonance in a number of contemporary accounts of EU constitutionalism).[67]

If seen in this light, soft law could also be a part of the solution to the EU's competence conundrum. Soft law's very problematisation of the distinction between 'national' and 'EU' competence up-ends our assumptions about how legal authority in the EU is currently exercised. If soft law's rise further demonstrates the difficulties of controlling competence through the boundaries of 'categorical federalism',[68] it will surely also force national and EU decision makers to think more freely about how the EU's political power can be constrained and controlled in the future.

At the very least, soft law's connection with bio-power should provoke scholarly reflection—if modern law and regulation increasingly carries a positive, regulatory, and networked character, a whole host of doctrines of EU law (from direct effect to supremacy to fundamental rights review) may need further re-evaluation too. The same applies to the competence debate: we need to re-think competences precisely because we need to re-think the nature of power and authority in contemporary EU law.

[66] S Garben, 'Confronting the Competence Conundrum: Democratising the European Union through an Expansion of its Legislative Powers' (2015) 35 *Oxford Journal of Legal Studies* 1, 26–30.

[67] Garben, ibid; M Dawson and F De Witte, 'From Balance to Conflict: A New Constitution for the EU' (2016) 22 *European Law Journal* 2, 204–24; G Davies, 'Democracy and Legitimacy in the Shadow of Purposive Competence' (2015) 21 *European Law Journal* 1.

[68] On this category in US and EU law, see J Resnik, 'Categorical Federalism: Jurisdiction, Gender and the Globe' (2001) 111 *Yale Law Journal* 3; R Schütze, *From Dual to Cooperative Federalism: The Changing Structure of European Law* (Oxford, Oxford University Press, 2009).

15

Refining the Division of Competences in the EU: National Discretion in EU Legislation

TON VAN DEN BRINK*

INTRODUCTION

MUCH EU LEGISLATION includes a degree of legislative freedom for Member States. It is indeed quite rare for EU legislation to completely absorb national legislative authority. Minimum harmonisation is a well-known phenomenon in this regard, but there are more ways for the EU legislature to leave national authorities some—implicit or explicit—measure of discretion. This enables, and sometimes requires, the Member States to make policy choices of their own in giving effect to EU legislation. EU legislation, which includes national discretion, directly affects the division of legislative authority between the EU and the Member States.

The division of competences between the EU and the Member States has always been a fundamental issue in EU integration and a key element in discourses on the future of the European Union. In the Laeken Declaration the 'better division and definition of powers' was formulated as one of the four challenges for the future of the European Union. This resulted, ten years later, in the Treaty of Lisbon, of which a number of elements are proof of this ambition. Legal bases for the EU to act have in some instances been better circumscribed and subjected to conditions. Principles for the exercise of powers, most notably subsidiarity, have been further elaborated and national parliaments have acquired a key role in monitoring the compliance thereof.

How does national discretion fit, if at all, into discourses on the division of powers between the EU and the Member States? National discretion is, obviously, an issue of specific and concrete EU legislative policies, but it also directly impacts upon the division of authority between the EU and its Member States. An assessment from a perspective of national discretion distinguishes itself from more

* Ton van den Brink is associate Professor of European Law at the Europa Institute of Utrecht University and is member of the management team of the Utrecht Centre for Regulation and Enforcement in Europe (RENFORCE).

classic approaches to the issue of the division of competences by a bottom-up approach. It seeks to unravel how concrete legislative choices at the EU level impact on the relation between the EU and the Member States. By contrast, constitutional approaches to the issue focus on the founding Treaties and on how constitutional principles and Treaty powers shape the constitutional relation between the EU and its Member States. Such approaches have gained political importance as they directly link to public and political debates on concerns over excessive regulation by the EU, the desire to contain the powers of the EU and the need to create a better balance between Member States' and EU powers. This is, indeed, equally true for national discretion.

The central aim of this chapter is, therefore, to assess how national discretion may contribute to the discourse on the division of competences as an additional or alternative approach to enhancing the legitimacy of the EU and its policies. First, some examples of national discretion in EU legislation will be elaborated to acquire a better understanding of the many manifestations and degrees thereof. Next, a typology of national discretion will be developed, followed by an exploration of the constitutional effects and issues it raises. Following on from this, the added value of considering national discretion as a factor for the division of competences will be explored. This part will, however, also address fundamental and practical issues that arise.

NATIONAL DISCRETION: A FIRST ENCOUNTER

Framework Decision on Probation Measures and Alternative Sanctions

The Framework Decision on the European Arrest Warrant is the best-known example of EU criminal procedure law. After its adoption in 2003, it has been complemented by a number of other legislative acts regulating co-operation between judicial authorities on the basis of mutual recognition and mutual trust. One of those acts is the Framework Decision on probation measures and alternative sanctions.[1] If probation measures or alternative sanctions have been imposed on a person who resides in another EU Member State, the Framework Decision allows the supervision of such measures to be carried out in the Member State of residence. Whereas the European Arrest Warrant is based on a single criminal sanction that is common to all EU criminal law systems—detention—this Framework Decision applies to various sanctions and probation measures. In contrast to the European Arrest Warrant, the Framework Decision brings along positive effects to the persons to whom it applies, for example, as courts will be more willing to impose alternative sanctions rather than detention if the convicted person resides in another Member State.

[1] Council Framework Decision 2008/947/EU on the application of the principle of mutual recognition to judgments and probation decisions with a view to the supervision of probation measures and alternative sanctions OJ 2008 L 337/102.

This context determines the freedom for Member States to transpose the Framework Decision into national legislation. Some of the legislative discretion of the Member States is similar to that of the European Arrest Warrant. The Framework Decision is based on a system of automatic recognition for the offences listed (the list of offences is the same as under the European Arrest Warrant). For sanctions resulting from other offences, the double criminality requirement applies. This effectively allows the Member States to determine to which requests the Framework Decision applies. With regard to the type of sanctions and measures to be taken over, a similar system has been adopted. A list of alternative sanctions and probation measures defines which sanctions and measures must be taken over. For other sanctions and measures, Member States may decide unilaterally whether they are prepared to supervise these as well.[2] Moreover, the Framework Decision allows the Member States to adapt the measure or sanction (in terms of nature and duration) if the original decision is 'incompatible with the law of the executing State'.[3] Another form of national discretion relates to the list of optional refusal grounds.[4]

Proposal on GMO Food and Feed

The Commission proposal on GMO food and feed is a rare example of EU legislation that actually seeks to increase Member States' discretion.[5] The current regulation is based on a system of granting authorisations for the placing on the market of genetically modified organisms (GMOs) and genetically modified food and feed at the EU level. Once authorised, the free movement rules apply and the Member States may, thus, not prohibit, restrict or impede the free circulation of that product within their territory. The Regulation contains a so-called 'safeguard clause' (Article 34 of the Regulation) allowing Member States to block authorised GMOs and genetically modified (GM) food and feed in exceptional circumstances. They can do so only if they can provide evidence for a severe risk to public health, animal health or the environment. With regard to GMOs, a Directive has been adopted in 2015 allowing the Member States to restrict or prohibit the cultivation of GMOs on other grounds as well.[6] The current proposal seeks to introduce a similar system for GM food and feed. It allows the Member

[2] Framework Decision 2008/947/JHA Art 4(2).

[3] ibid Art 9.

[4] ibid Art 11. This article is framed as giving discretion to the 'competent authority' of the Member States. Whether this amounts to legislative discretion is, thus, questionable as this provision could be read as an *obligation* on Member States' legislatures to allow their competent nation to refuse recognition if one of the situations listed is at issue.

[5] Proposal for a Regulation amending Regulation (EC) No 1829/2003 as regards the possibility for the Member States to restrict or prohibit the use of genetically modified food and feed on their territory, COM(2015) 177 final.

[6] Directive (EU) 2015/412 of the European Parliament and the Council of 11 March 2015 amending Directive 2001/18/EC as regards the possibility for the Member States to restrict or prohibit the cultivation of genetically modified organisms (GMOs) in their territory OJ 2015 L 68/1.

States to restrict or prohibit GM food and feed on the basis of national public interests ('compelling grounds' in the wording of the proposal), provided that the restriction or prohibition is reasoned, in compliance with EU law, proportionate and non-discriminatory. The Member States would effectively acquire the right to derogate ('opt out') from the EU system of authorisation giving access to the entire internal market. Some Member States' parliaments have considered that the proposal to 'renationalise' would infringe the Internal Market and would create new obstacles to free movement.[7] Such arguments are perhaps not among the most likely ones in subsidiarity scrutiny procedures at national level.

The proposal is indeed unique. It has a significant impact on the functioning of the Internal Market and it effectively entails a repatriation of competence from the EU. But it is equally unique in the type of discretion it provides for Member States. Their discretion is political in nature as it extends to the balancing of fundamental public interests. They may unilaterally decide whether the internal market and perhaps commercial interests prevail or whether they want to oppose GM food and feed based on other concerns. The impact of the proposal must be understood from the problems that the Member States had experienced with the current system. The Commission identified a number of issues.[8] Some Member States had unilaterally introduced bans on GM feed and food, which could not be justified on the basis of the existing EU legislation. Also, the Member States had never expressed a qualified majority in favour of, or against, a Commission authorisation decision in the context of the committee of national representatives that is involved in the decision making ('comitology'). Unlike most other committees, the lack of a qualified majority in favour, or against, had consistently resulted in a 'no opinion' situation. This undermines the legitimacy of EU Commission authorisations.

The future of the proposal is, however, very uncertain. The European Parliament has rejected the Commission's proposal and called on the Commission to withdraw it and submit a new one. To date, the Commission has not done so and the ball is therefore in the corner of the Council.

Family Reunification Directive

The Family Reunification Directive is a compromise between the interests of individuals to be able to live together with their families (in this sense the Directive elaborates the right to family life of Article 8 of the European Convention on Human Rights (ECHR)) and the preferences of the EU Member States to

[7] See eg the Belgian House of Representatives' Reasoned opinion in the framework of the Subsidiarity Early Warning Mechanism, at www.ipex.eu/IPEXL-WEB/scrutiny/COD20150093/bechb.do at 10.

[8] Explanatory Memorandum to the Proposal, see above n 5.

be able to effectively control migration.[9] The Member States have different views on how restrictive immigration policies should be and which demands should be imposed on immigrants. The preference to control migration is therefore translated into conditions and requirements that the Member States may impose, such as housing requirements, sufficient income requirements and compliance with integration requirements. The Directive only applies to third-country nationals that seek family reunion with other third-country nationals (sponsors) in the EU. The Member States are free to regulate the rights of third-country nationals that seek family reunion with EU citizens who reside in their own country.

Apart from optional material requirements and conditions, the Directive contains other elements of national discretion. A general provision enables the Member States to adopt or maintain more favourable provisions for individuals.[10] Member States may also extend the scope of application of the material rights, by extending the group of relatives eligible for family reunification to dependent parents, unmarried adult children and unmarried partners.[11] The Directive is based on dependent residence rights for family members (that is, residence rights being dependent on the sponsor) but the Member States may decide to grant independent residence rights as well.[12] Also the previously mentioned integration measures entail discretion for the Member States as the Directive leaves the concept of 'integration' undefined.[13]

To fully understand the scope of the discretion left to the Member States, a couple of CJEU decisions must be considered. In 2006, the CJEU had to decide on the request of the European Parliament to annul the Directive. The European Parliament submitted that the Directive violated the fundamental right of family life, as well as other fundamental rights. The CJEU disagreed as the right to family life does not 'create for the members of a family an individual right to be allowed to enter the territory of a State and cannot be interpreted as denying States a certain margin of appreciation when they examine applications for family reunification'.[14] The Court furthermore determined that the Member States remain bound to respect fundamental rights when implementing the Directive. Also, it pointed at the obligation for the Member States to take into account the specific circumstances of concrete situations and the competing interests at stake. Thus, Member States' executive authorities should be able to consider the merits of each situation and be obliged to take the interests into account as they flow from the Directive and the applicable fundamental rights. National legislative discretion is thus limited by the obligation to respect the required executive discretion

[9] Council Directive 2003/86/EC on the right to family unification OJ 2008 L 251/12.
[10] ibid Art 3(5).
[11] ibid Art 4(2).
[12] ibid Art 15.
[13] This point was submitted by the European Parliament as an argument to annul the Directive. The CJEU concluded, however, that such discretion could in itself not amount to a breach of the fundamental right to family life: Case C-540/03 *Parliament v Council* [2006] ECR I-05769, para 41.
[14] ibid para 59.

(national legislation may, *inter alia*, not prescribe the automatic application of the derogations provided for by the Directive).

In *Chakroun*, the CJEU had to address the issue of national discretion in a more direct manner. It formulated the following limitations:

— The conditions and exceptions in the Directive had to be interpreted narrowly, in light of the main purpose of enabling family reunion. To that end, the concepts from the Directive that did not refer to national law had to be interpreted uniformly.
— The Directive had to be interpreted and implemented in accordance with human rights (most notably the right to family life as elaborated by the ECHR and the EU Charter of Fundamental Rights).
— The Member States might not use their discretion to undermine the objectives of the Directive.

Concluding Remarks

The examples of national discretion elaborated in this section reveal its multifaceted nature. The EU legislature has found a variety of ways to enable the Member States to make their own policy choices within the context of EU legislation and the implementation thereof. The reasons for doing so may be related to political controversy, as the case of the Family Reunification Directive and the GMO food and feed proposal demonstrate. Also a high level of diversity in national legislation and practices may be a reason to grant Member States a considerable degree of appreciation, as the case of the Framework Decision on alternative sanctions and probation measures demonstrates. An additional, but thus far also unique, factor identified from the GMO example was that the existing EU legislative framework was found to be dysfunctional. The Family Reunification Directive example furthermore shows that not only the text, but also the context of EU legislation defines national discretion. In this case, the position of the Directive within the broader framework of EU fundamental rights protection is key to understanding the scope of national discretion. The example of the Family Reunification Directive also demonstrates that national discretion is not simply a binary issue of legislative freedom versus legislative confinement.

TOWARDS A TYPOLOGY OF NATIONAL DISCRETION

The examples elaborated in the previous section demonstrate that national discretion in EU legislation is not merely a matter of 'more' or 'less'. It comes in a wide variety of forms. A closer investigation of these different forms is therefore warranted, especially in light of the limited attention the subject has drawn in legal doctrine. In the remainder of this section, I will elaborate a typology of national discretion[15] that is expedient for a better understanding of the relation between the EU and the Member States. The types of national discretion are, however, not mutually exclusive. Concrete EU legislation may indeed carry characteristics of several types.

Minimum Harmonisation

The lack of doctrinal attention for national discretion arguably does not apply to minimum harmonisation. It has developed into a key aspect of the EU legal order both at the Treaty level and at the level of EU secondary law.[16] It has been incorporated in the Treaties as the prescribed method of legislation to shape policies ranging from environmental protection and social protection to criminal law. Even in areas for which the Treaties have not prescribed minimum harmonisation, legislation is regularly based thereon. The Family Reunification Directive is a case in point. The Directive contains material conditions for the right to family reunification. The Member States may, however, apply more favourable conditions, eg by not applying housing or sufficient income requirements.[17]

Minimum harmonisation seems a rather straightforward form of national discretion. EU legislation creates a basis of common rules but the Member States are free to maintain or introduce stricter rules to offer a higher level of protection. Several factors complicate this view, however. Minimum harmonisation may be implied by EU legislation and need not be made explicit, for example by adding the standard formula phrase that 'the Member States may adopt or retain in force stricter provisions/a higher level of protection', and so on. It may only be implied by the wording or the context of EU legislation. In *Gallaher* the CJEU decided that the requirement from the Tobacco Labelling Directive 89/622/EEC that the prescribed health warnings associated with smoking should cover 'at least 4 per cent' of cigarette packages should be read as meaning that the Member States could prescribe a higher surface percentage.[18] The Court rejected the view put forward in the proceedings that the phrase 'at least' referred to discretion of the industry, rather than of the Member States. Article 8 of the Directive prohibits the Member States from banning or restricting the sale of products which comply with this Directive. The consequence thereof was that the British higher standard of

[15] Partly based on my earlier chapter 'Towards an Ever Clearer Division of Authority between the European Union and the Member States?' in A van den Brink, MM Luchtman and M Scholten (eds), *Sovereignty in the Shared Legal Order of the EU—Core Values of Regulation and Enforcement* (Intersentia Publishers, 2015) ch 10.

[16] Although it has been a relative latecomer in the history of EU harmonisation, as Slot has argued. See PJ Slot, 'Harmonization' (1996) 21 *European Law Review* 378.

[17] For an overview of the different choices the Member States have made in this regard see K Groenendijk et al, *The Family Reunification Directive in EU Member States; The First Year of Implementation* (Wolf Legal Publishers, 2007), especially ch 5.

[18] Case C-11/92 *The Queen v Secretary of State for Health ex parte Gallaher* [1994] ECR I-03545.

6 per cent of cigarette package surface could only be imposed on domestic traders and would thus amount to reverse discrimination.

Even if it is clear that EU legislation leaves the Member States the discretion to adopt stricter norms, they may only do so within the confines of the broader EU law framework. In the context of internal market policies, minimum harmonisation is a solution to the tension between the aim to create a level playing field inherent to the Internal Market objectives, and other (social, environmental, etc) objectives.[19] The Internal Market objectives may not be disregarded by the Member States even though the concept of minimum harmonisation implies a distortion of the ideal of a level playing field between economic actors.[20] Thus, in setting stricter standards, the Member States need to comply with the Treaty provisions on the Internal Market, but also with fundamental rights.[21] An example of the former is the CJEU decision in *Dusseldorp*.[22] The Court decided that a national environmental measure, applying stricter standards than the EU Regulation it was based on, could not be applied by the national authorities. The reason was that the national measure not only benefited the environment, but also resulted in a distortion of competition.[23] Similarly, in *Gourmetterie van den Burg* the Court ruled on the limits of legislative discretion included in the Wild Bird Directive.[24] It decided that the Dutch ban on importing and marketing red grouse was incompatible with EU law, although it was based on the possibility to set stricter standards of bird protection. The Court argued that the Netherlands could not apply the discretion left to the Member States to protect birds which were neither part of a migratory nor an endangered species.

Elaboration Discretion

Elaboration discretion refers to the further fleshing out of EU legislation in national legislation. This may involve the further elaboration of open-textured norms into concrete norms which may be applied by public authorities, and invoked by individuals in court proceedings. It may also refer to the freedom of Member States to decide on appropriate measures to achieve concrete and specific policy objectives set by the EU. Elaboration discretion is perhaps one of the most common forms of national discretion in EU legislation and may result from the

[19] M Dougan, 'Minimum Harmonization and the Internal Market' (2000) 37 *Common Market Law Review* 853–85.

[20] ibid 865.

[21] The exact effect of Treaty provisions on national 'stricter standards' is, however, not clear, eg whether they may apply to imports as well. Dougan argues that minimum harmonisation should be accompanied by a provision clarifying the relation to Treaty provisions.

[22] Case C-203/96 *Chemische Afvalstoffen Dusseldorp* [1998] ECR I-4075.

[23] See eg Case C-71/02 *Karner v Troostwijk* [2004] ECR I-3325, in which Austrian stricter measures on misleading advertisement were scrutinised in light of the fundamental right of free expression.

[24] Case C-169/89 *Gourmetterie van den Burg* [1990] ECR 2143.

compromise nature of EU legislation or from the desire to shape more concrete norms in accordance with local expertise and peculiarities. Unlike minimum harmonisation, elaboration discretion does not necessarily concern the possibility to adopt, or retain in force, stricter standards in light of the objectives of EU legislation. Conversely, minimum harmonisation EU legislative acts may not need further concretisation, such as the provision from the Tobacco Labelling Directive that was the central point in the *Gallaher* case, on health warnings on cigarette packages. Another difference is that whereas minimum harmonisation leaves the Member States free to make use of the option to set stricter standards, the further fleshing out of EU legislation may well be an obligation on the Member States. This may be so in order to make EU law effective (and, as such, flow from the principle of loyal co-operation and *effet utile* of EU law) and to provide legal certainty on the legal position of individuals.[25]

A concrete example is the Universal Service Directive in the field of Telecommunications law.[26] This Directive aims to correct market failures by imposing universal service obligations. The Directive specifies the services that need to be provided, but leaves the Member States considerable freedom on how to achieve this in practice. Article 3(2) of the Directive contains the general elaboration of this division of authority between the EU and the Member States by stating that: 'Member States shall determine the most efficient and appropriate approach for ensuring the implementation of universal service, whilst respecting the principles of objectivity, transparency, non-discrimination and proportionality.'

This general principle is elaborated in specific provisions of the Directive. The Member States have the freedom to designate one or more undertakings to provide universal services (Article 8); to adopt measures to ensure the affordability of services (Article 9); and on the quality of service of designated undertakings. They may also opt for price regulation.

Implicit national discretion is very common in cases of elaboration discretion. Such discretion regularly relates to the enforcement of EU legislation. Although there is a trend towards more specific enforcement provisions, the general provision is still often found that the Member States must ensure a sanctioning system which is 'effective, proportionate and dissuasive'.[27] This gives the Member States the freedom to opt for enforcement models that fit within the national legal order.

Implicit elaboration discretion may equally result from vague and non-defined notions in EU legislation. In the context of EU environmental criminal legislation, Faure has discussed the notions of 'substantial damage', 'dangerous activities',

[25] *cf* A Prechal, *Directives in EU Law* (Oxford, Oxford University Press, 2005) section 5.2.1.

[26] European Parliament and Council Directive 2002/22/EC on universal service and users' rights relating to electronic communications networks and services (Universal Service Directive), OJ L 108/51.

[27] See, eg, Council Directive 2000/43/EC implementing the principle of equal treatment between persons irrespective of racial or ethnic origin (Race Equality Directive) OJ 2000 L 180/22 Art 15.

'dangerous substances' and the 'significant deterioration of a habitat'.[28] These notions are crucial for establishing criminal liability for environmental offences, but the EU legislature leaves it to Member States' legislatures and judicial practice to further flesh them out. This raises serious issues in light of the *lex certa* principle (individuals should be able to know in advance whether certain behaviour could infer criminal liability). Legal certainty is equally an issue for the Member States, as this type of national discretion may raise doubts on what the correct way of implementation is and to what extent the Member States indeed enjoy discretion.[29] This type of discretion is, thus, generally viewed as problematic and seen as an important factor affecting the quality of EU legislation. Although better law-making initiatives in general and the Inter-Institutional Agreement on Better Law-making in particular seek to increase the quality of EU legislation, no particular strategy has been developed to address the issue in that context.

'Scope' Discretion

Somsen[30] and Van Roermund[31] have introduced the notion of what could be called 'scope' discretion, that is, the freedom of Member States to decide to what situations EU legislation applies. This is regularly left open, or at least in part, by EU legislation itself. Just as other forms of national discretion, scope discretion may be the result of an explicit choice of the EU legislature. For the definition of a worker, the Posted Workers Directive relies explicitly on the laws of the host Member State.[32] Another example is the Recast Asylum Procedures Directive.[33] Article 3 of the Directive allows the Member States to apply the Directive to any applications for protection falling outside the Recast Qualification Directive (Recast QD). It has been observed that this concerns a significant expansion of the scope of the Directive in light of the practical importance of statuses that Member States grant as a matter of national discretion (as has been demonstrated during the current Syrian refugee crisis).[34]

[28] M Faure, 'Vague notions in environmental criminal law' (2010) 18 *Environmental Liability* 119–33.

[29] See also below, on the problems associated with national discretion.

[30] H Somsen, 'Discretion in European Community Environmental Law: An Analysis of ECJ Case Law' (2003) 40 *Common Market Law Review* 1413–53.

[31] B van Roermund, 'Law at Cross-Purposes: Conceptual Confusion and Political Divergence' in S Prechal and B van Roermund (eds), *The Coherence of EU Law; The search for unity in divergent concepts* (Oxford, Oxford University Press, 2008) 315–41.

[32] Directive 96/71/EC concerning the posting of workers in the framework of the provision OJ 1996 L 18/1 Art 2(2).

[33] Directive 2013/32/EU on common procedures for granting and withdrawing international protection (recast) OJ 2013 L 180/60.

[34] C Costello and E Hancox, 'The Recast Asylum Procedures Directive 2013/32/EU: Caught between the Stereotypes of the Abusive Asylum Seeker and the Vulnerable Refugee' in V Chetail, P De Bruycker and F Maiani (eds), *Reforming the Common European Asylum System: The New European Refugee Law* (Leiden, Brill/Nijhoff, 2016) ch 12, para 4.1.1.

The EU legislature may explicitly leave Member States the freedom to apply EU regulations and directives beyond a 'core' that is defined by the EU legislature itself, or it may explicitly refer to national legislation. The Framework Decision on the mutual recognition of probation measures and alternative sanctions is an example of the former. Scope discretion has been created with regard to the types of alternative sanctions and probation measures that need to be recognised. The 'core', that is the sanctions which the Member States are required to recognise, is listed in Article 4 of the Framework Decision. However, the Council concluded that such substantial differences exist between the Member States in probation measures and alternative sanctions and even in the nature of such measures and sanctions that a general universal recognition requirement would be undesirable.[35] It might indeed imply that executing Member States might be forced to carry out a sanction or probation measure that would not necessarily exist in the domestic criminal legal system. Thus, the Framework Decision leaves this decision to the Member States which may extend the scope of application to other sanctions and probation measures.[36]

EU legislation may also contain scope discretion in the form of exceptions that Member States may apply. Article 5 of the Copyright Directive[37] contains a list of exceptions that Member States may implement to restrict copyright protection (such as home use, educational use, etc). This list is exhaustive, but Member States have a 'broad discretion', as the CJEU puts it, in interpreting these exceptions.[38] The double criminality requirement in European Arrest Warrant procedures may equally be seen as an example of scope discretion in the form of exceptions. If a requested person is asked for surrender, the executing Member State must investigate whether the offence for which surrender is requested is a criminal offence in the host state, or is a so-called listed offence. If not a listed offence, the criminal law system of the host state thus defines the scope of application of the obligation to surrender. The Framework Decision on Alternative Sanctions and Probation Measures goes even a step further. It allows the Member States to derogate from the listed sanctions and probation measures altogether and apply the double criminality requirement to all requests.[39]

[35] Council conclusions from the presidency of 8 December 2010, 17628/10 at 5.

[36] An example is Article 2(2) Directive 2004/38, which enables the Member States to extend the rights of family members to partners in a registered partnership if they treat registered partnerships as equivalent to marriage. Another example of an extension of the scope of application is the decision of the French authorities to extend the right of granting a residence permit to those who denounce their traffickers to Bulgarian and Romanian nationals, whereas Directive 2004/81/EC limits this right to third country nationals. See T Marguery and BC Oude Breuil, 'Freedom, Security and Justice for Whom? The Case Study of Bulgarian Street Prostitution in France' in A van den Brink, M Luchtman and M Scholten (eds), *Sovereignty in the Shared Legal Order: Core Values of Regulation and Enforcement* (Antwerp, Intersentia Publishers, 2015) ch 9, 8.

[37] Directive 2001/29/EC on the harmonisation of certain aspects of copyright and related rights in the information society OJ 2001 L 167/10.

[38] Case C-145/10 *Painer* [2011] ECR I-12533.

[39] Art 10 Framework Decision 2008/947/JHA.

Implicit national discretion to decide on the scope of application exists when the Member States can decide on the interpretation of key concepts in EU legislation. Somsen has elaborated on the concepts of 'waste' and 'information relating to the environment' in the field of EU environmental law.[40] As the definition of these concepts determines to what situations EU legislation applies, the Member States enjoy substantial freedom to decide on the actual scope of application of EU legislation.

But even if EU legislation defines key concepts, Member States may still possess the power to influence the scope of application, for example by further elaborating such definitions, or—as Somsen has observed—by the qualification and classification of factual situations in light of these definitions. A good example flows from the Natura 2000 regime. The designation of protected areas defines the territorial scope of application of a number of environmental and nature protection measures. As Princen observed,[41] the identification of national areas of protection is for a large part determined by the individual Member States, which thus have a substantial influence on the territorial application of the EU protection measures.

Constitutional Dimensions of National Discretion

National discretion is primarily an issue of legislative choice. Nevertheless, there are various constitutional dimensions to it as well. These dimensions involve:

— the legitimacy paradox created by the protection of Member States legislative autonomy on the one hand and more complex division between Member States' and EU competences on the other;
— the link with EU constitutional law principles, most notably subsidiarity and proportionality;
— national discretion being an instrument to accommodate the balance between diversity and unity in the European Union and, as such, providing an alternative to existing forms of differentiated integration.

A Legitimacy Paradox

The discourse on the division of competences is a legitimacy discourse. The European Council's call in 2001 to design a 'better division and definition of competence in the European Union' (Laeken Declaration) originated from the desire to fix the perceived mismatch between citizens' expectations of the EU and the

[40] H Somsen, 'Discretion in European Community Environmental Law: An Analysis of ECJ Case Law' (2003) 40 *Common Market Law Review*, 1413, 1436.

[41] S Princen, *Het Moet van Brussel: de verhouding EU en lidstaten tussen retoriek en werkelijkheid*, (Inaugural Lecture, Utrecht University, 3 October 2014).

way in which these are—or are not—fulfilled.[42] The European Council identified three main tasks in fixing this mismatch. First, the division of competences should be clarified and made more transparent. Second, it should be determined whether a reorganisation of competences was needed, including guarantees that national 'spheres of competence' would not be affected. Third, it should be guaranteed that any reorganisation of competence would not increase the risk of creeping EU competences and an encroachment of Member States' autonomy.

In light of these legitimacy aims, national discretion creates a legitimacy paradox. National discretion fosters some of the legitimacy aims, in particular the protection of the legislative autonomy of the Member States. It enables the EU legislature to limit the encroachment on national spheres of competence as much as possible. As such, it creates ways to transform the balancing of effective EU action and national autonomy into concrete legislative solutions.

On the other hand, national discretion does not contribute to greater transparency and clarity of the division of competences between the EU and the Member States. On the contrary, it increases the complexity thereof. This is caused in part by the variety of forms of national discretion (see above) and by the sometimes implicit nature thereof (see below). But most of all, including national discretion in EU legislation is a concrete decision made in the context of specific legislation. Thus, the division of authority between the EU and the Member States may only be assessed ex post. By contrast, the aim in terms of clarity in the division of competences in the EU constitution has been to delineate national and EU powers more distinctly to make EU action better foreseeable. Apart from Treaty-prescribed minimum harmonisation, national discretion contributes little to the foreseeability of EU/national relations.

Containment is another aim to which national discretion contributes little. National discretion is not the result of the external limitation of the powers of the EU legislature (again, with the exception of Treaty-prescribed minimum harmonisation). Instead, it is a matter of legislative choice. Moreover, the CJEU only exercises low-intensity control over such choices.[43] Thus, the aim of containment of EU powers relies exclusively on self-restraint of the EU legislature in the context of national discretion.

Subsidiarity

National discretion in EU legislation would seem an obvious manifestation of subsidiarity. Indeed, as subsidiarity seeks to balance the exercise of EU and national competences—with a preference for lower levels of government—national discretion would seem a more than appropriate mechanism to flesh out

[42] European Council, 14–15 December 2001, SN 300/1/01 REV 1, 21–22.

[43] See below.

subsidiarity in concrete legislation. Yet, the link between the subsidiarity principle and national discretion in EU legislation is less obvious than it may seem. In a strict reading of Article 5(3) TEU, subsidiarity only regards the binary question whether or not the EU should act with regard to a specific issue. Discussing the content of EU legislation implies in this view that the subsidiarity question has already been answered in the affirmative. The question what freedom EU legislation should leave to the Member States is then exclusively a proportionality issue. Consequently, subsidiarity presupposes a dichotomy between EU competence and Member State autonomy. National discretion cannot be reconciled easily with such a dichotomy. It is possible, however, to embrace a broader notion of subsidiarity.[44] Craig argued that an EU subsidiarity strategy may involve that certain aspects of the regulatory regime are left to the Member States or that the EU rules are general in nature, leaving more scope for national input and variation (the latter has been qualified as elaboration discretion earlier in this contribution).[45] Thus, the subsidiarity question not only relates to the entirety of the regulatory regime, but also to specific aspects thereof. This would indeed be in line with several of the rationales underlying subsidiarity.[46] Most notably the desire to avoid excessive centralisation and the need to foster pluralism and the diversity of national values would be well served by such a view on subsidiarity. It would enable the interests of the Member States to be considered even if for the regulatory regime as a whole the subsidiarity calculus would be in favour of EU action.

Nevertheless, the Commission seems to uphold a stricter definition of subsidiarity. This definition leaves no room to consider national discretion in EU legislation. The Commission's approach to subsidiarity emerges most prominently from its position in the framework of the Subsidiarity Scrutiny mechanisms (the Early Warning Mechanism and the Political Dialogue). It should be noted that the Commission has a procedural interest in a strict definition of subsidiarity as this limits the likelihood of its proposals being confronted with 'yellow' or 'orange' cards. Particularly insightful for this approach is the Commission's response to the Reasoned opinions to the Proposal to establish a European Public Prosecutor's Office (EPPO).[47] The Commission distinguished 'true' subsidiarity arguments from other arguments and refrained from examining the latter. This involved various arguments of national parliaments that sought to protect national interests such as the argument that the proposal would be too far-reaching in general, that the powers of EPPO would be excessive, that the proposal would go beyond

[44] The distinction between a 'thin' and a 'thick' concept of subsidiarity has been elaborated in A van den Brink, 'Towards an Ever Clearer Division of Authority' in A van den Brink, M Luchtman and M Scholten (eds), *Sovereignty in the Shared Legal Order: Core Values of Regulation and Enforcement* (Intersentia Publishers, 2015) 231 ff.

[45] PP Craig, 'Subsidiarity: Political and Legal analysis' (2012) 50 *Journal of Common Market Studies* 72–87, especially 75.

[46] ibid 73.

[47] COM(2013) 851 final.

what was necessary to achieve its objective and that it would entail significant disadvantages for the Member States. All arguments that could be seen as arguments to allow the Member States more discretion were, thus, dismissed as not related to subsidiarity. The only accepted arguments related to the added value of the proposal and to the evaluation of the proposal in light of the existing mechanisms and forms of action of the Member States, in other words only those arguments that relate to the proposal as a whole and in general. On the other hand, the Commission's approach to subsidiarity involves more than an abstract consideration of whether an issue should be regulated at all. The Commission's assessment included the actual proposal at issue as a point of reference to decide whether the EU is better suited to act. The Commission examined the added value of the EPPO proposal by considering concrete elements thereof. Yet, this has not opened the way for the Commission to consider some parts of the proposal to be 'subsidiarity-proof' and others not, let alone that it would use national discretion as a way to do better justice to subsidiarity. This demonstrates that national discretion is not a direct and unconditional product of the subsidiarity principle according to current legislative policies.

Proportionality

The proportionality principle might be an alternative principle to lay the constitutional foundation for national discretion. Proportionality requires the EU legislature, inter alia, to 'not exceed what is necessary' to achieve EU objectives. This may indeed involve leaving discretion to Member States rather than regulating a topic into great detail. Davies has argued that a broad proportionality principle, which includes a balancing between EU objectives and national policies, should be the mechanism to consider national interests.[48] Currently, however, proportionality review is limited to a consideration of the suitability and necessity of EU action in light of EU objectives and has thus a strong bias toward EU integration.[49]

Moreover, in current EU legislative policies, proportionality is mainly geared to protect the interests of citizens, business and European societies in general. In its Impact Assessment Guidelines, the Commission has identified various impacts of proposed EU action that need to be part of proportionality review, such as distributional effects, social impacts, impacts on business, including SMEs and administrative burdens and environmental impacts.[50] No mention is made of the effects on national legislative autonomy. This approach to proportionality is actually in line with the origins of the principle. These origins are the liberal

[48] G Davies, 'Subsidiarity: The wrong idea, in the wrong place, at the wrong time' (2006) 43 *Common Market Law Review* 63–84, see especially s 7.

[49] T Tridimas, *The General Principles of EU Law* (Oxford, Oxford University Press, 2006) 193.

[50] European Commission Impact Assessment Guidelines 2009, SEC(2009)92, 29 ff.

state and its relation to its citizens as well as principles of justice.[51] They have in common that they protect individuals from excessive exercise of public authority. This also explains why proportionality has evolved into a forceful principle for the CJEU to scrutinise EU legislation when fundamental rights are at stake.[52]

Proportionality in the EU is, thus, strongly geared towards the protection of citizens, business and European societies against overregulation. This does not exclude the protection of national legislative authority against excessive EU action. It might indeed be part of a proportionality check for the EU legislature to consider whether EU legislative proposals could include discretion for national legislatures. This is, however, not the reality of the existing legislative policy of the EU (it should be noted in this regard that the recent Inter-Institutional Agreement on Better Law-making is silent on national discretion in EU legislation). But there are more fundamental issues involved. Leaving legislative choices to the Member States may be in conflict with the interests of individuals and may amount to a disproportionate limitation of their rights. The EU legislature has, for instance, enabled the Member States to limit family reunion in the Family Reunification Directive (discussed above). Such limitations (as well as their application by the Member States) need to be proportionate in light of the limitations of fundamental rights. In such circumstances, the CJEU would focus its proportionality review on the infringement of fundamental rights rather than on the intrusion of national legislative autonomy (for which it would only apply its 'softer', more restrained approach to proportionality). Proportionality may, thus, encompass national discretion, but the latter would only be protected by the principle in a limited way and in any case be overshadowed by the protection of the interests of individuals.

National Discretion and Differentiated Integration

National discretion is a tool to balance unity and diversity and allows in particular for the accommodation of the latter. In this sense, national discretion may be seen as an alternative to the various forms of differentiated integration that have emerged.[53] Differentiated integration is thus a broad concept. It encompasses EU Treaty based (eg EMU) and non-EU Treaty based forms of differentiation

[51] J Schwarze, *European Administrative Law* (London, Sweet & Maxwell, 2006) 679 ff.

[52] Conclusion of Advocate General Cruz Villalón in *Digital Rights Ireland*, Joined Cases C-293/12 and C-594/12. He held that the principle of proportionality 'acquires, in the context of the Charter, a particular force, which it does not have under Article 5(4) TEU. See also SA de Vries, 'The EU Single Market and Fundamental Rights' in SA de Vries, U Bernitz and S Weatherhill (eds), *The EU Charter of Fundamental Rights as a Binding Instrument. Five Years Old and Growing* (Oxford, Hart Publishing, 2015) 235–60.

[53] See for a—also from a legal perspective—useful classification of the different models of differentiated integration K Holzinger and F Schimmelfennig, 'Differentiated Integration in the European Union: Many Concepts, Sparse Theory, Few Data' (2012) 19 *Journal of European Public Policy* 292–305.

(eg the ESM), as well as secondary law based forms of differentiation (enhanced co-operation). Following the widely accepted definition that differentiated integration relates to the differential validity of formal EU rules, national discretion may not be qualified as a particular form thereof. Indeed, EU legislation that includes national discretion does not result in a differential validity thereof as the norms apply to all Member States.[54] National discretion must therefore rather be viewed as an alternative to differentiated integration.

After a first wave of attention in the 1990s, differentiated integration is now again in the spotlight. The second decade of the twenty-first century has shown a number of notable examples of differentiated integration (including the Brussels III Regulation and the creation of European patent protection as forms of enhanced co-operation). Some even claim that differentiated integration, or specific models thereof, is key to solve the current legitimacy crisis of the EU.[55] Politicians across Europe have equally embraced differentiated integration.[56]

In terms of equal application of EU rules national discretion is to be favoured over differentiated integration. The principle of equality is a constitutional principle of EU law laid down in Article 4 TEU, and is based on the basic principle of sovereign equality of states in the law of international organisations and common international law.[57] Differentiated integration challenges the equality of EU Member States as it creates a distinction between participating and non-participating states. Most of the conditions the TFEU imposes on enhanced co-operation therefore seek to respect equality and contain various guarantees to that end.[58]

Consequently, enhanced co-operation offers less flexibility in EU decision making than is often associated with it. Most notably, it may only be adopted as a measure of last resort.[59] This is a second advantage of national discretion over enhanced co-operation. Nevertheless, a couple of examples of the latter have seen the light, despite predictions that the strict conditionality would make enhanced co-operation practically useless. These examples demonstrate that enhanced co-operation indeed balances EU objectives and the need to consider and respect national diversity. In the case of the Rome III Regulation[60]—the first example in which recourse was taken to enhanced co-operation—the rationale

[54] F Schimmelfennig and T Winzen, 'Patterns of Differentiated Integration' *Journal of Common Market Studies*, forthcoming.

[55] eg JC Piris, *The Future of Europe: Towards a Two-Speed EU?* (Cambridge, Cambridge University Press, 2012).

[56] N Koenig, 'A Differentiated View of Differentiated Integration' (2015) *Jacques Delors Institute Policy papers* 140.

[57] J Wouters, 'Constitutional Limits of Differentiation: The Principle of Equality' in B De Witte, D Hanf and E Vos (eds), *The Many Faces of Differentiation in EU Law* (Antwerp, Intersentia Publishers, 2001) 301–45.

[58] See ibid for a discussion of these conditions.

[59] Art 20(2) TEU.

[60] Council Regulation 1259/2010/EU implementing enhanced co-operation in the area of the law applicable to divorce and legal separation OJ 2010 L 343/10.

has been to create legal certainty on which national rules apply in cases of international divorce.[61] Not all Member States wanted to take in part the measure. Consequently, a group of Member States have adopted the measure under enhanced co-operation. The non-participating Member States include some with more liberal divorce policies than average in the EU (the Netherlands) and some Member States which have implemented more conservative divorce policies and are thus at the opposite end of the scale (Poland).

Is national discretion now an alternative to enhanced co-operation? The example of the Rome III Regulation suggests otherwise. The Regulation regulates conflicts of laws and implies the recognition of foreign laws if the Regulation so prescribes. It is difficult to imagine a version of the Regulation that would be acceptable for all Member States even if it would entail a maximum of national discretion. Member States with fundamental objections to recognising divorce laws would indeed deny the very foundation of the recognition of foreign divorce laws. National discretion accommodates the balance between national diversity and EU policy objectives at a less fundamental level. The Rome III Regulation in fact includes various elements of national discretion, such as the public policy objection.[62] This is, however, meant for Member States that still accept the recognition of foreign divorce laws as a matter of principle.

All in all, national discretion serves the same purpose of accommodating unity and diversity as differentiated integration in general and enhanced co-operation in particular. Some principled drawbacks of differentiated integration do not apply to national discretion and including national discretion in EU legislation may facilitate acceptance among the Member States and thus avoid having recourse to enhanced co-operation. In the case of more principled objections, enhanced co-operation or other forms of differentiated integration form the most probable way.

NATIONAL DISCRETION: INDISPENSABLE TO THE COMPETENCES DISCOURSE?

Benefits

The discourse on the division of competences between the EU and the Member States would benefit from including national discretion as a key factor therein. First, it would contribute to a better understanding of the division of legislative authority between the EU and the Member States. The competences discourse has had particular strength in addressing the capacity of the EU to act and

61 D Leuffen, B Rittberger and F Schimmelfennig, *Differentiated Integration: Explaining Variation in the European Union* (Basingstoke, Palgrave Macmillan, 2013) 236.

62 Regulation 1259/2010/EU implementing enhanced co-operation in the area of law applicable to divorce and legal separation OJ 2010 L 343/10, Art 12.

the constitutional limits thereto. The Treaty powers and their classification form the heart of this part of the competences discourse. This, however, reveals only part of the picture of the division of legislative authority between the EU and the Member States. Including national discretion in the division of competences discourse allows us to explain how Member States may still enjoy discretion even if the EU legislature has the power to act; a subsidiarity review points towards EU action and the EU legislature has indeed adopted legislation. Even in such circumstances, national interests may indeed be guaranteed, contrary to what an assessment on the basis of the EU's capacity to act may suggest. Thus, national discretion fills a void in the wider public understanding of the relation between the EU and the Member States and it directs the attention to the actual legislative impact of the EU on the Member States, on citizens and on business. What is more, highlighting which policy choices still lie, despite EU legislation, at the national level may be an effective way to address the 'blaming Brussels game'. One side note should be made here: national discretion concerns EU legislation, which means that it is of little help for the understanding of other impacts of the EU. In the field of economic policy making (EMU), the division of authority between the EU and the Member States is more difficult to assess as it is based on a dialogue between EU and national—executive rather than legislative—institutions. In any case, for the impact of the EU in this ever more important field of EU action, national discretion in EU legislation is not a relevant factor.

A second benefit of including national discretion in the discourse on the division of competences would be to enhance EU legitimacy. This would require national discretion to become an explicit and structural aspect of decision-making processes. At this point in time, not even national parliaments systematically scrutinise EU legislative proposals on national discretion and on the preferences they have in this regard, although it is true that the scope for national decision making is a consideration in individual scrutiny processes. Also, and perhaps more importantly, it would be a significant step forward if the decision on the degree and type of national discretion would be included as an explicit and separate element of Commission Impact Assessments.

Issues and Obstacles

A more substantial role for national discretion in the division of competences discourse also raises a number of issues and obstacles, which will be elaborated in the following subsections.

'Gold Plating'

National discretion is closely connected to gold plating, which can be defined as the practice of Member States to add provisions of national law (norms, administrative and procedural requirements and the like) beyond what is necessary to implement EU legislation. Gold plating has a bad reputation. It is generally viewed as increasing legislative complexities, raising administrative burdens and adding unnecessary costs for businesses and public authorities. At the EU level it is seen as a risk that such negative effects are mistakenly attributed to EU legislation rather than to national policy choices, thereby affecting the legitimacy of EU policies and the EU itself. Thus, in the context of Better Law-making policies, the Commission has encouraged the Member States to avoid gold plating.[63]

At the national level, discouraging gold plating is a common strategy as well. In the Netherlands, for instance, a general government policy on this point has been translated into legally binding guidelines[64] that prohibit that in EU implementation legislation 'other rules than those which are necessary for the implementation' are included.[65] These guidelines specify such 'unnecessary rules' as those rules which are 'not related' to the legally binding EU act or which are 'unnecessary refinements' thereof. The main reason is different from those mentioned above: the Dutch government points to the need to implement EU legislation that would be endangered if the implementation of EU legislation is taken as the starting point for a broader revision of the regulatory framework. By contrast, the 2011 UK government principles to end gold plating are inspired by the need to avoid putting UK business at a competitive disadvantage.[66]

Strategies to avoid gold plating suggest little room for national discretion in the implementation of EU legislation. There are several problems with that view, however, especially in light of the reasons for avoiding gold plating. First, as demonstrated in the previous section, some forms of national discretion require action *per se* on the part of the Member States. EU legislation may require the Member States to choose between different alternatives or leave central notions undefined. Such forms of national discretion do not entail a choice between basic and more comprehensive EU implementation and can therefore not be linked to any gold plating prohibition.

Second, creating a level playing field for business, undistorted by different national legal regimes, is an important but not an absolute policy interest. The very reason that EU legislation includes—regularly explicitly—national discretion is to allow the Member States to balance the interest of creating a level playing field for business against other public interests. Overriding environmental, social or other interests may thus lead the Member States to set higher and/or additional standards. Moreover, going further than EU legislation requires may in some instances indeed contribute to a level playing field for business. This is particularly so if EU legislation does not regulate purely internal situations and Member States wish to extend the benefits thereof to domestic traders or service providers.

[63] See eg Commission, 'Better regulation for better results—An EU agenda', COM(2015) 215 final.

[64] ie legally binding for the government, but not for Parliament.

[65] Aanwijzingen voor de regelgeving, No 331, available in Dutch at http://wetten.overheid.nl/BWBR0005730/2011-05-11.

[66] *Guiding Principles for EU legislation*, in particular no 5 available at www.gov.uk/government/publications/guiding-principles-for-eu-legislation.

Timely implementation is in itself a convincing reason to avoid gold plating, but it can be attained in other ways as well. Setting longer implementation deadlines in case of national discretion would be an obvious strategy. This would deserve to be included as a general consideration in the framework of Better Law-making policies. The Member States could also take the initiative themselves by starting EU implementation processes early if they want to add national policy to the implementation of EU legislation. Such procedural solutions fit the procedural issue of timely implementation better than a strategy of making it impossible to use legitimate opportunities to include national policies in the implementation of EU legislation.

The Problem of Identification

National discretion is regularly unclear in terms of its scope or even its very existence. The compromise nature of EU legislation is an important factor in this respect. Even the CJEU has had difficulty in defining where EU obligations end and national discretion starts. A good example is its decision in *Robins*.[67] The CJEU had to decide on Article 8 of the old Insolvency Directive from 1980 that prescribed that the 'Member States shall ensure that the necessary measures are taken to protect the interests of employees (…) in respect of rights conferring on them immediate or prospective entitlement to old-age benefits, including survivors' benefits, under supplementary company or inter-company pension schemes outside the national statutory social security schemes'.

The Court considered that this wording leaves the Member States some latitude as to the means to be adopted for the purposes of that protection. The Court even went a step further and explicitly stated that it is impossible 'to establish with any precision the minimum level required in order to protect' the rights laid down in the Directive. Rather trying to fix the exact minimum level prescribed by the Directive, the Court investigated what levels of protection would definitely fall within and outside the scope of protection. On the one hand, the provision does not require that the rights to benefits at issue need necessarily be funded by the Member States themselves or even that these benefits are funded in full. On the other hand, the UK system—which had led to a guarantee of benefits of only 20 and 49 per cent of the benefits to which an employee was entitled for the applicants in the main procedure—could not be considered to fall within the definition of the word 'protect' used in Article 8 of the Directive, according to the Court.

Uncertainty on national discretion may also exist with regard to the scope of EU legislation. These may include indeed issues of scope with significant relevance to the functioning of markets and the legal position of citizens and business. A case in point concerns the application of the Services Directive in purely internal

[67] Case C-278/05 *Carol Marilyn Robins and Others v Secretary of State for Work and Pensions* [2007] ECR I-1053.

matters. The Directive itself is silent on the matter, but the European Commission is of the opinion that the Directive indeed applies to internal situations.[68] Davies came to a similar conclusion, based on the wording of the Directive; the effects on equality and free competition; and the fact that the notion of the internal situation comes from the case law of the CJEU on situations in which only the Treaty provisions apply whereas in cases of harmonisation usually no distinction is made between goods or services from domestic and foreign origin.[69]

The reality is, however, that the issue remains unresolved even if the Directive has been in force for more than 10 years now. The issue has been raised before the CJEU in Joint Cases *Trijber* and *Harmsen*.[70] In *Trijber* the application for an authorisation for the transportation of passengers by water was at stake whereas *Harmsen* applied for authorisation for the operation of two window prostitution businesses in Amsterdam. No prima facie cross-border aspects had been identified and the referring court explicitly asked the CJEU whether the Establishment Chapter of the Services Directive would apply in such circumstances. Despite the arguments put forward by Advocate General Szupunar[71] that the Court should actually answer this question, the CJEU avoided that by pointing to the possibility that the recipients of the services at issue might originate from other Member States. Although this seems a weak basis, for the Court it was sufficient to assume the cross-border element. It is questionable whether the CJEU will be able to maintain this position. Member States' courts, administrative authorities as well as businesses and citizens have a strong demand for clarification of the issue. In a recent case a national court has again asked for clarification on this point.[72]

Ex Post Decision by the CJEU

The cases elaborated above illustrate another issue with regard to national discretion in EU legislation. It is ultimately the CJEU that decides on the existence and the scope of national discretion in EU legislation. Such a decision may come only years after the EU directive or regulation has entered into force and long after the Member States have had to implement it. Even if EU legislation contains no definition of its key concepts, the uniform application of EU law may require that an independent and uniform interpretation throughout the EU is given by the CJEU.

[68] Commission Handbook on the implementation of the Services Directive 2007, 24.

[69] G Davies, 'The Service Directive: extending the country of origin principle and reforming public administration' (2007) 32 *European Law Review* 232–45, especially 241–42. See also C Barnard, 'Unravelling the services directive' (2008) 45 *Common Market Law Review* 323–96, especially 351–352, who adds as arguments in this regard the legislative history and the preamble of the Directive as well as the approach taken by Member States to abrogate national provisions in full if the CJEU declares these to be incompatible with EU free movement provisions.

[70] Joined Cases C-340/14 and C-341/14 *RL Trijber v College van Burgemeester en Wethouders van Amsterdam and J Harmsen v Burgemeester van Amsterdam* [2015], not yet published.

[71] Opinion delivered on 16 July 2015 in Joined Cases C-340/14 and C-341/14, not yet published.

[72] Case C-31/16 *Visser Vastgoed Beleggingen v Raad van de gemeente Appingedam* [2016], not yet published.

A case in point is the CJEU decision in *Brüstle*.[73] This case, decided in 2011, concerned the interpretation of Directive 98/44/EC concerning legal protection of biotechnological inventions. The CJEU had been asked to interpret the notion of 'human embryo', of which the Directive contained no definition, although it concerned a crucial unpatentability exception. The Court argued that the definition of such concepts should not be left to the Member States but rather be determined at the EU level. They should be determined by considering 'the context in which they occur and the purposes of the rules of which they form part'.[74] The Directive has been adopted to remove obstacles to trade and to the smooth functioning of the internal market, and thus to encourage industrial research and development in the field of genetic engineering, according to the Court. This might suggest that the Court would adopt a narrow interpretation of the notion of 'human embryo', limiting the scope of the exception. Instead, the CJEU argued that 'any human ovum must, as soon as fertilised, be regarded as a "human embryo"', and even a non-fertilised human ovum may in specific circumstances qualify as a human ovum. The preamble to the Directive and its content indicate that human dignity is a core value upheld by the Directive, according to the Court. The context and aim of the Directive thus indicate that the EU legislature intended to exclude any possibility of patentability where respect for human dignity could be affected. This case therefore illustrates that national discretion (in this case to adopt a national definition of the concept of human embryo) may in hindsight—in this case 14 years after its adoption—prove to never have existed at all. And even if Member States acted in good faith in the implementation of the Directive, their approach may have proved wrong after all should they have adopted too narrow an interpretation of the concept.

Brüstle shows that the role of the CJEU in defining and limiting national discretion may cause legal uncertainties, not only for individuals but also for Member States. Only the EU legislature can address this issue effectively, either by defining key notions itself, or by explicitly express referring to the law of the Member States.

Implementation Delays

National discretion may be a cause for implementation delays. It is, admittedly, difficult to substantiate this claim on the basis of existing empirical research. A vast body of literature on EU implementation and transposition deficits exists, but it has to date not been studied to what extent national discretion in EU legislation causes implementation delays. Instead, a considerable part of existing research deals with procedural variables, such as the length of transposition periods,[75]

[73] Case C-34/10 *Oliver Brüstle v Greenpeace eV* [2011] ECR I-9821.

[74] ibid para 31.

[75] B Steunenberg and M Rhinard, 'The transposition of European law in EU member states: between process and politics' (2010) 2 *European Political Science Review* 495–520.

the national organisation of EU implementation and transposition and national politicisation of EU legislation.[76] An exception is Kaeding, who indeed included national discretion as a variable to explain EU transposition delays.[77] His findings support the claim that national discretion has a negative impact on timely implementation. There are reasons, though, to be cautious in using these findings as an argument here. His definition of national discretion concerns national executive discretion and is based on *de facto* discretion (for example, taking into consideration the freedom of national executive authorities in light of the limited resources of the Commission to monitor compliance) rather than legal discretion.[78] His findings may thus not be applied to national discretion as it has been defined in this chapter.

Yet, it is beyond doubt that national discretion complicates EU implementation. It may be more difficult to negotiate at the national level which choices to make to flesh out EU legislation. Moreover, national mechanisms to speed up EU implementation are less appropriate for the implementation of EU legislation with a high level of national discretion. National authorities will be more inclined to implement EU legislation by primary legislation if national political decisions need to be made. In the Netherlands, this has even been formalised.[79]

CONCLUSION

The relationship between the central level and sub-central levels of government is a key issue in all federal-type political systems. This is even more true in the EU, in which EU membership is increasingly viewed in terms of its effects on national sovereignty. However, the constitutional system of the EU has not remained untouched by the increased political and public sensitivity to the division of competences between the EU and the Member States. On the contrary, it has proved itself to be responsive thereto and the Treaties now contain a range of elements to delineate EU and Member States' competences more clearly and elements which protect national competences better. Equally, the division of competences has become a more prominent feature of EU legislative processes.

National discretion in EU legislation equally relates to the division of competences—or of authority—between the EU and the Member States. It exists in all areas of EU law and is, as such, a systemic element of the EU legal order. It serves to balance not only national and EU interests but also diverging or even

[76] T König and B Luetgert, 'Troubles with Transposition? Explaining Trends in Member-State Notification and the Delayed Transposition of EU Directives' (2009) 39 *British Journal of Political Science* 163–94.

[77] M Kaeding, *Better Regulation in the EU. Lost in Translation or Full Steam Ahead? The Transposition of EU Transport Directives across Member States* (Leiden, Leiden University Press, 2007).

[78] ibid at 98.

[79] A van den Brink, 'Implementing European Union Law in the Netherlands: the Current System, its Limitations and Possible Alternatives' (2006) 12 *European Public Law* 111–26.

conflicting public interests in politically sensitive issues. The Family Reunification Directive is arguably the most pertinent example thereof from the examples discussed in this chapter. National discretion is thus indispensable to balance uniformity in achieving EU objectives and national policy preferences, practices and peculiarities.

Remarkably, no connection has been made thus far between national discretion and the division of competences between the EU and the Member States. Yet, taking national discretion into account is crucial for a proper understanding of how EU and national legislative competences are divided. The GMO example discussed in this chapter represents perhaps not the average of EU legislation, but it is nonetheless exemplifying of how an exclusive focus on the capacity of the EU to act without considering the actual content of EU legislation creates an incomplete picture of the EU's impact on the Member States. It may indeed conceal a reality of a much greater margin of discretion for national legislatures. The relationship between the EU and the Member States is indeed not merely determined by the Treaty-based system of allocation of competences and the interpretation thereof by the CJEU. Currently, however, a mismatch exists between national discretion on the one hand and constitutional principles and provisions that seek to clarify EU–Member States relations on the other. Although national discretion is a systemic element of EU legislation, it is not addressed systematically by the EU legislature (or by EU law scholarship for that matter).

The understanding of the division of competences between the EU and the Member States may be enhanced even further by considering the type of national discretion included in EU legislation. The typology of national discretion defines which policy choices may still be made at the national level. This is thus a crucial factor to be able not only to identify but also to qualify national autonomy.

Paradoxically, national discretion should equally be addressed in a more systematic fashion in EU legislative processes for its ability to adversely affect the understanding of EU–Member States relations. National discretion is in some cases implicitly rather than explicitly part of EU legislation; its limits may be difficult to identify (and the position of the CJEU thereon difficult to predict) and the borders between national discretion and gold plating (additional or adjacent national policy making rather than elaborating EU legislation) may be indistinct. This may blur the public understanding of EU–Member States relations and may make it easier for national politicians to play the 'blaming-Brussels' game. It may equally create problems for national authorities which must implement EU legislation correctly. Last but not least, the legal position of citizens and business may be affected as they may face legal uncertainties. Such issues need not necessarily be resolved or prevented by stricter EU legislation, but rather with a more careful consideration of national discretion in EU legislative processes.

16

The Shifting Powers of the European Parliament: Democratic Legitimacy and the Competences of the European Union

GREGORIO GARZÓN CLARIANA*

GENERAL

THE EXISTENCE OF a Parliament composed by members directly elected by citizens and closely associated to the exercise of the competences conferred to the European Union is certainly one of the most salient features of the Union's institutional system as it stands today,[1] and it results from a long evolution where Parliament itself has often played an active role.[2]

The powers of the European Parliament are a key factor when assessing the democratic legitimacy of actions taken by the European Union.[3] The Treaty on European Union now states that 'the functioning of the Union shall be founded on representative democracy' and that 'Citizens are directly represented at Union level in the European Parliament';[4] and the Court of Justice had already stressed Parliament's legitimising role in its landmark *Van Gend en Loos* case[5] and further developed it, notably in the well-known *Isoglucose* case after the first direct election, stating that consultation of the European Parliament 'reflects at

* Gregorio Garzón Clariana is Professor of Law at Universitat Autonoma de Barcelona.

[1] *cf* eg F Mosconi and A Padoa Schioppa, 'Making Better Use of the European Parliament's Powers' in G Bonvicini (ed), *Democracy in the EU and the Role of the European Parliament* (Rome, Istituto Affari Internazionali, Quaderni IAI, March 2009) 13. This chapter is partially inspired by the seminars on 'the institutional role of the European Parliament' that its author conducted in the Natolin campus of the College of Europe until 2011.

[2] *cf* J Priestly, *Six Battles that Shaped Europe's Parliament* (London, John Harper, 2008).

[3] Democracy inspires other elements of European integration such as the citizen's initiatives. It has also been seen as the justification for taking into account demographic considerations in the Council's voting system: see JC Piris, *The Constitution for Europe* (Cambridge, Cambridge University Press, 2006) 94.

[4] Art 10 TEU.

[5] '[I]t must be noted that the nationals of the states brought together in the Community are called upon to cooperate in the functioning of this Community through the intermediary of the European Parliament and the Economic and Social Committee', Case 26/62 *NV Algemene Transport- en Expeditie Onderneming van Gend & Loos v Netherlands Inland Revenue Administration* EU:C:1963:1.

Community level the fundamental democratic principle that the peoples should take part in the exercise of power through the intermediary of a representative assembly'.[6]

PARLIAMENT'S MISSION

The mission of the European Parliament has changed dramatically since the times of the Coal and Steel Community, when it was confined to the exercise of 'supervisory powers'.[7] The Treaty of Rome enlarged Parliament's role by conferring it also 'powers of deliberation',[8] but even this looks like a slight modification when compared with later evolutions, partially reflected in the new wording after the Lisbon Treaty according to which 'the European Parliament shall jointly with the Council exercise legislative and budgetary functions. It shall exercise functions of political control and consultation as laid down in the Treaties. It shall elect the President of the European Parliament'.[9]

At the same time, the European Parliament has undergone a process of progressive 'Europeanisation'. What had begun as an Assembly of delegates appointed by national parliaments is today a Parliament 'composed of representatives of the Union's citizens'[10] that cannot have another mandate as members of a national Parliament,[11] enjoy a European Statute[12] and belong to plurinational parliamentary groups[13] and often also to European political parties.[14] These developments have enhanced Parliament's role as a distinct, independent actor and favoured its proactive approach in exploiting (or even anticipating) the full potentialities of the legal provisions concerning its own prerogatives, in practices consistent with the constitutional traditions of the Member States and based in Parliament's Rules of Procedure[15] or in inter-institutional agreements or understandings.[16]

However, this evolution has not always been clearly perceived by the citizens, the media or even scholars not acquainted with the real life of European institutions. This may be partly due to the fact that the exercise of political power by supra- or post-national institutions remains a novelty that does not correspond to deeply rooted paradigms, but also to the language in the EU Treaties negotiated,

[6] Case 138/79 *SA Roquette Frères v Council of the European Communities* EU:C:1980:249 para 33.
[7] Art 20 of the Treaty of Paris.
[8] Art 137 of the Treaty establishing the European Economic Community.
[9] Art 14 of the Treaty on the European Union in the consolidated version after the Treaty of Lisbon.
[10] ibid.
[11] This incompatibility was introduced in Art 6 of the Electoral Act by an amending Decision of 2002, OJ L 283/2002.
[12] OJ L 262/2005.
[13] Art 32 of the European Parliament Rules of Procedure.
[14] Regulation (EU, Euratom) No 1141/2014 of the European Parliament and of the Council of 22 October 2014 on the statute and funding of European political parties and European political foundations, OJ L 317/2014.
[15] *cf* Art 232 of the Treaty on the Functioning of the European Union (TFEU).
[16] *cf* Art 295 TFEU.

in most cases, following non-transparent diplomatic routines. Perhaps the best example of the latter is the non-description of the European Parliament's mission in the Maastricht Treaty, as it replaced the previous wording by an abstract reference to the effect that Parliament 'shall exercise the powers conferred upon it by this Treaty'.[17] This opaque formula survived the Treaty modifications introduced by the Intergovernmental Conferences of Amsterdam and Nice and could only be replaced after the significant change of approach brought along by the European Convention.

SUPERVISION

In the 1990s the European Union was endowed, for the first time, with a system for parliamentary supervision on the lines of what exists in its Member States.[18] In addition to the old rules on MEP's questions and the motion of censure, the Maastricht Treaty introduced the right of petition and the Committees of Enquiry, building upon practices already initiated by the European Parliament;[19] furthermore, citizens were allowed to complain to a new European Ombudsman[20] and scrutiny of public expenses was considerably reinforced. The Treaty of Nice added a legal basis for the resignation of Commissioners on demand of their President, with indirect but clear consequences in their relations with Parliament.[21] These provisions were later implemented through legislation or amendments to Parliament's Rules of Procedure, and also by means of bilateral inter-institutional agreements[22] such as the Framework Agreement with the European Commission (intended to facilitate more fluent relations after the experience of the collective resignation of the Santer Commission)[23] or the more recent agreement with the European Central Bank.[24]

[17] Art 189 of the European Community Treaty, in the consolidated version after the Nice Treaty.

[18] *cf* G Garzón Clariana, 'El control parlamentario del ejecutivo en la Unión Europea' in F Pau i Vall (ed), *El control del Gobierno en democracia* (Madrid, Tecnos, 2013) 19–40; G Garzón Clariana, 'L'Évolution du contrôle parlementaire de l'exécutif dans l'Union Européenne' in I Govaere and D Hanf (eds), *Liber Amicorum Paul Demaret*, (Brussels, PIE Peter Lang, 2013) 199–210.

[19] *cf* R Kovar and D Simon, 'La citoyenneté européenne' (1993) *Cahiers de Droit européen*, 285–300; N Görtlitz, 'Le Droit d'enquête du Parlement européen' (2013) *Cahiers de Droit européen*, 783–819.

[20] *cf* R Gosalbo Bono, 'Médiateur' in *Répertoire de droit communautaire* (Paris, Dalloz, June 1995); P Magnette, 'The European Ombudsman: Protecting Citizen's Rights and Strengthening Parliamentary Scrutiny' in N Diamandouros et al, *The European Ombudsman—Origins, Establishment, Evolution* (Luxembourg, OPEC, 2005) 106.

[21] Art 217 CE as amended by the Treaty of Nice. This provision has a precedent in a practice set up by President Prodi.

[22] Bilateral agreements between the European Parliament and other Institutions have traditionally met with the opposition or reluctance of the Council, but this has not been an obstacle for the Council to conclude at least one of them, concerning access to confidential defence documents, see OJ C 298/2002.

[23] For the latest version see OJ L 304/2010.

[24] OJ L 320/2013.

Even if these improvements coincide with new legal bases accruing the competences of the European Union, they seem more closely related to other factors, like the establishment of a Citizenship of the Union[25] or the insistence of the British Government to strengthen supervision on the financial management of the European Commission.[26] On the other hand, the European Parliament's supervisory powers were (and remain) comparatively rather limited in some areas, even where the Union enjoys a well-established competence, for different reasons. Thus, the inter-institutional agreement with the European Central Bank focus on 'democratic accountability and oversight' within the framework of the Single Supervisory Mechanism, while in other areas scrutiny appears seriously restricted by the rigid rules of the Treaty concerning respect of the independence of the ECB.[27] Another example is the often problematic supervision of the activity of the decentralised agencies set up by legislative acts of the Union adopted by the Council, despite the common approach on the Agencies adopted by the three political institutions in 2012.[28]

LEGISLATION

The Treaty of Maastricht also marked a turning point in the European Parliament's role in European legislation, which had been previously limited to the phase of preparation of legislative acts, even if Parliament had managed in practice to influence their contents, especially after the introduction of the 'co-operation' procedure in the Single European Act. Thanks to a new co-decision procedure inspired by its 'Spinelli' Draft Treaty of 1984[29] the European Parliament became a branch of the legislative power, legally co-responsible for the legislative acts adopted jointly with the Council.[30] There was also an extended application of the consent procedure implying a Parliament's right of veto, which can be regarded as tantamount

[25] Both the right of petition and the right to submit complaints to the European Commission appear today in Title V (Citizen's Rights) of the Charter of Fundamental Rights. See *cf* G Garzón Clariana, 'Les droits politiques des citoyens de l'Europe: les vingt premières années' (2013) 13 *ERA Forum* 545–67, 549–51.

[26] *cf* J Cloos et al, *Le Traité de Maastricht* (Bruxelles, Bruylant, 1993) 435.

[27] *cf* JV Louis, 'Democracy and the European Central Bank' in G Garzón Clariana (ed), *Democracy in the New Economic Governance of the European Union* (Madrid, Marcial Pons, 2015) 109–50.

[28] *cf* S Laurent, 'Les agences communautaires facteur d'incohérence institutionnelle?—De la nécéssité du renforcement du contrôle parlementaire des agences' in V Michel (ed), *Le Droit, les Institutions et les politiques de l'Union Européene face à l'impératif de la coherence* (Strasbourg, Presses Universitaires, 2009) 107–30; E Bernard, 'Accord sur les agences européennes: la montagne accouche d'une souris' (2012) 3 *Revue du Droit de l'Union européenne* 399–446; M Chamon, 'Les agences de l'Union européenne: origines, état des lieux et défis' (2015) *Cahiers de droit européen* 293–318.

[29] Draft Treaty Establishing the European Union, Art 36, OJ C 77/1984 33.

[30] *cf* D Blanc, 'Le Parlement européen législateur' in M Blanquet (ed), *La prise de decision dans le système de l'Union européenne* (Bruxelles, Bruylant, 2011) 91–126; G Garzón Clariana, 'El Parlamento Europeo y la evolución del poder legislativo y del sistema normativo de la Unión Europea' (2015) 50 *Revista de Derecho Comunitario Europeo* 43–83, 47–62.

to co-decision,[31] albeit in a mitigated form not allowing for the submission of amendments, even if in practice this procedure often involves inter-institutional negotiations.[32] These significant developments led the European Court of Human Rights to consider, in its well-known *Matthews* case, that the European Parliament was 'part of the legislature' of Gibraltar.[33]

These impressive developments in the Treaty of Maastricht were, however, somewhat concealed from public opinion in sharp contrast with the ready awareness of many corporations and interest groups. This was undoubtedly favoured by the fact that 'the "co-decision" procedure' (as the Court of Justice has called it)[34] did not receive that name in the Treaty, in order to facilitate the agreement of the British government;[35] instead, there was only a numeric reference to the provision describing the procedure, which was kept until the Treaty of Lisbon, leaving some room for confusion or ambiguity for uninitiated readers.[36]

Co-decision was initially provided only in some legal bases, but the Treaty of Amsterdam considerably extended it, even if it has not been of application to important areas such as agriculture or trade, until the entry into force of the Lisbon Treaty, where it appears as the 'ordinary legislative procedure' following the approach of the European Convention.[37] At the same time, the role of the European Parliament in legislation has been enhanced by improvements in the procedure and the development of good practices;[38] but the fact that the Council is the other branch of the legislature is not without consequence on the contents or the flux of European legislation, inter alia because the European Commission is traditionally not inclined to submit legislative proposals when it does not see them as acceptable to the Council. National Parliaments are now also active in preventing European legislation, in particular through the new procedures for the supervision of respect of the subsidiarity principle.[39]

The Treaty of Lisbon has also reinforced Parliament's position as co-legislator through the introduction of two relevant complements. First, it requires parliamentary consent in the conclusion of international agreements in the fields where

[31] *cf* Case 302/87 *European Parliament v Council of the European Communities* EU:C:1988:461 paras 13 and 26.

[32] Rules of Procedure of the European Parliament, Art 99.

[33] [GC] No 2483/94 *Matthews v United Kingdom* paras 51–54, ECHR 1999-1.

[34] Case C-155/07 *European Parliament v Council of the European Union* EU:C:2008:605, para 79.

[35] *cf* eg Cloos, above n 26 at 308. In the *Matthews* case the agent of the United Kingdom tried to convince the ECHR that the new legislative procedure introduced in the Maastricht Treaty did not amount to 'co-decision'.

[36] *cf* Garzón Clariana, above n 30 at 59–60. Similarly, the consent procedure was then known as the 'assent' procedure, or appellations in other languages that were not totally clear as to the role Parliament was to play.

[37] Art 289 TFEU.

[38] *cf* E Barón Crespo, 'El desarrollo de la codecisión como procedimiento legislativo de la UE' (2012) 46 *Cuadernos europeos de Deusto* 19–48, 32–42; C Pennera y J Schoo, 'La codécision—Dix ans d'application' (2004) *Cahiers de droit européen* 531–66, 534–35.

[39] Protocol No 2 added by the Treaty of Lisbon.

co-decision or consent apply for legislation.[40] Second, it places Parliament and Council on an equal footing as regards supervision of 'delegated acts' supplementing or amending legislation.[41] These improvements correspond to repeated demands of the European Parliament.

BUDGET

The European Parliament has been seen as part of the budgetary authority since the amendments of the budgetary provisions in the Treaties of the 1970s, and it asserted its position in the adoption of the budget soon after the first direct election.[42] Bearing this in mind, the successive reforms of the Treaty have perhaps been less impressive here than in the case of the prerogatives of the European Parliament. In fact, some slight changes in the Treaty of Lisbon even encouraged the Council and the Kingdom of Spain to claim (unsuccessfully) that the annual budget could no longer be signed by the Parliament's President alone.[43] More substantially, the powers of the Parliament in the annual budget remain limited as regards both the expenditure and the resources.

The Treaty of Lisbon has left behind the distinction between 'discretionary' and 'compulsory' expenditure that had often complicated negotiations between Parliament and Council, but expenditure is always subject to the ceilings determined in the Multiannual Financial Framework; what is more, the Framework is now adopted by the Council acting with the consent of Parliament,[44] whereas previously it was established in an inter-institutional agreement. As regards expenditure resulting from international agreements, the need for Parliament's consent on the grounds that an agreement has 'important budgetary implications for the Union'[45] should seldom arise in view of the praetorian strict interpretation of this notion by the Court of Justice.[46]

As regards resources, there has not been very substantial progress in Parliament's position since the introduction of the system of 'own resources', despite successive attempts in the preparation of the Maastricht Treaty[47] and the Constitution

[40] Art 218(6)(a)(v) TFEU.

[41] *cf* eg K Bradley, 'Delegation and Conferral of Powers in the European Union: Political Problems, Legal Solutions?' in CF Bergström and D Ritleng (eds), *Rule Making by the European Commission: the New System* (Oxford, Oxford University Press, 2016); G Garzón Clariana, 'Los actos delegados en el sistema de fuentes de Derecho de la Unión Europea' in J Cardona Llorens et al (eds), *Estudios de Derecho Internacional y Derecho Europeo en Homenaje al Profesor Manuel Pérez González* (Valencia, 2012, II 1491–1526); G Garzón Clariana, 'Les actes délegués dans le système des sources du droit de l'Union Européenne' (2011) 12 *ERA Forum* 105–34; J Schoo, 'Comments to Art 290 TFEU' in J Schwarze (ed), *EU-Kommentar* 3rd edn (Baden-Baden, Nomos Verlag, 2012) 2337–41.

[42] *cf* Priestly, above n 2 at 6–22.

[43] *cf* Case C-77/11 *Council of the European Union v European Parliament* EU:C:2013:559.

[44] Art 312(2) TFEU.

[45] Art 218(6)(a) (iv) TFEU.

[46] *cf* Case C-189/97 *European Parliament v Council of the European Union* EU:C:1999:366.

[47] *cf* Cloos, above n 26 at 443–44.

for Europe:[48] the participation of the European Parliament in the procedure is always limited to a consultation. As for the Decision of the Council, it enters into force only after the approval of the Member States. Member States approve it in accordance with their respective constitutional requirements, 'respecting national sovereignty'[49] and involving national Parliaments, inasmuch as they are associated to this procedure according to their own Constitutions. Moreover, issuing loans is expressly forbidden by the Financial Regulation in the context of the 'principle of equilibrium' of the budget.[50]

CONSULTATION AND APPOINTMENTS

The mission of the European Parliament, as it now appears in the Treaty on the European Union, also comprises the exercise of a function of consultation and the election 'of the President of the Commission'.[51] Consultation (including, when appropriate, re-consultation) has become a marginal, archaic procedure as regards legislation, even if it is now provided for in some legal bases in the field of economic governance,[52] in one of the rare steps back of the Treaty of Lisbon. As regards appointment of Members of other European Institutions, the present wording of the Treaty may be misleading, as it minimises Parliament's role as if it had remained unaltered since the times of the Maastricht Treaty. The reality is quite different: according to provisions already applied in the pre-Lisbon era, the Commission as a body—and not only its President—is appointed only after a 'vote of consent' of the European Parliament,[53] and Parliament is consulted before the appointment of the Members of the Court of Auditors[54] and of the European Central Bank Executive Board.[55] What is more, Parliament's role in these appointments has been enhanced by good practices grounded on its Rules of Procedure to the extent that it has often had a decisive say even where the Treaty provided for a simple consultation.[56] Developments after the Lisbon Treaty include the well-known election of President Juncker as the candidate of the European People's Party,[57] and the much more modest Parliament's participation in the appointment

[48] *cf* MJ Martínez Iglesias, 'Les finances de l'Union' in G Amato, H Bribosia and B De Witte (eds), *Genesis and Destiny of the European Constitution* (Brussels, Bruylant, 2007) 599, 619–20.

[49] Second recital, OJ 168/2014 at 105. The consent of the European Parliament is, however, required at the stage of the implementing measures of the Council Decision (Art 311 TFEU).

[50] Art 17, OJ 298/2012. This is not the place to discuss whether this prohibition is a necessary consequence to be drawn from the Treaty provisions, as has been maintained in C Delon Desmoilin, *Droit budgétaire de l'Union européenne*, (Paris, LGDJ, 2011) 155–56.

[51] Art 14(1) TEU.

[52] *cf* Blanc, above n 30 at 115.

[53] Art 17(7) TEU.

[54] Art 286(2) TFEU.

[55] Art 283(2) TFEU.

[56] *cf* Priestley, above n 2 at 45–77.

[57] *cf* N Peñalver García and J Priestley, *The Making of a European President* (Basingstoke, Palgrave Macmillan, 2015).

of the Members of the Court of Justice of the European Union, lagging well behind Parliament's legitimate expectations on this matter.[58]

FINAL REMARKS

The powers of the European Parliament depend mostly on the extent and the quality of European integration, as illustrated by the application of the so-called Community method to the matters of the old 'third pillar'. It is for this reason that, in the domain of the new economic governance, the 'report of the five Presidents' has linked the improvement of the democratic accountability and legitimacy to an increased 'sovereignty sharing'.[59] There remain, however, some relevant exceptions, where Parliament's role is attenuated in matters that belong to the hard core of the Union's competences, as a result of a deliberate choice of the Union's Treaties, for example, in the 'special legislative procedures' where the Council appears as sole legislator or in the appointment of judges of the Court of Justice. These may be seen as transitory in view of past experience, although the difficulty of amending the present rules should not be underestimated.

A different aspect is the continuing effect of acts adopted in the past in accordance with obsolete procedures that are no longer applicable to their subject matter, or even that no longer exist in the law of the European Union. This is, of course, a significant part of the Union's acts, both legislative[60] and regulatory. The point here is not just that they were adopted with an insufficient involvement of the European Parliament by current standards, but also that they perpetuate inappropriate limitations to parliamentary scrutiny (as in the case of legislation establishing most of the Agencies of the Union,[61] or providing for implementation by means of the old 'comitology'). Respect of the *acquis* should not prevent alignment to the present, more democratic procedures in this regard.

[58] Art 255 TFEU. See G Garzón Clariana, 'Le role du Parlement europé̀en dans le dé̀veloppement de la Cour de Justice' in N Colneric et al (eds), *Festchrift für Gil Carlos Rodríguez Iglesias* (Berlin, Berliner Wissenschafts-Verlag, 2003) 21–39, 26–27.

[59] *cf* European Commission, *Completing Europe's Economic and Monetary Union—Report by Jean-Claude Juncker in close cooperation with Donald Tusk, Jeroen Dijsselbloem, Mario Draghi and Martin Schulz*, Brussels, 22 June 2015, 17–18.

[60] The *poids du passé* is more important in legislation than it appears at first sight, as part of the legislative acts adopted through co-decision result from the codification of previous acts adopted in accordance with old procedures, without modifications of substance.

[61] The issue of parliamentary scrutiny of the agencies' activities should be worrying now that the Court of Justice has made it clear that their acts can have legal effects on the European citizens: see Case C-270/12 *United Kingdom of Great Britain and Northern Ireland v European Parliament and Council of the European Union* EU:C:2014:18 paras 17–18.

17

De-constitutionalisation of European Law: The Re-empowerment of Democratic Political Choice

FRITZ W SCHARPF*

EUROPEAN INTEGRATION HAS long relied on the democratic legitimacy of its Member States without paying much attention to the increasing importance of its multi-level governing processes. At this time, however, Europe is caught in the intersection of multiple crises, all of which—the Brexit as well as the euro crisis, the refugee crisis as well as the crises in Europe's relations with its eastern and southern 'near abroad'—are challenging the effectiveness as well as the democratic legitimacy of government on European and national levels. These dual challenges are connected: democratic legitimacy presupposes effective governing and problem-solving capacity. Hence the failure of output legitimacy may undermine or even destroy the possibility of input legitimacy—a risk for which the fate of the Weimar Republic remains a most disturbing memento.[1] At the same time, however, the lack of input legitimacy in the present European context will constrain and may ultimately destroy the effectiveness of measures based on non-accountable supranational authority. Since these propositions go beyond my previous conceptualisation of output-oriented and input-oriented legitimating arguments,[2] I will elaborate them briefly before addressing my main theme, the specific factors constraining the capacity of democratically legitimate political action to deal effectively with the multiple crises challenging the multi-level European polity.

DEMOCRATIC ASPIRATIONS

Democracy is a contested normative concept. And even if Lincoln's triad of 'government of the people, for the people and by the people' should find broad

* Fritz W Scharpf is Professor and Emeritus Director of the Max Planck Institute for the Study of Societies in Cologne.

[1] A Brecht, 'Die Auflösung der Weimarer Republik und die politische Wissenschaft (1955) *Zeitschrift für Politik NF* 2 (4) 291–308.

[2] F Scharpf, *Governing in Europe. Effective and Democratic?* (Oxford, Oxford University Press, 1999).

agreement, different traditions of normative democratic theory put the emphasis on different elements. Thus the dominant emphasis of 'output-oriented' legitimating arguments is on government *for the people*—that is, on the fundamental justification[3] for the coercive powers of governing authority by the function of protecting life, liberty and property and promoting the common interest of the governed. 'Input-oriented' normative arguments focusing on government *by the people* emphasise the institutions and processes facilitating collective self-government or, in representative democracies, ensuring the responsiveness of governors to the interests and preferences of the governed. 'Community-oriented' arguments, finally, focusing on government *of the people* emphasise the precondition of a political community or *demos* that qualifies as the collective 'self' of democratic self-government.

Obviously, these distinctions are at best suggestions of different dimensions of normative concerns regarding the critique and justification of governing power. In the critical and affirmative discourses of constitutional democracies, arguments in all three dimensions are obviously pertinent, and the lack of conceptual precision is more of an academic than a political concern. In discussions of an alleged 'European democratic deficit', however, such underlying agreement could not be presupposed. Critics had primarily focused on the *no-demos* issue and the lack of effective channels of input-oriented political communication and electoral accountability,[4] and they have sometimes treated output-oriented concerns as normatively irrelevant.[5] Their opponents, by contrast, tended to deny the relevance of applying input-oriented criteria to EU decision processes, pointing to the low political salience of typical EU policy choices. Instead, EU legitimacy was seen to depend on the rule of law, popular trust in EU institutions, generalised output satisfaction, and ultimately on the central role of politically accountable national governments representing their constituencies in EU affairs.[6]

But whatever may have been said until recently for the empirical plausibility of these output-oriented arguments, their legitimating power has declined dramatically under the cumulative impact of the present crises. These illustrate and demonstrate the fact that neither at the European nor at the national level does

[3] Bernard Williams defines the 'first' political question 'as the securing of order, protection, safety, trust, and the conditions of cooperation. It is "first" because solving it is the condition of solving, indeed posing, any others' in B Williams, *In the Beginning Was the Deed: Realism and Moralism in Political Argument* (Princeton, Princeton University Press, 2005). In that sense, the representation of *buon governo* in Ambrogio Lorenzetti's fresco in the Sienese Palazzo Pubblico (1338–39) does indeed symbolise the basic precondition of any discourse on political legitimacy.

[4] D Miller, *On Nationality* (Oxford, Clarendon Press, 1995); S Hix, *What's Wrong with the Europe Union and How to Fix It* (Cambridge, Polity, 2008).

[5] MT Greven, 'Can the European Union Finally Become a Democracy?' in MT Greven and LW Pauly (eds), *Democracy Beyond the State? The European Dilemma and the Emerging Global Order* (Lanham, MD, Rowman & Littlefield, 2000) 35–62.

[6] A Moravcsik, *The Choice for Europe. Social Purpose and State Power from Messina to Maastricht* (Ithaca, Cornell University Press, 1998); A Moravcsik, 'In Defence of the "Democratic Deficit"' (2002) *Journal of Common Market Studies* 40 (4), 603–24.

government have the capacity to provide effective solutions for manifest common problems and common aspirations. In short, the present crises demonstrate the political salience of challenges to the output legitimacy of government in the multi-level European polity.

Now obviously, once we have moved beyond the fundamental state functions of the Hobbesian Leviathan, the criteria for output legitimacy, or its failure,[7] are all socially constructed. They did and do change with the evolution of state functions and with the rise and fall of expectations and normative aspirations. In the abstract, however, the relevant dimensions are well defined by the oaths of office in constitutional democracies, which commit presidents, heads of government and ministers to employ the powers of government for promoting the common welfare, protecting the people from harm, and doing justice to all.[8] These oaths reflect output-oriented rules on the actor level, which may matter in personalised political critiques, political scandals and impeachment procedures. Manifest output failure on the system level, however, may have less to do with the misconduct of office holders than with the inadequacy of governing capacities in relation to the magnitude of the challenges confronting the polity. In other words, Moravcsik's sanguine assessment of the Community's output legitimacy may have been quite plausible, given his focus on the progress of European integration in the decades before existing governing capacities at European and national levels were overwhelmed by the cumulative impact of global and self-inflicted challenges and crises.

If that is so, however, input-oriented democratic legitimacy will be frustrated as well. For some, to be sure, political participation is a value in itself—and the present European Union provides few opportunities for its realization. But for most of us, politics is about policies shaping the legal, economic and social conditions of our collective existence through purposeful political action. Yet, if the polity whose policies we hope to influence should lack the capacity to shape these conditions, input-oriented democratic participation loses its meaning and its legitimating power as well. And neither could 'communitarian' legitimacy arise under conditions where the prospective European political community so obviously lacks the capacity for effective self-government. In other words, under the present conditions of the multilevel European polity, the lack of output legitimacy would undermine input-oriented and community-oriented legitimacy as well.

In this chapter, I will not return to my earlier publications suggesting that the governance of the single currency is afflicted with a manifest failure of output

[7] As Amartya Sen pointed out referring to the concept of '*justice*', agreement is much more likely to be reached if discussion focuses not on a positive definition but on its opposite, the identification of cases of manifest '*injustice*'. See A Sen, *The Idea of Justice* (Cambridge, Harvard University Press, 2009) 103–04.

[8] For example, Article 56 of the German Basic Law stipulates: 'I swear that I will dedicate my efforts to the well-being of the German people, promote their welfare, protect them from harm, uphold and defend the Basic Law and the laws of the Federation, perform my duties conscientiously, and do justice to all.'

legitimacy and that its present regime amounts to an exercise of technocratic-authoritarian governing powers that is destructive of input-oriented democratic legitimacy in the Member States.[9] Instead, I will here focus on how the European Union itself is constraining the capacity for democratic political action on the level of its Member States through the excessive 'constitutionalisation' of the European Treaties. Since these constraints have institutional causes, there is at least a possibility that they might also be relaxed through politically feasible institutional reforms.

THE ASYMMETRIC IMPACT OF EXCESSIVE CONSTITUTIONALISATION

In the European Union, the Treaties are legally binding for European and national authorities and their legislative, executive, administrative and judicial actions. In that regard, they perform the functions ascribed to the 'basic law' in constitutional democracies; they are even harder to change than most national constitutions; and just like national constitutional courts, the European Court of Justice (ECJ) has the final say in authoritative interpretation. But the Treaties differ from national constitutions in crucial respects: A 'lean' federal constitution must have rules organising the federal level of government; it must also allocate governing competences to the levels of government; and it will usually stipulate a number of fundamental rights protecting basic human and citizen rights and freedoms against the exercise of governing powers. The European Treaties, however, go far beyond these core functions by regulating in considerable detail a wide range of matters that democratic constitutions would leave to be determined by political legislation.[10] In other words, there is more constitutional law in the EU than in constitutional federal states.

The Problem

By itself, the greater coverage of the Treaties affects the horizontal and the vertical balance of powers. In the horizontal dimension, it reduces the domain of political legislation and it enlarges the space for authoritative judicial interpretation—which becomes the only mode through which changes in primary

[9] F Scharpf, 'Legitimacy Intermediation in the Multilevel European Polity and Its Collapse in the Euro Crisis' in K Armingeon (ed), *Staatstätigkeiten, Parteien und Demokratie* (Wiesbaden, Springer, 2013) 567–96. Also available as Discussion Paper 12/6, Cologne, Max Planck Institute for the Study of Societies, www.mpifg.de/pu/mpifg_dp/dp12-6.pdf.

[10] D Grimm, 'The Democratic Costs of Constitutionalization: The European Case' (2015) *European Law Journal* 21 (4) 460–73. D Grimm, 'Europe's Legitimacy Problem and the Courts' in D Chalmers, M Jachtenfuchs and C Joerges (eds), *The End of the Eurocrats' Dream: Adjusting to European Diversity* (Cambridge, Cambridge University Press, 2016) 218–40. D Grimm, *Europa ja—aber welches? Zur Verfassung der europäischen Demokratie* (München, CH Beck, 2016).

law can be brought about without a unanimous Treaty amendment. In the vertical dimension it also constrains Member States in areas where, in the absence of federal legislation, policy could have been shaped by national political action. What matters most for Member States, however, is the fact that the Treaties have also come to incorporate an *economic constitution* placing the rules governing economic relations and economic policy beyond political determination.

This idea, which is alien to the constitutions of democratic states, federal or unitary, originated in Germany in the 1930s in the 'ordo liberal' variant of normative economic theory. Opposed to *laissez-faire* liberalism as well as to state interventionism, it advocated a rule-based economic regime in which state intervention would be necessary but essentially limited to ensuring the stability of money and preventing the self-destruction of competitive markets through economic concentration and cartels. After World War II, ordo liberal principles had considerable influence on German economic and legal theory[11] and also on the monetary and competition policies shaping the German 'social market economy'. But efforts to have the underlying principles constitutionalised failed in the assemblies drafting the Basic Law and also in the Federal Constitutional Court which, in an early decision,[12] held that democratically accountable governments and parliaments, though bound by the basic human and citizen rights protected by the constitution, were not constrained by the doctrines of any economic theory in their choice of economic policies and market interventions.

However, what had failed in Germany succeeded in the European Economic Community, whose competition rules were framed under German influence and whose early practice was shaped by a German head of the Competition Directory committed to ordo liberalism.[13] What mattered even more in long run, however, was the ECJ's interpretation of Treaty provisions postulating the abolition of tariffs and the free movement of goods, services, capital and workers. They might have been treated as the political commitment to a goal that was to be realised through European legislation. Instead, the Court elevated them to the status of 'economic liberties'—that is, of subjective rights of individuals and corporations that, invested with the properties of 'direct effect' and 'supremacy',[14] came to have the legal force of fundamental rights which must be respected by all levels of government.

The Treaty of Rome had, of course, not included any of the typical constitutional rights of life, liberty, property, free speech, free press or free association that are

[11] H Ehmke, *Wirtschaft und Verfassung: Die Verfassungsrechtsprechung des Supreme Court zur Wirtschaftsregulierung* (Karlsruhe, CF Müller, 1961) 7–55.

[12] BVerfGE 4, 7, 20 July 1954.

[13] From 1958 to 1967, Hans von der Groeben, a high civil servant in Ludwig Erhard's ministry of economic affairs, was the first Director General for Competition in the European Commission. See also DJ Gerber, 'Constitutionalizing the Economy: German Neo-liberalism, Competition Law and the 'New' Europe' (1988) *American Journal of Comparative Law* 42 (1) 25–84; M Wegmann, *Der Einfluss des Neoliberalismus auf das Europäische Wettbewerbsrecht 1946–1965* (Baden-Baden, Nomos, 2008).

[14] Case 26–62 *Van Gend & Loos v Netherlands* [1963]; Case 6–64 *Costa v Enel* [1964].

generally protected by national constitutions. Instead, the Court's interpretation of economic liberties transformed issues which in national constitutions would be settled by political legislation into constitutional rights that are constraining political choices on European and national levels. By hindsight, this interpretation may be construed as a revolutionary act of judicial self-empowerment[15] which placed the Court's interpretation of economic liberties not only above Member State laws and constitutions, but also beyond the political choice of European legislation. Its doctrinal bases had been developed and disseminated by a transnational network of 'Euro-Law' associations;[16] politically, the Court's authority was not effectively challenged by the 'Masters of the Treaty';[17] and it is by now generally accepted by national courts as well.[18]

As a practical consequence of the constitutionalisation of economic liberties, private litigants are empowered to challenge national law in ordinary courts—which then are obliged to submit claims not yet supported by the settled case law to the ECJ for a preliminary opinion. It is this combination of self-interested litigation pushing against the boundaries of the current case law with the Court's methodological commitment to 'teleological interpretation',[19] the *effet utile* principle, and its own role as a 'motor of integration',[20] which has dynamically extended the protection of economic liberties—moving from intervention against protectionist discrimination to the removal of non-discriminatory potential 'impediments' of economic choice,[21] from the free movement of goods to all other economic liberties, and from the free movement of workers to mobility rights derived from European citizenship.[22]

In light of the obvious difficulty of harmonisation through consensual legislation, judicial legislation promoting 'integration through law'[23] was widely

[15] K Alter, *Establishing the Supremacy of European Law: The Making of an International Rule of Law in Europe* (Oxford, Oxford University Press, 2001); Grimm, above n 10.

[16] A Vauchez, '"Integration through Law": Contribution to a Socio-history of EU Political Commonsense' (2008) *EUI Working Papers* RSCAS 2008/10, Florence, European University Institute; KJ Alter, 'Jurist Advocacy Movements in Europe: The Role of Euro-Law Associations in European Integration 1953–1975' in KJ Alter, *The European Court's Political Power. Selected Essays* (Oxford, Oxford University Press, 2009) 63–91.

[17] KJ Alter, 'Who Are the "Masters of the Treaty": European Governments and the European Court of Justice' in KJ Alter, *The European Court's Political Power. Selected Essays* (Oxford, Oxford University Press, 2009) 109–36.

[18] A Stone Sweet, *The Judicial Construction of Europe* (Oxford, Oxford University Press, 2004); RD Kelemen, *Eurolegalism: The Transformation of Law and Regulation in the European Union* (Cambridge, Harvard University Press, 2011).

[19] G Itzcovich, 'The Interpretation of Community Law by the European Court of Justice' (2011) *German Law Journal* 10 (5) 537–60.

[20] T Horsley, 'Reflections on the Role of the Court of Justice as the "Motor" of European Integration: Legal Limits to Judicial Lawmaking' (2013) *Common Market Law Review* 50 (4) 931–64.

[21] C Barnard, 'Restricting Restrictions: Lessons for the EU from the US?' (2009) *Cambridge Law Journal* 68 (3) 575–606.

[22] S Schmidt, 'Who Cares about Nationality? The Path-dependent Case Law of the ECJ from Goods to Citizens' (2012) *Journal of European Public Policy* 19 (1) 8–24.

[23] M Cappelletti, M Secombe and JHH Weiler (eds), *Integration through Law: Europe and the American Federal Experiment*, 5 Vols (Berlin, De Gruyter, 1985).

considered a welcome 'bypass' to avoid potential political blockades.[24] And indeed, the famous *Cassis* decision[25] of 1978 was then used by the Commission to promote political agreement on the Single European Act and the move from unanimity to qualified majority voting, as even governments as yet unconverted to the neoliberal creed[26] came to prefer the legislative harmonisation of basic standards to the uncertainties of judicially imposed 'mutual recognition'.[27]

Yet, even after the Single European Act had generated an avalanche of European legislation on product standards promoting work safety, environmental and consumer protection, the leadership of judicial 'negative integration' and liberalisation was maintained through the progressive widening and deepening of the reach of economic liberties and of European competition law. Thus the domain of free service provision was extended to include public-sector banks[28] and a wide range of functions that had been performed by public infrastructure and public or publicly subsidised social services in most Member States.[29] The right of free establishment was extended by the *Centros*[30] decision to prevent the application of national company law to firms established as letter-box companies abroad for the sole purpose of operating domestically;[31] and free capital movement was seen to be violated by national attempts to constrain tax evasion[32] and to strengthen stakeholder representation in shareholder assemblies.[33] And finally, in a series of (in) famous decisions in 2007 and 2008,[34] the freedom of service

[24] P Genschel, 'One Trap, Many Exits, but No Free Lunch: How the Joint-Decision Trap Shapes EU Tax Policy' in G Falkner (ed), *The EU's Decision Traps: Comparing Policies* (Oxford, Oxford University Press, 2011) 54–72.

[25] Case C-120/79 *Louise de Cavel v Jacques de Cavel* [1980] 70.

[26] N Jabko, *Playing the Market: A Political Strategy for Uniting Europe, 1985–2005* (Ithaca, Cornell University Press, 2006).

[27] S Schmidt, 'Mutual Recognition as a New Mode of Governance' (2007) *Journal of European Public Policy* 14(5) 667–81.

[28] D Seikel, *Der Kampf um öffentlich-rechtliche Banken: Wie die Europäische Kommission Liberalisierung durchsetzt* (Frankfurt am Main, Campus, 2013).

[29] This is not meant to deny the influence of OECD-wide beliefs supporting the neoliberal transformation of the post-war 'mixed economies' since the 1980s (for a comparative account, see H Wollmann, I Koprić and G Marcou (eds), *Public and Social Services in Europe: From Public and Municipal to Private Sector Provision* (Basingstoke, Palgrave Macmillan, 2016). But the ECJ's case law facilitated the implementation in Member States that were resisting. See also W Sauter, *Public Services in EU Law* (Cambridge, Cambridge University Press, 2014).

[30] Case C-212/97 *Centros Ltd v Erhvervs- og Selskabsstyrelsen* [1999] I-01459.

[31] J Lowry, 'Eliminating Obstacles to Freedom of Establishment: The Competitive Edge of UK Company Law' (2004) *The Cambridge Law Journal* 63 (2) 331–45.

[32] Genschel, above n 24.

[33] B Werner, *Der Streit um das VW-Gesetz: Wie Europäische Kommission und Europäischer Gerichtshof die Unternehmenskontrolle liberalisieren* (Frankfurt am Main, Campus, 2013).

[34] Case C-438/05 *International Transport Workers' Federation and Finnish Seamen's Union v Viking Line ABP and OÜ Viking Line Eesti* [2007] I-10779; C-341/05 *Laval un Partneri Ltd v Svenska Byggnadsarbetareförbundet, Svenska Byggnadsarbetareförbundets avdelning 1, Byggettan and Svenska Elektrikerförbundet* [2007] 809; C-346/06 *Dirk Rüffert v Land Niedersachsen* [2008] 189; C-319/06 *Commission of the European Communities v Grand Duchy of Luxembourg* [2008] 350.

provision was also held to override national wage regulations, rights of collective bargaining and collective action.[35]

In this context it is worth noting that the Court's enforcement of economic liberties and European competition law is not constrained by the allocation of governing competences between the Union and its Member States, or even by Treaty clauses such as Article 153(5) or Article 168(7) TFEU, which explicitly preclude the exercise of European competences.[36] This effect appears constitutionally appropriate where basic human rights are at stake. But in light of the fact that in modern capitalism economic interactions have come to pervade all aspects of society, the Court may now intervene in the full range of national governing powers—whenever there are litigants, individuals or corporations, who find it in their interest to push for the greater extension of economic liberties or the rules of unfettered competition.

This is not meant to say that such efforts will invariably succeed. The Court may use its version of the *proportionality* test to tolerate some national constraints on economic liberty. Nevertheless, the balance between economic interests and public purposes is no longer defined by democratically accountable national governments and parliaments but ultimately by a Court that is committed not only to the priority of European over national competences but also to the promotion of a liberal economic constitution.[37]

In effect, the extension of judicial surveillance over the exercise national competences has created a highly asymmetric regime for the heterogeneous political economies of EU Member States.[38] Given the historical, institutional and political differences between 'liberal' and 'coordinated market economies'[39] and between 'liberal', 'Bismarckian' and 'social democratic' welfare states,[40] European states had defined different boundaries between state, market and civil society. They had adopted different mixes of tax-financed, work-based and commercial social security and of public, not-for-profit and private social services; and their industrial relations and wage-setting institutions were corporatist, statist or decentralised, to mention just some of the differences. In general, therefore, in the non-liberal Scandinavian and Continental 'social market economies', capitalism was more

[35] F Rödl, 'Private Law, Democracy, Codification. A Critique of the European Law Project' in C Joerges and T Ralli (eds), *European Constitutionalism without Private Law—Private Law without Democracy*, ARENA Report 3/2011, 11–157.

[36] The standard argument is that even in the exercise of their undisputed governing competences Member States must of course respect the subjective rights of individuals and corporations that are protected by the Treaties (eg C-158/96, *Raymond Kohll v Union des caisses de maladie* [1998] 171, 19–20).

[37] M Höpner, 'Der Europäische Gerichtshof als Motor der Integration: Eine akteursbezogene Erklärung' (2011) *Berliner Journal für Soziologie* 21, 203–29.

[38] The same is of course true of the present euro regime, except that the asymmetries there are favouring 'Northern' over Southern political economies, rather than 'liberal' over 'coordinated market economies' and 'liberal' over 'Bismarckian' and 'social-democratic' welfare states.

[39] P Hall and D Sokice (eds), *Varieties of Capitalism: The Institutional Foundations of Comparative Advantage* (Oxford, Oxford University Press, 2001).

[40] G Esping-Andersen, *The Three Worlds of Welfare Capitalism* (Cambridge, Polity, 1990).

'organised' and the provision of goods, services and infrastructure was to a larger part 'mixed' between the state or societal organisations and the market than was generally the case (but not without significant exceptions, like the British National Health Service (NHS)) in the more 'liberal' Anglo-Irish political economies. These differences had three crucial implications.

First, since the non-liberal institutional configurations and policy legacies had been historically shaped by national policy choices reflecting the contingent outcomes of class battles and political compromises, they differed significantly from one country to another. By the same token, further policy changes were likely to have high political salience as well.

Second, to the extent that these non-liberal national solutions (including the NHS) had the effect of limiting the domain of market competition, they were obviously the primary target of the ECJ's protection of economic liberties against 'impediments' to their exercise. Equally important, however, were the differences among non-liberal national solutions. Even if these could pass the Court's 'proportionality' tests individually, transnational differences would still constitute 'non-tariff barriers' to economic mobility—with the consequence that the ECJ's requirement of 'mutual recognition' would undermine the economic and political viability of more demanding national solutions.[41] In practical effect, therefore, the impact of the judicially defined and enforced expansion of the domain of Treaty-based economic liberties was necessarily, and almost exclusively, targeted on the institutions and policy legacies of the non-liberal Member States of the Community and the Union.

Third, the 'legitimate diversity'[42] among non-liberal political economies also frustrated the promise of a 'social dimension' of European integration which Jacques Delors had associated with the completion of the 'Single Market' programme in 1992.[43] Even after the mid-1990s and before Eastern enlargement, when centre-left governments for a while had a majority on the European level, there was no progress in creating non-liberal regimes on the European level, and no agreement on legislative harmonisation that could stop the erosion of non-liberal national systems of social protection, industrial relations and corporate governance,[44] whereas a series of Treaty amendments that tried to protect national autonomy in such fields as education, health care and industrial relations by explicitly limiting European competences could not, for the reasons mentioned above, stop the progress of judicial liberalisation.

[41] Schmidt, above n 27; S Schmidt, 'Law Making in the Shadow of Judicial Politics' in R Dehousse (ed), *The Community Method: Obstinate or Obsolete?* (Basingstoke, Palgrave, 2009) 43–59.

[42] F Scharpf, 'Legitimate Diversity: The New Challenge of European Integration' (2003) *Zeitschrift für Staats- und Europawissenschaften* 1 (1) 32–60.

[43] J Delors, 'The Social Dimension', Address by President Delors at the Trades Union Congress—Bournemouth, 8 September 1988, file:///C:/Users/FS/Downloads/SPEECH-88-66_EN%20(1).pdf.

[44] C Barnard, 'EU Employment Law and the European Social Model', Paper No. 43/2014, University of Cambridge, Legal Studies Research Papers.

In effect, therefore, the advancement of European economic integration through the judicial extension and enforcement of Treaty-based economic liberties has generated an asymmetric negative impact on the institutions and policy legacies of non-liberal political economies—whereas Member States with liberal economic institutions and practices are hardly affected.[45] This asymmetry cannot be corrected on the European level because the historically shaped configurations of non-liberal Member States are 'parochial'[46] in the sense that none of them could find acceptance as the template of uniform European solutions. Under these conditions, the legal erosion of national non-liberal systems will have a default outcome that approaches the liberal model, while legislation on the European level will be under constitutional and political constraints favouring the codification of the ECJ's case law and market-making consensual rules.[47] In other words, the EU cannot become a social-market economy.[48]

In Member State politics, however, the progressive expansion of legal constraints on non-liberal institutions and practices had generally low political salience. One reason is that judicial legislation works through decisions in individual cases which, on their specific facts, will often appear unspectacular or even trivial and will catch the attention of political parties, trade unions and the media only under exceptional circumstances—as was partly true in the *Laval-Viking* series of interventions in collective action or in the *Volkswagen* case.[49] And even if governments are aware of the negative policy implications of the decisions, there is no legal remedy against Treaty-based ECJ judgments; political responses that would have to mobilise support for a unanimous Treaty amendment appear quite unpractical; and open defiance through explicit non-compliance[50] would bring governments in conflict with their own national legal order and their commitment to the rule of law. It is not surprising, therefore, that even governments strongly opposed to a ruling have generally accepted not only the decision of the specific case but also accommodated their administrative responses and subsequent policy choices.[51]

[45] In this regard, the asymmetric impact of the European regime of economic liberties on 'liberal' and 'non-liberal' political economies resembles the asymmetric impact of the regime upholding the European Monetary Union on 'Northern' and 'Southern' political economies. In both cases, the asymmetry arises if a uniform European regime is imposed on structurally heterogeneous national polities, economies and societies. See F Scharpf, *The Costs of Monetary Integration* (Cologne, Max Planck Institute for the Study of Societies, forthcoming).

[46] W Streeck, 'German Capitalism: Does It Exist? Can It Survive?' (1997) *New Political Economy* 2 (2) 237–56.

[47] S Schmidt, *The European Court of Justice and the Policy Process: The Shadow of the Case Law* (Oxford, Oxford University Press, 2016).

[48] F Scharpf, 'The Asymmetry of European Integration or why the EU Cannot Be a Social Market Economy' (2010) *Socio-Economic Review* 8 (2) 211–50.

[49] C-112/05 *Commission of the European Communities v Federal Republic of Germany* [2007] 623. M Höpner, 'Integration durch Usurpation—Thesen zur Radikalisierung der Binnenmarktintegration' (2009) *WSI Mitteilungen* 8/2009 407–15; Werner, above n 33.

[50] There is, of course, a lot of tacit non-compliance in the EU which, however, will not be able to challenge the legal validity of the Court's rule for law-abiding Member States. See L Conant, *Justice Contained: Law and Politics in the European Union* (Ithaca, Cornell University Press, 2002).

[51] M Blauberger, 'With Luxembourg in Mind ... the Remaking of National Policies in the Face of ECJ Jurisprudence' (2012) *Journal of European Public Policy* 19 (1) 109–26.

A similar avoidance of open conflict has characterised responses of the Council and the European Parliament to Treaty-based ECJ decisions that nullified or modified European legislation.[52]

By and large, therefore, 'integration through law' has not only progressed through non-political processes relying on the institutional independence and supranational authority of the ECJ;[53] it has also generated remarkably little open opposition on national and European levels; and it has hardly been touched by the increasing politicisation of European issues.[54] In that sense, its impact on the exercise of democratic governing powers in the multi-level European polity has remained politically latent. Whereas the piecemeal erosion of the institutions of non-liberal economies, industrial relations and welfare states is widely lamented in comparative political economy and welfare-state research, it is usually ascribed to the competitive pressures of economic globalisation and the dominance of a neo-liberal *Zeitgeist*. By comparison, studies combining legal and politico-economic analyses with a focus on the liberalising effects of the judicial constitutionalisation, expansion and enforcement of 'economic liberties' have remained quite rare.[55]

What is more widely recognised by now is the constraining effect on political democracy arising from excessive constitutionalisation in general[56] and from European constitutionalism in particular.[57] It operates not only through actual interventions against specific national laws and institutions, but even more so through 'non-decisions',[58] that is through the deterrent effect on political initiatives which, arguably, might violate supreme European law. The effect is greatly extended by the large penumbra of legal uncertainty associated with judicial legislation evolving through decisions in individual cases rather than through the general rules of European legislation.[59]

[52] DS Martinsen, *An Ever More Powerful Court? The Political Constraints of Legal Integration in the European Union* (Oxford, Oxford University Press, 2015); G Davies, 'The European Union Legislature as an Agent of the European Court of Justice' (2016) *Journal of Common Market Studies* 54 (4) 846–61; S Schmidt, above n 47.

[53] RD Kelemen, 'The Political Foundations of Judicial Independence in the European Union' (2012) *Journal of European Public Policy* 19 (1) 43–58; C Joerges, 'Integration Though Law and the Crisis of Law in Europe's Emergency' in D Chalmers, M Jachtenfuchs and C Joerges (eds), *The End of the Eurocrat's Dream. Adjusting to European Diversity* (Cambridge, Cambridge University Press, 2016) 299–338.

[54] S Hutter, E Grande and H Kriesi (eds), *Politicising Europe: Integration and Mass Politics* (Cambridge, Cambridge University Press, 2016).

[55] M Höpner und A Schäfer, *Die Politische Ökonomie der europäischen Integration* (Frankfurt am Main, Campus, 2008); Scharpf, above n 48; Rödl, above n 35; Werner, above n 33; Seikel, above n 28; Barnard, above n 44.

[56] R Bellamy, *Political Constitutionalism: A Republican Defence of the Constitutionality of Democracy* (Cambridge, Cambridge University Press, 2007).

[57] A Menéndez, 'The Existential Crisis of the European Union' (2013) *German Law Journal* 14 (5) 453–526; Grimm, above n 10; S Garben, 'Confronting the Competence Conundrum: Democratising the European Union through an Expansion of its Legislative Powers' (2015) *Oxford Journal of Legal Studies* 35 (1) 55–89.

[58] P Bachrach and M Baratz, 'Two Faces of Power' (1962) *American Political Science Review* 56 (4) 947–52.

[59] S Schmidt, 'Beyond Compliance: The Europeanization of Member States through Negative Integration and Legal Uncertainty' (2008) *Journal of Comparative Policy Analysis* 10 (3) 299–308; Schmidt, above n 47.

Given the constitutional supremacy and practical irreversibility of Treaty-based case law combined with the expansive dynamism of interest-driven litigation, there is a ratcheting effect of ever tighter legal constraints on non-liberal political action on the national as well as on the European level. And quite apart from the liberalising transformation of non-liberal political economies, the consequence is a progressive narrowing of the action space and hence of the problem-solving capacity of democratic politics in the face of increasing external and internal challenges and crises. In other words, the judicial constitutionalisation, extension and enforcement of economic liberties has the effect of incapacitating democratic political action at a time where the multi-level European polity is challenged by the interaction of multiple crises that have the potential of undermining not only the democratic legitimacy but also the political viability of government on European and national levels.

But what could be done about this?

A Precedent: The New-Deal Revolution in US Constitutional Law

The present European constellation is institutionally unique. But there is a remarkably close parallel in the constitutional history of the United States in the first third of the twentieth century[60] where the Supreme Court had used three bases of constitutional law to create ever tighter constraints on political action by the states as well as the federal government. With regard to state action, constitutional constraints were derived from Article I, Section 8, Clause 3 of the original constitution stating that 'the United States Congress shall have power to regulate Commerce with foreign Nations and among the several States' and from the 14th Amendment providing that 'no State … shall deprive any person of life, liberty or property without due process of law'. In the Court's interpretation, however, the empowerment of federal legislation also implied a 'negative (or dormant) commerce clause' which even in the absence of legislation constrained state action impeding interstate commerce.[61] Moreover, the 14th Amendment, which had been adopted after the Civil War to protect former slaves against discriminatory state action, was read as a guarantee of 'substantive or economic due process' that protected the freedom of contract of economic actors against state regulation.[62] In combination, the Supreme Court's interpretation of these two

[60] MP Maduro, 'We The Court: The European Court of Justice and the European Economic Constitution. A Critical Reading of Article 30 of the EC Treaty' (Oxford, Hart, 1998); Barnard, above n 44.

[61] J Eule, 'Laying the Dormant Commerce Clause to Rest' (1982) *Yale Law Journal* 91 (3) 425–85.

[62] Ehmke, above n 11 at 334–80; Note 'Resurrecting Economic Rights: The Doctrine of Economic Due Process Reconsidered' (1990) *Harvard Law Review* 103 (6) 1363–83; M Philips, *The Lochner Court, Myth and Reality: Substantive Due Process from the 1890s to the 1930s* (Westport, Praeger Greenwood, 2001).

clauses imposed roughly the same liberalising constraints on state action which is presently imposed on EU Member States by the ECJ's interpretation of 'economic liberties'.[63]

At the same time, however, the federal legislation under the commerce clause was also constrained by the Court's 'bi-polar' interpretation of the constitutional allocation of competences.[64] Treating the 'police power' as the core of the residual competences of the states, the Court intervened against federal laws purporting to regulate interstate commerce that also appeared to serve the typical public health, safety and general-welfare purposes of police-power measures. In a landmark case, therefore, a federal statute excluding the products of child labour from interstate commerce was held to conflict with the police power reserved to the states[65] whereas the child labour regulations of individual states were frustrated by out-of-state competition that could not be excluded under the dormant commerce clause.

These issues came to a head in the Great Depression of the 1930s, when the Supreme Court in a series of dramatic decisions struck down core elements of Roosevelt's New Deal programme. As the conflict had become a major issue in the 1936 elections, outright resistance and a 'Court packing plan' seemed imminent when the Democrats won by a landslide. The confrontation was barely avoided when the Court in 1937 reversed itself[66] by removing the constitutional constraints on the economic policy choices of democratically accountable governments on both levels. After the 'constitutional revolution of 1937', therefore, state governments were only bound by federal legislation but no longer by the judicial doctrines of economic due process and of the dormant commerce clause.[67] At the same time, federal legislation under the commerce clause was no longer prevented from pursuing the public health, safety and general-welfare purposes that are also matters for the concurrent police power of the states.[68] In other words, even though the United States continues to be an extremely liberal political economy, policy choices on both the federal and the state level have ceased to be constrained by a judicially defined 'economic constitution'.

[63] Technically, the constraints imposed by the American case law were even tighter as the application of economic due process did not even require a potential trans-border impediment to the exercise of economic liberty. See also Maduro, above n 60.

[64] Scharpf, above n 48.

[65] *Hammer v Dagenhart*, 247 US 251 (1918).

[66] The 'switch in time that saved nine' was actually achieved by one Justice (Roberts) changing sides in a divided Court—but then consolidated by Roosevelt's subsequent judicial appointments. See W Leuchtenburg, *The Supreme Court Reborn: The Constitutional Revolution in the Age of Roosevelt* (New York, Oxford University Press, 1995).

[67] Note, above n 62; Barnard, above n 21.

[68] Ehmke, above n 11 at 381–402; FW Scharpf, Grenzen der richterlichen Verantwortung: *Die political-question-Doktrin in der Rechtsprechung des amerikanischen Supreme Court* (Karlsruhe, CF Müller, 1965) 325–46; Eule, above n 61; M Redish and S Nugent, 'The Dormant Commerce Clause and the Constitutional Balance of Federalism' (1987) *Duke Law Journal* 36 (4) 569–617.

European Solutions?

In the United States, the 'constitutional revolution of 1937' was brought about through judicial self-correction under the threat of a frontal collision between judicial authority and highly politicised democratic majorities. As these conditions are unlikely to arise in the European Union, hopes for a judicial self-correction are also unlikely to be fulfilled. The question is whether a similar result could be achieved through an amendment of the European Treaties—perhaps in the context of a broader revision of the European institutional set-up in response to present crises and the Brexit negotiations?

Dieter Grimm has suggested a radical de-constitutionalisation of the European Treaties.[69] In his view, a future Treaty on the European Union (TEU) should contain only rules of genuine constitutional status. These would have to constitute governing authorities on the European level, regulate their roles in the decision-making procedures of the Union, specify EU governing competences in relation to the Member States, and define the fundamental principles, human rights and citizen rights which are binding on European and national authorities. Most other rules in the present Treaty on the Functioning of the European Union (TFEU) should then be downgraded to the status of ordinary or secondary European law.

This fundamental revision of the Treaties would of course require the settlement of a vast number of difficult and controversial issues. If it could be achieved, it would indeed liberate political and legislative choices on the European level from the ever tighter and ever more rigid constitutional constraints of the overextended primary European law. As a consequence, it would rebalance the relationship between judicial and legislative authority in such a way that the judiciary would have to respect the primacy of potentially reversible policy choices of politically accountable actors, but would nevertheless have the mandate and the authority to review political legislation by reference to the institutional ground rules, basic human and citizen rights and the fundamental principles of the European constitutional Treaty.

From the perspective of EU Member States, however, the immediate effect of this fundamental reform would be quite limited. The present *acquis* of European law, even if much of it should lose constitutional status, would of course remain in force. And according to the general rule of federal constitutions, European law and its judicial interpretation would still override the law of the Member States; it could still be invoked by individual and corporate litigants in national courts; and it would still be policed by the Commission in infringement proceedings (Article 258 TFEU). Specific rules could, of course, now be relaxed or abolished through European legislation. But given the diversity of non-liberal national

[69] Grimm, above n 10.

solutions and political preferences, individual governments would have to fight steep uphill battles trying to mobilise broad political support on the European level for removing a particular element of the *acquis*.

From the perspective of American states, at any rate, the constitutional revolution of 1937 had a narrower thrust: it merely had to reverse the judicial creation and enforcement of subjective constitutional rights based on the doctrines of the 'dormant commerce clause' and of 'economic due process'. And from the perspective of EU Member States, it would be equally sufficient if the same effect could be achieved for the 'economic constitution' which the Court had created by interpreting Treaty clauses promoting the integration of the internal market as 'economic liberties' which it treated as directly applicable and enforceable subjective rights. Since we cannot count on the Court to reverse its interpretation, the question is whether a similar effect could be achieved through Treaty amendments that would not require a total revision of the European legal order.

One such possibility might be the insertion of a general clause at the beginning of Part Three TFEU stating that under Titles I–IV, VI and VII litigation and infringement proceedings may only be based on regulations and directives adopted under Articles 289, 290 and 291 TFEU.[70] A similar clause might also be inserted with regard to Article 16 of the Charter of Fundamental Rights. By not including the prohibition of discrimination on grounds of nationality under Articles 18 TFEU and 22(2) of the Charter, however, the proposed amendments would still allow litigation and infringement proceedings challenging protectionist measures impeding the access of foreign suppliers or consumers to national markets.[71]

If this or a similar solution were to be adopted, there is no reason to fear that it could destroy the single market. The huge body of European legislation on economic integration, much of it codifying the *economic liberties* case law, would of course remain in place. From the perspective of member governments, therefore, the proposal would make most of a difference in policy areas like capital taxation, industrial relations, corporate governance, social and public services and public infrastructure, where the diversity of national traditions, institutions and preferences has so far impeded effective European legislation.[72] Where European legislation does exist, it could now be changed—but it would still be hard to mobilise European majorities for issues that may have political salience only in one or a few Member States. In a previous article, however, which had not focused on

[70] Thus, Commission directives adopted under Article 106(3) TFEU would not qualify.

[71] This would amount to a return to the Court's case law before the *Dassonville* and *Cassis* decisions had moved from intervening against protectionist discrimination to intervention against all national rules or practices 'that are capable of hindering, directly or indirectly, actually or potentially' the exercise of a Treaty-based liberty. A return to non-discrimination would also correspond with the very cautious use of the 'dormant commerce clause' in recent case law of the US Supreme Court. See Barnard, above n 21.

[72] See Scharpf, above n 2, ch 3.

constitutional issues, I had proposed a procedure that would allow Member States to ask for politically controlled individual opt-outs from the European *acquis*.[73] It could well be combined with the present proposal.[74]

From the perspective of European legislation, the present proposal would change the function of economic liberties: instead of displacing European legislation they would empower it to define (and re-define) the wider or narrower limits of competitive markets in the political economies of the European Union. And where the effective boundaries between markets, civil society and the state have not been (or will no longer be) defined by political legislation on the European level, the competence would revert to political choices on the national level. In other words, the proposed amendments should and could impede and also reverse the expansion of a judicially defined European economic constitution at the expense of political action on European as well as national levels.

[73] See FW Scharpf, 'After the Crash: A Perspective on Multilevel European Democracy' (2015) *European Law Journal* 21 (3), 384–405.

[74] Under the procedure, a Member State should notify the Commission of a national legislative initiative that would conflict with existing European legislation. After being reviewed in light of the issues at stake in the particular case, such initiatives could be denied by Parliament and Council. In effect, the possibility of re-examining the *acquis* on a case-by-case basis should result in a more fine-grained pattern of European law that is based on a political assessment of the actual need for Europe-wide uniformity, and it should eventually limit the body of binding European law to rules that serve a positive European purpose and that have the political support of current legislative majorities at the European level.

18

Restating the Problem of Competence Creep, Tackling Harmonisation by Stealth and Reinstating the Legislator[1]

SACHA GARBEN*

INTRODUCTION

AS ALAN DASHWOOD has argued rightly, the 'Community caravan' should not be moved forward at every opportunity and at all costs, especially not by 'night marches'.[2] Those 'night marches' can be taken to refer to the phenomenon of 'competence creep', whereby the EU somehow manages to legislate and/or otherwise act in areas where it has not been conferred a specific competence.[3] This problem has occupied scholars, legal practitioners and politicians for a long time, but no consensus seems to have been reached as to its precise manifestations, causes and solutions. The actions undertaken at political level to address this 'competence problem'[4] have mainly taken the form of various Treaty revisions aimed at delimiting the competences of the EU more clearly and forcefully. Particularly the Treaty of Lisbon has made an effort at such enhanced containment, as has been explained in Chapter 1 of this book. However, the current competence constellation still fails to effectively limit European integration precisely where it purports that it does. Regardless of the various reiterations of the conferral principle, national autonomy clauses, the principle of national identity, prohibitions of harmonisation and other ostensibly 'red lines' in terms

* Sacha Garben is Professor of EU Law at the College of Europe, Bruges.

[1] This chapter builds on the insights presented in S Garben, 'Confronting the Competence Conundrum, Democratising the European Union through an Expansion of its Legislative Powers' (2015) 35(1) *Oxford Journal of Legal Studies* 55.

[2] A Dashwood, 'The Limits of European Community Powers' (1996) 21 *European Law Review* 113, 113.

[3] For a discussion, S Weatherill, 'Competence Creep and Competence Control' (2004) 23 *Yearbook of European Law* 1.

[4] P Craig, 'Competence: Clarity, Conferral, Containment and Consideration' (2004) 29 *European Law Review* 323.

of division of competences, areas of Member States competence[5] can be deeply integrated at European level.

Attempting to provide a meaningful contribution to the rich and perennial debate about the legal limits to European integration, this chapter proposes a systematic conceptualisation of the phenomenon of competence creep, redefining it as the slightly broader notion of 'harmonisation by stealth', which includes a range of platforms and methods of Europeanisation beyond EU law *stricto sensu*. It examines to what extent such harmonisation by stealth is problematic, focusing on the legitimacy deficit arising from its displacement of the legislative process on the national and European level, and argues that its manifestation that is most commonly understood as competence creep and on which virtually all containment action has focused to date, namely the adoption of EU legislation on the basis of 'indirect' competence, is actually the least troublesome form of harmonisation by stealth from a legitimacy perspective. Accordingly, this chapter proposes to refocus both the discussion and the actual containment measures on the more worrying forms of harmonisation by stealth, and puts forward several reforms with the aim of reinstating the legislative process on the national and European level.

THE VARIOUS MANIFESTATIONS OF HARMONISATION BY STEALTH

There are various interpretations of the phenomenon of competence creep. Following its most narrow understanding, it refers to the adoption of EU legislation in areas in which the EU is not considered to have been conferred a specific legislative competence—areas of Member State competence. The EU's broad, functional powers under Articles 114 and 352 TFEU are often the focal point in this regard. However, as several authors have pointed out, like Gareth Davies and Christiaan Timmermans in this book, in addition to such positive, legislative powers, the EU's negative competences are equally relevant. Member State (and individual) action can be constrained by virtue of the Court's application of the prohibitions of restrictions on free movement and of distortions of competition, and of general principles of law.[6] Sacha Prechal has furthermore correctly added

[5] For the purposes of this discussion, the terms 'Member State competences' or 'retained powers' shall be used interchangeably, and shall be understood broadly as those policy areas as regards to which no specific power has been conferred on the EU, areas where the Member States are considered to retain their 'autonomy', and specific issues which fall outside the powers conferred on the EU. This includes the area of national security that is considered the 'sole responsibility' of the Member States on the basis of Art 4 TEU, policy areas that qualify as 'complementary EU competences' as defined in Arts 2(5) and 6 TFEU, as well as issues that have been excluded from direct EU competence in areas of shared powers, such as the issues of pay and the right to strike in the context of Art 153(5) TFEU, or the possibility of setting maximum standards (full harmonisation) when the specific direct EU competence only allows the adoption of minimum standards, again such as in the area of social policy under Art 153(4) TFEU.

[6] S Prechal, 'Competence Creep and General Principles of Law' (2010) 3(1) *Review of European Administrative Law* 5, 18.

that while 'competence creep is first and foremost associated with the liberal interpretation of the legal basis provisions by both the EU institutions and the ECJ', nevertheless 'other methods of intervention by the EU may be included as well', such as the use of soft law instruments or the Open Method of Coordination, financial incentives, coordination, and the development of policies.[7] Particularly coordination has developed into a powerful method of integration in recent times, with European economic governance touching on a wide range of sensitive issues that are excluded from EU legislative competence. Finally, in its broadest form, competence creep could also be considered to include parallel integration of areas of Member State competence taking place outside the EU's institutional framework, through international Treaties or intergovernmental co-operation.[8]

If one is to capture the full complexity of the dynamics of the phenomenon, a broad definition is appropriate to include all those variations of European integration, particularly because these different modes are linked to each other. They can be alternatives, causally linked or co-dependent in different situations. Awareness of this interconnection is not only of theoretical interest, but bears high practical relevance. Reforms aimed at containing European integration should be careful to take all forms of integration into account, if such reforms are to be effective. After all, the limitation of one form of integration may encourage the use of another, when they can be used alternatively (for example, parallel integration instead of EU soft law). Equally, such reform should be mindful of the interaction between various forms of integration in order to avoid unintended consequences. For instance, limitation of one form of integration without equally limiting another may provoke a regulatory gap, when the former serves to compensate for the loss of regulatory capacity caused by another form of integration (for example, indirect legislation to react to negative integration).

To denote such an encompassing interpretation, the term 'competence creep' does not seem particularly well fitted, however, as it carries a certain association with the issue of legal basis and legislation, the EU's accrual of formal powers and with the 'expanding reach and scope of EU law'[9] and is not as easily and naturally connected to the other methods of Europeanisation beyond EU law *stricto sensu*.[10] The terms 'integration by stealth' and 'covert integration' have been used in political science literature to denote similar dynamics, but these accounts are, logically, focused more on the political dimensions of the problem than on its legal implications. Majone has linked 'integration by stealth' to the functionalist approach to integration, where spill-over of economic integration is used to further political integration of other areas.[11] Adrienne Héritier defines 'covert integration' in areas

[7] ibid.

[8] S Garben, *EU Higher Education Law—The Bologna Process and Harmonization by Stealth* (Kluwer Law International, 2011).

[9] P Eeckhout, 'The Growing Influence of European Union Law' (2010) 33 *Fordham International Law Journal* 1490, 1491.

[10] The same applies to 'EU law creep' coined by Sacha Prechal. See S Prechal, above n 6 at 7.

[11] G Majone, *Dilemmas of European Integration: the ambiguities and pitfalls of integration by stealth* (Oxford University Press, 2009).

of core state powers as 'a process that takes place outside the formal European political decision-making arena' and usefully maps various patterns thereof.[12] Both oppose this type of integration to 'frankly political integration' explicitly mandated by 'formal political actors'. This chapter will seek to integrate these insights into the discussion, but will propose to use yet another term, that of 'harmonisation by stealth',[13] in order to set it apart as a primarily legal phenomenon or, in any event, to make clear that this discussion focuses on the legal dimensions of the phenomenon.

Five main forms of such harmonisation by stealth can be distinguished in line with the above discussion: indirect legislation, negative integration through the case law of the CJEU, economic governance, EU soft law, and parallel integration. All these modes of integration have in common that they induce the approximation of national laws, regulations and/or administrative practices by reference to a common European norm. This norm, and the resulting integration, can be 'negative', for example in the form of a prohibition excluding certain national rules or practices, or 'positive', such as in the form of a commonly applicable substantive standard. It can be of general application, or specific in the sense that it applies only to a single Member State. The norm can be 'hard', in the sense of a legally binding requirement, or 'soft', in that it lacks formal binding-ness but nevertheless produces indirect effects on national law and policy. But it always results from a European-level decision of some kind, whether by the European legislator, European judiciary or European and/or national executives, and induces convergence of national policies, rules or practices. All these forms of integration furthermore have in common that they take place 'by stealth'. This refers to the fact that the area in which the integration takes place belongs to Member State competence, in that it has not been defined as an area of exclusive or shared EU competence, that harmonisation has been specifically excluded in the specific legal basis applicable to that area, or that it takes place without a legal basis in the Treaties altogether.

Indirect Legislation

The first form of harmonisation by stealth is the one that is most commonly understood to be the core of the competence problem, namely the adoption of EU

[12] A Héritier, 'Covert integration of core state powers: renegotiating incomplete contracts' in P Genschel and M Jachtenfuchs (eds), *Beyond the regulatory polity? The European integration of core state powers* (Oxford University Press, 2014) 230.

[13] I have previously used the term 'harmonisation by stealth' to denote integration in parallel to the Treaties in the particular example of the Bologna Process in S Garben, *EU Higher Education Law—The Bologna Process and Harmonization by Stealth*, above n 8 and S Garben, 'Confronting the Competence Conundrum, Democratising the European Union through an Expansion of its Legislative Powers', above n 1. It seems entirely possible and appropriate, however, to expand the use of the term to cover all forms of integration in areas of Member State competence, whether by law or by policy, and whether within or outside the EU's institutional framework.

legislation in areas where the EU's direct legislative competence is limited. First, this can happen by virtue of specific Treaty provisions that provide competence on a particular issue related to an area that as a whole is qualified as a Member State competence. For instance, in the case of education, which is a complementary EU competence that excludes the adoption of harmonising legislation, Article 53 TFEU grants the EU the power to adopt harmonising measures for the purposes of diploma recognition. Such *lex speciali* unhelpfully add to the confusion on what powers the EU does and does not have in certain fields. Second, and more importantly, the Treaty's functional powers—mostly, but not exclusively related to free movement such as Articles 46, 50, 56, and 114 TFEU—can cut horizontally through virtually all policy areas, including those where the EU has no, or only complementary, competence. This means that the EU can, through such indirect powers, legislate in areas that are considered to fall within national autonomy. As Bruno De Witte has pointed out, there are many examples of this phenomenon in the legislative practice of the EU,[14] such as the Directive on return of works of art illegally removed from the territory of Member States, the Television Without Borders Directive, the large body of legislation on the recognition of diplomas, the Citizenship Directive, and the Patients' Rights Directive.

Although this dynamic largely follows from the interaction of various Treaty provisions themselves, the CJEU has been instrumental in its validation, by categorically refusing to shield any type of policy field from such indirect EU action.[15] A striking example is the judgment in Case C-176/03 *Commission v Council*, where the Court recognised a power for the EU legislator to specify that EU obligations in a legislative measure for environmental protection had to be implemented through criminal law, even if the EU did not at the time possess any specific competence to do so.[16] The obvious question of how such indirect legislation can be reconciled with the exclusions of harmonisation featured in the provisions on complementary competences, has been answered by the Court in *Tobacco Advertisement*.[17] Germany challenged a directive that imposed a general ban on the advertising or sponsorship of tobacco products in the EU, maintaining that it had been adopted ultra vires. As the EU did not have a general power to legislate in the area of public health, the measure had been adopted on the basis of Articles 114, 53(2) and 62 TFEU. Article 168 TFEU on public health contains

[14] B De Witte, 'Clarifying the Delimitation of Powers: a Proposal with Comments' in European Commission (ed), *Europe 2004: le grand débat. Setting the agenda and outlining the options* (European Commission 2002).

[15] In *Casagrande*, the Court held that: 'although educational and training policy is not as such included in the spheres which the Treaty has entrusted to the Community Institutions, it does not follow that the exercise of powers transferred to the Community is in some way limited if it is of such a nature as to affect the measures taken in the execution of a policy such as that of education and training'. Case 9/74 *Donato Casagrande v Landeshauptstadt München* [1974] 773.

[16] Case C-176/03 *Commission of the European Communities v Council of the European Union* EU:C:2005:542.

[17] Case C-376/98 *Germany v European Parliament and Council* [2000] 8419.

a prohibition of harmonisation, which according to the German government led to the invalidity of the Directive. It is worth quoting AG Fennelly:

> Although it is not contested that the Directive could not have been adopted on the basis of Article [168(4) TFEU], it would be surprising (and inimical to legal certainty) if the authors of the Treaty on European Union had, when providing new Treaty powers in respect of public health, so severely restricted existing competence in a different field simply because it sometimes has a bearing on health. Articles [114] and [168] are not, in any respect, inconsistent. As we have seen, Articles [114(3)] and [168(1)], third indent, combine to show that Article [114] may be used to adopt measures which aim at the better protection of health. The limitation expressed in Article [168(4)] is not in conflict with these provisions. It affects, in its own terms, only the incentive measures for which it provides.[18]

In essence, the Court agreed with the view expressed by the Advocate General. It held that the prohibition of harmonisation did not mean that harmonising measures adopted on the basis of other provisions of the Treaty were prohibited from having any impact on the protection of human health. Although other Treaty articles were not to be used in order to circumvent the express exclusion of harmonisation of Article 168(4) TFEU, this did not mean that the European legislator was prevented from relying on the legal basis of Articles 114, 53(2), and 62 TFEU on the ground that public health protection was a decisive factor in the choices to be made. Although the Court ultimately annulled the Directive, as the internal market rationale could not justify a general ban on advertisement, this was not because Article 168(4) prohibited all harmonisation per se. In the area of public health, the Patients' Rights Directive clearly proves this point,[19] and there is nothing to suggest that this does not apply to the other areas which feature harmonisation prohibitions, such as culture[20] and education.[21] Thus, as Van Bogdandy and

[18] ibid, Opinion of AG Fennelly.

[19] Directive 2011/24/EU of the European Parliament and of the Council of 9 March 2011 on the application of patients' rights in cross-border healthcare, adopted on the basis of Art 114 TFEU. The second consideration of the preamble states: 'Article 114 TFEU is the appropriate legal basis since the majority of the provisions of this Directive aim to improve the functioning of the internal market and the free movement of goods, persons and services. Given that the conditions for recourse to Article 114 TFEU as a legal basis are fulfilled, Union legislation has to rely on this legal basis even when public health protection is a decisive factor in the choices made. In this respect, Article 114(3) TFEU explicitly requires that, in achieving harmonisation, a high level of protection of human health is to be guaranteed taking account in particular of any new development based on scientific facts'.

[20] Indeed, several pieces of internal market legislation pursue cultural policy goals alongside their economic aims, such as the Copyright Directive 2001/29/EC and the Resale Right Directive 2001/84/EC, enacted pursuant to Arts 53(2), 62 and 114 TFEU. As Psychogiopoulou notes, the 'very essence of Article 167(4) TFEU resides in the fact that other provisions of the Treaty may be used to adopt measures with cultural implications'. E Psychogiopoulou, 'The Cultural Mainstreaming Clause of Article 151(4) EC: Protection and Promotion of Cultural Diversity or Hidden Cultural Agenda?' (2006) 12 *European Law Journal* 585.

[21] See G Gori, *Towards an EU Right to Education* (Kluwer Law International, 2001) 88 and S Garben, *EU Higher Education Law—The Bologna Process and Harmonization by Stealth*, above n 8. As is also clear from, for example, the legislation on the recognition of diplomas, the Student Residence Directive and the Citizenship Directive, there are numerous legal bases in addition to Art 114 TFEU that can affect education.

Bast have argued, since 'it is foreign to [EU] law to create areas that are hermetically sealed off from [EU] influence through measures based on recognized [EU] competences', provisions such as harmonisation prohibitions have only a limited reach and they should be understood as a negative condition belonging to a specific enabling norm and not as a cross-sectoral norm limiting all EU competence.[22]

The only exception is the flexibility clause of Article 352 TFEU, which since the Lisbon Treaty specifically provides that it cannot be relied on to harmonise national law where such harmonisation has been excluded by the Treaties. Nevertheless, that provision has often been identified as one of the main causes of 'competence creep', and although the unanimity requirement has always provided an important brake on this integration accelerator, it remains a powerful provision also in its post-Lisbon manifestation. It mandates the adoption of EU measures 'if action by the Union should prove necessary, within the framework of the policies defined in the Treaties, to attain one of the objectives set out in the Treaties, and the Treaties have not provided the necessary powers' and is no longer confined to the attainment of objectives in the context of the common market. According to the German Constitutional Court, Article 352 TFEU:

> meets with constitutional objections with regard to the ban on transferring blanket empowerments or on transferring Kompetenz-Kompetenz, because the newly worded provision makes it possible substantially to amend treaty foundations of the European Union without the constitutive participation of legislative bodies in addition to the Member States' executive powers.[23]

It has therefore vowed to strictly police the use of Article 352 TFEU in the future, requiring prior bicameral ratification in Germany for its application.[24]

CJEU Case Law

The second way in which areas of Member States' competence can be integrated is when the Court of Justice considers a national provision contrary to EU law and it will therefore have to be disapplied regardless of whether it falls within an area of Member States' retained powers.[25] Already in 1968, the Court of Justice was faced with the question whether an Italian tax on the export to other Member States of articles having an artistic, historic, archaeological or ethnographic value was caught by the prohibition on export restrictions laid down by the EEC Treaty.[26] Italy argued that such articles could not be assimilated to 'consumer

[22] A von Bogdandy and J Bast, 'The European Union's Vertical Order of Competences: the Current Law and Proposals for its Reform' (2002) 39 *Common Market Law Review* 227, 238.

[23] *BVerfG*, 2 BvE 2/08 vom 30.6.2009, Absatz-Nr (1-421) para 328.

[24] For a discussion, see P Kiiver, 'The Lisbon Judgment of the German Constitutional Court: A Court-Ordered Strengthening of the National Legislature in the EU' (2010) 16(5) *European Law Journal* 578–88.

[25] See also L Azoulai, 'The "retained powers" formula in the case law of the European Court of Justice: EU Law as total law?' (2011) 2 *European Journal of Legal Studies* 192.

[26] Case 7/68 *Commission v Italy*.

goods or articles of general use' and were therefore not subject to the Treaty provisions which applied only to 'ordinary merchandise'. The Court firmly rejected the idea that there was a general cultural exemption.[27] In subsequent years, the Court has continuously confirmed this approach, emphasising that practices, goods and services are not excluded from the Treaty simply because they fall in areas where the competence of the EU is limited, or even non-existent. In that vein, the Court has held that teachers qualify as 'workers' in the sense of Article 45 TFEU,[28] and that privately funded education constitutes a 'service' in the meaning of Article 56 TFEU.[29] Similarly, it qualifies medical care as a 'service'[30] and has held that the activities of tourist guides cannot exempted from the Treaty.[31]

Perhaps one of the best known examples, in EU law and beyond, is the *Bosman* case.[32] At issue were certain transfer rules in professional football that restricted the free movement of workers in the EU. Several governments argued that Article 45 TFEU was not applicable to sporting activities as in most cases sport was not an economic activity, and since sport and culture fell within Member State autonomy and should therefore be shielded from EU interference. The Court replied that, considering the EU's objectives at that time when there was not yet (even) a complementary EU competence in this field, 'sport is subject to [EU] law only in so far as it constitutes an economic activity'.[33] As regards the difficulty of severing the economic aspects from the sporting aspects of football, the Court held that EU law does not 'preclude rules or practices justified on non-economic grounds which relate to the particular nature and context of certain matches'. However, this could not 'be relied upon to exclude the whole of a sporting activity from the scope of the Treaty'. Also the argument based on the limitation of EU competence was firmly rejected, since the question was not about 'the conditions under which [EU] powers of limited extent, such as those based on Article [167 TFEU], may be exercised but on the scope of the freedom of movement of workers guaranteed by Article [45 TFEU], which is a fundamental freedom'. As a result of the judgment, the entire football transfer system had to be changed.[34]

As *Bosman* clearly shows, the Court is eager to enforce the *effet utile* of EU law and as such is highly reluctant to carve policy areas out of the scope of the Treaty,

[27] R Craufurd-Smith, 'Community intervention in the cultural field' in R Craufurd-Smith (ed), *Culture and European Union Law* (Oxford University Press, 2004), 28.

[28] Case 66/85 *Deborah Lawrie-Blum v Land Baden-Württemberg.*

[29] Case C-76/05 *Herbert Schwarz and Marga Gootjes-Schwarz v Finanzamt Bergisch Gladbach.*

[30] Case C-158/96 *Raymond Kohll v Union des caisses de maladie.*

[31] Cases C-154/89 *Commission of the European Communities v French Republic,* C-180/89 *Commission of the European Communities v Italian Republic* and Case C-198/89 *Commission of the European Communities v Hellenic Republic.*

[32] Case C-415/93 *Union royale belge des sociétés de football association ASBL v Jean-Marc Bosman, Royal club liégeois SA v Jean-Marc Bosman and others and Union des associations européennes de football (UEFA) v Jean-Marc Bosman.*

[33] This confirmed its earlier judgment in Case 36/74 *BNO Walrave and LJN Koch v Association Union cycliste internationale, Koninklijke Nederlandsche Wielren Unie and Federación Española Ciclismo.*

[34] See S Van den Bogaert, *Practical Regulation of the Mobility of Sportsmen in the EU Post Bosman* (Kluwer Law International, 2005).

even if they fall within Member State competence. Especially if certain (aspects of) activities can be regarded as economic, the Treaty freedoms will apply to them in that capacity, no matter whether they belong to a field where the EU has competence. The Court explicitly confirms that the free movement provisions fully apply even if they cut through areas where the EU possesses no, or only limited, legislative powers. The Court does recognise that certain non-economic objectives might have to be considered, but refers to the possibility of objective justification to accommodate these concerns. In that justification assessment, the Court does not explicitly take into account whether an area falls within the scope of EU competence or not. While it could be argued that the Court is slightly more deferential in the application of the proportionality test in these areas,[35] being less hostile towards justifications of an economic nature[36] or towards directly discriminatory measures,[37] the rigour with which the Court applies the Treaty provisions and the proportionality assessment in these policy areas remains striking.

While most often associated with the free movement and competition law provisions, such negative integration in areas of Member State competence can be considered to take place whenever the Court of Justice interprets a provision of primary or secondary EU law broadly, when this structurally limits the Member States' freedom to act and their margin of appreciation in an area, or on an issue, that was believed to be a matter of national powers.[38] Whenever the CJEU expands the scope of application of EU law, this not only constitutes a potential 'harmonisation by stealth' in itself, it also opens the door to the application of the general principles of EU law as well as the fundamental rights laid down in the EU Charter to this newly 'colonised' area. The general principles and fundamental rights can significantly constrain national action, both in terms of negative and positive duties. It may for instance lead to the disapplication of national legal provisions

[35] See L Boucon, 'EU Law and Retained Powers of Member States' in L Azoulai, *The Question of Competence in the European Union* (Oxford University Press, 2014).

[36] The Court has recognised the risk of 'seriously undermining the financial balance of the social security system' in health care cases and the objective of 'ensuring that the grant of assistance to cover the maintenance costs of students from other Member States does not become an unreasonable burden which could have consequences for the overall level of assistance'. See Case C-157/99 *BSM Geraets-Smits v Stichting Ziekenfonds VGZ and HTM Peerbooms v Stichting CZ Groep Zorgverzekeringen*, Case C-209/03 *The Queen, on the application of Dany Bidar v London Borough of Ealing and Secretary of State for Education and Skills*.

[37] In sport cases, the Court has allowed directly discriminatory measures (which normally can only be justified on the basis of explicit Treaty derogations and not on the unwritten list of objective justifications) to be considered under the objective justifications scheme, even if these justifications have not always passed the proportionality test. See eg Case C-415/93 *Bosman*, Case C-176/96 *Jyri Lehtonen and Castors Canada Dry Namur-Braine ASBL v Fédération royale belge des sociétés de basket-ball ASBL (FRBSB)*, Case C-438/00 *Deutscher Handballbund eV v Maros Kolpak*, Case C-325/08 *Olympique Lyonnais SASP v Olivier Bernard and Newcastle UFC*. K Pijetlovic, 'Another classic of EU sports jurisprudence: Legal implications of *Olympique Lyonnais SASP v Olivier Bernard and Newcastle UFC* (C-325/08)' (2010) 35 *European Law Review* 857. In cultural cases, the Court has generally been less lenient, but see as regards fixed book prices: Case C-531/07 *Fachverband der Buch- und Medienwirtschaft v LIBRO Handelsgesellschaft mbH*.

[38] S Prechal, above n 6 at 19.

on age restrictions or to the need to create new remedies for the effective enforcement of EU law. The extension of the scope of EU law by the Court therefore has a double effect on limits to European integration: it first 'annexes' new issues and areas to the scope of EU law, and second thereby also displaces the limits on EU competence as regards procedural rules and human rights.[39]

EU Soft Law

It is a difficult conceptual question whether all forms of EU soft law necessarily amount to harmonisation by stealth. For one, it could be argued that when a policy or initiative relates to an area of Member State competence without inducing convergence to a particular norm, it should not be included in the definition. Examples could be funding for regional infrastructure or for a European youth choir. But this seems a matter of degrees rather than a categorical distinction, since it will probably always be possible to distinguish some kind of general, underlying norm behind any European action, such as 'fostering co-operation between Member States' or 'developing infrastructure across the EU territory'. A second difficulty is that when the soft measures or policies are adopted on the basis of a Treaty provision that specifically provides for them in relation to that policy area, like in the case of many complementary competences which allow the EU to adopt 'incentive measures', it would seem inappropriate to argue that such integration takes place 'by stealth'. Nevertheless, one could counter-argue that the 'stealthy' or 'covert' element results from the fact that while harmonising legislation is excluded by the legal basis, the action nevertheless exerts a normative power that in certain ways is not very different from harmonising legislation, but is adopted without the checks and balances and safeguards imbued in the legislative process. From that point of view, the 'harder' the effects of the soft action, the more appropriate it is to include it in the concept of harmonisation by stealth.

Because of its power to structurally converge national laws and policies in sensitive areas of Member State competence, the Open Method of Coordination is probably the most important source of harmonisation by stealth through soft law.[40] In the OMC, Member State executives (guided by the European executive) agree on certain objectives, such as common quantitative benchmarks, but remain free to implement them in the way they see fit, taking into account their system differences, and they are not sanctioned for failures. As such, the OMC has been described as respectful of national identity and subsidiarity.[41] But while the OMC

[39] The EU Charter provides in Art 51(2) that it 'does not establish any new power or task for the Community or the Union, or modify powers and tasks defined by the Treaties' and that it 'applies to the Member States only when they are implementing Union law'.

[40] See C de la Porte, 'Is the Open Method of Coordination Appropriate for Organising Activities at European Level in Sensitive Policy Areas?' (2002) 8 *European Law Journal* 38.

[41] See D Hodson and I Maher, 'The Open Method as A New Mode of Governance: The Case of Soft Economic Policy Co-ordination' (2001) 39 *Journal of Common Market Studies* 719.

is certainly less coercive than legislation, case law and economic governance, to characterise it as entirely compatible with national autonomy and subsidiarity nevertheless underestimates the OMC's tangible effects in opening up sensitive national sectors. As Erika Szyszczak has stated, 'there are arguments to be made that, despite being viewed as an aspect of subsidiarity, the OMC penetrates into national systems changing internal policy, re-configuring political institutional frameworks'.[42] International standard-setting and -comparing are very effective means for putting pressure on 'underperforming' states to make them conform to the European common standard.[43] As Mark Dawson sets out in detail in Chapter 14, the influence of 'soft law' may not be easily understood in traditional legal conceptions of norms and power, but it structures and influences national actors and standards all the same.

The TFEU does not mention the OMC by name, but it does introduce its characteristic elements in specific Treaty provisions. Although the phrasing varies somewhat per article, it generally mentions coordination, the establishment of guidelines and indicators, the organisation of exchange of best practice, and the preparation of the necessary elements for periodic monitoring and evaluation. The areas for which the OMC is now provided in the Treaty are: Article 149 TFEU on employment, Article 153(2)(a) TFEU and Article 156 TFEU on social policy, Article 168(2) TFEU on public health, Article 181(2) TFEU on research and development, and Article 173(2) TFEU on industry. As such, the OMC is now generally founded on a direct legal basis in the Treaties, although this is not always the case. For instance, the OMC is also applied in the area of education, which is, quite unhelpfully, not mentioned in the Treaties. Admittedly, the OMC could be considered 'co-operation between Member States' which the EU is allowed to contribute to on the basis of Article 165 TFEU, but it nevertheless seems inconsistent to mention the specific features of the OMC in some areas, but not in others. In any event, however, as has been argued, the 'covert' or 'stealthy' element of this particular form of integration is not derived from the use of an indirect legal basis, but instead from the avoidance of the procedural and substantive requirements and limits imposed on harmonising legislation, while achieving similar effects.

[42] E Szyszczak, 'Experimental Governance: The Open Method of Coordination' (2006) 12(4) *European Law Journal* 486.

[43] Although not constituting an OMC, this finding can nevertheless be exemplified in the area of education by the Programme for International Student Assessment (PISA) study. In Germany, as a reaction to the country's unsatisfactory results in the PISA study, national attainment standards for compulsory schools have been introduced. Not only does this amount to the creation of national standards in a country where such standards are uncommon, it might also impair the constitutional autonomy of the German Länder, which are normally in charge of educational matters. See H Ertl, 'Educational Standards and the Changing Discourse on Education: The Reception and Consequences of the PISA Study in Germany' (2006) 32 *Oxford Review of Education* 619.

Economic Governance

A deep tension between the need for containment and for conferral of the EU level underlies the area of economic policy. On the one hand, in light of its pervasive nature, Member States are legitimately concerned about granting the EU a hard competence in this area, as they fear it may become a blank cheque for the EU to decide on highly sensitive decisions of a redistributive nature at the core of their sovereign powers, and arguably beyond the EU's limited legitimacy.[44] Yet, the closely intertwined European economies and the common currency would seem to necessitate a strong European-level capacity to decide on the crucial elements of the economic and monetary union to which the Member States have committed themselves. In the wake of the economic crisis, this latter consideration has become particularly poignant, and alongside monetary policy, economic policy coordination at the European level has gained in importance and intensity. In this, it is affecting a wide range of other policy areas in unprecedented ways. As such, while perhaps the most recent manifestation of harmonisation by stealth, it could be argued to be the most powerful. For that reason, it deserves to be mentioned as a separate category, even though it overlaps to a certain extent with the categories of EU soft law and parallel integration.

First and foremost, the economic and sovereign debt crisis threatening the stability of the Euro-zone and the EU economy more generally has necessitated the grant of financial assistance to Member States in economic peril, and the conditions on which such assistance has been granted have amounted to a powerful form of European integration of national law and policies in areas of Member State competence. The Commission, through the European Stability Mechanism and its siblings,[45] coordinates the financial support provided by euro countries and the IMF in the form of economic adjustment programmes, requiring reforms to address economic imbalances, specified in Memorandums of Understanding. Such Memoranda have been signed under the ESM, the EFSF and earlier financial assistance agreements, with Cyprus, Greece, Hungary, Ireland, Latvia, Portugal, Romania and Spain. The detailed conditionalities specified relate to many areas and issues that are otherwise considered to lie outside the scope of EU competence, such as the organisation of health, education, pension and social protection systems, as well as the standards and methods of wage setting.

[44] For a comprehensive overview of the debate about the EU's legitimacy: A Føllesdal and S Hix, 'Why there is a Democratic Deficit in the EU: A Response to Majone and Moravcsik' 44 *Journal of Common Market Studies* 533–62.

[45] The European Stability Mechanism (ESM) and the European Financial Stability Facility (EFSF) are intergovernmental support mechanisms created by the euro Member States in response to the financial crisis. EFSF was created as a temporary rescue mechanism, following the decisions of 9 May 2010 within the framework of the Ecofin Council. In October 2010, it was decided to create a permanent rescue mechanism, the ESM, on the basis of an international Treaty, entering into force on 8 October 2012. The ESM, taking the form of an intergovernmental organisation under public international law, is now the main instrument to finance new programmes. Parallel to the ESM, the EFSF continued with the ongoing programmes for Greece, Portugal and Ireland. Previous to the ESM and EFSF, so-called Balance-of-Payments programmes had been agreed between the IMF and the EU with Latvia, Hungary and Romania.

Furthermore, the crisis has given momentum to the so-called European Semester, in which the Council on proposal of the Commission adopts country-specific recommendations (CSRs) as part of the coordination of Member States' economic and employment policy. As Zeitlin and Vanhercke note, the Semester brings together within a single annual policy coordination cycle a wide range of EU governance instruments with different legal bases and sanctioning authority, from the Stability and Growth Pact, the Macroeconomic Imbalances Procedure, and the Fiscal Treaty to the Europe 2020 Strategy and the Integrated Economic and Employment Policy Guidelines.[46] Under the Excessive Deficit Procedure and the Excessive Imbalance Procedure, the recommendations are backed up by the possibility of financial sanctions if Member States repeatedly fail to take action on public finances or macroeconomic imbalances.[47] There have been highly detailed CSRs concerning areas of retained powers or limited EU competence, such as minimum pay levels and social protection measures, in a great number of Member States.[48] While some of these recommendations encourage Member States to increase social inclusion and worker protection,[49] which would be in line with the legal basis for EU action under the Social Policy Title, many others entail the opposite.[50]

The CSRs, adopted by the European Council on proposal of the Commission, are non-binding and thereby formally leave the ultimate decision to the national level. Nevertheless, the political pressure they exert on national standards should not be underestimated, especially as they take place in a structured framework with an eventual possibility for sanctions. Admittedly, CSRs are followed only in a minority of cases,[51] perhaps because national parliaments can indeed refuse to legally implement them. Nevertheless, governments can play into a lack of

[46] J Zeitlin and B Vanhercke, 'Socializing the European Semester? Economic Governance and Social Policy Coordination in Europe 2020' (2014) *Swedish Institute for European Policy Studies* 7.

[47] No sanctions have been imposed to date.

[48] 16 Member States in 2015.

[49] For instance, Poland has been criticised for its high share of temporary contracts. However, the proposed solution is to facilitate dismissals. See COM(2015) 250 final.

[50] For instance, in 2015, Belgium was to reduce 'align wage growth more closely with productivity and to make wage-setting more flexible', the Commission criticised Bulgaria (which has the lowest minimum wage in the EU) for the 'substantial' increases since 2011 as such 'sharp discretionary shifts in the Government's wage-setting policy could be distortive for the labour market', although the Council watered this down in the final recommendation, Croatia was asked to 'tighten the definition of arduous and hazardous professions' for the purpose of retirement and to increase flexibility in wage-setting, Finland was asked to eliminate early retirement, France was to lower its minimum wage and to increase working time, Italy should promote 'second-level bargaining, which could help to better align wages with productivity and encourage the adoption of innovative solutions within firms', Luxembourg was to reform its wage-setting system so as to reduce wages in all sectors apart from the financial sector, and Portugal was criticised for its minimum wage which 'has risen significantly faster than the average wage in nominal terms since 2008' and needs to ensure that collective bargaining 'allows firms to adjust to specific circumstances'. See http://ec.europa.eu/europe2020/making-it-happen/country-specific-recommendations/2015/index_en.htm.

[51] According to the European Parliament, only 'around 9% of the CSRs were fully implemented by the Member States in 2013', European Parliament resolution of 11 March 2015 on the European Semester for economic policy coordination: Annual Growth Survey 2015.

transparency and sense of urgency to (selectively) push through the implementation of the reforms, arguing that 'international obligations' have to be met, perhaps pointing at the threat of sanctions or reduced EU-level funding. As for the Memoranda of Understanding in the context of euro-crisis governance, their exact legal status in EU law is unclear.[52] In light of their scope and breadth, 'including very detailed instructions regarding the state budgets both on the revenue and on the spending side' 'affect[ing] policy choices in areas which are not within the EU legislative competence', this could be considered highly troublesome.[53]

Parallel Processes of Integration

The fifth and final form of harmonisation by stealth is constituted by action outside the EU framework, through intergovernmental processes governed by international law, undertaken by all Member States or a group of Member States with constitutional significance (for example, all euro-Member States). Under the current interpretation of the Treaties, such parallel action is prima facie in conformity with EU law when the EU does not possess a 'specific competence' to undertake the same action within the EU's legal and institutional framework.[54] As such, the Court validated in the *Pringle* judgment the Treaty on the European Stability Mechanism (ESM) that was concluded outside the EU framework. Although the Member States had considered it necessary to amend Article 136 TFEU specifically to allow the establishment of such a mechanism outside the Treaty, the Court held that the parallel action by the Member State was legal with or without such formal authorisation. In a way, the case also concerned the question whether parallel action could be used to circumvent a limit on EU competence, *in casu* the 'no bail-out clause' of Article 125 TFEU. The CJEU held that neither the ESM nor the Member States who participate therein are liable for the commitments of a Member State which receives stability support, nor do they assume those commitments within the meaning of Article 125 TFEU, and thus that there was no incompatibility. This could be implicitly taken to mean that if there had been such a conflict between the ESM and the no-bail-out clause, this would not have been allowed under EU law. It should be considered, however, that the no-bail-out clause is not a standard limitation on EU competence but is rather a specific prohibition of a certain course of action of the EU and the Member States, and a breach thereof—whether inside or outside the Treaties—would therefore be quite clearly at odds with the duty of loyal co-operation. The same

[52] C Kilpatrick, 'Are the Bailouts Immune to EU Social Challenge Because They Are Not EU Law?' (2014) 10 *European Constitutional Law Review* 393, M Schwarz, 'A Memorandum of Misunderstanding' (2014) 51 *Common Market Law Review* 398–99.

[53] B De Witte, 'Euro Crisis Responses and the EU Legal Order: Increased Institutional Variation or Constitutional Mutation?' (2015) 11 *European Constitutional Law Review* 452.

[54] Case C-370/12 *Thomas Pringle v Government of Ireland, Ireland, The Attorney General* EU:C:2012:756 para 18.

does not necessarily apply to other limits on EU competence, such as prohibitions of harmonisation.

In the earlier *Bangladesh* judgment, the Court had dismissed the action for annulment brought by the European Parliament against an act adopted at the 1487th session of the Council with a view to the grant of special aid to Bangladesh and of the means adopted by the Commission for the implementation of that act. As the contested act was not an act of the Council but an act taken by the Member States collectively, the application brought by Parliament against the Council was declared inadmissible. The Court stated that 'the Community does not have exclusive competence in the field of humanitarian aid, and that consequently the Member States are not precluded from exercising their competence in that regard collectively in the Council or outside it'.[55] The formulation used in the subsequent *Pringle* judgment is notably more restrictive, in that it considers such action admissible not because the EU's competence was not exclusive, but because it was not specific. As Christiaan Timmermans has argued in Chapter 2, this could be read as a confirmation that when the EU does possess such specific competence for a certain action, Member States may not resort to the parallel international framework. However, even if this reading is correct, this still leaves a great number of areas open to such parallel integration, particularly the areas of Member State competence.

This can be seen in the area of education, where EU direct legislative competence is limited and cannot entail the harmonisation of national laws by virtue of Article 165 TFEU. This is often explained by the fact that education is a core national power, closely related to national identity and sensitive societal choices. However, over the past 15 years, national higher education systems across Europe have been effectively harmonised, most notably into a common three-tier Bachelor's–Master's–Doctorate structure as commonly found in Anglo-Saxon systems of higher education. This harmonisation by stealth has taken place through the so-called Bologna Process, which is arguably the most powerful example of this kind of parallel integration by stealth.[56] The Bologna Process is based on the Sorbonne and Bologna Declarations, two intergovernmental statements devoid of any formal legal effect. Nevertheless, the Declarations, and the process of policy exchange and intergovernmental co-operation that has resulted from them, have effectively structurally harmonised the higher education systems of the participating countries, which includes all EU Member States. The Bologna Process has launched the 'European Higher Education Area', and is being applied through a wide range of national implementation measures such as accreditation and quality assurance processes, often anchored in national laws and regulations

[55] C-181/91 *Parliament v Council and Commission* EU:C:1993:271.

[56] For an extensive discussion, see S Garben, *EU Higher Education Law: The Bologna Process and Harmonization by Stealth*, above n 8 and S Garben, 'The Bologna Process from a European Law Perspective' (2010) 16 *European Law Journal* 186.

and thus binding on higher education institutions. The Bologna Process is a very curious phenomenon, especially considering the traditional resistance of Member States against EU 'interference' in the area of education and their insistence to remain fully competent in this area that is often considered to be a bastion of national identity, and as such raises questions about the real reasons for Member States to oppose EU action and the expansion of EU competences if they so readily give up their national autonomy in the context of another Europeanisation process.

THE DEMOCRATIC DEFICIT OF HARMONISATION BY STEALTH

The preceding discussion has shown that all five forms of harmonisation by stealth are, under the current interpretation of EU law, perfectly legal. The various limits to EU competence, such as harmonisation prohibitions, autonomy clauses and the exclusion of specific issues, only apply in relation to the legal basis to which they directly relate, and not to action undertaken on the basis of *other* legal bases.[57] Arguably, this is for good reason: as policy areas are not watertight compartments but closely inter-related, and as a single regulation will usually address various aspects of human life and thus touch on various policy areas, such 'spill-over' or 'cross-cutting' may be an inevitable feature of, and precondition for, effective government. For that same reason, as Judith Resnik has explained in the US context and Robert Schütze has argued in relation to the EU, a system of 'categorical'[58] or 'dual'[59] federalism, characterised by strict competence demarcation between different levels of government in a multi-level polity, is bound to fail. From a legal perspective, the fundamental principles of effectiveness and primacy of EU law mandate such indirect effects of action undertaken on the basis of one legal provision on other policy areas. But although there may be good practical, conceptual and legal reasons for cross-cutting governance and 'co-operative federalism'[60] in the European Union, the various forms of harmonisation by stealth as set out above raise profound legitimacy problems. Apart from the lack of clarity and openness inherent in the use of these 'stealthy' forms of integration, it is argued here that the most serious problem is the democratic deficit that arises from their effect of displacing at the same time the national *and* the European legislator. Decisions of enormous political consequence are not taken by the legislator but instead taken by the judiciary or the executive, and parliaments are left in a passive, rubber-stamping role, if any at all.

[57] With the exception of harmonisation prohibitions and Art 352 TFEU, where the latter provides that it cannot be used in areas where harmonisation is excluded.

[58] J Resnik, 'Categorical Federalism: Jurisdiction, Gender, and the Globe' (2001) 111 *Yale Law Journal* 619, 620.

[59] R Schütze, *From Dual to Cooperative Federalism—The Changing Structure of European Law* (Oxford University Press, 2009) 346.

[60] ibid.

Indirect Legislation: Displacement of the National Legislator by the European Legislator

It is ironic that the one form of harmonisation by stealth that arguably suffers the least from these legitimacy concerns is the one that is most commonly understood to be the core of the problem of competence creep: that of indirect legislation. Of course, this is not to deny that such indirect legislation poses certain problems. Indirect legislation is often used because the Member States consider it 'politically expedient to achieve certain extraneous objectives through common action but regardless of the constitutional niceties associated with the principle of attributed powers'.[61] Dougan notes the main, essentially federal, concern with such action in areas of Member State competence:

> the power to harmonise involves an effective transfer of regulatory initiative to the Union legislature in a manner which can ultimately not merely displace but replace individual national political choices,

and

> such transfers [sic] of competence is of especial constitutional significance not only because such transfers imply in every case fundamental reconfigurations in the exercise and accountability of public power, but also because such an approach poses specific legitimacy problems for the Union—problems arguably aggravated since the entry into force of the Lisbon Treaty, since the Union's primary law now places renewed emphasis on the principle of the Union as an organisation of only limited powers, and contains a more formalised system of differentiated competences explicitly attached to different policy spheres.[62]

This is a powerful critique. Furthermore, in addition to these constitutional concerns, to the extent that the assumption is still valid that the legislative process on the national level is more democratic than that on the EU level, such a transfer implies a loss of democratic legitimacy.

However, while it is true that indirect legislation such as on the basis of Article 114 TFEU has touched on a wide array of policy issues that seem only remotely connected to the internal market, the extent to which this indirect legislation is responsible for displacing the national legislator can be questioned. A similarly wide range of policy issues that seem only remotely connected to the internal market has been brought within the internal market's scope in the context of the free movement provisions by the Court of Justice in its case law. If the national legislator is already disempowered and displaced through such negative integration, then the concerns about European-level re-regulation by the legislator are much less convincing. The initial, relevant transfer of competence in such cases takes place through the Court's case law, rather than the European legislator's re-regulation on the basis of 'indirect' provisions. Re-regulation may in such cases

[61] M Dougan, 'Legal Developments' (2010) 48 *Journal of Common Market Studies* 172.
[62] ibid.

actually be necessary, to prevent, or prevent aggravating,[63] a de-regulatory bias in the integration process. Halberstam calls this the 'federal conservation of powers principle: unless a loss of competent state authority is made up for by a gain in authority at the center, federalism institutionalizes a bias in favour of deregulation'.[64] Scharpf has powerfully warned us about the risk of an imbalance between negative and positive integration in the EU context.[65] In order to combat the potentially corrosive effects of negative integration on the vital areas in question such as education, health and culture, it is necessary to be able to 'plug the holes' on a European level. As Handoll argues, 'where the Court has recognized the intrusiveness of "functional" rules of free movement and non-discrimination into areas of national competence, the [Union] will have to be competent to take positive action to resolve resulting difficulties'.[66] A broad interpretation of the legislative powers of the same functional provisions that have caused this intrusion in the first place is therefore necessary.

Furthermore, when it comes to Article 114 TFEU, which is perceived as one of the main culprits of this kind of harmonisation by stealth, it can be challenged whether such legislation is indeed really 'indirect'. Article 114 TFEU itself explicitly and specifically foresees its own use in a range of other policy areas, including where the EU's competence is limited, such as public health. Similarly, Article 352 TFEU, the other focal point of competence creep criticism, is clearly a catch-all legal basis, and its use in a wide range of areas can therefore hardly be considered surprising or, for that matter, surreptitious. The only stealthy element of legislation on the basis of 114 and 352 TFEU in areas of Member State competence is that it contradicts (but not contravenes) the prohibitions of harmonisation (as regards Article 352 TFEU) and categorisation of competences as introduced by Maastricht and Lisbon respectively. It thus seems that from a clarity point of view, these reforms have made the problem worse rather than better. The powers of Article 114 and 352 TFEU have been broad from the beginning of the European

[63] Even where competence exists and is uncontested, it is difficult to achieve positive integration due to the high majority thresholds needed to pass legislation and the great diversity of national systems and views.

[64] D Halberstam, 'Federalism: a Critical Guide' (2011) 251 *University of Michigan Public Law Working Paper* 20, 21.

[65] F Scharpf, 'The Asymmetry of European Integration, or Why the EU Cannot be a "Social Market Economy"' (2010) 8 *Socio-Economic Review* 211.

[66] J Handoll, 'Foreign Teachers and Public Education' in B De Witte (ed), *European Community Law of Education* (Nomos Verlagsgesellschaft, 1989) 36. AG Sharpston, in her opinion to Bressol, implicitly seemed to follow this approach. The Opinion recognised the difficult situation that Austria (and by extension Belgium) found itself in, remarking that: 'the EU must not ignore the very real problems that may arise for Member States that host many students from other Member States'. Indeed, the AG sought the solution at the European level, inviting 'the Community legislator and the Member States to reflect upon the application of these criteria [of subsidiarity] to the movement of students between Member States'. Case C-73/08 *Nicolas Bressol and Others, Celine Chaverot and Others v Gouvernement de la Communaute française* [2010] 02735, Opinion of AG Sharpston, paras 151 ff. See on this point also S Prechal, above n 6, on the 'activation' of legislative competence in the area of public health by the CJEU's case law on patient mobility.

integration process, and could always have been expected to draw a range of issues and areas into the slipstream of economic integration. The EU has been explicitly charged with the task of achieving certain policy objectives, such as the creation of the common market with the free movement provisions and the principle of non-discrimination at its centre, and has been granted accompanying legislative powers. It is in recognition of the fact that carrying out these tasks may require changes in all kinds of sectors that the Treaty endows the EU with functional powers. Articles 114 and 352 TFEU play a crucial role in this system and are clearly and deliberately broadly formulated in consideration of the flexibility for which they are intended to allow, necessarily implying uncertainty about their reach. Although they do not confer an unlimited competence, they do not tie down legislative action to particular sectors,[67] but arguably there is little stealthy about that.

Most importantly of all, the choice to legislate, 'indirectly' as much as 'directly', is made explicitly by the European legislator, which entails the involvement of the Commission, the Council, the European Parliament as well as national parliaments, under high consensus requirements and following a balanced procedure accommodating all the different institutional, national and federal interests. Efforts have furthermore been made to increase the transparency of decision making[68] and public consultation in the EU legislative process in recent years. While indeed still not as democratically legitimate as national legislation, European legislation is adopted through the most democratic form of international decision making that is available. It benefits from high levels of input and 'throughput legitimacy',[69] especially when compared to all the other forms of harmonisation by stealth. This is not intended to argue that the problems connected to indirect legislation in areas of Member State competence should be neglected, but instead to point out that from a democratic perspective it is the least worrisome form of harmonisation by stealth and that as such, it is curious—and not particularly effective—that it has been singled out as the target for all the containment action undertaken in the various Treaty revisions.

Negative Integration: Displacement of the National and European Legislator by the Judiciary

In contrast to indirect legislation, harmonisation by stealth through the case law of the Court of Justice does not benefit from that same measure of democratic

[67] S Weatherill, above n 3.

[68] On this 'transparency shift' in the Council, M Hillebrandt, D Curtin and A Meijer, 'Transparency in the EU Council of Ministers: An Institutional Analysis' (2014) 20 *European Law Journal* 1–20. For proposals for further improvement, D Curtin and P Leino, 'Openness, Transparency and the Right of Access to Documents in the EU' (2016) *European Parliament Research Paper*, available at www.europarl.europa.eu/supporting-analyses.

[69] V Schmidt, 'The Eurozone's Crisis of Democratic Legitimacy—Can the EU Rebuild Public Trust and Support for European Economic Integration?' (2015) 15 *ECFIN Discussion Paper*.

legitimacy. Nevertheless, it could be considered constitutionally legitimate, at least to a certain extent, since the Treaties endow the CJEU explicitly with the task and power to interpret EU law. That mandate could therefore be used as a different source of legitimacy and justification for situations where the Court expands the scope of EU law to situations not strictly foreseen by the text of the law. It does not, however, give the Court a carte blanche. Negative integration by the CJEU is particularly problematic when it displaces sensitive national policy choices in areas of Member State competence. In that context, it is in fact much more problematic than the displacement of the national legislator through indirect legislation, because in that latter scenario national governments and national parliaments have collectively, following the various majority rules, decided to replace national decisions by European ones. In the case of CJEU case law, there is no such involvement of the national democratically legitimate actors, nor of the elected European Institutions.

Despite these fundamental concerns, the Court regularly engages actively in the displacement of the national legislator in areas of Member State competence, particularly in the context of the free movement provisions. Its cross-cutting approach, driven by the *effet utile* objective, has had particularly far-reaching consequences in the area of public health.[70] By qualifying restrictions on (reimbursement of) care obtained in other Member States as restrictions of the services provision, the Court's case law has meant that individuals may access other treatments than those allocated in the national package and they can escape waiting lists, which has profound consequences for national health systems by challenging domestic practices governing the allocation of these public services.[71] National autonomy to decide on important political questions, weighing the cost and benefit of health care to the public and the individual, is thereby limited by EU law. Furthermore, even though certain restrictions can be justified to protect the stability of the health care system, the Court imposes high standards of rationality through a strict proportionality assessment, which most of the national arrangements have failed. So it can indeed be said that the explicit stipulations in the Treaty that health is primarily an area of Member State competence have proven not to be the guarantees against EU interference in national health care services that they were often believed to be.[72]

The same holds true for the area of education. Although the Court has held that unlike medical treatment, publicly funded education does not constitute a

[70] See G Davies, 'Welfare as a service' (2002) 29 *Legal Issues of Economic Integration* 27; P van Nuffel, 'Patients free movement rights and cross-border access to health-care' (2005) 12 *Maastricht Journal of European and Comparative Law* 253; C Newdick, 'Citizenship, free movement and health care: Cementing individual rights by corroding social solidarity' (2006) 43 *Common Market Law Review* 1645.

[71] D Martinsen, 'Inter-institutional dynamics in the cross-border provision of healthcare services' (2009) 5 *ARENA Working Paper* 6. For a comprehensive discussion, see A Wunder, *Grenzenüberschreitende Krankenbehandlung im Spannungsfeld von Grundfreiheiten und vertraglicher Kompetenzverteilung* (Peter Lang, 2008).

[72] E Mossialos, *Health systems governance in Europe: The role of European Union Law and Policy* (Cambridge University Press, 2010) 1.

'service',[73] the case law has arguably had an even greater impact on national education systems than it has had on health systems. First, privately funded education does constitute a service.[74] Second, the Court's judgments on diploma recognition for professional and academic purposes require transparent and reasonable procedures operating from the assumption that equivalent diplomas should be recognised as such.[75] Most importantly, the Court has developed a progressive line of case law on mobile students' right to equal treatment, which has meant in particular that Member States cannot impose restrictions or higher fees on mobile EU students.[76] This is controversial because neither the economically inactive students nor their parents will have paid taxes in the host state, and there is no guarantee that they will settle there after their studies.[77] As such, EU law requires Member States which choose to devote significant public resources to maintaining a high quality further education system for the benefit of their own populations to subsidise, through the principle of equal access, in addition potentially large numbers of foreign students.[78] As an important illustration, in the situation of Austria and Belgium, which were flooded by German and French medical students that were escaping their country's *numerus clausus* system, this led to a situation where it became impossible to maintain their deeply valued tuition-fee-free and open-access higher education systems.[79]

The phenomenon of harmonisation by stealth through the case law of the CJEU is not limited to areas of complementary competence. Equally problematic is the CJEU's case law where it, on the basis of one Treaty provision, undermines and circumvents the objectives and limits to EU action specified in relation to another area of shared competence. A notable example is that of national labour standards, where Article 153 TFEU authorises the EU to adopt measures laying down minimum requirements for the protection of workers, without preventing any Member State from maintaining or introducing more stringent protective measures. Article 153(5) excludes, *inter alia*, the issues of pay and the right to strike from such EU action. However, the CJEU has held that some of those national labour standards can be a restriction on companies' free movement rights. While initially the Court conducted a relatively relaxed proportionality review,

[73] Case C-263/86 *Belgian State v René Humbel and Marie-Thérèse Edel.*

[74] Case C-76/05 *Herbert Schwarz and Marga Gootjes-Schwarz v Finanzamt Bergisch Gladbach.*

[75] Case C-313/01 *Christine Morgenbesser v Consiglio dell'Ordine degli avvocati di Genova* and Case C-19/92 *Dieter Kraus v Land Baden-Württemberg.*

[76] Case C-293/83 *Françoise Gravier v City of Liège.* See G Davies, 'Higher education, equal access, and residence conditions: Does EU law allow member states to charge higher fees to students not previously resident?' (2005) 12 *Maastricht Journal of European and Comparative Law* 227, M Dougan, 'Fees, grants, loans and dole cheques: Who covers the costs of migrant education within the EU?' (2005) 42 *Common Market Law Review* 943, AP van der Mei, 'EU law and education: Promotion of student mobility versus protection of the education systems' in M Dougan and E Spaventa (eds), *Social Welfare and EU Law* (Hart Publishing, 2005).

[77] AP van der Mei, above n 76.

[78] M Dougan, above n 76.

[79] See S Garben, 'Case C-73/08, *Nicolas Bressol and Others, Céline Chaverot and Others v Gouvernement de la Communauté française*' (2010) 47 *Common Market Law Review* 1493.

upholding most measures as justified,[80] the situation changed with the *Laval*, *Viking* and *Rüffert* judgments.[81] Widening simultaneously the definition of 'restrictions' and narrowing the scope for justification on social grounds, these judgments fundamentally expand the displacement of national social rules such as on minimum pay, regardless of any seemingly hard limits, or safeguards, included in the social policy legal basis. What is more, the European legislator has been unable to re-regulate the issue, due to the opposition of national parliaments, partially in light of the EU's limited legislative competence.[82] Indeed, the CJEU's negative integration not only displaces the national legislator, it also partially displaces the European legislative process.

A good example is C-576/13 *Commission v Spain*,[83] in which the Court held that the Spanish dock work system, which required all companies wishing to perform cargo-handling services to register with the dock workers' company and to hire with priority workers belonging to that company, among which a certain number on permanent contracts, constituted an unjustified restriction of the freedom of establishment. In rejecting the justifications that were inter alia based on worker protection, the Court followed a lowest common denominator approach, pointing to other Member States' more liberal systems as proof that the measures were not necessary for the protection of workers. The ruling puts pressure on social standards in a sector that is highly symbolic for the power of unionisation, where in the face of harsh and precarious working conditions workers' solidarity has been able to procure high standards of protection through a variety of complex systems

[80] See eg Case 279/80 *Criminal Proceedings against Alfred John Webb* EU:C:1981:314; Joined Cases 62 and 63/81 *Société anonyme de droit français Seco and Société anonyme de droit français Desquenne & Giral v Etablissement d'assurance contre la vieillesse et l'invalidité* EU:C:1982:34; Case C-113/89 *Rush Portuguesa L^{da} v Office national d'immigration* EU:C:1990:142; Case C-272/94 *Criminal proceedings against Michel Guiot and Climatec SA, as employer liable at civil law* EU:C:1996:147; Joined Cases C-369/96 and C-376/96 *Criminal proceedings against Jean-Claude Arblade and Arblade & Fils SARL and Bernard Leloup, Serge Leloup and Sofrage SARL* EU:C:1999:575; Case C-165/98 *Criminal proceedings against André Mazzoleni and Inter Surveillance Assistance SARL, as the party civilly liable, third parties: Eric Guillaume and Others* EU:C:2001:162.

[81] Case C-341/05 *Laval un Partneri Ltd v Svenska Byggnadsarbetareförbundet, Svenska Byggnadsarbetareförbundets avdelning 1, Byggettan and Svenska Elektrikerförbundet* EU:C:2007:809; C-438/05 *International Transport Workers' Federation and Finnish Seamen's Union v Viking Line ABP and OÜ Viking Line Eesti* EU:C:2007:772.

[82] In response to the (critical reception of the) judgments, the Commission proposed a Council regulation on the exercise of the right to take collective action within the context of the freedom of establishment and services. However, in June 2012, the Commission received the first-ever 'yellow card'. Twelve national parliaments expressed subsidiarity-related concerns regarding this so-called 'Monti II Regulation' amounting to 19 votes. Upon the mandatory revision of the proposal, the Commission decided to withdraw it. See 'Commission decision to withdraw the Proposal for a Council Regulation on the exercise of the right to take collective action within the context of the freedom of establishment and the freedom to provide services—COM(2012) 130'. The Commission's recent proposal to revise the Posting of Workers Directive also received a yellow care. Proposal for a Directive of the European Parliament and the Council amending Directive 96/71/EC of the European Parliament and of the Council of 16 December 1996 concerning the posting of workers in the framework of the provision of services, COM(2016) 128 final.

[83] Judgment of the Court (Sixth Chamber) of 11 December 2014, EU:C:2014:2430.

across ports in Europe. This social organising power was able to block the EU's attempts to liberalise port services in 2001[84] and 2004,[85] with fierce union protest actions leading the European Parliament to an unprecedented vote-down of the proposed directive after having already reached a compromise in the conciliation phase.[86] A new proposal for a Regulation is pending, but has excluded that cargo handling be opened up to the market.[87] The *Commission v Spain* judgment, rendered without the Opinion of an Advocate General and available only in Spanish and French, now does just that, thereby showcasing the surreptitious power of negative integration, achieving outcomes that would be more difficult to procure in a democratic arena.

In the particular area of EU social law, the Court has recently adjusted its case law, taking a slightly more deferential stance towards national standards, in *Elektrobudowa*[88] and *Regiopost*,[89] the *AKT* ruling[90] on the Temporary Agency Work Directive,[91] as well as the recent case law on access to benefits for non-economically active EU migrants.[92] These judgments show that the Court is responsive to societal concerns about its case law. But it does not fundamentally change the decisive role that the case law plays in the essentially political questions about the balance between 'the market' and 'the social', making one wonder whether it is acceptable that the Court (pre)determines political outcomes to such an important degree. The role of any judiciary in making sensitive policy decisions is a

[84] Proposal for a Directive of the European Parliament and of the Council On Market Access to Port Services, COM(2001) 0035 final.

[85] Proposal for a Directive of the European Parliament and of the Council on market access to port services, COM(2004) 0654 final.

[86] P Verhoeven, 'Dock Labor Schemes in the Context of EU Law and Policy' (2011) *European Research Studies*.

[87] Proposal for a Regulation establishing a framework on market access to port services and financial transparency of ports, COM(2013) 0296 final.

[88] Case C-396/13 *Sähköalojen ammattiliitto ry v Elektrobudowa Spółka Akcyjna* EU:C:2015:86.

[89] Case C-115/14 *RegioPost GmbH & Co KG v Stadt Landau* EU:C:2015:760.

[90] Case C-533/13 *Auto- ja Kuljetusalan Työntekijäliitto AKT ry v Öljytuote ry and Shell Aviation Finland Oy* EU:C:2015:173.

[91] This Directive was adopted based on Art 153 TFEU, allowing minimum harmonisation for the protection of workers. However, in line with the 'flexicurity' approach, the Directive also contains Art 4, stipulating that 'prohibitions or restrictions on the use of temporary agency work shall be justified only on grounds of general interest relating in particular to the protection of temporary agency workers, the requirements of health and safety at work or the need to ensure that the labour market functions properly and abuses are prevented'. This clearly evokes other prohibitions in the Treaty, looking like a directly effective right to challenge national restrictions on temporary agency work. This was indeed advocated by a company, in defence against an enforcement action of a trade union for breaking a provision in the applicable collective agreement specifying that agency work would only be used to cover temporary needs. If this interpretation were followed, temporary agencies and user undertakings could challenge all kinds of restrictions on temporary agency work. This would, furthermore, apply in wholly internal situations meaning a complete liberalisation of this precarious type of employment, brought about by means of an EU labour law directive. The AG supported this approach, arguing that the substantive obligation of Art 4 was already contained in Art 56 TFEU. The CJEU disagreed, denying direct effect to Art 4, and thereby arguably prevented another *Laval*.

[92] Case C-333/13 *Elisabeth Dano and Florian Dano v Jobcenter Leipzig* EU:C:2014:2358, Case C-67/14 *Jobcenter Berlin Neukölln v Nazifa Alimanovic and Others* EU:C:2015:597.

thorny enough issue, let alone in the EU's constitutional order, where the 'correction' by the political process of such judgments is exceedingly difficult. The EU may lack the competence altogether to 're-regulate' the issue, or it must rely on the internal market legal bases which lead to an economic bias by demanding that the measure serve the functioning of the internal market.[93] The EU legislator is subject to high consensus requirements, that is must fulfil in the context of a very diverse EU28, with national parliaments posing an additional hurdle. The effect of the case law on the bargaining conditions in the Council makes it difficult for the legislator to deviate from that case law in practical terms.[94] Moreover, a fundamental deviation is difficult also in legal terms, as the Court's interpretations of the internal market provisions are of a constitutional nature. The legislative process is powerless in that case to fundamentally alter the interpretation given by the CJEU; only a Treaty revision would suffice. Of course, ultimately, the final power therefore lies with the Masters of the Treaties, but the picture clearly emerges that it is the Court that, to a very large extent, decides on the political question of the place of the market in our societies, and on the power of our societies to regulate the market. The Court's case law on the basis of the free movement provisions thereby displaces not only the national legislator, but also to a certain degree, the European one. While as Claire Kilpatrick rightly points out we should be equally careful not to sanctify the legislative process,[95] its legitimacy to decide on the fundamental political questions, such as about the balance between 'the market' and 'the social', must be accepted as being significantly higher than the judicial process.

Soft Law, Economic Governance and Parallel Integration: Displacement of the National and European Legislator by National and European Executives

What soft law, economic governance and parallel integration have in common is that they mainly involve non-binding measures, or measures that are not binding by virtue of EU law, and as such that they formally leave the ultimate decision to the national level, and thus the national legislator. The principles of primacy and effectiveness of EU law are not applicable, and the duty of loyal co-operation seems only to have a very weak force in these contexts. As such, one could question whether they entail any displacement of the legislator, either on the national or European level, at all. The clear answer is, however, that only on the most narrow,

[93] G Davies, 'Democracy and legitimacy in the shadow of purposive competence' (2015) 21 *European Law Journal* 2–22.

[94] F Scharpf, 'The Asymmetry of European Integration, or Why the EU Cannot be a "Social Market Economy"', above n 65.

[95] The legislative process and output can be sub-optimal: 'slow or absent responses to changing circumstances, entrenched positions, the construction as addressees rather than as producers of norms of key actors and unclear and contradictory legislative bargains are central and well-known problems'. C Kilpatrick, above n 52 at 19.

formalistic and legalistic understanding of power and authority could one argue that this would not be the case. All these forms of harmonisation by stealth carry important normative power and constrain national action in various ways, and they do so largely without the free involvement of the legislator and particularly the European and national parliaments. As such, these forms of harmonisation by stealth contribute to the de-parliamentarisation of European integration, the legitimacy deficit of which has been examined at length particularly in political science literature.[96]

As Erika Szyszczak notes, the OMC has been left deliberately outside of the (re)organisation of competences in the Lisbon Treaty, probably to maintain its flexibility.[97] In a way, its rationale is precisely to overcome the limits on EU legislative competence: a complementary form of governance, as a 'third way' to be deployed when 'harmonisation is unworkable but mutual recognition and the resulting regulatory competition may be too risky'[98] for instance 'to encourage the Member States to coordinate sensitive policy areas that are being eroded by the rulings of the Court of Justice'.[99] But as also has been pointed out above, the OMC does have the capacity to exercise a certain degree of coercive power, and at the same time its lack of transparency and failure to engage with the (more) democratic institutions of the EU such as the European Parliament, the ESC, and the Committee of the Regions as well as a broad participation of civil society have been noted to run counter 'to the principles of good governance that have emerged (transparency, accountability, democratic input) as well as the fundamental principle that the [Union] is governed by the rule of law'.[100] The OMC might seem respectful of national autonomy, but its executive-dominated nature and exclusion of transparent procedures and parliamentary involvement means it lacks democratic legitimacy.[101] This is all the more worrying considering that the adopted common standards to which convergence is directed are usually not as neutral as they may appear. Although often surrounded by figures and statistics that add to their air of scientific neutrality, these benchmarks are concrete expressions of policy choices

[96] See eg F Duina and M Oliver, 'National Parliaments in the European Union: Are There Any Benefits to Integration?' (2005) 11 *European Law Journal* 173, K Auel and A Benz, 'The Politics of Adaptation: The Europeanisation of National Parliamentary Systems' (2005) 11 *Journal of Legislative Studies* 372, J Richardson (ed), *European Union Power and Policy-Making* (Routledge, 2006) and A Cygan, *Accountability, Parliamentarism and Transparency in the EU, The Role of National Parliaments* (Edward Elgar, 2013).

[97] E Szyszczak, above n 42.

[98] D Trubeck and JS Mosher, 'New Governance, EU Employment Policy, and the European Social Model' in J Zetlin and DM Trubeck (eds), *Governing Work and Welfare in a New Economy: European and American Experiments* (Oxford University Press, 2003) at 21.

[99] E Szyszczak, above n 42.

[100] E Szyszczak, above n 42 citing Case 294/83 *Parti Ecologiste 'Les Verts' v Parliament* [1986] 1339 and Case T- 135/96 *UEAPME v Council and Commission* [1998] 2335.

[101] See V Hatzopoulos, 'Why the Open Method of Coordination Is Bad For You: A Letter to the EU' (2007) 13 *European Law Journal* 325. For an in-depth analysis of the OMC see M Dawson, *New Governance and the Transformation of European Law: Coordinating EU Social Law and Policy* (Cambridge University Press, 2011), in particular 203, 207 and 280 on the role of national parliaments.

that the OMC relocates from the national democratic arena to the European technocratic one. As such, it is difficult to understand why it would be an admissible course of action either when there is scope for the Community Method,[102] or when there is not.

European economic governance through the European Semester is, in a way, a particularly advanced form of the OMC. The CSRs are, technically speaking, soft law, in that they are not legally binding. Nevertheless, the CSRs' lack of direct legal effect does not make them inconsequential. First and foremost, they are issued in the context of a structured framework, which features an ultimate possibility of financial sanctions in case of non-compliance. While such sanctioning authority is only connected to CSRs under the macroeconomic imbalance procedure and excessive deficit procedure, the yearly package of CSRs is often presented as a whole and it is difficult to specify precisely which individual recommendation is based on what legal basis. In practice, therefore, all CSRs operate under the shadow of financial sanctions. Furthermore, soft norms construct a narrative and influence institutional actors' behaviour in subtler ways,[103] and although difficult to establish empirically, a certain opportunity cost is involved, in that a number of potential policies on the European and national level may not be initiated because of this narrative. Furthermore, the fact that CSRs are non-binding means that they are not reviewable under the EU Charter of Fundamental Rights,[104] and that they can circumvent the limitations on EU competence in the areas of health, education and particularly social policy, undermining the EU's social legal basis of Article 153 TFEU and its safeguard principles of social dialogue, minimum harmonisation, non-regression and the exclusion of issues such as pay, with impunity.

Very similar legitimacy problems plague the other leg of European economic governance: the euro-crisis measures. The international ESM Treaty is not reviewable under the EU Charter,[105] and the Memoranda much like the CSRs allow 'circumvention' of the EU's limited competences on social policy, education and health.[106] The coercive power of the Memoranda of Understanding is unlike anything previously seen in the process of European integration, as a country faces bankruptcy if it does not accept and comply with the European-level decisions. Its power to displace an entire national democratic process was for the whole EU to witness in the 2015 Greek 'bail-out', where a newly elected national government with an explicit mandate concerning the euro-crisis was unable to change

[102] In its White Paper on European Governance, the European Commission argues that the OMC should not be used when the Community Method is available. European Commission, *White paper on European governance*, COM(2001)428.

[103] M Dawson, Chapter 15.

[104] This could be different if sanctions were imposed for non-compliance, as indicated by Koen Lenaerts, President of the CJEU, in a lecture in Leuven on 26 April 2013, reported by J Zeitlin and B Vanhercke, above n 46 at 57.

[105] As regards the ESM, the Court confirmed this in the *Pringle* judgment: Case C-370/12 *Thomas Pringle v Government of Ireland, Ireland and The Attorney General* EU:C:2012:756.

[106] M Dawson and F De Witte, 'Constitutional Balance in the EU after the Euro-Crisis' (2013) 76 *Modern Law Review* 817–44.

anything about the measures that would fundamentally impact on its national law and policy. As Scharpf notes, 'these conditionalities were not defined by European legislation under the Community Method or through consensus-oriented voting in the Council but through extremely asymmetric bargaining between creditor and debtor governments that resembled conditions of an unconditional surrender'.[107]

More than in the case of the OMC, however, law does play an important role in the context of economic governance. The 'first generation' of financial assistance programmes was adopted on the basis of Article 122(2) TFEU, as a stop-gap, until the adoption of the ESM Treaty was made possible by Article 136(3) TFEU through a Treaty revision. Indeed, it has been correctly pointed out that Member States in their handling of the euro-crisis have in fact resorted to legal measures to a much greater extent than could perhaps be expected and than sometimes seems to be suggested.[108] Moreover, the most important euro-crisis decisions were taken by Heads of State, which undeniably enjoy an important measure of legitimacy, and politicians of the highest level remain involved in the follow-up processes alongside the Commission, the ECB and the IMF, and in the formulation of the concrete financial assistance measures and their conditionalities. Also the European Semester does have a legal mandate, a formal basis in the Treaties, and an elaborate framework of secondary legislation.[109] Economic policy coordination itself is thus firmly rooted in EU primary and secondary law. However, the actual, substantive decision making by contrast takes place in a non-transparent, exclusionary and undemocratic way, mainly between the Commission and the Council. The problem is that the role of law in this case is to legalise the 'outsourcing' of highly sensitive, political questions that from a democratic perspective should be taken through the legislative process, to an executive, non-transparent forum. The parliamentary complicity in setting up the framework is understandable in light of the crisis situation at the time, but cannot validate the indefinite displacement of substantive decision making on highly crucial issues, locating it outside the democratic legislative process.

Economic governance has made use of parallel integration in the form of international Treaties. The Court has validated these practices in the *Pringle* judgment, but nevertheless such intergovernmental law making on the borders of the EU legal and institutional framework could be considered to raise concerns about democratic legitimacy. It is especially national executives that are empowered in such intergovernmental settings. As Moravcsik has argued, 'international

[107] F Scharpf, 'After the Crash: A Perspective on Multilevel European Democracy' (2015) 21 *European Law Journal* 3, 389.

[108] B De Witte, 'Euro Crisis Responses and the EU Legal Order: Increased Institutional Variation or Constitutional Mutation?', above n 53 at 434–57.

[109] The TFEU provides the three central provisions: Art 121 on multilateral surveillance, Art 126 on excessive deficits, and Art 136 on specific economic policy guidelines for the euro area. These provisions have allowed the adoption of secondary legislation, elaborating the framework and providing further legal basis for action in the European Semester, such as the Stability and Growth Pact, the Six-pack and Two-pack regulations. The intergovernmental Fiscal Compact Treaty lays down the 'balanced budget' rule.

cooperation redistributes domestic power in favour of national executives by permitting them to loosen domestic constraints imposed by legislatures, interest groups, and other societal actors'.[110] These concerns apply equally to international soft law such as the Bologna Process, in which there are no pre-determined procedures, and decision making is limited to governmental officials and does not require ratification. Such international soft law avoids not only the checks and balances of the legislative process but also those imbued in the EU's institutional framework altogether. Although national parliaments could in theory have refused to legally implement the Sorbonne and Bologna Declarations, governments have been able to play into a lack of transparency and sense of urgency to push through the Declaration's implementation, arguing that 'international obligations' had to be met,[111] thereby subjecting national higher education systems to an unprecedented level of reform and Europeanisation without an effective national or European-level debate.

It might seem puzzling why Member States embark on such far-reaching Europeanisation processes in areas of national autonomy. Apart from the fact that, as discussed above, a certain need or desire collectively to reform these areas can follow from the effects of the Court's case law, there is also a more cynical explanation on offer. Areas of Member State competence such as health and education tend to be highly contentious and politically charged on the national level, which is exactly one of the reasons why it has been attempted to explicitly limit the EU's competence in these fields. At the same time, however, this fact provides national governments with a strong incentive to divert to the European level if they want to reform these policy areas. The European level allows them to play 'two-level games' whereby they can side-step national lobbies, stakeholders, and general public scrutiny.[112] Indeed, this has been offered as the main driving force behind the Bologna Process.[113] Although all EU or European action empowers national governments *vis-à-vis* all other national actors, EU legislative procedures at least offer checks and balances that are largely absent in intergovernmental processes. In the words of Chalmers et al:

> Indeed, it is positively perverse for those who criticise the European Union because it is executive-oriented or does not sufficiently involve national parliaments to hark back nostalgically to [the] intergovernmental model. It leads to an even higher executive dominance and even greater parliamentary exclusion.[114]

[110] A Moravcsik, 'Why the European Union Strengthens the State: Domestic Politics and International Cooperation' (1994) 52 *Harvard University Centre for European Studies WPS* 1.

[111] See on this issue P Ravinet, 'From Voluntary Participation to Monitored Coordination: why European Countries feel increasingly bound by their Commitment to the Bologna Process' (2008) 43 *European Journal of Education* 353, V Papatsiba, 'Making Higher Education more European through Student Mobility? Revisiting EU Initiatives in the Context of the Bologna Process' (2006) 42 *Comparative Education* 93, C Racké, 'The Emergence of the Bologna Process: Pan-European instead of EU Governance' in D de Bièvre and C Neuhold (eds), *Dynamics and Obstacles of European Governance* (Edward Elgar Publishing, 2007).

[112] A Moravcsik, above n 110.

[113] C Racke, P Ravinet, V Papatsiba, above n 111.

[114] D Chalmers, G Davies and G Monti, *European Union Law* (Cambridge University Press, 2010) 132.

Contrary to the EU legislative process, whether used directly or indirectly, soft law, economic governance and parallel integration lead to a structural and fundamental displacement of the national and European legislator by national and European executives, with all the legitimacy problems that this entails.

SOLUTIONS TO HARMONISATION BY STEALTH

Could we address harmonisation by stealth through a better and stricter enforcement of the division of competences between the EU and the Member States? To be effective, this would entail eradicating all cross-cutting functionality, all elements of co-operative federalism as well as the principle of *effet utile* from the Treaties. The adoption of such a strict system of dual federalism as the new constitutional settlement for the European Union is perhaps not impossible. In concrete terms, the Treaty titles and legal bases relating to specific policy areas could specify that the limits on EU action featured therein apply to any action undertaken by the EU on any legal basis in the Treaties, including the case law of the Court of Justice. To reinforce that same point, the internal market provisions could all be amended to specify that they do not apply to policy areas where EU legislative action is limited on the basis of the Treaties, or where the Treaties do not provide for any EU action at all. The implicit references to the OMC could be deleted from the provisions on complementary competence. In the mandate of the Court of Justice in Article 19 TEU, it could be made clear that it shall ensure that in the interpretation and application of the Treaties the law is observed, 'and that the division of competences between the EU and the Member States is respected'. It could furthermore be added that 'in particular, the Court of Justice shall ensure that policy areas which do not belong to the areas of competence of the European Union, or in which the Union's legislative competence is limited, shall not be subject to the application of Treaty provisions relating to other policy areas'. Finally, a protocol could be annexed to the Treaties on the principle of effectiveness, specifying that it shall not lead to the application of EU law in areas that belong to the competence of the Member States.

These changes would require a fundamental Treaty revision, and would imply an important regression of the European integration process. For instance, if this approach were to be followed, all the current legislation that relates to areas of Member State competence would have to be repealed, such as a whole body of health standards for goods in the internal market, and the principle of mutual recognition would no longer apply in these areas. Clearly, this approach would hamper the EU's capacity of effective governance, even in its core areas such as the internal market. It would turn an inherently dynamic process and polity into a static one. As stated above, policy areas are not watertight compartments but closely inter-related, and a single regulation will usually have to address various aspects of human life and thus touch on various policy areas. Preventing such 'spill-over' or 'cross-cutting' would paralyse the EU, and hamper its output legitimacy. Furthermore, it is not clear that handcuffing the EU to such a degree is in line with the preferences of the European electorate. Even in current times of rising Euro-scepticism, support for the integration process remains in the majority across the EU, and it is noteworthy that this support includes common policies in 'sensitive' policy areas closely related to Member States' powers, such as an EU-wide civil protection policy,[115] student exchange programmes such as Erasmus[116] and a common European policy on migration from third countries.[117]

Most importantly, such strict containment of EU integration would probably result in a vast increase in harmonisation by stealth through integration outside the Treaties. It would seem impossible to prevent such parallel European integration: especially in such a dualist system as foreseen by this approach, the EU would not have the authority to tell Member States what to do or what not to do, individually or collectively, outside the scope of the Treaties in areas of Member State competence. This would therefore amount to throwing the baby out with the bathwater: in a concern to increase the legitimacy of EU integration it would force European integration through less legitimate means. Such integration outside the Treaties would avoid all the checks and balances built into the EU legislative process, and all the institutional safeguards built into the EU framework. Indeed, although also EU soft law and negative integration by the CJEU avoid the democratic features of the EU legislative process, they still benefit from the involvement of the European Commission and the Court of Justice, which have a degree of legitimacy of their own, and they take place in the context of a carefully built supra-national constitutional framework. Parallel integration, by contrast, combines the worst of all worlds, and could be argued to be the least legitimate form of harmonisation by stealth. To elevate it to being the main motor of European integration, which would be likely to happen if a strict dual federalist approach were to be adopted for the EU, would therefore be undesirable.

In light of the foregoing, it does not seem feasible to prevent the EU from continuing to integrate areas of Member State competence. But it is equally undesirable to do nothing about the problematic phenomenon of harmonisation by stealth. Especially the displacement of the national and European legislator should be addressed somehow, as they pose fundamental legitimacy concerns far beyond the well-known complaints about the democratic deficit in the EU's legislative process. In order to square this circle, it is proposed here to both limit the various forms of integration by stealth and to enhance the EU's formal, legislative powers.

[115] 88% of EU citizens support EU action in this area. Special Eurobarometer 433 on civil protection, available at http://ec.europa.eu/echo/files/eurobarometer/2015/reports/CP_en.pdf.

[116] 21% of EU citizens report this as the EU's biggest overall achievement in the 2016 Eurobarometer, available at http://ec.europa.eu/public_opinion/archives/eb/eb83/eb83_first_en.pdf.

[117] 73% of EU citizens support such a common policy, 2016 Eurobarometer, above n 116.

Re-empowering the National (and European) Legislator: Limiting Harmonisation by Stealth through Negative Integration

How can the foregoing insights be concretely operationalised, in terms of possible reforms? As regards negative integration, many authors have identified the problematic consequences of the Court's case law concerning areas of Member State competences. For EU lawyers it is perhaps natural to seek the solution in trying to convince the Court to change its approach, either in the margins or more fundamentally. One proposal that has been made by Barnard is to 'to restrict restrictions' of the free movement provisions, in order to better protect Member States' regulatory powers in the social area but also other fields of general interest.[118] Under this approach, non-discriminatory rules, such as labour laws on salaries and occupational health and safety, would not constitute *prima facie* restrictions of the freedom to provide services, establishment or the free movement of goods or capital, and therefore do not have to pass the proportionality assessment. As regards the justification stage, in all cases where the EU possesses no competence to harmonise, the national rule in question should benefit from a 'presumption of compliance'[119] and the Member State should be granted a wide margin of appreciation. Such rules are only to be struck down in case of a manifest error, where for instance the measure in question in no way serves the interest that it is supposed to protect. This would apply to areas of complementary EU competence, such as sport, health and education, but also to other areas if harmonisation is explicitly excluded, such as pay and the right to strike under Article 153(5) TFEU.

However, it is unlikely that the Court itself would come to this change of heart, and even if it did, it could change back at any point. The previous time the Court did something similar, with the *Keck* doctrine,[120] it found it very difficult to stick to this deferential approach and many consider *Keck* to have been overturned, for all intents and purposes, by later case law.[121] To take matters out of the Court's hands, the above approach could instead be adopted by means of a Treaty amendment. The free movement provisions could be amended to make clear that they do not apply to non-discriminatory measures, and that Member States are granted a wide margin of discretion in the assessment whether the pursuit of a public interest

[118] C Barnard, 'Restricting Restrictions: Lessons for the EU from the US?' (2009) 68 *Cambridge Law Journal*.

[119] ibid.

[120] Joined cases C-267/91 and C-268/91 *Criminal proceedings against Bernard Keck and Daniel Mithouard* EU:C:1993:905.

[121] Case C-110/05 *Commission v Italy* EU:C:2009:66. There are still judgments where the Court carries on *Keck's living memory: C-387/01 Weigel v Finanzlandes direction für Vorarlberg* EU:C:2004:256; Joined Cases C-544/03 and C-545/03 *Mobistar SA v Commune de Fleron* EU:C:2005:518. See C Barnard, 'Restricting Restrictions: Lessons for the EU from the US?', above n 118 at 601. In tax cases especially Case C-374/04 *Test Claimants in Class IV of the ACT Group Litigation v Commissioners of Inland Revenue* EU:C:2006:773; Case C-446/04 *Test Claimants in the FII Group Litigation v Commissioners of Inland Revenue* EU:C:2006:774. See K Banks, 'The application of the fundamental freedoms to Member State tax measures: guarding against protectionism or second-guessing national policy choices' (2008) *European Law Review* 504.

justifies a restriction of the free movement provisions in areas where the EU's legislative competence is limited. While this option is perhaps just as unlikely to succeed as the Court changing its case law, it would be the more effective option in the long term.

Perhaps the most effective proposal, albeit very far-reaching, has been made by Fritz Scharpf, namely to 'de-constitutionalise' the internal market provisions altogether.[122] This would entail removing the four freedoms from the Treaties and the EU Charter of Fundamental Rights as part of a more general 'reduction of the domain of constitutional law in the EU',[123] where the EU legal order would be reorganised with at the highest level only a lean constitution, comprising human (political and social; but not economic) rights, institutional provisions, provisions on competence division and legislative procedures. The internal market would be demoted to a specific policy domain, to be regulated exclusively by secondary legislation. This would lower the standing of the free movement provisions in the hierarchy of norms, granting a priority to certain other rights and objectives, and it would make the case law of the Court concerning the internal market much more adaptable by the European legislator. These changes would have to be made unequivocally and clearly pronounced in the text of the new Treaty, to prevent the Court from reintroducing the constitutional nature of the four freedoms via the back door as 'general principles of EU law'.

Limiting Harmonisation by Stealth through Soft Law, Parallel Integration and Economic Governance and Re-empowering the European Legislator through an Expansion of the EU's Legislative Powers

While concerns about the democratic deficit of soft law in the context of the OMC and parallel integration did not go unnoticed, it is especially the glaring legitimacy problem in the area of economic governance that has compelled scholars to contemplate radical and fundamental constitutional reforms. Maduro[124] and Kumm[125] have made far-reaching proposals that certainly have merits, but as Dawson and De Witte note, their proposals are 'problematic in so far as they call for a democratisation of the Commission, but not for a democratisation of the Union'.[126] Habermas,[127] Collignon[128] and Hix[129] have proposed genuine

[122] F Scharpf, 'After the Crash: A Perspective on Multilevel European Democracy', above n 107 at 401.

[123] ibid.

[124] M Maduro, 'A New Governance for the European Union and the Euro: Democracy and Justice' (2012) *RSCAS Policy Papers*.

[125] M Kumm, 'What Kind of a Constitutional Crisis is Europe In and What Should Be Done About It?' (2013) *WZB Discussion Paper*.

[126] M Dawson and F De Witte, 'Self-Determination in the Constitutional Future of the EU' (2015) 21 *European Law Journal* 380.

[127] J Habermas, *Zur Verfassung Europas. Ein essay* (Suhrkamp, 2011).

[128] S Collignon, *The European Republic: Reflections on the Political Economy of a Future Constitution, Federal Trust* (2003).

[129] S Hix, *What's wrong with the European Union and How to Fix It* (Polity, 2008).

democratisation of the EU as a whole, proposing to transform the Union into a parliamentary democracy, the Commission in a parliamentary government and to replace the veto positions of national executives through majority rule in a bicameral European legislature, but such majoritarian democracy poses normative problems in the present EU context by lacking protection of persistent minorities.[130] While such far-reaching reforms may indeed be necessary in the longer run, in the meantime it may be best to work with the democratic instruments that are already available: the European legislative process.

Indeed, it would seem that any effective change in this respect would have to directly challenge the crucial fact that these processes of harmonisation by stealth are allowed to operate outside the EU's legal and/or legislative framework. Of course, the Court of Justice has explicitly validated the legality of parallel integration in its *Bangladesh* and *Pringle* judgments, and the OMC and CSRs (usually) have a legal basis in the Treaty or secondary legislation, making it difficult to argue that they are illegal. But, as discussed above, even if they have formal validation under the Court's current interpretation of EU law, these processes are illegitimate from a democratic perspective and that of the rule of law. It should be recalled that under Article 10 TEU, the functioning of the Union is founded on representative democracy, citizens have the right to democratic participation and decisions shall be taken as openly and as closely as possible to the citizen. While this provision does not grant citizens a directly effective 'right to democracy', the Court could still use it as a source of interpretation. Furthermore, under the principle of sincere co-operation, Member States are to refrain from any measure which could jeopardise the attainment of the Union's objectives. Finally, the rule of law is one of the EU's most important foundational principles, as stipulated in Article 2 TEU.

On the basis of these principles, a case could be made that it is not permissible for Member States and EU Institutions to engage in parallel action outside the EU legal framework.[131] While the EU legal framework suffers from a democratic deficit, the intergovernmental model is much worse as it leads to an even higher executive dominance and even greater parliamentary exclusion.[132] Therefore, there should be a general principle of precedence of the EU framework over parallel action—as a kind of sibling to the subsidiarity principle and derived from the duty of sincere co-operation. Similarly, on the basis of those same principles, it could be argued that integration through EU soft law, such as the OMC and the CSRs, should not be allowed to set European-level norms that displace parliamentary decision making in highly political areas such as social policy, education and public health. As such, there should be a general principle of precedence of the legislative process over any other action.

[130] F Scharpf, 'After the Crash: A Perspective on Multilevel European Democracy', above n 107 at 393.

[131] B De Witte, 'Internationale verdragen tussen lidstaten van de Europese Unie' in R Wessel and B De Witte, *De plaats van de Europese Unie in het veranderende bestel van de volkenrechtelijke organisatie, Mededelingen van de Nederlandse Vereniging voor Internationaal Recht* (Asser Press, 2001) 104.

[132] D Chalmers, G Davies and G Monti, *European Union Law*, above n 114.

This argument is of course most convincing if the EU would have had the competence to do legislatively what the harmonisation by stealth envisages. In that case, the very decision to operate outside the EU legislative framework if competence existed to operate inside it, should be considered as contrary to sincere co-operation, the rule of law and the commitment to democratic governance, negatively affecting the EU's existing policy or its objectives. It could be argued that for that reason, counter-intuitive as it may sound, the EU should be granted a general legislative competence.[133] That would prevent the counter-productive situation that areas of national competence would be more vulnerable to illegitimate European integration than those where the EU has been authorised to harmonise. The central idea is that as a general rule the Union would be afforded all the powers that prove necessary, within the framework of the policies defined in the Treaties, to attain one of the objectives set out in the Treaties. It would essentially place what is now Article 352 TFEU at the centre of the competence constellation, by moving it to the beginning of the Treaty and appointing the ordinary legislative procedure as the relevant legislative process. The current legal bases could co-exist with the new general legislative competence, operating as *lex speciali*. This means that the intricate system of scattered and overlapping functional and subject-specific legal bases would continue to exist, but departing from a fundamentally different position as there would be no doubt or secrecy about the broadness of the EU's legislative powers. Such a general legislative competence for the EU to achieve the aims of the Union set out in Article 2 TEU, checked by an empowered control of subsidiarity and proportionality, could serve to curtail technocracy and re-politicise EU policies, thereby enhancing democratic participation and thus legitimacy. Although it could of course be projected to widen the scope of possible legislation to be adopted at Union level, the extent of this extension is questionable. We have seen that through the functional competences, the flexibility clause, and intergovernmental policy making, the Member States can already use the EU or European platform for almost every imaginable policy initiative. Under a general legislative competence, the greatest difference would be the fact that these policies would have to pass through the appropriate legislative procedures and would stir the necessary public debate, something that seems far more desirable than the current solutions in place. In fact, it could very well mean that the Union becomes less productive in terms of its output. The Union's activities would thereby be curtailed by the democratic process, rather than an artificial and inefficient demarcation of competences. Formal extension of powers could lead to practical limitation of their exercise.

A more modest version of this proposal would be to abolish the prohibitions of harmonisation and to recognise a (limited) legislative competence in

[133] S Garben, 'Confronting the Competence Conundrum: Democratising the European Union through an Expansion of its Legislative Powers', above n 1 at 55–89.

the current areas of complementary competence. Perhaps more than any other feature of the Treaty, prohibitions on harmonisation in areas of complementary competences represent the flawed nature of the current competence scheme. They do not limit negative integration in these fields in any way, nor do they prevent indirect harmonisation through other legal bases in the Treaty. This makes them deceptive as well as ineffective. Furthermore, quite unhelpfully they do limit the kind and extent of harmonisation possible in these fields, in that they prevent the development of comprehensive and holistic policies. This leads to areas of complementary competence being affected rather as a side issue to free movement than a main objective, and often in a fragmentary and reactive fashion. Additionally, as we have seen, this encourages Member States if they desire integration in these fields to act informally, either within or outside the EU's institutional framework. One advantage of removing the prohibitions of harmonisation would simply be to no longer deny the power that already largely exists in these fields, thereby making the competence-constellation less deceiving and dishonest. It would no longer be hidden from national parliaments, stakeholders and citizens that EU action can and does affect these fields, which will hopefully make them more alert and responsive to EU legislative proposals, in turn allowing them more effectively to influence legislative output through both national and European democratic processes. Furthermore, to delete the prohibitions of harmonisation from the Treaty text would still broaden the legal basis for EU legislative action in fields concerned to an important extent, since harmonising measures could now also be adopted on the basis of these provisions and not only indirectly through other Treaty provisions or outside the EU legal framework. Apart from increased transparency, the potential to fill regulatory gaps and to promote socio-cultural concerns *vis-à-vis* economic ones, this would allow the EU to develop a certain degree of self-standing policy in areas like education and public health, thereby potentially pushing action 'though the front door', diminishing the amount of legislation adopted on other legal bases or informal action embarked on outside the EU legal framework.

Such a simple elimination of the harmonisation prohibitions from the affected Treaty provisions would in itself achieve substantial recognition and extension of the EU's legislative powers, as explained above. This option could, however, be taken a step further, introducing new clauses into the affected Treaty provisions that face the competence conundrum head-on by explicitly recognising and consolidating the potential for EU integration in these fields, and directing such potential action in a way that respects that subsidiarity and national identity deserve special protection. This could, for example, be given shape in the legislative procedure to be followed and the voting requirements in the Council (for example, assent procedure with unanimity in the Council), and by specifying that legislative action should aim to fill regulatory gaps created by negative integration through the Court's case law. Additionally, such negative integration could itself be constrained by explicitly granting Member States a wide margin of discretion in the context of their objective justifications for derogating from the application of other Treaty provisions. For instance, Article 165 TFEU on education could be rephrased as follows:

> 1. … When Union action on the basis of other provisions in this Treaty affects education, regard should be had in the adoption of those measures to the specific socio-cultural value of education and the primary responsibility of the Member States in this field.
>
> In recognition of Member States' primary responsibility in this area, they shall be afforded a wide margin of appreciation in the assessment whether educational measures that restrict free movement and equal treatment rights, as laid down in other provisions in this Treaty, pursue a legitimate objective and are proportionate and suitable to achieve that objective.
>
> …
>
> 4. In order to contribute to the achievement of the objectives referred to in this Article: the Council, acting unanimously on a proposal from the Commission and after obtaining the consent of the European Parliament, after consulting the Economic and Social Committee and the Committee of the Regions, shall enact measures aimed at achieving the aims set out in the first paragraph of this provision and at addressing the need for common action arising out of the European Court of Justice's case law, especially in the context of free movement and European Citizenship.

FINAL THOUGHTS

In an attempt to provide a comprehensive overview of the problem of competence creep in its broadest manifestation, this chapter has distinguished five main forms of 'harmonisation by stealth': indirect legislation, the case law of the CJEU, economic governance, EU soft law and parallel integration outside the Treaties. Such harmonisation in areas of Member States' retained powers is possible, because the various limits to EU competence only apply in relation to the specific legal basis to which they directly relate, and not to action undertaken on the basis of *other* legal bases or outside the Treaties. Arguably, this is for good reason: as policy areas are not watertight compartments but instead closely inter-related, and as a single regulation will usually address various aspects of human life and thus touch on various policy areas, effective government inevitably entails and requires such 'spill-over' or 'cross-cutting'. From a legal perspective, the fundamental principles of effectiveness and primacy of EU law indeed mandate such indirect effects of action undertaken on the basis of one legal provision, into other policy areas. As such, organising the EU's constitutional settlement as a system of 'categorical'[134] or 'dual'[135] federalism, characterised by strict competence demarcation between different levels of government, is bound to fail.

[134] J Resnik, above n 58.
[135] R Schütze, above n 59.

Nevertheless, as this chapter has also sought to demonstrate, the incontestable need for cross-cutting governance and 'co-operative federalism'[136] does not necessarily legitimise the various forms of harmonisation by stealth. While these practices may be legal under the current interpretation of EU law, serious democratic deficiencies damage the legitimacy of all but one of these forms of integration. The main concern is that they displace at the same time the national *and* the European legislator in taking decisions of high political consequence, relocating this power to the judiciary or the executive, and leaving parliaments largely disempowered. It is ironic that the one form of integration by stealth that suffers the least from this concern is the one that is most commonly understood to be the core of the problem of competence creep: that of indirect legislation. While it is true that legislation on the basis of, for instance, Article 114 TFEU has touched on a wide array of policy issues that seem only remotely connected to the internal market, this can often be defended in light of the wide range of policy issues that seem only remotely connected to the internal market that have nevertheless been brought within its scope by the CJEU in the context of the free movement provisions. When negative integration disempowers the national legislator, then the European one should be (re-)empowered correspondingly. Moreover, this form of integration still takes place through legislation, and thus a (relatively) democratic process with a range of checks and balances. That same goes for use of the flexibility clause of Article 352 TFEU.

Building on these findings, the chapter has made a case to address the legitimacy problems arising from especially the other forms of integration by stealth. While the EU system 'must retain its necessary capacity for dynamism and adaptability'[137] and for effective, cross-cutting governance, such governance must surely also be democratically legitimate. This will require a fundamental overhaul of the current competence constellation. While slightly different in terms of the concrete solutions proposed, the ideas for constitutional reform presented in this chapter have been very much in line with those put forward by Fritz Scharpf in his 'democratic vision of Europe' in Chapter 17. The ultimate goal is to reinstate and reinforce the position and powers of both the national and European legislator in taking the important decisions that impact, directly or indirectly, the lives of European citizens. This chapter has argued that this could be done by, on the one hand, limiting the various possibilities of integration by stealth and, on the other hand, expanding the possibilities for the adoption of EU legislation particularly through the Community Method. Admittedly, these are very ambitious proposals, but while their adoption may be a million miles from political likelihood, exploring such revolutionary *pistes de réflexion* is warranted in light of the seriousness of the legitimacy crisis facing the European integration process at present.

[136] ibid.
[137] S Weatherill, above n 3.

Index